The Transmedia Construction of the Black Panther

The Transmedia Construction of the Black Panther

Long Live the King

Bryan J. Carr

LEXINGTON BOOKS
Lanham • Boulder • New York • London

Published by Lexington Books
An imprint of The Rowman & Littlefield Publishing Group, Inc.
4501 Forbes Boulevard, Suite 200, Lanham, Maryland 20706
www.rowman.com

86-90 Paul Street, London EC2A 4NE, United Kingdom

British Library Cataloguing in Publication Information Available

Library of Congress Cataloging-in-Publication Data Available

ISBN 9781793631831 (cloth : alk. paper) | ISBN 9781793631848 (epub)

∞™ The paper used in this publication meets the minimum requirements of American
National Standard for Information Sciences—Permanence of Paper for Printed Library
Materials, ANSI/NISO Z39.48-1992.

*For Pang and the cats, who helped and humored
me on this journey through Wakanda*

Contents

Acknowledgments

I am indebted to many people from this project's start as a conference paper to the finished product you hold in your hands. I must first thank my editor Jessie Tepper and the production crew at Lexington Books for helping to shepherd this project into existence, as well as Dr. Robert Westerfelhaus and Dr. Claudia Bucciferro, who organized the panel for and responded to the original paper respectively. I am also grateful to my fellow comics scholar J. Dr. Richard Stevens, who acted as a sounding board, offered helpful advice, and assisted in helping me track down some key back issues, as well as my esteemed mentor Dr. Meta G. Carstarphen for her wisdom and advice on this project and in general. I must also express my gratitude to my long-time friend Steve Watts, who not only offered helpful feedback and encouragement but also brought his wonderful wife Nina and his children in to see me present (if there's one thing kids love, it's academic conferences), as well as my other source of friendly feedback, Drew Proctor. I would be remiss if I did not thank Evan Narcisse for taking time out of his busy schedule to talk about the Black Panther and his work on the character, as well. I also appreciate the support of my colleagues and administrators at the University of Wisconsin—Green Bay. I should also extend my gratitude to all the writers, artists, programmers, actors, directors, composers, and other creatives that have contributed to the Black Panther's legacy over the years and given this book purpose and a reason to exist. Finally, and most importantly, I am grateful to my wife Pang, who cheered me on and challenged me to clarify and explain what the goal of this book was and why I was writing it, keeping me focused and on task—I could not have done it without her.

Chapter 1

Introduction

A King of Many Faces

It is hard now, after 2018, to imagine a world where "T'Challa" and "Wakanda" are not household words. 2018's *Black Panther* film was, to put it mildly, a cultural moment. The film won three Academy Awards (the first-ever Oscars for Marvel Studios, as well as the first-ever wins for African-American women in the Costume and Production Design categories) and became the first superhero movie to be nominated for Best Picture.[1] *Black Panther* also became the highest-grossing film ever helmed by an African-American director, earning over $1.3 billion worldwide.[2] The film also inspired creativity in other media, including a Grammy award-winning Kendrick Lamar concept album and a special Wakanda-themed exhibition at the 2018 New York Fashion Week.[3] Industry experts estimated merchandise based on the film was on track to generate nearly $250 million for Marvel and Disney in 2018, despite some complaints that the relative paucity of toys and other merchandise compared to other Marvel properties was not sufficient to keep up with demand.[4] The film was also critically well-received, appearing on many critics' lists of favorite 2018 films and earning one of the highest overall scores for a superhero film on movie review aggregator site *Rotten Tomatoes*.[5] It was a significant coming-out party for a character who, prior to the last few years, had largely been a relative obscurity compared to his contemporaries.

WHO IS THE BLACK PANTHER?

In 2005, multi-hyphenate media producer and writer Reginald Hudlin posed a question to the reader as the title of his first *Black Panther* story arc: "Who is the Black Panther?" At the time, this was a fair question. The character was still a relative obscurity in the larger Marvel canon compared to heavyweights

1

like Hulk and Spider-Man. By now, of course, the reader likely has at least some passing familiarity with the Black Panther, created by Stan Lee and Jack Kirby in 1966 as part of Marvel Comics' then-flagship title *Fantastic Four*. For the unaware, however, Black Panther is the *nom de guerre* of T'Challa, the king and political leader of the fictional African nation of Wakanda and son of its late former leader, T'Chaka. Clad head to toe in an identity-obscuring black bodysuit and a helmet with feline ears and features representing his role as leader of the Panther Clan and their patron god Bast, he fights primarily using hand-to-hand combat with sharpened metal claws. His intellect, superior technology, heightened senses, and agility make him a formidable combatant and ally as he battles supervillains either alone or as part of one of many changing super-teams across the Marvel Universe.

Unlike many superheroes, whose identities and powers are the product of happenstance or tragedy, T'Challa's are ancestral—he is part of a long line of Black Panthers, each of whom has led Wakanda through different eras in the nation's history, and each of whom earned the right to the title through a combination of birthright and ritual combat.[6] Wakanda is as important to the Panther's identity as his name or his costume—a mysterious African nation hidden from the prying eyes of the world and comprised of many different tribes and clans, it is a technologically-advanced utopia historically untouched by the creeping hand of European colonialism. That technological advancement comes because of the country's stockpile of vibranium, a nearly indestructible and malleable metal capable of absorbing vibrational energy used for purposes from weaponry to medicine. As a result of its near limitless supply of vibranium, Wakandan technology is advanced beyond that of even the Marvel Universe's greatest inventors and rarely present outside the nation's borders, save for an odd exception like Captain America's shield. The Black Panther is at once scientist and scholar, unmatched warrior, and esteemed political and spiritual leader.

That is the broad story, of course, but details can differ across media. In the comics, for instance, T'Challa's father T'Chaka is murdered by the villain Klaw as he attempts to steal Wakanda's vibranium for himself; in the films T'Chaka's end comes as the collateral result of a complex plot to pit the Avengers against each other. In some iterations, Black Panther's costume is laced with vibranium and capable of capturing and redirecting kinetic energy, while in others his costume is a relatively standard fabric susceptible to rips and tears. In some incarnations his sister Shuri takes on the role of Black Panther for herself while in others she is content in her laboratory, developing the gadgets and armor her brother uses to fight threats to Wakanda. Some interpretations of the character have him cast in living plastic as a LEGO figurine going on slapstick adventures or trading punches with *Street Fighter* characters in a video game. In short, like many superheroes, Black Panther's story is a song with a melody we all can hum, but with lyrics that change depending on the audience. The question of "Who is the Black Panther," then, really should be—"Who is the Black Panther *today*?"

Without question, the Marvel Cinematic Universe films deserve much of the credit for raising the cultural profile of the Black Panther. The character rarely appeared in media outside of printed comics to a notable degree until the 2000s and then only sparingly until Marvel showed renewed interest in developing theatrical films with the hero in the latter part of the 2010s, when the film made Black Panther into a pivotal part of the company's larger product universe. Yet focusing primarily on that film, as much contemporary academic discourse on the character does, leaves out a significant part of his history and the real-world contexts that shape it. The fictional story of the Black Panther runs parallel to the Civil Rights movement, apartheid in South Africa, and ongoing questions of racial inequality in America. As a character defined by his relationship to the African Diaspora and arguably Marvel's most prominent Black character, Black Panther's stories and publishing presence have ebbed and flowed alongside the willingness of the company to address these issues. Few of Marvel's heroes have the potential to be as socially relevant and important as the Black Panther, and that potential has rarely been realized until recently.

Moreover, the economic imperative of superhero fiction means the character's story is not limited to just one medium. A thorough understanding of the relevance and importance of the Black Panther cannot begin and end in the multiplex; rather, it requires a critical and historiographical analysis of the range of media and social contexts that have fed into this contemporary moment. Similarly, focusing solely on the comics ignores the reality that Marvel and other major superhero producers no longer see these characters as constrained to that medium. Rather, the zeitgeist of media conglomeration means that the character is a brand, and Marvel and its parent company Disney have a multitude of channels at their disposal to tell stories and market to different audiences. A transmedia approach is necessary to reflect this cultural reality and ascertain what the character represents to the audience.

Corporate-owned superhero narratives exist at the confluence of multiple interpretations of a given character over multiple decades of existence—effectively, critical inquiry into these narratives require at least some grounding in how the popular perception of these concepts have developed over time. This is especially important because of the inherent symbolic tension at the core of the Black Panther character. He was created at least in part as a response to colonial narratives of Africa and acted as a rare Black superhero in mainstream comics, but primarily developed by white creators until late in his history. To develop a comprehensive picture of the rhetorical significance and potential of the character to address contemporary sociopolitical issues, it is therefore necessary to address the Black Panther not just through one performance but as a larger discourse spanning multiple decades and existing in a larger cultural space that the franchise has spoken to with varying degrees of care and efficacy.

With that in mind, this book argues the *Black Panther* franchise is uniquely important among superhero media in terms of its inclusivity and sociopolitical relevance. It also can act as a powerful counter-narrative to Eurocentric and colonialist narratives in a predominantly white genre. There are consistent elements across the whole of the *Black Panther* franchise that speak to modern and historical concerns and questions of blackness and African identity. These elements have been developed over time via collaborative and iterative input from a variety of creative professionals. By identifying and connecting these elements, we can identify how the Black Panther can be used to start important and wide-ranging conversations about sociopolitical and racial equality, as well as the potential and problems of trying to find those ideas in corporatized media systems. To tease out these elements, this volume attempts to connect critical and theoretical streams of thought to an in-depth analysis of the work to speak to the cultural validity of the Black Panther and how his stories represent genuine issues such as Black identity, Civil Rights, the African Diaspora, and more through the decades of creative work and sociohistorical context surrounding the character.

CONCEPTUAL FRAMEWORK

The Black Panther character was created in 1966, and in the over half a century since his debut the real-world cultural context surrounding the character has informed the way he and his contemporary superheroes have been depicted. Superheroes are no longer just characters in a story, they are brands leveraged across comics, film, animation, video games, toys, and other merchandise. All of these elements form a larger meta-narrative of who the characters are as a constellation of media touchpoints—but the salient touchpoints of that constellation will vary depending on the audience and which media they choose as an entrée point. In many cases, fans may pick or choose which versions are the most accessible, personally salient, or interesting and could even reject specific incarnations and decisions.[7]

As such, a transmedia approach is necessary to understanding how these texts interact with the audience and intersect with cultural and market forces, and in so doing explain how these ideas manifest across different converged media forms and audiences.[8] Like most Marvel heroes, the Black Panther is a notion that writers and artists and programmers can put their own unique spins on so long as they hold on to the basic aspects of that notion. As such,

Black Panther (like his contemporaries Spider-Man and Iron Man) has been interpreted as a Hollywood action hero, a Lego figure, a video game avatar, and played numerous roles on the comics page—all of these are valid pieces in the broader mosaic. However, unlike most of his contemporary superheroes, the Black Panther carries the rhetorical weight of being both a Black superhero and an African one—and this is a crucial part of understanding the character that can never be removed from the notion. For instance, while it is difficult to imagine in a post-Marvel Cinematic Universe world, the character was marginalized by Marvel for many years due in no small part to a lack of confidence the adventures of a Black hero would sell, and politically neutralized out of institutional fear of association with the real-life Black Panther Party.[9] The multimillion-dollar *Black Panther* transmedia franchise exists now despite decades of cultural and economic timidity on the part of Marvel. Moreover, the entire conceit of the character exists as a direct response to centuries of social and economic injustice toward Africa and its descendants that may not always be accepted by a wide audience.

It is an oft-repeated notion that Lee and Kirby wanted to challenge the stereotypes of African savagery that were so prominent in comics and other media, and indeed this volume seeks to explore how that counter-narrative is constructed across the different forms of Panther media.[10] However, the rhetorical potency of the character goes beyond that, and the idea of an Afrofuturist nation wherein Black excellence and advancement is allowed to prosper has been described as the sort of "recuperative" narrative that is key to critical race theory.[11] It is also important to note this viewpoint is not universal. Apart from the ideological challenge of considering corporate intellectual property as revolutionary, the *Panther* franchise has its share of critics who particularly view the film as a neoliberal rejection and demonization of Black revolution.[12] Superheroes have become a broader subject of political discourse, but the Black Panther in particular merits a comprehensive transmedia analysis to see how the character fits into political areas where most heroes dare not tread.

This book also argues that the Black Panther exists in specific economic, historical, and cultural contexts from which he cannot be separated. Consider, for instance, how the 2018 film and its depiction of Wakanda as a technologically and socially advanced nation was considered by cast, crew, and fans as a rejection of and rebuttal to former president Donald Trump's comments referring to Haiti, El Salvador, and African nations generally as "shithole countries" with undesirable immigrants in a meeting with Senators prior to the film's release.[13] Such attitudes are not new and did not begin with the former president. While the primary intent of this work is media criticism, to ensure proper academic diligence it is important to consider the historical origins of media depictions of Africa and of Blackness (and where those ideas come from) more generally and how the Black Panther franchise succeeds (or falls short) as a counter-narrative. That last parenthetical is especially important because the Black Panther is part of a much larger media ecosystem that may not be interested in revolutionary content or controversial perspectives. An honest analysis must account for Marvel's economic and cultural ubiquity and its historical inconsistency in its sociopolitical stances. At the same time their titles have historically championed a more progressive political agenda, they have also intervened in areas that could affect their bottom line and looked the other way on racial issues behind the scenes. Consider Marvel's decision to remove an Art Spiegelman essay critical of President Trump from a collection of the company's Golden Age comics, or the fact that current Editor-in-Chief C.B. Cebulski surreptitiously wrote under a Japanese pseudonym for a time to make Marvel's writer pool appear more diverse, a fact the company hid for years.[14] A transmedia approach to this character must take these actions into consideration, even if the company is so large that its film and publishing arms operate relatively independent of each other.

TRANSMEDIA CHARACTERS

Of course, crafting a narrative of the totality of the multimedia character that is the Black Panther is a daunting task. Not only has the character existed for over half a century, demand for superhero content and the fragmentation of media audiences across diverse demographics have made transmedia characters aimed at different audiences in different contexts an economic imperative. The popularity of the film has led to an unprecedented explosion of new Black Panther content in the last few years. Like many heroes, the Black Panther also leans into the "multiverse" conceit in which intellectual property holders create multiple iterations of the same characters and concepts that exist on different but notionally connected planes of reality. To switch fictional universes for a moment, consider Batman and the Joker. These characters exist in children's films (*The Lego Batman Movie*) as well as in comics and video games aimed at the teen-and-older audience, young adult novels, and films and television shows aimed specifically at adults like the *Harley Quinn* streaming series and the R-rated *Joker* film. Each of these versions is canonical onto itself and uses the same broad strokes of the characters but present them in a manner relevant to their intended audience (which may "grow up" or "grow down" to enjoy the others over time) and frequently homage each other. It may help to view superhero media as a comprehensive product line, with multiple products under the subsection of each character aimed at distinct target audiences and life stages—effectively allowing the franchises to endure and remain profitable in perpetuity. Henry Jenkins calls this concept "multiplicity," and views it as a key part of the transmedia model. Jenkins suggests that multiplicity "allows fans to take pleasure in alternative retellings" and also allows a degree of participation as fans "sort out not only how the pieces fit together but also which version of the story any given work fits within"—key enticements for the superhero audience.[15]

Contemporary superhero media is inherently intertextual, repurposing and referencing previous works. There is a long history of superhero comics providing complex footnotes and callbacks to previous issues via editorial window boxes and references to encourage readers to track down reprints and back issues, a tradition spiritually carried forward to the connected cinematic universes they inspire. As Kinder suggests, this intertextuality means we must therefore consider individual texts in context of how they relate to each other and promote each other.[16] In the Marvel context, for instance, published comics often are timed to tie into major theatrical releases—reprints of the *Captain Marvel* series releasing concurrently with the 2019 film bore photos from the film on their covers, and the prominence of the villain Thanos in the *Avengers: Infinity War* and *Avengers: Endgame* films resulted in an ongoing comic series starring the character. Superheroes act as a perfect example of vertical integration for media conglomerates—consider that Disney owns the characters, the studios that make the films, the publisher that prints the comics, the streaming services where the films are screened, and the stores in which merchandise for the characters are sold. In this environment, intertextual synergy is not just expected, it is required.

Henry Jenkins originally viewed transmedia as one story told across multiple media platforms.[17] As an example, Jenkins offers *Star Wars,* a film franchise in which much of the backstory and lore are covered in tie-in comics, novels, games, and other media—the films are comparatively a small part of the sheer tonnage of storytelling material. In Jenkins' original definition, the story is a consistent whole parceled out through a variety of different means. Mainstream superhero franchises complicate these definitions by consisting of canonically distinct media properties happening in separate continuities that can be enjoyed fully independently of each other. Yet there is still intertextual influence between the different forms of each character. Nnedi Okarafor's *Shuri* series reimagined the title character as a young scientist more in line with her depiction in the 2018 film (with a costume to match), and the contemporary *Guardians of the Galaxy* comics borrow the design aesthetics and musical affinity of the hero Star-Lord from those films. As these movies reach a much wider audience than the comics, new readers would expect recognizable characters in those pages, creating a form of transmedia focused on character rather than narrative.

To focus only on the modal delivery of content and a shared narrative world as a defining quality of transmedia ignores the practical usage and

prominence of modern media characters. The twin forces of platform convergence and media consolidation have based entire publishing and promotional
empires on the *idea* of a character and how that idea can be represented to
different market segments. To that end, this book proposes that the Black
Panther is not necessarily a transmedia story, but rather a transmedia *character*, to borrow a concept from Paolo Bertetti. Bertetti suggests that transmedia
characters "are cultural and social constructs" that exist as the "result of tex-
tual procedures."[18] Bertetti identifies heroes like Harry Potter and Spider-Man
as characters who are not defined or contained by a single text and can
"become living objects in the mind of the reader" as the sum of the creative
works featuring the character.[19] Bertetti draws from the work of Gianfranco
Marrone, who made a similar argument about the fictional Italian detective
Inspector Montalbano. Marrone suggests that characters like Montalbano,
who appear in novels, television series, and more, "[exceed] the narrative
proper [. . .] to live in larger and at the same time more rarified imaginary
universes" that intersect with "journalistic, political [and] promotional" discourses to "change his nature as an object semiotic."[20] The Black Panther,
a subject of ongoing political and social discourse and often a response to
global politics and history, certainly fits these criteria.

To Bertetti, such characters have both existential identity (the proper name
and appearance of the character, their role in the story, and relationships to
other characters) and fictional identity (how the character is operationalized
in different modal forms and the values that guide their acts).[21] These characters may appear in a variety of different forms and texts, but there are still
common elements that appear in all versions. In the Black Panther's case, it
could be the distinctive black costume modeled after his namesake, Wakanda
as a sovereign hidden nation, or any number of other elements. Characters
like the Panther, in Bertetti's view, are based on "multiple courses of events"
that do not contradict each other but rather refer to a "single diegetic universe" of characters that relate to each other—within this, a character like
Black Panther can diverge thematically (in terms of what he is doing or represents in a story) from medium to medium as well as figuratively (his costume,
powers, and appearance can all change to varying degrees as well).[22]

The Black Panther is not singular in this regard. A character like Sherlock
Holmes, for instance, has recurring characteristics that may change depending
on medium and adaptation but ultimately speak to a universally understood
depiction of the character. Roberta Pearson offers a competing model for
understanding transmedia characters, arguing that fictional characters more
generally are defined by factors like their speech patterns, psychological traits
and behaviors, physical appearance, and biography.[23] For instance, the Black
Panther always struggles with the duties of kinghood and his responsibilities
to his nation even as he allies himself with costumed adventurers from around

the globe, he is always depicted as an athletic man wearing a head-to-toe outfit modeled after a black cat, and he is always the king of Wakanda having received that title due to either a successful challenge for the throne or the death of his father. Such characteristics keep the character consistently recognizable. Yet, as Pearson argues, while corporately owned characters like the Black Panther inevitably outgrow a single text and "migrate across media platforms and the globe," that guiding corporate hand "[imposes] a greater degree of coherence and consistency." Such entities, Pearson argues, have a material interest in "[protecting] long-term profitability even as they exploit the copyright across multiple platforms" and gradually replace previous iterations of the character with more marketable ones as economics dictate, as DC did when they replaced the campier 1960s Batman with a grittier one in the 1980s.[24] Therefore, if it is in the financial interest of the company to retool the comics incarnation of the character or his supporting cast to align more closely with the films for synergy, then those fictive elements can and will change to be more consistent—as we will see later, elements from the films like the character's powers and Wakandan "salute" have made their way into the comics to create a more cohesive transmedia character.

This is important, because while individual authors and fan communities can take those elements and reimagine them, ultimately it is the work of the copyright holder and the historical context of a character that determine what is most salient and relevant and canonical. Yet at the same time, the reassignment of these "floating signifiers," as Pearson calls them, to different media contexts allows for the rhetorical significance of those fictive elements—the Panther and what he stands for—to reach different audiences and speak to them in different ways at different times.[25] Like with Batman and the Joker, the Black Panther can be discovered in one form in one age or context and rediscovered in a different as one grows older or more sophisticated in their media consumption habits, creating the opportunity for a character that grows and changes with the audience—a child may discover the character in a cartoon aimed at preschoolers and grow up to read the more adult-oriented comics work of Ta-Nehisi Coates or Don McGregor featuring the character, carrying their fandom forward as they age (and providing multiple marketing contact points for Disney).

The same concept applies to broader social and cultural trends—the *Black Panther* film would not have been such a watershed moment had Black-led superhero films (and indeed, media by and about Black protagonists) not historically been passed over due to studio and corporate uncertainty and unease, nor would the comics have led to that moment without the contributions of various writers and artists to revitalize and champion the character internally. The Black Panther, as a transmedia character speaking to a broader human experience owned as intellectual property of an enormous media conglomerate, acts at a locus of control somewhere between the meaning assigned to those fictive elements by individual creators and fans and the broader corporate vision for the character. This book suggests those elements are often used to explore key concepts that recur throughout these forms and pertain to his symbolic value of African identity and Blackness—and that these recurring key concepts, even if not necessarily recounting parts of a contiguous multimedia story, establish a clear narrative and image of who the character is and what he represents.

CRITICAL RACE THEORY AND MEDIA LITERACY

If the Black Panther character is a response to Eurocentric narratives, exploring the rhetorical dimensions of how that response is crafted is important to understanding the continuing relevance of the character. Measuring that relevance requires some understanding of how the Black Panther narrative can act as counterbalance or salve to historical narratives of degradation and disempowerment. Critical race theory offers a window through which we can explore the "story-telling" potential of the character and his stories.

Critical race theory, far from the anti-American bogeyman recently evoked by much of the conservative right, is essentially just a form of study that "foregrounds race and racism in all aspects of the research process," exploring how discourses of race and power shape cultural phenomena from education to the mass media with a goal of working to eliminate racism and other "forms of subordination."[26] In CRT, race and racism are endemic and must be understood on both micro and macro-levels. CRT approaches are then centered in an interdisciplinary approach focused on social justice and the valuation of the experiential knowledge of people of color.[27] Originating in legal scholarship, CRT uses this interdisciplinary approach to challenge "post racialism's agnosticism on race"—the actual goals of such work can be varied in scope and intent.[28]

For the purposes of this book, we are primarily interested in what CRT can tell us about media representations and discourse. A significant component of this approach involves the contextualization of media content "within power relations" in a manner centered on the "lived experience of People of Color."[29] When applied to media narratives, critical race theory is useful for deconstructing "prevailing dominant narratives in media content" as well as how they can be challenged and in so doing place minority voices at the center of the discourse.[30] Richard Delgado suggests that the challenging of these dominant racial narratives is a vital means of challenging "the status quo"; the act of storytelling serves to build consensus and a "common culture of shared understandings."[31] More importantly, he suggests the act of counter-storytelling identifies how the dominant narrative selects facts and structures them to benefit the in-group majority. In this way, counter-story-telling is an important means of "survival and liberation" for the oppressed and an essential means of "deepen[ing] and humanizing" the members of the in-group by seeking these stories out.[32] Moreover, as Goessling suggests in her study of an urban photography narrative project, the production of coun-ter-narratives illustrates the relationship between the self and society as well as the "material consequences" of those dominant social narratives.[33] Stories, the theory argues, are powerful and they can shape our social reality—and in that way, stories from outside the dominant in-group can act as a means of empowering those who do not fall into the majority.

Importantly, however, a Critical Race Media Literacy approach goes beyond simply exploring how non-white individuals are represented in the media; rather, it also encourages audiences to "'read' racism through media texts, images, and discourses that promote deficit renderings of Non-White cultures and race social consciousness."[34] It also uncovers how media pro-mote specific narratives of race while downplaying or suppressing others.[35] The principles of media literacy—that media is constructed as the product of a creative language to audiences that receive it differently with its own viewpoints in a system aimed at generating profit and power—are helpful to understand here.[36] Media messages are not naturally-occurring phenom-ena, but are instead the product of individual creators who are themselves influenced by their own experiences and media consumption. Therefore, the present analysis of the *Black Panther* meta-franchise should seek to explore how these influences shape and contextualize these texts—and critically engage with how authentic the counter-narratives that originate from massive corporations can feasibly be.

In that spirit I must also acknowledge my own positioning and privilege as a white scholar and my outsider status in much of this discussion. I cannot assume and do not claim the research I have done for this book and elsewhere is a replacement for the lived experiences of people of color, nor does analyz-ing a pop culture text offer unique insight into these experiences or allow me to speak for them. Throughout this project I have done my best to de-center my own experience by putting these works in their proper social and histori-cal context and refer to the work of scholars of color as much as possible. Ultimately, I concur with Amy Aldous Bergerson's view that CRT research requires white scholars to be cautious but also poses significant value in chal-lenging dominant attitudes in the academy.[37]

As alluded to above, the Black Panther character and narrative are hardly genuine outsider stories—to suggest otherwise is to ignore the character's locus at the center of a gigantic transmedia franchise owned by one of the largest media conglomerates in history. Yet, the anecdotes surrounding the film—of people flocking to theaters to see the film dressed in traditional clothing and adopting "Wakanda Forever" as a rhetorical device of empowerment—suggest that fans have adopted it as a symbolic counter-narrative. As such, the Black Panther cannot be divorced from the real contexts of race and racism that inform the creation of his character and the popularity of his stories. A full reckoning with the character requires the identification of the parameters of the counter story he (and by extension the writers, artists, directors, and actors who portray him) tells. The *Black Panther* film and transmedia franchise may only be revolutionary within the narrow framework of corporate intellectual property ownership, but it still acts as a means through which hegemonic white narratives of Africa and Blackness could be challenged in mainstream spaces.

To do this, this book will be using a form of synthesis based on the generative criticism model, in which the critic attempts to discern what is rhetorically interesting about a text or how it creates a reaction without having a specific question in mind.[38] Hall argues that generative criticism is about "assembling relational mappings" and should account for all forms of a concept.[39] Such a perspective is useful when considering the Black Panther or any such transmedia character—this book embraces the multiplicity of the concept, attempting to craft a cohesive vision of how the character negotiates with questions of colonialism, Black identity, and Diaspora as well as upholding a unique transmedia identity of his own.

This multiplicity poses a unique challenge, considering that there is no one definitive Black Panther text under the rules of transmedia other than the one that an individual fan may deem as definitive for their personal preferences. Even the original *Fantastic Four* comics in which the character debuted cannot be the definitive version, as the modern concept of the character varies in important ways. Therefore, this volume begins from the standpoint that such a definitive version of the character cannot exist, and the constellation of various takes on the character—with all its contradictions and conflicting audiences—is in fact as close as we can get; the *idea* of Black Panther is the canon, not a particular issue, game, or film. To understand this canonical notion of the character, the book seeks to contextualize the corpus of work across discrete publishing and media eras from his inception to the current moment. While I have endeavored to identify and include as many relevant transmedia depictions of the character as I can, I have erred on the side of focusing on specific authorial eras and meaningful evolutions in the character rather than recounting every single appearance of the character no matter how minor. I also largely limited the purview of the book to media in which the Black Panther or a close associate was the primary or a very significant character—meaning that many works by necessity are left out. I feel the material analyzed in this volume is the material most relevant and significant to the character's transmedia identity and counter-narrative status as well as the most contextually relevant material. In that spirit, prior to initiating a long-form analysis of the character, it is helpful first to understand the media environment in which he was created and continues to exist.

NOTES

1. Watercutter, "Black Panther's Oscar wins made history."
2. Mendelson, "Box Office: 'Black Panther' tops 'Last Jedi' and 'Avengers.'"
3. Maloney, "Backstage at the Black Panther"; White, "'Black Panther wins two Grammys."
4. Berr, "'Black Panther' merchandise is also striking gold"; Robinson, "Toy companies have not kept up with the demand for 'Black Panther' merch."
5. Rotten Tomatoes, "72 Best Superhero Movies of All Time."
6. Culver, *Black Panther: The Illustrated History of a King.*
7. Lamerichs, "An Introduction to Character Studies."
8. Jenkins, "Transmedia 202: Further Reflections"; Kinder, *Playing with Power.*
9. Kinos-Goodin, "9 Key Moments."
10. Narcisse, "Wakanda was the way Stan Lee spoke to me."
11. Nama, *Super Black*; Delgado, "Storytelling for Oppositions and Others."
12. Wilt, "How Black Panther liberalizes Black Resistance for White Comfort."
13. Lenker, "Black Panther cast and crew"; Vitali, Hunt, & Thorp V, "Trump referred to Haiti and African nations as 'shithole' countries."
14. Romano, "Art Spiegelman"; Elbein, "The Secret Identity of Marvel Comics' Editor."
15. Jenkins, "Revenge of the Origami Unicorn."
16. Kinder, *Playing with Power.*
17. Jenkins, *Convergence Culture.*
18. Bertetti, "Toward a Typology of Transmedia Characters," 2344–5.
19. Ibid, 2345.
20. Marrone, "Montalbano: Affirmations and transformations of a media hero," 2–3; the Italian-to-English translation cited here is the product of Google Translate.
21. Bertetti, "Toward a Typology," 2348–9.
22. Ibid, 2353–4.
23. Pearson, "World Building Logics and Copyright," 119.
24. Ibid.
25. Ibid, 120.
26. Solórzano & Yosso, "Critical Race Methodology," 24–25.
27. Solórzano, "Images and Words that Wound."
28. Crenshaw, "Twenty Years of Critical Race Theory."
29. Yosso, "Critical Race Media Literacy," 59–60.
30. Alemán & Alemán Jr., "Critical Race Media Projects."
31. Delgado, "Storytelling," 2413–14.

32. Ibid, 2436 & 2440.
33. Goessling, "Increasing the Depth of Field," 671.
34. King, "The Media and Black Masculinity," 36.
35. Ibid.
36. Center for Media Literacy, "MediaLit Kit."
37. Bergerson, "Critical race theory and white racism."
38. Foss, "Generative Criticism."
39. Hall, "A Case for Generative Criticism," 315.

Chapter 2

Context of the King

Africa, the Media, Blackness, and Hegemony

Understanding why the Black Panther is so important—and why he endures—requires the critic to understand the circumstances surrounding his creation and existence. Lee and Kirby, of course, put ink and words to paper to give the character life, but without the then-contemporary influence of the Civil Rights movement and centuries of toxic media narratives denigrating the African continent and Black Americans he may not have seemed so necessary—or his debut so revolutionary. In a larger sense, the media and popular culture bear much of the blame for the narratives against which these counter-stories push—and the attitudes and stereotypes presented across news and entertainment are without a doubt reflective of underlying patterns of discrimination that have existed for those centuries. It is one thing to identify a stereotyped portrayal in popular culture—it is another to step back and look at the systemic power imbalances and privilege that led to it being adopted and then repeatedly decontextualized over time to simply become part of the discourse's background.

This chapter attempts to provide an explanation and overview of media coverage of and attitudes toward African and African American individuals and culture, as well as how these representations reflect systemic inequity and white hegemony. I do not claim these experiences are identical. However, as this book is focused on the Black Panther, it is necessary to talk about these representations in tandem as well as find the places where sociopolitical discrimination toward American citizens based on their race spills over to discrimination and marginalization of the continent and culture more broadly. The Black Panther was created at once both to challenge the then-contemporary attitudes of the jungle pulps and stories that were so popular on newsstands and on the screen as well as—at least in Lee and Kirby's telling—to address a distinct lack of diversity in their own work made more immediately apparent by the struggle for equality going on outside their door. T'Challa is African, not African American (and in fact this distinction is crucial to many of his stories, as will be discussed later in this volume), but as one of the few Black heroes of that era he ultimately acts as a representative of both interests.

As such, this chapter attempts to explore multiple threads of historical and media depictions to understand how these perspectives have evolved and developed alongside the forces of history. It is not an exhaustive overview of Civil Rights, the African Diaspora, or any other vital phenomena in the history of these stories, nor can it catalog the sum of media depictions and negotiations of these racial identities. This chapter is, however, an attempt to draw a line between hegemonic white attitudes toward Africa and Black identity and how those attitudes manifest in the news and entertainment media, creating at least the rough outlines of the larger media story that the Black Panther mythology and its fan appropriation is intended to counter.

AFRICAN DIASPORA AND A SEARCH FOR PLACE

In his essay on the *Black Panther* film for the *New Yorker*, writer Jelani Cobb suggests that the Panther's home of Wakanda serves an important purpose as a "redemptive counter-mythology" to long-held Eurocentric narratives about Africa and its people, suggesting the film's casting and narrative choices reinforce a narrative of connection between "the continent's scattered descendants."[1] Wakanda, in Marvel Comics lore, is a prosperous sovereign African nation that hides its wealth, vibranium, and technological advancement from the world to avoid exploitation by outside forces. This last point is especially important—to understand the Black Panther is to understand that he is largely what Adilifu Nama identifies as an idealized and restorative vision of an alternate history in which at least some part of Africa was not subject to European and white hegemony.[2]

Understanding why that alternate history resonates must begin with a brief discussion of the impact of slavery. The first African slaves were brought into the English colony of Jamestown in 1619, instituting "a system of bondage" that "[reserved slavery] exclusively for black Africans and their descendants."[3] European slaveowners benefited from a ready supply of labor that was effectively cut off from their homeland or any sort of "external political support."[4] Over time, attitudes normalizing and justifying the inhumane treatment of slaves were adopted, effectively justifying the practice due to perceived biological and intellectual differences. For instance, female slaves were forced into nudity when being sold and labored in hiked-up skirts, creating the white perception that African women were promiscuous in comparison to their Victorian counterparts and thereby excusing sexual violence visited upon them.[5] The exploitation of African bodies was systemic and easily self-justified by the white European majority over the long and tragic history of slavery.

The consequence of this imperialist adventurism and the slave trade was a global separation of generations of Africans from their homeland. Over time, their descendants would reclaim their identity and ancestral ties, connecting their African heritage to their Black identity and seeking a return to their political and spiritual homeland. This concept, called the African Diaspora, broadly applies to anyone of African descent around the world and is defined by the African Union Commission as "peoples of African origin living outside the continent, irrespective of their citizenship and nationality and who are willing to contribute to the development of the continent and the building of the African Union."[6]

The Atlantic slave trade is only one of the "diasporic streams" that scholars argue contribute to the global African Diaspora. Other streams include the movement of Africa's earliest people, immigration from Nigeria and Cameroon, and global networks of trade.[7] Data released by the World Bank suggests members of the African Diaspora are spread across the globe and numerous in amount, and that the African Union considers the Diaspora to be the "sixth region" of the continent.[8] Great diversity exists within this group, but the common characteristic of Diaspora members is a sense of belonging to both worlds and the ability to bridge between cultures.[9] Moreover, there is an attempt on the part of the members of the Diaspora to find a way to exert their own sense of place and identity in the countries they inhabit, through active participation, festivals, protests, and other efforts to reinforce their cultural identity.[10]

The implicit meaning of the Wakanda metaphor in the Black Panther mythology is therefore central to this discussion—the idea of a free, untouched place in which Black excellence can thrive is an undeniably powerful one considering the Diaspora (though, as we will discuss later, Wakanda is not always a perfect metaphor in this regard, and that imperfection can often drive the plot). Similar place-making efforts exist throughout real world history, as well. In 1804, after a lengthy civil war in which the French general and former slave François-Dominique Toussaint L'Ouverture led a revolution against the white slaveowners of the colony of San Domingo, the nation of Haiti was formed as a state free of the practice of slavery. In historical retellings, Toussaint himself is held up as a heroic figure advancing a cause of liberty, representing the "determination of his people never, never to be slaves again."[11] The Haitian Revolution, scholars argue, effectively created a counter-state to the prevailing system of African slavery around the world.

Yet, as historian Randall Robinson explains, this act remained a sore spot in white consciousness:

> Deeply interwoven in the modern Haitian subconscious are themes of origin, the middle passage, the heroic revolution, and the terrible price black Haitians were forced to pay for it by a white world that has never forgotten or forgiven it [. . .] The leaders of the white world simply do not accord to the constitutions and laws of black countries the near sanctity they accord to their own.[12]

Haiti, was of course, not the only nation that rejected colonialism or outright avoided it. Implicit in the discussion of Wakanda as a metaphor—as the hypothetical and fictional lone holdout from colonization—is the idea that the whole of Africa was colonized during European expansion. However, this is not the case. Many African nations were colonized during the so-called "Scramble for Africa" of the late 1800s and early 1900s in which thirteen European countries divided up the continent under the guise of attempting to suppress the slave trade.[13] Two nations, Ethiopia and Liberia, are claimed to have never been colonized, though these claims come with caveats. While Liberia was founded in 1822 by the American Colonization Society, a group that saw the return of Black Americans to Africa as a desirable alternative to domestic emancipation, some scholars argue the ACS controlled too little territory in the country prior to its declared independence to be considered a true colony. Similarly, while Italy occupied Ethiopia from 1936 to 1941, Ola Olsson notes this five-year span "did not result in a lasting colonial adminis-tration."[14] Naturally, the independence of these countries and the initial suc-cess of the Haitian Revolution did little to change Western attitudes toward Black independence, and in fact led to further antipathy.

In the spirit of counter-narratives, there is evidence that at least some Black fans saw attending the *Black Panther* film in its theatrical release as a form of place-making. For instance, while the film is fictional and the tribes and cul-tures represented within it are equally so, the production and costume design of the film reflected the traditional and ceremonial clothing of many African nations and tribes. As Teen Vogue writer Amira Rasool noted, the film offered an attempt to restore "a sense of freedom and power" to global Black communities "once stripped of so many of their traditional garbs"; dressing up to go to the film, in Rasool's mind, reflected "the variety and beauty of African nations and [projected] a vision of ourselves that is not only royal but accurate to our experiences as a diverse and successful group."[15] Indeed, Rasool and countless other fans appeared at their local cineplexes dressed in traditional African clothing and other ensembles befitting a larger social and cultural event, flooding social media with selfies and photographs to mark the occasion. It is hard to argue that this is not a form of place-making, an effort to claim space in the predominantly white blockbuster film industry more generally and the overwhelmingly white superhero genre more generally. Skepticism of such an idea is understandable—filling Disney's coffers is not exactly a revolutionary act—but something, informed by history, in the metaphor of Wakanda and the Black Panther spoke to the audience.

EUROCENTRISM AND COLONIALISM IN POPULAR NARRATIVES OF AFRICA AND BLACKNESS

White popular narratives of Africa and its people as a lesser culture were built on a long process of Othering and Eurocentric hegemony. In the late nineteenth century, scientists like Frederick Coombs pushed phrenology and other pseudoscientific theories to justify subjugation of Africa and its people, while contemporary media depictions of the time portrayed Africans as uncivilized savages.[16] Naturally, such attitudes fed into and further underscored the sense of innate Eurocentric superiority that had served to justify the subjugation of a people.[17] These attitudes spilled over into popular media, reinforcing the systems of exploitation that had perpetuated for centuries. Even after the abolition of slavery and gradual slow rollout of civil rights in America, representations of Africa and by association Blackness were often tied inextricably with narratives of a savage "Other," as well as a monolithic view of the continent itself defined by its extremes of weather, poverty, and other factors.[18] In short, Africa and its people had become a monolithic caricature in the predominantly white popular culture around the world with the implicit goal of justifying Eurocentric attitudes.

Part of the challenge of any form of critical approach to reconstructing these attitudes is that there is no one overarching body of thought that guides media narratives or cultural attitudes, but rather these attitudes must be reconstructed from many different forms of discourse.[19] The decisions of what stories are told, what is included in the text, and what is not are all dictated by underlying—and even unconscious—attitudes that must then be reconstructed.[20] Moreover, media messages are created in the context of the creator's beliefs, experiences, and influences—meaning ideologies can propagate and repeat themselves.[21] As Foucault suggests, understanding these narratives requires exploration of many different texts and documents to reconstruct historical discourses.[22] Such a task is well-suited for a transmedia analysis.

The comics industry that would eventually spawn the Black Panther was no stranger to these narratives. A genre of works called "jungle comics" like *Sheena, Queen of the Jungle* often featured white protagonists doing battle with the native population, regularly portraying African natives as slow-witted characters speaking in "an imbecilic hybrid of pidgin English and African-American slang."[23] At the height of World War II, these titles inserted themselves into the African theater of war, suggesting that native uprisings served only to further the Nazis' interest in the region and as such anticolonialism was antithetical to Western freedom.[24] The bigoted implication of these comics was clear—native African backlash against white colonialism was either ill-advised or actively fomented by America's fascist enemies taking advantage of an ignorant populace. In this way, the WWII-era "jungle comics" served to reinforce an exploitative depiction of Africa and its diasporic people in the American eye at a time when many Black Americans were starting to demand greater representation and rights at home.

These comics were hardly alone in taking a dim view of Africa and its people. In fact, they largely mirrored the representation of Africa seen in other media. Even venerated scientific publications like National Geographic repeated colonialist attitudes of savagery and exoticism at the same time they downplayed genuine political and social strife in African countries as well as other parts of the world.[25] *Tarzan* novels and stories spoke of the titular white character's mastery over savage natives and carried with them creator Edgar Rice Burroughs' belief in eugenics and white superiority.[26] As political scientist Kevin Dunn suggests, films of the 1930s depicted Africa as both a "beautiful, unspoiled land ripe for settling" as well as a "terrible, untrained wilderness that requires taming by whites" populated by "savage natives," promoting colonialism both as unquestioned good and moral imperative.[27] Contemporary media is less overt about this ideology but still advances it—a 2019 reality series called "The British Tribe Next Door" saw a white British family bring a replica of their house to the tribe of a Namibian village to show off accoutrements like hair straighteners.[28] Even as these attitudes are widely challenged in the marketplace of ideas, the underlying colonialist ideology can find ways to creep through.

News coverage has also advanced the negative framing of Africa—a 2014 *Newsweek* story speculating that the consumption of "bushmeat" led to the then-contemporary Ebola outbreak was roundly criticized for using outmoded stereotypes and contributing to a sense of Othering that may have ultimately endangered public health.[29] This is emblematic of much of the coverage of Africa in the wider international news media, which too often focuses on poverty, violence, and patriarchal attitudes. In an article for the Columbia Journalism Review, Karen Rothmyer argues this is largely the product of NGOs trying to raise awareness and funding by focusing on problems rather than advancement, leading to paternalistic and inaccurate stories.[30] Remi Adekoya echoed these sentiments on the impact of such coverage in an editorial for *The Guardian*, arguing both that the broader media system tends to prefer covering negative stories about the continent and there is no outward-facing African media network on the scale of a BBC or Al Jazeera to counter these perceptions.[31]

There is no question that media narratives about Africa, its culture, and its residents as well as those of who are of African descent have been largely driven by the global media, a mammoth system in which Africa has a comparatively smaller voice than other countries. While again care must be taken not to conflate these two media experiences, there is commonality in that the African American experience is also underreported and has historically been skewed in a negative direction largely to support Eurocentric ideological systems. The political and social domain of these belief structures—often designed to reinforce existing systems of power and dominance—must be considered to understand why the Black Panther mythology is so rhetorically potent.

THE NEWS MEDIA, CIVIL RIGHTS, AND CONTEMPORARY ISSUES

The media are undeniably powerful, though how powerful is a matter open to at least some debate. It is unlikely that media alone can inspire direct action or thought. But as George Gerbner suggested with his study of media violence that led to his theory of cultivation, the more violent media we consume, the more likely we are to believe the world is a dangerous and frightening place—a fact that also determines how we treat others who we see as a potential threat as well as what attitudes are mainstreamed.[32] The media and the stereotypes they carry promote specific interpretations of reality and create belief structures that not only govern our perspective but can also "play an important role in reconciling individuals to discriminatory treatment."[33] Repeated stereotyped images like those discussed in the previous section as well as this one, then, not only provide a skewed vision of reality—both positive and negative—and can skew the audience's perception of racial issues in the real world.

In this light, the media's coverage of Black social movements is vital to the conversation. The media has historically played a primary role in shaping public opinion on issues related to race and equality. Unfortunately, that role has rarely been impartial or positive throughout history. The mainstream press in both the North and South insulted, libeled, and denigrated Black people and interests in the pre-Civil War era with the primary interest of reifying the exploitative existing economic system.[34] The lack of representation in the press and a need to advocate for themselves led leaders in the Black community to create their own newspapers—over forty existed prior to the beginning of the Civil War in 1861, including Frederick Douglass's widely-read

North Star.[35] *Freedom's Journal*, instituted in 1827, cast itself as a publication seeking to correct misconceptions about the African American population and to provide that same population a platform to speak for themselves.[36] While these publications provided a subjugated minority with the chance to tell their own stories, their publication histories tended to be fairly brief as a product of both small budgets and a target audience that had been denied education and literacy.[37] While these and other minority-owned-and-targeted publications advanced the causes of abolition and equality, the white majority press remained largely unconcerned or hostile toward these issues.[38]

Post-war efforts by the press to cover ongoing campaigns of inequality and brutality against free Black people met with often violent antagonism. Ida B. Wells' journalistic campaign against lynching in the South in the late 1800s unveiled the truth that the majority of victims were falsely accused; she published her reports in the *Memphis Free Speech* and spoke on the issue around the world. Wells' work can rightly be considered some of the most influential in the history of investigative journalism, but her offices at the Free Speech were also famously destroyed in an act of intimidation.[39]

Even as overt hostility decreased, underreporting continued. Mainstream press rarely covered stories pertaining to segregation and the Jim Crow South, and white reporters covering these stories often did so at great personal risk.[40] The advent of television was a turning point. The 1954 *Brown v. Board of Education of Topeka* case and the ensuing school desegregations that followed made for compelling visuals and raised awareness of the civil rights struggle, though many outlets struggled to cover the story without alienating advertisers.[41] Martin Luther King Jr. was exceptionally proficient in the language of television and its impact, cognizant of the role "cameras and glaring lights" could play in offering some degree of protection to protesters.[42] King held media-friendly events and worked to maintain positive relationships with reporters—an arrangement that was not terribly difficult because segregationists despised and even in many cases tried to sabotage media coverage. However, the prevalence of civil rights issues in the media was a double-edged sword—as Alexis Madrigal put it in The Atlantic, media coverage essentially reinforced the "nationally acceptable message" that "the suffering of black people made for good television if it was violent enough" and created "two buckets out of black protesters [. . .] the 'good' peaceful ones and the 'bad' radical ones."[43] While Madrigal ultimately concludes that television did help grow public support for the Civil Rights Act of 1964 and the Voting Rights Act of 1965, this schism exists to this day in media coverage of civil rights issues.

In 1967, spurred by ongoing unemployment, poverty, educational disparity, and police brutality (among other factors), the "long, hot summer" of race riots began in cities across America—most notably Detroit, where rioting lasted for five days and resulted in 43 deaths and over 7,000 arrests.[44] In response to the unrest, then-President Lyndon Johnson commissioned a group to study the root causes of the problem. The National Advisory Commission on Civil Disorders (or as it would be known colloquially, the Kerner Commission) took a multifaceted approach to the study of race relations in America and laid the blame for the riots on systemic factors like police brutality, economic inequality, and racial discrimination.[45] The full report, weighing in at over 708 pages, was a surprise to Johnson, who tacitly rejected its findings—he had expected it to return findings that Communist agitators were responsible. It also failed to change public opinion; in fact, white support for civil rights waned after its release while support for tougher police crackdowns went up.[46]

Yet despite this, and especially in the current moment, the Kerner report remains a key moment in the discussion of how the media has constructed narratives around Black identity and civil rights. While the report does not wholly blame the 1967 unrest on the media—in fact, it assumes a greater degree of good faith than reporting perhaps merited at the time—it is prescient about where it finds the underlying flaws in the media's approach. The Commission's words were written in 1968 and echo a less thoughtful time in their language, but the meaning is as relevant as ever:

> The media report and write from the standpoint of a white man's world. The ills of the ghetto, the difficulties of life there, the Negro's burning sense of grievance, are seldom conveyed. Slights and indignities are part of the Negro's daily life, and many of them come from what he now calls "the white press"—a press that repeatedly, if unconsciously, reflects the biases, the paternalism, the indifference of white America.[47]

As the Commission report alluded to, the major issue with press diversity is a simple one—the majority of so-called "gatekeepers," those who make the editorial decision of which stories to cover and which ones to publish, have historically been white males.[48] Producers and editors are overwhelmingly still white and male, according to the American Society of News Editors— only 21.9 percent of salaried employees reported by all newsrooms in the ASNE's 2019 survey were people of color.[49] These numbers, remarkably, are improvements—a 2017 study of five of the country's largest newspapers (including *The New York Times* and *The Washington Post*) found that minority representation in newsrooms lagged well behind minority representation in the cities and communities they served—for instance, only 31 percent of the Washington Post's newsroom was comprised of minorities compared to 54 percent of people living in the metropolitan area it serves.[50] A 2015 study by Color of Change found that major network affiliate stations in the New York media market exaggerated the proportion of Black individuals involved in crime by 24 points on average, even going so far as to represent 3 out of every 4 criminals reported on as Black, creating a "culture in which the benefit of the doubt is not distributed evenly—we see a hostile society for some, and a privileged society for others."[51]

The vast majority of scholarship is consistent that these skewed media perceptions not only reinforce a bifurcated American society but also perpetuate toxic racial stereotypes and implicit bias that serves to dehumanize and criminalize Black people.[52] Such stereotyping contributes to racial profiling in policing, as well as higher levels of incarceration.[53] Black men are also disproportionately sentenced to capital punishment, with roughly 42 percent of the national death row population identified as Black.[54] Black people are also three times more likely than white people to be killed by the police; 2018 data suggested they were also nearly four times as likely to be arrested.[55] Simply pointing out these facts often leads to accusations of anti-Americanism, with protesters taking to the streets to demand action after the killing of unarmed Black Americans being painted as imaginary anti-state agitators by the government. Nor does celebrity grant the benefit of the doubt: just ask former NFL quarterback Colin Kaepernick, whose gesture of kneeling during the national anthem to call attention to inequality and police brutality cost him his job with the San Francisco 49ers and likely caused the league to blackball him from being re-signed to a team later.[56] While Kaepernick would settle a collusion lawsuit with the league in 2019, the narrative had already been cast. As sportswriter Howard Bryant puts it in his essential book *Full Dissidence*, the attack on Kaepernick for criticizing police meant that "white America had exposed itself yet again in its willingness to sacrifice black life, in its complete and criminal lack of interest in justice."[57] How could a character like Black Panther not resonate in such an environment?

CO-OPTION AND ERASURE OF BLACK IDENTITY AND ISSUES IN THE MEDIA

Outside of the news media, popular culture has done little to challenge these narratives—and in fact, in many cases, has served to romanticize a brutal history. The prominence of blackface and minstrel shows in vaudeville and early broadcast entertainment is well-documented and served both to ridicule Black Americans and justify their subjugation to a receptive white audience.[58] While shows like *Amos and Andy* and films like *The Jazz Singer* brought blackface to the mainstream well after, arguably one of the most famous—and heinous—forms of blackface was the 1915 D.W. Griffith film *The Birth of a Nation*, which cast the Ku Klux Klan as noble heroes seeking to retake their homeland after the Civil War. Griffith's heroes perpetuate a campaign of violence and lynching against Black men, played as buffoonish and sexually aggressive villains by white actors wearing blackface makeup. The wildly popular film was famously praised by then-President Woodrow Wilson as "like writing history with lightning" in spite of its lack of any sort of resemblance to actual history.[59] The film inspired condemnation and protests, most notably those in Boston led by the newspaper editor Monroe Trotter that author Dick Lehr would argue acted as a prototype for the civil rights movement.[60] Despite the film's well-documented racist bona fides—in the 1970s, KKK Grand Wizard David Duke screened the film at Klan recruitment rallies—it was and is still widely shown in college film courses, including the one I took as an undergraduate in the early 2000s, with its innovations in the technique of filmmaking offered as justification for its curricular inclusion.[61] Another student subjected to the film in their undergraduate film class, the Academy Award-winning director Spike Lee, was so infuriated by the film's content and the faculty's seeming indifference to its meaning that he made a first-year film project called *The Answer* about a Black filmmaker tasked with writing a big-budget remake of the movie; he would later revisit the film and its legacy in a pivotal scene in his 2018 film *BlacKkKlansman* intercutting a raucous Klan screening of the film with a heartbreaking recounting of the real-life lynching of Jesse Washington.[62]

More mainstream than *The Birth of a Nation* but no less insidious in its own right is *Gone with the Wind*, the overlong and wildly financially successful 1939 adaptation of the Margaret Mitchell novel romanticizing the postwar South era as "a utopia of tranquil living" with "docile and content" enslaved Black servants—as Jason Bailey wrote in the *New York Times*, it positions the freed Reconstruction-era slaves as "morally dangerous and politically naïve" in a manner similar to Griffith's film.[63] The film, still the highest-grossing ever when adjusted for inflation, is often lauded as a sweeping epic and for Hattie McDaniel's reception of the first ever Oscar granted to an African American performer for her role as a Black servant. It has also been the subject of harsh criticism from voices ranging from Malcolm X to filmmaker (and recently-minted *Black Panther* writer) John Ridley, who in an op-ed for the *Los Angeles Times* called the film out for romanticizing the Confederacy as "something more, or better, or more noble than what it was—a bloody insurrection to maintain the 'right' to own, sell and buy human beings." After the essay was published, the film was temporarily removed from the HBO Max streaming service and raced to the top of the Amazon sales charts in physical and digital versions; HBO put up a recontextualized version later.[64] *Gone with the Wind* offered a romantic version of the racist "Lost Cause" narrative—and one that persists through the Instagram-ready "plantation weddings" it inspires to this day.

While Black characters and performers appeared in deeply stereotyped form in media like *Our Gang* and reruns of the aforementioned *Amos & Andy* well into the 1960s and 1970s, pressure from the Civil Rights movement leaded to greater diversity and more realistic portrayals—but even the less overtly stereotyped portrayals lagged well behind real-world trends and issues.[65] Moreover, new stereotypes were added that reinforced Black performers as secondary to white performers, casting them in stereotyped roles as asexual and marginalized sidekicks.[66] Black characters were still largely tokenized to be less threatening to white audiences, and while *Roots* brought the story of slavery in America to a massive audience in 1977, most Black appearances were in sitcoms like *Good Times* and *Sanford and Son* rather than dramas.[67] Even the popular and often politically radical Blaxploitation genre, which cast Black actors and actresses in lead roles where they often violently fought back against racism and oppression, ran into criticism from the NAACP and other organizations; while the genre offered Black actors and creators opportunities in the industry its films were still largely "made by white directors, aimed at primarily white audiences."[68]

Unfortunately, Black actors and creatives still struggle for opportunity in front of the camera and behind it. A UCLA study demonstrated that only 15.7 percent of roles in the top films of 2019 went to Black performers—an increase from 2018 and well ahead of other minority groups but dwarfed by the over 67 percent of roles that went to white performers.[69] Black actresses were even less likely to appear in prominent film roles, with only 64 Black women being cast in the total sample; behind the camera only 5.5 percent of films were helmed by Black directors.[70] As of 2021, only 20 acting Oscars have been awarded to Black actresses and actors—and Halle Berry is the only Black actress to win the Best Actress prize.[71] While hardly the sole arbiter of a film's quality or worth, Academy Awards are nonetheless crucial to the economics of film and can help performers and directors negotiate higher pay rates—meaning that the lack of diversity in nominees and winners has genuine consequences. In 2015, activist April Reign created the #OscarsSoWhite campaign to call out a lack of diversity in the voting body of the Academy and its nominees; in an editorial reflecting on the impact of the campaign she wryly noted that membership went from "92% white and 75% male" all the way to "84% white and 68% male" five years later as a result.[72] It should be noted that both Spike Lee and Jordan Peele received writing Oscars in recent years, but their films (*BlacKkKlansman* and *Get Out,* respectively) were largely shut out of other categories.

Moreover, speaking out about social issues can have genuine repercussions in the industry. In 2014, director Ava DuVernay and the cast of *Selma* wore

T-shirts bearing the phrase "I Can't Breathe" in support of protests surrounding the police killing of Eric Garner to the film's premiere in New York. Amid the nationwide protests over the death of George Floyd, star David Oyelowo claimed that the statement was the reason the critically acclaimed film was snubbed at the Oscars; a claim backed up by DuVernay on Twitter.[73] While the Academy put out a tweet of apology shortly after Oyelowo's interview, the story clearly illustrates an industry in which Black voices are still largely marginalized.

SUPERHEROES, LEGACY, AND AFROFUTURISM

The superhero genre into which Black Panther and his eponymous film fall into has traditionally been predominantly white as a result of the twin forces of nostalgic gatekeeping in the comics sector and executive reluctance on the film side—consider, for instance, the popularity of the John Stewart Green Lantern character (the first Black Green Lantern and one of the earlier prominent Black superheroes in DC comics) as part of the early-2000s era *Justice League* animated series. His appearance in that wildly successful series made him the most visible Green Lantern prior to the release of the ill-advised 2011 film, which cast Ryan Reynolds as the white Green Lantern Hal Jordan.[74] As with many such issues in the superhero genre, synergy is to blame. While Stewart was beloved by fans and especially Black fans, when it came time to reboot the comic series DC editorial specifically requested writer Geoff Johns bring the white Hal Jordan character back.[75] This had the ultimate effect of essentially pushing Stewart to the sidelines in merchandising and other media in perpetuity.

Another popular Black character, the late Dwayne McDuffie's Static, was the star of the successful *Static Shock* afternoon cartoon series on the now-defunct Kids' WB network, but as McDuffie suggests, executive concern over the lack of ability to sell toys based on the show killed it despite excellent ratings.[76] Finally, in 2018 Sony's *Spider-Man: Into the Spider-Verse* was released to rave reviews and eventually won an Academy Award for Best Animated Feature, drawing praise for its portrayal of hero Miles Morales and his biracial identity—including un-subtitled Spanish spoken at home. Yet some, like *Washington Post* reporter David Betancourt, criticized relegating the character to an animated film while the live-action *Spider-Man: Homecoming* and *Spider-Man: Far from Home* films assigned elements of his story and support network to Tom Holland's Peter Parker in the live-action Marvel Cinematic Universe.[77] The mythic power of the superhero is undeniable, but that power too often remains limited to a very narrow spectrum of experiences.

Certainly, Black Panther, as a creation of two white Americans that is owned by a massive international entertainment conglomerate, does not innately wrest the microphone away from the white majority (though Black creatives would ultimately steer the character in pivotal directions over time). However, in some small way, it can at least start a conversation about challenging these situations—especially because of the franchise's close entanglement with the Afrofuturist movement, which attempts to explore these genres through an African lens as opposed to a Eurocentric one. As writer Ytasha Womack puts it, Afrofuturism is "both an artistic aesthetic and a framework for critical theory" combining "elements of science fiction, historical fiction, speculative fiction, fantasy, Afrocentricity, and magic realism with non-Western beliefs" to comment and critique past and present while prognosticating about the future.[78]

Daylanne English and Alvin Kim reinforced the political importance of the movement, calling it a form of "African American cultural production and political theory that [imagines] less constrained black subjectivity in the future."[79] The political is the point in most Afrofuturist works, which often portray futures in which "black people use technology to become leaders of their worlds" and use sci-fi tropes to comment on real-world difficulties.[80] Author (and *Black Panther* contributor) Dr. Nnedi Okorafor called science fiction "one of the greatest and most effective forms of political writing" in a 2017 TED Talk and lauded its ability to inspire "new technologies, ideas, and sociopolitical changes."[81] The 2018 release of the *Black Panther* film is often credited with a revived interest in Afrofuturism as a concept, though it is important to note that a plethora of authors, artists, and creators have contributed to it that have nothing to do with Marvel, some of the most noteworthy being the artist Jean-Michel Basquiat and musicians George Clinton and Janelle Monáe.[82] Still, it is worth exploring the Black Panther mythos—and how it postulates a scientifically advanced African nation hidden from the rest of the world—in this light, as well as why it does and how it brings the idea of Afrofuturism into greater mainstream prominence.

In summary, the narrative of Black identity in the news and entertainment media is one of distortion, omission, and marginalization, but also one that speaks to the power of counter-narratives and the necessity of exploring the media from a transmedia perspective informed by context and history. The Black Panther character is not only the product of pen and ink but the social and historical forces that shaped the zeitgeist surrounding a medium that has often reflected the biases of the world around it. It is into this world that Lee and Kirby first brought the character to light, and it is there our analysis should begin.

NOTES

1. Cobb, "'Black Panther' and the invention of 'Africa.'"
2. Nama, *Super Black.*
3. Smedley & Smedley, *Race in North America*, 96.
4. Ibid, 113.
5. Harris-Perry, *Sister Citizen.*
6. African Union Commission, "The Diaspora Division."
7. Palmer, "Defining and Studying the Modern African Diaspora."
8. World Bank, "African Diaspora."
9. Kanjunju, "Africa's secret weapon: The diaspora."
10. Allen, Lawhon, & Pierce, "Placing race."
11. James, *Black Jacobins*, 198.
12. Robinson, *An Unbroken Agony*, 24 & 26.
13. Saul, "Slavery and the 'Scramble for Africa.'"
14. Little, "How a Movement to Send Freed Slaves to Africa Created Liberia"; Ertan, Fiszbein, & Putterman, "Who was colonized and when?"; Olsson, "On the democratic legacy of colonialism."
15. Rasool, "Why I'm dressing up to see Black Panther."
16. Seay & Dionne, "The Long and Ugly History."
17. Smedley & Smedley, *Race in North America.*
18. Bunce, Franks, & Paterson, "Introduction."
19. McGee, "Text, Context, and the Fragmentation of Contemporary Culture."
20. Biesecker, "Rethinking the Rhetorical Situation."
21. Hardt, *Critical Communication Studies.*
22. Foucault, "The Archaeology of Knowledge."
23. Wright, *Comic Book Nation*, 37.
24. Ibid.
25. Goldberg, "To Rise Above the Racism of the Past, We Must Acknowledge It."
26. Weeks, "Tarzan and the race card."
27. Dunn, "Lights . . . Camera . . . Africa," 169.
28. Hirsch, "Racist African stereotypes."
29. Seay & Dionne, "The Long and Ugly History."
30. Rothmyer, "Hiding the Real Africa."
31. Adekoya, "Why Africans worry."
32. Croteau & Hoynes, *Media/Society.*
33. Rothenberg & Mayhew, *Race, Class and Gender in the United States*, 576.
34. Ford, McFall, & Dabney, "African American Media Today."
35. Ibid.
36. Newkirk, "The Minority Press."
37. Ibid.
38. Bramlett-Solomon & Carstarphen, "American Press and Multiculturalism."
39. Dickerson, "Overlooked: Ida B. Wells"; Public Broadcasting System, "Biographies: Ida B. Wells."
40. Bramlett-Solomon & Carstarphen, "American Press."

41. Ibid.
42. Madrigal, "When the Revolution was Televised."
43. Ibid.
44. Walsh, "50 Years After Race Riots, Issues Remain the Same."
45. George, "The 1968 Kerner Commission Got It Right, But Nobody Listened."
46. Ibid.
47. National Advisory Commission on Civil Disorders, *Report*, 366.
48. Dates & Pease, "Warping the World."
49. American Society of News Editors, "2019 Diversity Survey."
50. Frissell, Ibrahim, Raghavendran, & Yang, "Missed deadline."
51. Color of Change, "Not to Be Trusted."
52. Godsil & Johnson, "Transforming Perception."
53. Welch, "Black Criminal Stereotypes."
54. Ford, "Racism and the Execution Chamber."
55. Clayton, "The statistical paradox of police killings."
56. Ruiz, "It's already too late."
57. Bryant, *Full Dissidence*, 31.
58. Clark, "How the History of Blackface is Rooted in Racism."
59. Janik, "Writing History with Lightning."
60. Lehr, *The Birth of a Movement.*
61. Janik, ibid.
62. Vest, *Spike Lee*; Tenreyro, "Jesse Washington Was A Real Person."
63. Bailey, "'Gone with the Wind' and Controversy."
64. Ridley, "Hey, HBO"; Spangler, "'Gone with the Wind' Hits No. 1."
65. Bramlett-Solomon & Carstarphen, ibid.
66. Spears, "Race and Ideology: An Introduction."
67. Ibid.
68. Whitty, "Looking back at 'blaxploitation' films."
69. Hunt & Ramón, "Hollywood Diversity Report 2020."
70. Ibid.
71. Dixon, "Black Oscar winners"; Harris, "Daniel Kaluuya."
72. Reign, "#OscarsSoWhite Creator."
73. Romano, "*Selma* star says Oscar voters blacklisted film."
74. Polo, "Allow us to Explain."
75. Stone, "Green Lantern: Geoff Johns Looks Back."
76. Harvey, "The World's Finest Presents Static Shock."
77. Betancourt, "Miles Morales."
78. Womack, *Afrofuturism*, 9.
79. English and Kim, "Now We Want Our Funk Cut," 217.
80. Fitzpatrick, "It's Not Just Black Panther."
81. Elderkin, "Nnedi Okorafor Remarks"; It should be noted that Dr. Okorafor uses the term "Africanfuturist" rather than "Afrofuturist" to describe her work.
82. Sayej, "Beyond Black Panther."

Chapter 3

The Panther in the Silver Age

The King Arrives

After World War II, the bottom fell out of the superhero industry. As J. Richard Stevens suggests, the binary morality of superheroes became simultaneously less appealing in a more ambiguous Cold War landscape and their powers less impressive next to the horrifying power of the atomic bomb.[1] For years, the genre languished while other comic genres—notably crime, horror, and war stories—captured the public consciousness. Then, in 1956, the genre was reborn in a literal flash of lightning as DC Comics reintroduced their Golden Age hero The Flash with a new science-fiction direction to a warm reception and massive sales, followed by another successful revamp with the Green Lantern a few years later. Over the next few years, DC added to its costumed menagerie, culminating in the introduction of the Justice League of America and the superhero team-up concept in 1960.[2] Superheroes were a boom market again, and Marvel wanted in.

Seeking to challenge the market leader head-on, writer and editor Stan Lee and artist Jack Kirby collaborated on the introduction of a new team of superheroes, the Fantastic Four. Where many superhero teams were paragons of heroic perfection, the Fantastic Four was a family that bickered, moped, and struggled with their relationships.[3] The book was unlike anything else on the market, marrying high-concept science-fiction heroics and iconic villains like Doctor Doom and the Mole Man with grounded tales of domestic friction. Naturally, it became a massive success, rivaling the Justice League in popularity and laying the groundwork for a new era of comics that appealed to college students and the counterculture as much as they did to kids.

It is to this series that the Black Panther owes a debt, despite the fact he has since eclipsed the Four in current popular consciousness. Everything that the Black Panther has become starts in those inauspicious beginnings as a *Fantastic Four* guest character—and the elements that are now an indelible part of his transmedia brand came from two men who were neither African

31

nor Black, writing as sympathetic outsiders. However, there is no doubt that Black Panther was a marked improvement in representation over the books Marvel and other publishers had released before.

THE JUNGLE COMICS

So-called "jungle comics" were something of a cottage industry for Atlas Comics, the forebear of what is now known as Marvel.[4] Arriving late in the waning days of the Golden Age of Comics that had seen the creation of characters like Superman and Batman, the jungle books of Atlas Comics eschewed colorful superheroes for tales of white heroes fighting against the savagery of the jungle.[5] While none of the titles lasted more than a few years, Atlas made up for brevity with ubiquity—at least three "jungle" titles ran in the early to mid-1950s, and all of them reflected a mindset influenced by colonizing ideals.

The first, the anthology series *Jungle Tales*, ran from 1954 to 1955 and primarily featured white characters like Jann of the Jungle and big game hunter Cliff "The White Hunter" Mason alongside stories of African wildlife without human characters. While less overtly lurid than some of the earlier jungle comics discussed in the last chapter, *Tales* nonetheless carried forth their traditions, sandwiching overdramatic fictional prose about African exploration in between feature strips and ads for acne treatments. The racial politics of the series were set early on, with the second page of the first Jann of the Jungle story featuring a white director calling an African assistant "boy."[6] Jann, a white Hollywood stuntwoman filming a movie in the jungle, demonstrates her keen ability to tame the jungle by redirecting a stampede of animals away from the film shoot, after which she is revealed to be the granddaughter of another white woman who was revered by the tribe. In the Jann stories to follow, she often saved the natives from various threats like sickness and attacking animals, permanently relegating them to bystander or victim status when they are not actively fleeing the scene.

Similar white savior narratives ran through the characters featured in other books like *Lorna, the Jungle Queen* and the first run of *Jungle Action*. The latter, first published in October of 1954, was another anthology series that introduced the Tarzan knockoff Lo-Zar, Lord of the Jungle, the youthful hero Jungle Boy, and the leopard-print bodysuit-clad Leopard Girl—all of whom were white. Lo-Zar in particular is a shameless white savior character for the indigenous people of an unknown African locale, identified as the "one man who can help them in their most dreadful hour" over an image of a helpless African woman and her child about to be devoured by an attacking lion.[7] Lo-Zar's adventures echoed the earlier World War II jungle comics, although his foe was no longer the Nazis but rather the Communist "Reds" seeking to steal uranium from within the jungle—a reflection of Cold War anxieties and propaganda.[8] The usage of the Soviet Union as an antagonist was common in many of Atlas' comics, with Jann of the Jungle doing battle with a Soviet agent that duped her native friends in another issue.[9] In this way, not much had changed since the earlier jungle comics—foreign invaders were still taking advantage of African people who were either portrayed as helpless or maliciously complicit until "good white people" put a stop to it. All that changed, ultimately, was the banner under which the scoundrels fought.

When they weren't overtly political, the comics stereotyped the continent and its people in other ways. Many stories simply treated Africa as a monolithic entity of untamed jungle and mysterious danger, even going so far as to pit their heroes against dinosaurs and fantastic supernatural elements like zombies while making no acknowledgement of the then-real politics of apartheid or even identifying a specific country or location for their setting. In the pages of these titles, Africa was still less a real place with real people and real issues than an interchangeable backdrop for pulp tales of colonization and "savagery," a blank canvas on which the author could imagine any sort of barbaric threat to the heroes he wanted.

The only indigenous African lead in the Atlas jungle comics was Waku, Prince of the Bantu, who made his debut alongside Jann of the Jungle and Lo-Zar in the first issue of *Jungle Tales*. Predating the Black Panther by about a decade, Waku is arguably the first African lead in a Marvel publication; Marvel officially considers him their first regular Black lead character in an ongoing series.[10] While there are similarities between the two characters—notably that they were both the son of a chieftain who dies early in the story and are reluctantly thrust into leadership positions—the stories diverge from there, with Waku's tale being a more grounded one where he fights to save his people from enslavement by white poachers. He must also defeat Mabu, the man who sold them, in order to lead the Bantu tribe. While certainly less overtly racist by virtue of centering its narrative on an African character (and one it treats with general respect) and lacking some of the more abhorrent dialogue affectations of earlier comics discussed in the previous chapter, the art belies an implicit value judgment—the "good" Bantu, like Waku and his love interest Lalei, are drawn with more Anglicized features while Mabu and his allies are drawn with more overtly African ones and sharpened teeth.[11] This was far from the only example of stereotyped or racist art in the comics—in a later installment of "Jann of the Jungle," Jann's loyal native African sidekick Kuba is drawn and colored with pitch-black skin and large, bright white lips, echoing minstrel blackface.[12] Still, the Waku strips were unique amongst the Atlas anthologies for having a primarily African cast—something that would not be seen in a Marvel book set in Africa again until even a decade after the Black Panther debuted.

For the most part, contemporary Marvel has largely ignored these comics—while a search on their website returns crowdsourced wiki entries for characters like Jann (though largely in service of the character's cameo appearances in modern continuity) and an article referring to Waku, copies of the original *Jungle Action* and *Jungle Tales* series are nowhere to be found in reprints or digital platforms, likely for good reason. However, these comics are important to this book for one primary reason—they predate the Black Panther by only a decade or so and clearly inform the culture and the product Atlas was putting out in the years prior to the Silver Age and the beginning of Marvel's superhero stories. The Black Panther fundamentally acts as a means of updating and counter-arguing these original stories—and his roots in the era must be understood in terms of that context.

STAN, JACK, AND T'CHALLA

Stan Lee and Jack Kirby's place in comics history and in the pantheon of Marvel creative teams is indisputable, even while their partnership was occasionally fraught. Kirby, whose real name was Jacob Kurtzberg, was from the Lower East Side of New York and had started out doing some animation work for the Fleischer studios on series like *Popeye* and *Betty Boop* as well as work on syndicated comic strips—work that largely went nowhere. He eventually found employment at Timely Comics (the incarnation of Marvel before Atlas), partnering with his frequent collaborator Joe Simon where they eventually came up with their signature creation—a heroic figure draped in red, white, and blue named Captain America who fought the forces of fascism with patriotism and his powerful shield.[13] The *Captain America* series arrived on newsstands just before the start of America's involvement in World War II and became a massive hit for Timely Comics, selling a million copies and putting the new hero on the same playing field as titans like Superman and Batman at the same time it lifted Timely's fortunes.[14] While the Captain was a hit, it was not without controversy—the first issue featured the title character punching Adolf Hitler on the jaw, making its politics clear and causing some murmurs of disapproval from a war-weary public as well as outright threats on Kirby and Simon's life from Nazi sympathizers—as legend has it, Kirby went down to the lobby to deal with one such threat himself only to find out the instigators had fled.[15] Eventually, Simon and Kirby would collaborate with a young man who got in the door at Timely as the nephew of publisher Martin Goodman's business manager. That young man, Stanley Lieber, who had written works of his own at the publisher under the pseudonym Stan

Lee, kept that name as he worked on the Captain America series alongside Kirby and Simon. Their partnership would hit a roadblock when Kirby and Simon started moonlighting at DC Comics after learning that Goodman was garnishing their royalties. Somehow, Goodman found out and fired Kirby and Simon, who allegedly believed Lee was the culprit.[16] Lee stayed at Timely while Simon and Kirby left for DC.

Their comics careers were put on hold temporarily as Simon, Lee, and Kirby served in World War II. Kirby served in the Army first as a mechanic, then later as a rifleman and eventually a scout, where his art skills came in handy as he snuck behind enemy lines and drew maps to guide his unit across Europe. Here, Kirby's antipathy toward fascism and Nazis and fondness for diversity was honed, themes that would echo throughout his later work.[17] For his part, Lee enlisted in the Army's signal corps and eventually put his substantial writing skills to work crafting training films and other media for use in the war effort.[18] After the war, Lee would return to Timely and work his way up the ranks as both a writer and later an editor at the company during its Atlas days, taking on significant amounts of work. Feeling burned out, Lee nearly left the company but a resurgence in its fortunes allowed him to start hiring artists and writers again—and he started by reaching out to Jack Kirby.[19] Together, Lee and Kirby started working on imaginative science fiction and monster stories that "spoke to the anxieties of the atomic age" and laid the groundwork for what would eventually become the Marvel style of heroics and genre fiction mixed with genuine pathos.[20] Lee, ever the ebullient salesman, meshed particularly well with Kirby, himself a fan of high-concept storytelling, and while their partnership was often antagonistic it was nonetheless fruitful.

After receiving the edict from Goodman to start their own superhero team to challenge DC's *Justice League*, Lee and Kirby developed the Fantastic Four, a team of explorers granted superhuman powers by cosmic radiation during an accident on a research trip in outer space. The team's leader, Reed Richards, gained elasticity and the nickname "Mr. Fantastic," while his love interest and later wife Susan Storm received the power of invisibility and the infantilizing codename of the "Invisible Girl." Susan's brother Johnny became the modern version of the Golden Age Marvel hero the Human Torch, able to fly and manipulate fire, and Reed's best friend and trusted pilot Ben Grimm became the Thing, a hulking monster made of rock with a loveable spirit who struggled with his lot in life. Not only did the concept of relatable and often flawed heroes resonate with the public, Kirby's dynamic art and Lee's plotting and showmanship came together to create a series unlike anything else on the stands. In their essential memoir/superhero analysis *Supergods*, acclaimed comics author Grant Morrison described the first issue's cover, in which the team fought a giant monster, as something revelatory:

Comic-book covers of the fifties had shown ordinary people running from symbolic monsters of the id. Now four people were fighting back. [. . .] The Fantastic Four formed a living equation. The exploration of their constantly shifting, always familiar, family dynamic made them a perpetual-motion story engine.[21]

That perpetual-motion story engine made the Fantastic Four the talk of the industry and would later find its way to the African continent and the country of Wakanda, where Lee and Kirby would implicitly grapple with the Marvel titles of the past.

ENTER THE PANTHER

The Black Panther is many things, but he is not the first Black superhero. It would be doing a disservice to the history of the genre not to explore the complexity of the various "firsts" as they pertain to Black and African comic heroes. For instance, a timeline of Black superheroes that leaves out Lothar, the sidekick to Lee Falk and Phil Davis' 1930s comic strip hero Mandrake the Magician (occasionally referred to as one of the first superheroes) is incomplete. Lothar, presented first as Mandrake's muscular African assistant speaking in broken English and sporting stereotyped features, gradually evolved over the course of the strip—he is eventually revealed to be royalty, and by the 1960s was drawn in a less stereotyped fashion and speaks with proper English, with the two men becoming equal partners. The character was also an early transmedia hero, appearing in television, radio, and animation and even temporarily adopting the mantle of fellow pulp superhero The Phantom in a 2015 comic series.[22] Still, Lothar was a supporting character—the first African superhero who was also a lead character in a comic book would debut over a decade later.

Here, credit must be given to Orrin C. Evans, the editor of the short-lived and tragically overlooked in many historical comics narratives *All-Negro Comics* in 1947.[23] Like other titles of the era, *All-Negro* was an anthology series, but unlike other titles it was created by a Black writer and editor who sought to use the title to advance the careers of other Black creators—in a letter to the reader in the first issue, Evans promised that "every brush stroke and pen line" in the book was "by Negro artists" and that the series would give said artists gainful employment and "glorify Negro historical achievements."[24] *All-Negro Comics* presented new Black characters like the Dick Tracy-esque detective "Ace Harlem," the cherubic stars of the children's fantasy strip "Dew Dillies," and a series of one-panel gag strips about fashionable Black women called "Hep Chicks on Parade."

But it was George J. Evans Jr.'s "Lion Man" that was the book's superhero, and arguably the first Black superhero in American comics.[25] Identifying the character as a college-educated young scientist, Lion Man is tasked by the United Nations with watching over a uranium deposit on the African gold coast capable of making a bomb "that could destroy the world."[26] Along with his sidekick, the trouble-making orphan Bubba, Lion Man runs afoul of the villains Dr. Blut Sangro and his associate Brosser the Beachcomber, who come to the Gold Coast presumably looking for the uranium deposit (their exact goals or country of origin are never officially stated). After the hero is briefly taken hostage by the two villains, Bubba sneaks away—a brief skirmish ensues as Sangro and Brosser march Lion Man back to his secret lab, and Lion Man comes out victorious and ready to hand the men over to the United Nations for punishment. This victory is lost on Bubba, who finds a machine gun and opens fire on the villains to save Lion Man, killing Brosser and allowing Sangro to escape. The strip ends with Dr. Sangro swearing revenge, promising a second installment that would never come.[27]

Despite the somewhat disjointed narrative, Lion Man had enough of the hallmarks of a superhero—powers (at least a tremendous amount of hand-to-hand fighting skill and gadgets), a secret identity, a mission, and even something of a costume (if one counts a loincloth as a costume)—to qualify by the standards set forth by scholars like Peter Coogan.[28] Moreover, Lion Man lacks many of the negative stereotyped characteristics of the Black or African characters seen in the jungle comics before and after his debut, demonstrating clear independence and scientific acumen (although little about his identity or power set has anything to do with lions). Presumably he would have developed more as a character in follow-up stories, but *All-Negro Comics* never published a second issue because many newsstands would not sell the first issue and newsprint vendors refused to sell paper to Evans for another printing. Evans eventually left the comics industry to go back to journalism in Pennsylvania. Still, despite its short print run, *All-Negro* inspired other independent Black comic publications, and for his contributions to the medium Evans was inducted into the 2014 class of the Will Eisner Hall of Fame.[29] It is unclear whether Lee and Kirby ever saw the Lion Man story, but certainly another cat-themed Black superhero operating in Africa and protecting its natural resources nearly two decades beforehand merits mention.

Still, the Black Panther is easily the first African superhero in mainstream superhero comics—a title that comes with several qualifications but is even more significant for them. The mainstream comics industry had never seen anything quite like the Black Panther, though it took a while for the character to take shape. As Lee would tell it in later years, the concept was aimed at subverting audience and industry expectations:

There were no other black heroes that I knew about, and there were certainly no black heroes who were the king of their own country in Africa. [. . .] Underneath was that fantastic city that he had created, which was completely scientific and had all the latest equipment of every type in it. And we realize that the Black Panther is one of the world's great scientists—[just like] Reed Richards. So again, I wanted to go against stereotypes.[30]

Kirby had initially designed the character as the Coal Tiger, an unmasked hero with a more traditional yellow and black superhero costume, with a yellow-and-black striped tunic and a short cape. That costume was presumably changed when they decided to rename the character "Black Panther." The origin of the name is unclear, as is who should get full credit for the character's creation, as both Lee and Kirby attempted to claim sole credit over the years and neither was a wholly reliable source.[31] One telling has it that Kirby suggested the name in honor of the boxer Harry "The Black Panther" Wills and the African-American World War II 761st tank battalion, also known as the Black Panthers.[32] In 2005, Lee chalked the name up to a story he read as a child where a character had a black panther as a pet.[33] Regardless of the name's origin, the Black Panther officially debuted in 1966's *Fantastic Four* #52, opening with a splash page where the Panther, his face obscured by a black mask save for his eyes, looms large above the Fantastic Four as he leaps toward them from the background.

The story proper begins with the Fantastic Four taking a test drive of a highly advanced new flying vehicle delivered to them as a gift from the nation of Wakanda and its mysterious chieftain, the Black Panther. The Four meet up with the Wakandan emissary on the roof of their headquarters and agree to accept the chieftain's invitation to what the man calls "the greatest hunt of all time." Reed, supposedly the world's greatest scientist, is amazed when the diplomat transmits a message back to Wakanda using "cosmic channel waves which can blanket all of Earth"—setting up the expectation in the reader's mind early on that Wakanda is not the stereotyped African backwater they had seen in other media.[34] Flashing to Wakanda, the message reaches T'Challa, who summons a giant ceremonial panther statue from the ground that is revealed to hold within it a bank of supercomputers and his "stalking costume"—changing into it, he vows to greet the Fantastic Four "as they have never been greeted before!"[35]

Shortly after they arrive, the Panther introduces himself and attacks the team, using his superior agility, clever tactics, and advanced gadgetry to nullify them one-by-one by trapping the Human Torch inside an asbestos-lined vacuum, catching the Invisible Girl just as she turns visible because of intelligence he had gathered prior, poisoning the Thing with strength-sapping water, and trapping Mister Fantastic in indestructible titanium cuffs after a fight in the dark. Rather than posing a simple physical threat to the Four, the Panther utilizes obvious research and scientific acumen to best the heroes—demonstrating that this mysterious assailant is no mere brute. The Panther is bested only after the Human Torch's roommate Wyatt Wingfoot frees them and allows them to work together to defeat the Panther, who gives his word not to attack again and unmasks, identifying himself as the "chieftain of the Wakandas" and "perhaps the richest man in all the world!"[36]

The story continues in *Fantastic Four* #53, where the Panther reveals himself as T'Challa, the King of Wakanda. Wakanda is portrayed in the story as a wealthy and technologically advanced country, thanks to its "virtually inexhaustible" supply of the incredibly rare mineral vibranium.[37] T'Challa reveals that his father, the previous king, was murdered by a plunderer named Klaw (here clearly acting as symbol of colonization) seeking to take Wakanda's vibranium for himself. T'Challa reveals that his attempt to "hunt" the Fantastic Four was a means of showing that he would be ready to fight Klaw should he return, which he inevitably does. The Four help defend Wakanda from Klaw's forces but leave the marauding colonizer to T'Challa, who battles the villain and his new sonic arm cannon as well as a giant panther Klaw creates out of sonic energy. Not only does the Panther defeat the sonic panther—"His speed—his strength—he's like a human panther himself!" Klaw thinks—he ultimately destroys Klaw's sound converter by using his scientific knowledge to overload the machine's circuitry, saving the Fantastic Four and his home.[38] After the Fantastic Four encourage the Panther to continue the fight for good rather than retire, T'Challa commits himself to service beyond Wakanda's borders and gets a hero's origin: "I shall do it! I pledge my fortune, my powers—my very life—to the service of all mankind!"[39]

While later writers and artists would expand on the world of Wakanda, the broad strokes of the Panther mythos—Wakanda as an isolated and advanced nation, the rejection of inherent Western supremacy, the valuable and powerful metal vibranium, and the Black Panther as both ruler of a nation and a protective force against colonizing interests—are present from the start and represent a clear break from the media narratives surrounding Africa at the time. There is no denying that the Black Panther was unique in the Marvel pantheon, not only for the color of his skin and the country of his origin but also how he was presented to the reader. Unlike other masked heroes, T'Challa wore the panther cowl not to conceal his identity, but rather as a symbolic gesture of his culture and the "panther power" he possessed—his powers came not from a freak scientific accident or twist of fate, but a (at the time) vaguely defined cultural ritual. He was as much a spiritual leader as a martial one, with a persona representative of a "figurative god image" comparable to how "a cow is venerated in India," according to one of Lee's editorial comment boxes.[40] While the mystical elements of the character's origins echo some of the more problematic supernatural elements of the earlier jungle comics, Lee and Kirby cut them with the flavor of modernity and technology, creating a sort of early Afrofuturist work. Wakanda's rich natural resources and its demonstrable wealth were unique compared to the myriad portrayals of Africa as a poor and backwards continent at the time. Moreover, the idea of Black Panther as a noble and powerful ally whose trust must nonetheless be earned due to historical Western subjugation is formed here—the Fantastic Four are visitors in his country, and not automatically hailed or immediately accepted as liberators or saviors.

Yet even this more sympathetic vision of Africa carries with it echoes of Eurocentrism—the Thing expresses his disbelief with the flying car T'Challa's emissary gifts the team by asking "But how does some refugee from a Tarzan movie lay his hands on this kinda gizmo?"[41] Later, he mocks the Wakandans' ceremonial dance ("A bunch'a Fred Astaires they ain't!") and mocks T'Challa's backstory by claiming he's seen it too many times in other books and movies.[42] It is possible that Lee and Kirby intended the Thing in this story as a source of metatextual commentary on where their story challenged the larger oeuvre of jungle fiction, but the line between satire and replication can often be blurry. The Thing's boorishness may be in character, but it is also evocative of many readers' attitudes at the time. Moreover, his direct invocation of Tarzan reinforces an experience with African culture and people that is both heavily mediated and reliant on Eurocentric narratives—though he would hardly be alone at that point in history. Reed's remark that vibranium would "be worth a fortune to our missile program alone" also evokes the same mindset of Africa as a set of resources to benefit the global military and political hegemony of the United States seen in many of the earlier jungle comics, albeit from a less bigoted perspective.[43]

The Black Panther owed a great deal to the historical and cultural milieu in which he was developed. In his book *Super Black*, Adilifu Nama suggested that the character "signals a strident critique of African colonial and postcolonial politics" like those seen in the jungle comics but also acted as an "idealized composite of third-world black revolutionaries"—T'Challa is unquestionably a powerful advocate for his own nation but also a willing and respectful ally to the American heroes.[44] In a piece on the *Black Panther* film for the journal *Political Geography*, Robert A. Saunders suggests that contemporary global politics are necessary to understand the importance of a character like Black Panther—shortly before the character's creation, both Ghana and Kenya had claimed their independence and the system of apartheid had long since taken root in South Africa; meanwhile the pan-African movement and the formation of the Black Panther Party ushered in a heightened era for the Civil Rights movement. By introducing the character, Saunders argues "Marvel injected itself into a protean geopolitical space that proved to be impossible to predict"—indeed, how the character and his creatives responded to that geopolitical space would be a defining aspect of future stories.[45]

The politics of the Panther's debut are hard to miss, even if they are not overt. Martin Lund suggests this original story effectively portrays Wakanda and by extension Africa as a willing partner with America against the threat of the Soviets, represented in the story by Klaw—while T'Challa and Reed Richards do not lament the encroachment of "the Reds" as the jungle comic heroes of the 1950s did, the implication is nonetheless there. As Lund argues, the comic's setting of Klaw's first foray into Wakanda aligns roughly with the time period in the 1950s in which "the African continent had first become a Cold War concern" and the natural resource of vibranium acts as a clear stand-in for the African reserves of uranium that were of interest to America and other Cold war powers.[46] Here, the limits of the Black Panther as an African character created by white Westerners become apparent. The American characters practice their own form of entanglement and colonization welcomed by the stand-in for African nations, while their political adversaries represent a cruel and exploitative colonial interest; yet both parties are interested in what Wakandan technology and resources can do for their respective national goals.

Lee and Kirby's depiction of an African nation defined by its advancement and prosperity rather than Eurocentric depictions of savagery and poverty should be understood in the context of its time. While one must be careful not to over-romanticize the Silver Age Marvel comics, they were undoubtedly progressive for their era. Kirby, who grew up in an immigrant neighborhood and famously despised Nazis, fascists, and the politics of Joseph McCarthy, told *The Comics Journal* in 1990 that he came up with the character because despite growing up with many Black people and having a lot of Black readers, he felt he had ignored them by not having Black characters in his work.[47] Kirby has often been celebrated for his progressiveness and an apparent strong belief in social justice. His work on Black Panther and other comics was even famously adapted by visual arts professor John Jennings and artist Stacey Robinson in the form of the "Black Kirby" collaborative exhibition that tried to meld the style and concepts of Kirby's work and his Jewish background as well as the collaborators' own concepts of social justice and Black culture to explore the idea of Otherness and how his work inspired Black creators.[48]

For Lee's part, he would later explain that he saw the Panther as an opportunity to show that people were capable of great things "no matter what the color of your skin is"; it did not hurt that the Black Panther was an opportunity to poke chief rival DC Comics' lack of diversity in the eye while downplaying Marvel's own tendency toward tokenism in their comics.[49] He built on this reputation in a famous "Stan's Soapbox" essay published two years later in 1968, where he decried bigotry and racism as deadly "social ills" and called upon his readers to "fill our hearts with tolerance."[50] It is soaring rhetoric of the sort you would expect from the man who for years spun yarns about visitors from the stars and fantastic heroes, and there is no reason to believe that it was not genuine. While Lee's own connection to his Jewish identity was somewhat fraught, Kirby embraced his, as did many other Marvel creators at the time.[51] As scholar Harry Brod put it, these identities and the generally liberal politics and "strong support for the civil rights movement" at the Marvel offices led to Lee, Kirby, and many other creatives "[exploring] the theme of the persecuted outsider" in their works.[52] Even though these original stories were not written from a Black perspective, they and later Panther tales certainly had empathy for those lived experiences that inspired them.

However, as men of their time, it should be noted that Lee and Kirby's respective records on this matter were somewhat uneven and both men had work in the past that would not stand up to modern scrutiny. Lee had worked not only on the jungle comics but also titles like *Young Allies*, a series that spun out of the *Captain America* title in the early 1940s starring Cap's kid sidekick Bucky and a team of patriotic youths as they fought against the Axis. As part of that ensemble, Lee created Whitewash Jones, a Black youth who served as buffoonish comic relief and spoke in a stereotyped drawl to proclaim his love of watermelon; Kirby was on art duty for some of these stories.[53] In 2009, writer Roger Stern and artist Paolo Rivera wrote a story that retconned the Young Allies as actual wartime heroes in the Marvel Universe, casting the Lee and Kirby comics as government propaganda and having the actual Lt. Jones lament his portrayal as "something out of a minstrel show," thereby acknowledging and challenging that part of Marvel history.[54]

It is clear from their published words and professional demeanor that both Lee and Kirby were at least sensitive to the power their stories had as well as to the problem of limited and biased media representation. Indeed, T'Challa was quickly instituted as a major part of the nascent Marvel Universe, starring in stories where he fought alongside Captain America and even taking his spot on the Avengers in 1968.[55] However, it is important to note that Marvel was a business first and foremost—and resistant to anything that might be considered politically divisive or harmful to their bottom line. The publisher was hesitant to signify T'Challa's Blackness on the covers for his comic appearances—he was covered by a full body costume that obscured his face when appearing on comic covers until about 1968, allegedly to avoid problems with certain distributors.[56] Mark Evanier's biography *Kirby: King of Comics* includes the original, unpublished version of *Fantastic Four* #52, featuring a very different looking Black Panther with a belt, shorts, and contrasting gloves and a cape but most importantly a mask that showed the bottom half of his face.[57] Compared to the final published cover, Panther also takes up significantly more visual space and appears to be a more dynamic and less menacing character, leaping directly into battle with the Four as opposed to pouncing on them from behind in the published version. The subtext is hard to miss, and even just as a piece of art the finished cover is somewhat diminished by comparison.

If Marvel was, as the story goes, concerned about what newsstand distributors would think they were probably somewhat relieved to find that most of the response to the character from fans was positive—at least, based on what they published. While an "Alan Finn" was upset with the character in a letter published in issue #55 that proclaimed "The Black Panther stinks!", his objection seems to be that the character made short work of the Four in their fight and that the character was "ridiculous" rather than any specific racial animosity—another fan was thrilled to see the Panther, lauding his status as an African king and proclaiming him to be "the first great Negro hero-villain in comic book history!"[58] But it was a letter from a reader named Guy Haughton in issue #59 that illustrated the timeliness and tension of the character. Haughton, who identified as a "young Negro," had complex thoughts about the Black Panther. On one hand, Haughton commended the creators' "courage" and appreciated their "psychological uplifting" in the form of acknowledging "the Negro race," claiming the book was "doing more than entertaining the masses, for you are promoting human respect and bringing about a better world."[59] On the other, Haughton was less thrilled about how the character was conceived: "Alright, so you've got a Negro super-hero, but does he have to be an African chieftain and whatnot? Couldn't he have been a plain American? I mean if you had an Italian super-hero, would you make him the head of a pizza stand in Venice and call him the Masked Ferrari?"[60]

One wonders if other readers in Haughton's position reacted similarly to the first major Black superhero—a hero who was royalty hailing from another country, with limitless resources at his disposal but still deeply tied to the same ideological constructs that characterized the jungle comics. The Panther was an aspirational figure, certainly beyond upwardly mobile, but largely detached from the class constraints and the real civil rights struggle and inequity felt by many Black Americans of the era. While Marvel would introduce heroes that spoke more directly to the African American experience of the time later—notably Sam Wilson as the Falcon and Luke Cage—their first attempt arguably was as notable in some ways for what he wasn't as for what he was. Still, by 1968, the Panther was appearing in books alongside Iron Man and Captain America, an implicit endorsement of the viability and importance of the hero. He did not, however, appear in public-facing television or merchandise, sadly also illustrating the context in which he debuted.

THE REAL-LIFE PANTHERS

It is hard to imagine that Marvel's inaugural Black superhero being largely removed from the controversy and politics of the Civil Rights era was an accident. The character was timely but designed to largely avoid touching political live wires. That lack of engagement stands out in hindsight. Malcolm X had only been assassinated about a year earlier, and the Civil Rights Act had been signed into law two years prior, serving as one of the catalysts for significant political realignment amid white resentment.[61] The assassination of Martin Luther King Jr. and the "Long Hot Summer" were only a scant couple of years away. More immediately, however, Marvel was about to find itself thrust into a controversy they had not foreseen.

Just a few months after the Black Panther debuted in *Fantastic Four*, the Black Panther Party was also established in Oakland, California. Founded by Huey P. Newton and Bobby Seale, the organization was focused on combating police brutality, promoting the welfare of Black communities, and opposing capitalist exploitation of the same—as Joshua Anderson notes, the BPP was an organization that saw racial inequity and class disparity as connected issues, with a heavy focus on the concept of the United States as an imperialist force at home and abroad.[62] Such ideas, combining Marxism with a rejection of U.S. power and influence, did not go unnoticed and were attractive to the politically active Black youth of America, drawn to the group's promise of change and revolution and skeptical of the police as an "occupying force."[63] Members of the white mainstream were immediately wary of the group, with reactions ranging from dismissive skepticism to outright condemnation and fear.[64]

While the group was tarnished primarily as an insurgent one that posed a threat to law and order due to its pledge of armed resistance against police violence and occasional acts of violence, it also worked to provide health care through free clinics and social programs in order to address poverty—a story left out of much contemporary and current discourse around the group.[65] J. Edgar Hoover, then the director of the FBI, went so far to call the group "the greatest threat to internal security of the country," though government officials admitted the Party were "feeding more kids than we are" through their free breakfast program (which by many accounts was a major component of why Hoover found the group so threatening). Said program would eventually become a model for a similar effort at the federal level.[66] It would be revealed years later that the FBI's efforts to combat the Panthers on all fronts through tactics like sympathizer intimidation and the placement of deep-cover informants and agitators helped to feed the media narrative of the Panthers as a threatening and dangerous group. These ideas echoed again years later in a trumped-up scandal as right-wing media outlets accused members of the New Black Panther Party of voter intimidation in 2008 for appearing outside of a Philadelphia polling station in Panther regalia and carrying nightsticks. While the NBPP is generally considered a fringe group disowned by and unaffiliated with the original BPP, the media coverage in primarily conservative outlets failed to make that distinction, reanimating white animosity toward the group.[67]

The media depiction of the Black Panthers has historically been an antagonistic one, casting the group as threatening or as possessing directionless anger in both news coverage and entertainment media like *Forrest Gump* despite the complexity of the group's thought and its pro-social elements. In their own way, Marvel contributed to that cultural antipathy toward the group via aggressive course-correction—specifically, what to do about their prominent Black character who shared the name with a group that had been vilified in most of white America? Faced with the choice of sticking to their guns and keeping the name as Lee and Kirby intended or hastily rewriting a character's legacy out of fear for their bottom line, Marvel chose the path of least resistance.

1972's *Fantastic Four* #119, in which Marvel decided to rebrand the character, is otherwise a perfectly enjoyable and surprisingly politically aware comic by Roy Thomas and John Buscema in which The Thing and Human Torch leave on a mission to rescue T'Challa from the nation of Rudyarda, where he was captured when pursuing thieves who stole Wakandan technology. The nation of Rudyarda is a barely veiled stand-in for South Africa and identified in a video call by T'Challa's chief advisor as "one of the last remaining strongholds of white supremacy upon our continent."[68] After the American heroes enter the prison where T'Challa is being held, T'Challa corrects his allies when they call him by his ancestral title, identifying himself as the Black Leopard while gearing up to make his escape. When the Thing asks about the reason for the sudden name change, T'Challa suggests it was necessary to return to the United States, where the Black Panther's name had certain "political connotations," adding "I neither condemn nor condone those who have taken up the name—but T'Challa is a law unto himself"—an interesting example of Marvel trying to play both sides with the subtlety of an exploding garbage truck.[69]

The symbolic importance of Marvel's hesitance to embrace the character's name at this moment in history is an important part of his transmedia legacy, albeit a short-lived one (he would return to the "Black Panther" moniker shortly thereafter). As writer Clarkisha Kent argues, this was an example of an effort in which the creatives at Marvel tried to dance around the very real political symbology of T'Challa to avoid alienating audiences. Kent goes on to suggest that the character shares many of the BPP's core tenets and that the shared name actually made the character "more relevant and meaningful" as a result.[70] Beyond this, however, this particular incident in the Panther's career illustrates an important tension at the heart of the character—Marvel was then and is now eager to use the character to explore contemporary issues pertaining to African politics and black identity, but balances that need with the compelling desire to remain "apolitical" across its multimedia empire. The authors behind *Fantastic Four* #119 certainly touched on the very real problem of apartheid—a rarity for superhero comics—but rather than using the character to interrogate or challenge the attitudes that led to this system, ultimately reaffirmed them through the rhetorical act of changing the character's name to acquiesce to American political demands.

THE LEGACY

Lee and Kirby laid the groundwork for a character that is resonant and important to this day, but with that foundation came the challenging aspects of the Black Panther's character. While undeniably progressive, the Black Panther comics put forth in this era of Marvel Comics largely lacked willingness to interrogate the legacy of colonialism and Black oppression that the character could easily challenge, settling on a view of Africa and Black identity that was largely deferential to white concerns and characters. The Panther himself was a character that both reflected a necessary change in the broader media but also one overshadowed by his white counterparts and still largely and purposely removed from the genuine social issues of the day.

Still, there is in these original stories an awareness of the character's historical context. The Panther's first and most enduring villain serving as a rhetorical stand-in for white exploration and exploitation of native African resources is a telling choice of where the sympathies of the creators truly rested, and a powerful reversal from the "great white hunters" and heroes of the jungle comics in a very short time frame. While the choice of name change for the character was inspired by economically driven cowardice on the part of the publisher, it was in the service of a story that explored foreign policy and issues that many white readers would not have otherwise considered. Such steps are important in the larger narrative of the Black Panther and what he represents. However, in this era he is also largely a supporting character, the token Black friend of the Fantastic Four and Captain America. In comics, a superhero needs their own spotlight to truly be taken seriously in the discourse, and a company hesitant to even show T'Challa's Black skin on the cover was not about to take that leap unless the right set of circumstances and creative champions presented themselves. In the next decade, they would.

NOTES

1. Stevens, *Captain America, Masculinity, and Violence*, 58.
2. Wright, *Comic Book Nation.*
3. Ibid.
4. A thorough explanation of the complex rebranding and publication history of Marvel can be found in several other volumes, particularly Howe's "Marvel Comics: The Untold Story."
5. The history of the comics industry is usually separated into discrete "ages" defined by specific trends and storytelling; generally speaking, the pre-WWII to mid-1950s era is considered the Golden Age.
6. Rico et al., "Rampage!," 2.
7. Rico et al., "The Trail of Sudden Death!," 1.
8. Rico et al., ibid.
9. Rico & Pike, "The Screaming Terror!"
10. Wheeler, "Trace the Lineage of Marvel's Black Super Heroes."
11. Whitney, "Fire Spirit!"
12. Rico & Pike, "Fanged Fury!"
13. Howe, *Marvel Comics: The Untold Story.*
14. Evanier, *Kirby: King of Comics.*
15. Ibid.
16. Howe, *Marvel Comics*; Evanier, *Kirby.*
17. Peters, "8 Ways Comic Book Legend Jack Kirby Fought Fascism."
18. Stilwell, "Marvel legend Stan Lee."
19. Wright, *Comic Book Nation.*
20. Ibid, 202.
21. Morrison, *Supergods*, 91.
22. Carlson-Ghost, "Before Black Panther, there was Lothar!"
23. Davis, "Why the first black superhero was not the one you think."
24. Evans, All-Negro Comics, 1.
25. Evans Jr., "Lion Man," 28.
26. Ibid, 36.
27. Ibid.
28. Coogan, "The Hero Defines the Genre."
29. Davis, "Why the first black superhero," Howard, *Encyclopedia of Black Comics*, 74.
30. Culver, *Black Panther: The Illustrated History of a King*, 10.
31. Riesman, *True Believer*, 151–52.
32. Culver, *Black Panther*, 11–12.
33. Riesman, *True Believer.*
34. Lee & Kirby, "The Black Panther!" 3.
35. Ibid, 5.
36. Ibid, 20.
37. Lee & Kirby, "The Way It Began . . . !" 6.
38. Ibid, 18.

39. Ibid, 20.

40. Lee & Kirby, "The Black Panther!," 20; Lee & Kirby, "The Way It Began . . . !" 8.

41. Lee & Kirby, "The Black Panther!" 2.

42. Lee & Kirby, "The way It Began . . . !" 1 & 5.

43. Ibid, 5.

44. Nama, *Super Black*, 43.

45. Saunders, "(Profitable) imaginaries of black power," 141.

46. Lund, "Introducing the Sensational Black Panther!" 11.

47. Groth, "Jack Kirby Interview."

48. Hallwalls Contemporary Art Center, "John Jennings and Stacey Robinson: Black Kirby"; Womack, *Afrofuturism.*

49. Culver, *Black Panther*, 16; Howe, *Marvel Comics.*

50. Miller, "Stan Lee's Powerful 1968 Essay."

51. Brod, *Superman is Jewish?*

52. Brod, *Superman is Jewish?*, 92–93.

53. Davis, "Why the first black superhero"; Howe, *Marvel Comics.*

54. Cronin, "The Abandoned An' Forsaked."

55. Culver, *Black Panther.*

56. Evanier, *Kirby*; Kinos-Goodin, "9 Key Moments."

57. Evanier, *Kirby*, 1320.

58. Lee & Kirby, "When Strikes the Silver Surfer!" 22–23.

59. Lee & Kirby, "Doomsday," 23.

60. Ibid.

61. Oreskes, "Civil Rights Act."

62. Anderson, "A Tension in the Political Thought of Huey P. Newton."

63. Bloom & Martin Jr., *Black Against Empire*, 153.

64. Kreitner, "October 15, 1966."

65. Bassett, "Beyond Berets."

66. Massie, "The most radical thing."

67. Graham, "The New Black Panther Party"; Russonello, "Fascination and Fear."

68. Thomas & Buscema, "Three Stood Together!" 6.

69. Ibid, 14.

70. Kent, "On Black Panther."

Chapter 4

The Panther in the 1970s

Whitewashing and New Jungle Action

The late 1960s were a flashpoint for civil rights in the United States. Only a few months after 1967's "long, hot summer," Dr. Martin Luther King, Jr. was assassinated in Memphis on April 4th, 1968. The news hit the organizers who worked with King and on the civil rights movement hard. As activist Heather Booth reflected, the assassination "was like the breaking of a dream, the breaking of our hopes."[1] The psychic toll of King's assassination—especially coming so soon after Malcolm X's—was massive, but the movement continued apace. Across the ocean, Africa too was going through its own upheaval. While several African nations had declared independence from their colonizers in the early 1960s, the lack of interest on the part of those colonizing nations to assist in the transition of power to a functioning independent government or deliver any resources to help led to unrest and economic challenge across the continent.[2] Nelson Mandela was in the midst of his prison sentence in South Africa, where he would eventually become the face of the country's anti-apartheid movement (an irony, considering that images depicting him were illegal).[3] At home and abroad, Black liberation was a relevant and challenging part of the contemporary zeitgeist—and racism and white European resistance to it was hardly abating. Meanwhile on the comics page, an African king had become a much larger part of the Marvel universe—to a point.

THE PANTHER, THE AVENGER

The Black Panther regularly appeared as part of the Avengers lineup in the late 1960s and early 1970s, starting with *Avengers* #52 in 1968. The issue is relatively unassuming, though its cover, featuring the villain Grim Reaper slashing an X through the book's logo and the very cover itself, is visually striking. However, what is more significant amid the historical and social

49

upheaval is how the Panther is drawn on the same cover. While still clad in his traditional black garb, the bottom part of his cowl has been cut away to reveal his face, echoing the costume design of DC heroes like Batman or the pugilist Wildcat. More importantly, however, the cover signaled an apparent change in Marvel's alleged policy of distributor appeasement and an acknowledgement of T'Challa's Blackness. One could also suggest that one of the story's inciting moments, wherein T'Challa finds the heroes apparently dead and is immediately blamed for their murder despite a lack of evidence, echoes the questionable legal grounds on which police detained Black individuals both then and now—though it's unclear if that was writer Roy Thomas' intent. By the end of the issue, it is revealed that the heroes were merely incapacitated by the Reaper and T'Challa solves the mystery, being rewarded with unanimous induction into the Avengers as a result.[4]

From *Avengers* #53 onward, the Panther appeared alongside Hawkeye, Goliath and others in the cover corner boxes, signifying his membership as part of the team. However, he was also Othered from the start. In that issue, after T'Challa suggests he should not have joined the Avengers because "those who cannot govern themselves . . . are not worthy of my allegiance!" Goliath spits back, calling him a "self-centered, second-rate Tarzan."[5] Again, Marvel's writers elected to draw a rhetorical comparison between T'Challa and Tarzan—a comparison the character seemed unable to escape for the first decade of his existence, as this was one of the primary pop culture lenses through which Africa was viewed at the time and likely during the childhood of these authors. Such small slights were not limited to individual characters. *Avengers* #56 also saw the reinstitution of a mask that hid T'Challa's entire face as well as praise from Captain America for the Panther's "jungle senses"; the other Avengers also make regular comments about T'Challa's country and ethnicity like Hawkeye calling an excursion to Wakanda to battle the fire god Surtur and ice god Ymir "a little safari."[6] The implication that T'Challa is considered an exotic Other on a team that also features men who can grow to giant stature and indestructible androids says a great deal about the mindset of late 1960s Marvel and the world it inhabited.

Even T'Challa himself begins to question whether being a member of the Avengers is the best use of his time, first feeling the pull of his leadership responsibilities back home in *Avengers* #59.[7] Ten issues after his debut as part of the team, Avengers business finally takes them to Wakanda, where T'Challa makes the team aware that they are in the technological marvel of the nation at his whim – "The proud Wakanda do, indeed, dwell in part within a man-made jungle! No man—white or black—gains admittance to our land unless we desire it!"[8] Here, Wakanda's isolationist policies are reinforced for the benefit of newer readers, signifying that the Avengers—part of the in-group largely anywhere else—are now Others here, though by virtue of their nationality rather than their race.

In this issue, Thomas and artist John Buscema explore T'Challa's place as a traveler of the world and its political ramifications as well as introduce a crucial new character to the Panther mythology. The Panther learns that his chosen interim leader, M'Baku, has undercut his directive not to use guns in defense of the country; he does not know that M'Baku is also secretly planning to usurp the throne.[9] M'Baku drugs T'Challa and the other Avengers at a homecoming feast, where he reveals his plan to destroy the Wakandan religious structure built around the panther god Bast and replace it with the "forbidden" white gorilla, wearing the animal's pelt and declaring himself to be the Man-Ape.[10] As the two brawl, T'Challa laments that his fellow Wakandans have not risen up against M'Baku and that they no longer seem to value their freedom, to which the usurper replies "Freedom? You dare to speak of freedom? You, who have sold yourself to our white-skinned enemies?"[11] This theme—that T'Challa has sold out his people by signing on with the Avengers—is a recurring one throughout the character's history after this point. T'Challa is ultimately saved from certain and symbolic death after M'Baku's attempt to topple a giant Bast statue on top of him fails, crushing the "Man-Ape" instead. As the Vision wonders why M'Baku would attempt to kill Black Panther and undo the social and scientific progress of his country, T'Challa delivers what is arguably the issue's theme in a closing monologue: "He could do nothing else, my friend . . . for, he was a living anachronism . . . strange to the ways of civilization! [. . .] And so, faced with a world more complex, more subtle . . . he could only battle on, until the end!"[12]

The introduction of M'Baku to the Panther mythos again belied the pitfalls of having a predominantly white creative and editorial team working on the character. The obvious racial implications of a Black character named Man-Ape aside, M'Baku also arguably represents the same tribal stereotyping that had long permeated the comics industry and acted as a retrograde shorthand for Africa. While it is possible to read the issue as a metatextual disposal of that era and an ushering in of a new age of comics starring more progressive Black heroes, so too is it hard to ignore that this progressivism comes from a rejection of traditionalism and an embrace of Westernized culture and values deemed implicitly superior. This is especially notable considering then-contemporary Western pushes to "modernize" Africa and other Third World countries socially, politically, and economically in the 1950s and onward.[13] That M'Baku is destroyed by the statue representing the Panther—and therefore progress—also seems purposefully symbolic, and while the character no longer goes by "Man-Ape" he still generally represents a more militant traditionalism as foil to T'Challa's progressivism in the 2018 film and elsewhere. A few issues later, T'Challa largely drops out of the Avengers narrative as other heroes like Thor and Iron Man cycle back in. Despite his presence on cover pages suggesting his presence in many of these stories, he is largely left on the sidelines—during one issue where the Avengers battle in a high-stakes game for the future of earth, T'Challa and Yellowjacket merely watch the events unfold on a monitor.[14] In short—it is fairly clear that this era of *Avengers* really did not know what to do with the character.

Yet, in fairness, Roy Thomas' run on *Avengers* should receive some credit for being the first to use the Panther to engage with contemporary racial issues. T'Challa gets a starring role again in 1970's *Avengers* #73 doing battle with the white supremacist group the Sons of the Serpent. The Sons are busy in the opening pages of the story, bombing the offices of the Equal Employment Bureau and savagely beating the Black television presenter Montague Hale. After recovering from the attack, Hale debates the right-wing talk show host Dan Dunn on television, accusing Dunn of bigotry and sympathy toward the Sons. Dunn chides Hale with dog whistle language, claiming that they have a guest of "separate but equal importance," implying that Hale exaggerated the extent of his injuries, and praising his other guest, the Black singer Monica Lynne for being an example of "people who know their place" – a grim harbinger of the faux debate programs that would come to dominate the political airwaves in the next few decades.[15] Hale reaches out to Lynne, asking her to lend her celebrity and talents to "the right cause," which Lynne refuses. Hale is shocked, proclaiming "You can't mean that, girl! After what the establishment's done to our people . . . after what the Sons of the Serpent did to me . . . !" but Lynne is unmoved.[16]

On her way home, she is ambushed by the Sons but her assailants are quickly dispatched by the Black Panther while Lynne wonders why the police haven't arrived. When they finally show up after the brawl, Lynne confronts them about it, demanding "What I want to know is, where were the police until the danger was over? Didn't you want to dirty your hands . . . to rescue a Black girl?"[17] Unimpressed with the officer's non-answer, she storms off to presumably take Hale up on his offer.

Realizing that the Sons of the Serpent are trying to initiate a proxy civil war through inflammatory televised rhetoric, T'Challa turns down the Avengers' offers to help. Revealing himself to be a "soul brother" to Lynne (who is shocked by the news that the Black Panther is in fact Black), he asks her not to go on TV again and starts hunting down the Serpents, ultimately infiltrating their organization.[18] The plan goes awry when he is subsequently captured and held captive in the Sons' underwater fortress—meanwhile, a fake Panther working for the Sons commits crimes against business owned by Serpent supporters in order to further stoke racial tensions and frame T'Challa in the eyes of the media as "both Black . . . and the vanguard of a new type of marauding militant!"[19] Realizing that tensions are at a boiling point across the country, the Panther struggles to break free of his chains while Lynne and the Avengers locate the Serpents' broadcast studio. The heroes arrive too late to stop the unmasking of the false "T'Challa," who labels himself an enemy of America and declares "no Black American can rest . . . while a white American lives!"[2220] The Vision frees the Panther, who rips the mask off of the imposter and reveals him to be a white man; the Supreme Serpents orchestrating the broadcaster are revealed to be Dunn and Hale, who admit they had orchestrated the entire conflagration to benefit themselves.

Thomas' script goes out of its way to take a centrist view of the argument that casts doubt on both sides of the issue, largely undercutting its insight. The Wasp says she found Hale "something less than civil," and even T'Challa takes a neutral perspective by hoping "both sides realize they have responsibilities which match their rights."[21] Dunn may have moved from dog whistle to bullhorn on television, and the characters may openly criticize the media's proclivity to give free airtime to right-wing propaganda from the Serpents, but Hale's pro-Black stance is portrayed as equally inflammatory and exploitative. The entire enterprise, which includes a scene featuring the android Vision walking down the street as a Black man asks "He ain't white . . . and he sure ain't Black! Whose side are you on, baby?" feels overly cautious and hopelessly antiquated even for the time.[22] The story's ultimate reveal—that Hale and Dunn orchestrated the entire scheme to boost their ratings and attain power—is literally a "both sides are equally bad" ending, implying that the entire debate about civil rights and race relations is performance art manipulated by hucksters. While once can argue Thomas' heart was in the right place, it is still a story written from a position of privilege taking the utmost care not to cause discomfort to Marvel's perceived white majority of readers.

The Avengers comics of this era largely portrayed T'Challa as a noble character with a gifted scientific mind, but also more rigid and strait-laced than the rest of the Avengers, who benefited from more distinctive personality quirks. If T'Challa had a defined personality, it was largely as someone who felt an outsider no matter how close to the team he got, albeit less because of his race than his duties to Wakanda (a tension made obvious by an inner monologue in *Avengers* #68 *where he proclaims that his country's needs must come first: "I am an Avenger* . . . but I am also, first and foremost . . . a Wakanda!")[23] He later drops that line of thought just a few issues later in *Avengers* #73, remarking that Africa (which he refers to as a "dark continent" that "now blazes with the pulsing light of knowledge . . . of self-awareness!") no longer feels like home and that America, with all its "complexity and contrast," was his new one—another instance of Thomas' Panther toeing the line of the white moderate.[24]

This investment in America and its people played out in many of T'Challa's other adventures in the era—to hide his identity as the king of Wakanda and

to give back to America's Black population, the Panther moonlit as a school-
teacher named Luke Charles, educating the inner-city youth of New York. In
a guest appearance in *Daredevil* #69, the Panther works with Daredevil to
save the life of Lonnie Carver, a young boy in his class who runs afoul of the
Thunderbolts, a Black street gang, along with his newly-returned Vietnam
vet brother Billy. The gang demands Billy join them in order to protest the
"white man's war" and call him an "Uncle Tom" and viciously beat him when
Billy refuses; T'Challa stops the gang handily while lecturing them on their
methods, concluding as the gang scurries away "Those vermin aren't interested in Black power . . . only Thunderbolt power!"[25] Later, as Panther and
Daredevil fight the Thunderbolts under cover of darkness, one gang member
finds a lighter and reveals the Panther is one of their mystery assailants, calling him the "original Establishment Black man himself," to which Panther
replies "Don't try to palm off that 'Establishment' jargon on me, friend!
I'm old enough to tell the difference between a dissenter and a criminal!"[26]
The heroes triumph over the gang members with some help from Billy, who
reveals to his brother in the hospital that he had infiltrated the gang on behalf
of the District Attorney's office—a fact Daredevil was aware of the entire
time. And so, the status quo prevails, with T'Challa and Daredevil heading
into the night for a Coke.

Here the Panther arguably acts again as a mouthpiece for white centrism
through Thomas' words, painting the vaguely defined anti-war politics of
the Thunderbolts as a strawman and Panther as a sort of comfortable liberal
voice of Blackness to comment on the war without taking a firm stance on
the actual issue. While the story seems to have a generally positive view of
dissent (unsurprising given Marvel's popularity in the counter-culture movement of the era), the implication that good Black protest should only ever be
peaceful and unassuming in nature reinforces a paternalistic white ideology.
While the Panther argues that the Thunderbolts do not possess a genuine
interest in Black power, it is never expressly said what they do represent other
than a generic criminality—in Thomas' view, "Black power" rests in the more
moderate-friendly perspectives of T'Challa and Billy.

T'Challa's role as a teacher came up again years later in *Marvel Two-in-
One* #40, published in 1978. Still under the Luke Charles persona and wearing a dashiki while teaching a Black history class, T'Challa runs into his old
friend Benjamin "The Thing" Grimm as he drops off a wayward youth the
Avengers had taken in at school. T'Challa brings Grimm in on a mission to
investigate a string of disappearances targeting prominent and successful
Black New Yorkers. As the two investigate, they discover that a strange vam-
piric creature is possibly to blame, intervening as he attacks the famous musi-
cian C.L. Wadsworth. Wadsworth stakes the beast through the heart with his
bow, and the heroes leave, only for the creature to reanimate and be revealed

as a zuvembie.[27] Here it is worth noting that the term "zuvembie" means simply "zombie" – because the industry-wide Comics Code under which Marvel was required to publish at the time forbade the usage of many supernatural creatures and had only recently relaxed its restrictions on vampires, the term was borrowed from an old Robert E. Howard story to get around the censors.[28] The Comics Code, an involuntary industry policy put into place after the government investigated the industry over concerns of juvenile delinquency, could also be partially to blame for the far-from-revolutionary politics of this particular era of the Panther, as it generally held that the authority of government and law enforcement should be respected and honored in the pages of comic book stories.[29]

The creature sneaks into T'Challa's apartment and incapacitates him, leading the Thing to team up with the supernatural hero Brother Voodoo to find the missing king. It is revealed that the monster is actually the work of W'Sulli, a witch doctor from a "small emerging African nation bordering Uganda," and former Ugandan economic minister Dr. Obatu, the civilian identity of the supervillain Dr. Spectrum.[30] Obatu fled from his home country after Idi Amin, at the time the actual president of Uganda, sentenced him to death for his crimes, and with W'Sulli he makes a plan to bring the kidnapped Black luminaries (including a de-powered Panther) back to Uganda in exchange for Amin's commutation of his sentence. Here the book editorializes, informing the reader of Amin's status as a real-world dictator and labeling him in the words of one of T'Challa's fellow captives "the meanest mass murderer since Hitler."[31] W'Sulli uses a ritual to transfer the captives' spirits into a sacred urn for Amin to control, but the plan is disrupted by the appearance of Thing and Brother Voodoo, who cause Amin to flee for his safety. The urn is destroyed, and the spirits return to their rightful bodies, including granting the Panther back his stolen powers. No longer controlled by W'Sulli's power, the vampire kills the witch doctor and causes Obatu to fall to his death. The heroes leave, talking amongst themselves and remarking that Amin would be unlikely to retaliate lest he invoke the collective wrath of Wakanda and the United States.[32] This story is a rare one for the era that bridges both Panther's African identity and his Western one, casting him once again as a willing and enthusiastic ally of America against its enemies overseas—in this case, Idi Amin, who had been an adversary of the United States since the Carter administration and murdered over 100,000 people during his time as leader of the country.[33] Amin's close partnership with the Soviet Union during the 1970s likely also contributed to U.S. antipathy toward his regime, though several private American companies did business with the country despite this and the Soviets would eventually denounce him after he was ousted from power in 1979.[34] Amin was undeniably a cruel, brutal dictator—and this story offers an early instance of the Black Panther as a response by primarily white creators to African politics both as a potentially recuperative symbol and as a reinforcement of U.S. foreign policy.

Black Panther's run as an Avenger wound down 35 issues later in *Avengers* #87, a re-told origin story for the hero as he shares his past with his team. Many sections of the story are redrawn sequences from *Fantastic Four* #52 (which was long out-of-print), but Thomas takes the time to expand on the original story with additional material that fleshes out the Panther's origin and wrapped up his connection with the team. The story explains T'Challa chose to leave Wakanda to pursue education and training elsewhere on the advice of his father's confidant and shaman N'Baza, with his childhood friend B'Tumba in tow. Suspicious that N'Baza is working to consolidate his own power, he returns and completes the Panther ritual, only to discover that B'Tumba had been working with the A.I.M. crime syndicate to steal vibranium and that N'Baza is innocent. B'Tumba and T'Challa reconcile when B'Tumba is killed by A.I.M. N'Baza served as the steward of Wakanda until his death, which forced the Panther to decide whether to return to Wakanda and take over as king or renounce his title and stay in America "in the dual role of ghetto teacher and crime-battling Panther"; in the next issue, T'Challa reveals he has decided to return home and leaves the team.[35]

Despite their timidity on racial and political matters, this era of the Black Panther as part of the Avengers offered well-written and engaging work from two of Marvel's best at the time and made the character part of the company's flagship team of heroes—certainly a vote of confidence. Yet while these appearances certainly raised the Panther's profile, they did not do much to promote him as the equal of a Spider-Man or Incredible Hulk. As later writers would remark, the Panther had simply gone from guest star to ensemble cast member. Looking back, it is hard not to notice Marvel's apparent refusal to promote one of their few prominent Black characters to the front of the line as a team leader or star of his own series, whether out of caution or cowardice. It would fall to a new, untested writer given a long-defunct title to finally crown the king.

THE PANTHER AS PRESTIGE COMIC—
MCGREGOR'S *JUNGLE ACTION*

In the annals of Marvel history, there are several names that have contributed a great deal to the concept of the Black Panther. However, if there is a line of demarcation between the Silver Age Panther who became largely lost in the crowd as an Avenger and the more modern, vital one, it is hard not to argue that the line does not go directly through the work of Don McGregor. McGregor's seminal run on the character expanded upon the social and historical structure of the nation of Wakanda and added key elements to the narrative that would become forever intertwined with the character going forward. Most importantly, however, McGregor's run fleshed out the Panther himself, exploring who he is and what motivates him on a human level that made him more than just the token Black friend of the Avengers or Fantastic Four.

McGregor began his career at Marvel in 1972 as a proofreader. Eventually, he worked his way up to the role of editor and writer and consistently pressed for a chance to get a book of his own. As an editor, he was ultimately given two books to work on—the sci-fi series *Killraven* and a relaunch of the old *Jungle Action* series that Marvel had decided to publish with Black Panther in the lead role. The new focus on Black Panther was part of a larger effort by Marvel to diversify its product line alongside other books featuring characters like Luke Cage and Brother Voodoo (though those books still promoted the sort of moderate centrism with regard to race and equality that appeared in the earlier Avengers run).[36] McGregor, who was not a fan of the original Jungle Action series and later dubbed its focus on white saviors "horrendous material," decided to subvert the name with his approach to the character, correctly surmising that Wakanda's status as an isolated nation would mean that the cast should be entirely African and therefore would be the only comic at either Marvel or DC with an entirely Black cast.[37] By most accounts, Marvel did not expect the series to sell as well as its flagship titles, which may have given McGregor more freedom to take his preferred approach.

McGregor, along with a rotating cast of artists and supporting creators—most notably Rich Buckler and Billy Graham—took advantage of these low expectations to write a "dense, thirteen-chapter saga" named "Panther's Rage" in the pages of *Jungle Action*.[38] Graham, a Black artist, and McGregor were friends—but Graham was not assigned to the book for that reason. Rather, as McGregor would write years later, Marvel putting new Black artists onto "Black titles" was just what Marvel editorial did at the time.[39] The team took it upon themselves to expand the Panther mythos, mapping out Wakanda in supplementary material in each issue and drawing upon the foundational work of Lee and Kirby to flesh out a deeper history and context for the character and his country. Many of the elements that would be pivotal in the 2018 film, such as the Warrior Falls where the ritual battles for leadership are held and most importantly the antagonist Killmonger, are first introduced in this storyline.

Reading McGregor's *Jungle Action* run today, it is surprising how well it still holds up both as a cultural artifact and a piece of sequential storytelling. The "Panther's Rage" story arc takes place over 13 issues—a rarity in monthly comics at the time, where story arcs lasted at best two or three issues—and focuses on the rebellion of the villainous Killmonger against T'Challa's rule, with a constant stream of related antagonists, heroic feats and jungle landscapes illustrated in eye-catching splash pages and clever panel arrangements. A single villain being the primary antagonist of an ongoing story was an unusual move in this era of comics, and one that McGregor said was made a necessity by the more serialized nature of the story—as he put it in an interview, having a new antagonistic threat in each issue would eventually make the Wakandans (and, one would assume, the reader) wonder if they weren't actually better off with the Panther gone.[40] It's not just the structure of the story that makes it unique, but also the craft on display. While *Action* had no shortage of talented artists, Graham's art is particularly eye-catching, with ambitious splash pages, art that breaks and overtakes the standard panel format, and stunning title treatments that open each of his books. Graham's work also spoke to a sense of Black pride sorely missing in the predominantly white world of comics creatives. As Evan Narcisse, who would write the later *Rise of the Black Panther* series that synthesized and reconciled the work of McGregor and other creators into a cohesive whole, put it:

> You look at Billy Graham and the art he did in the Jungle Action run with McGregor, and it's gorgeous. To me, that's very much a "Black is Beautiful", self-love, self-pride, trying to eschew the stereotypes about African culture and African people that had been promulgated through Hollywood. To me, Graham was actively working against all that stuff and looking to establish a pro-Black aesthetic throughout the book.[41]

That aesthetic—Black and African characters rendered in accurate skin tones, living, fighting, and loving in a world of exotic wonder, meshed well with McGregor's poetic and multitudinous prose. Rather than simply having characters speak through word balloons, McGregor's words intertwined and weaved throughout the visuals and engaged in rhetorical themes of connection to the earth, distrust of outsiders, and the weight of T'Challa's role as king. A typically florid passage opens *Jungle Action* #11, the text arcing downward alongside the protagonist as he leaps and falls through the air:

> For this one moment, he does not have to be the Black Panther! As he leaps with graceful precision, a human paragon of the animal he is named after, he does not have to be T'Challa, king of the Wakandas, either [. . .] And then he lands at the bottom of the precipice . . . and the moment ends . . . and he is once more all of those things.[42]

In this opening crawl from relatively late in the run, McGregor makes his vision clear. By referring to the Panther as a "paragon of the animal he is named after," he deftly connects the character's innate nobility and physical prowess with the animalistic metaphor of his codename while simultaneously illustrating the character's duality by reminding the reader of the burden of nobility placed on his head. McGregor has the theme of Wakandan isolation-ism on his mind in "Panther's Rage" as well, building a subplot around the returning Monica Lynne, who is now romantically involved with T'Challa and living with him in Wakanda, where she is mistrusted by much of the nation's populace as a treacherous outsider. McGregor uses Lynne as an audience surrogate, overwhelmed by what she sees and concerned about how she is perceived. After a minor slight from one of T'Challa's handmaidens, she pontificates on her role in the country: "It's in her eyes . . . in her face. I feel less like a person every day I'm here. I'm more like a symbol to your people . . . a symbol of everything they've come to hate over the years."[43]

Later, Lynne is accused of the murder of Zatama, one of the royal advisors. When T'Challa worries that the "madness" of the outside world is affecting his people and causing them to mistrust her, Monica replies:

> No, T'Challa, it's more than a conflict of ideologies, now. I've seen suspicions and bigotry erupt into ripped flesh and dead bodies—and for less reason than your people think they have! They believe some heathen foreigner killed one of their people. [. . .] Maybe a hundred years from today they'll chastise them-selves for their actions and have talk show debates about their ancestors' barba-rism. But for today, they need a victim. And I'm it![44]

Elsewhere, W'Kabi, the Panther's second-in-command, tells him the "foreign shores" have changed him and he is "not the same man who took over as this country's leader when his father was murdered by outworlders!"[45] Here McGregor pokes at the idea of colonialism and T'Challa's unintended role in bringing it to the untouched land of Wakanda. Most superheroes have dual identities, but in McGregor's version of the character, the Black Panther has not only duality of role (masked hero and political ruler) but also inherent ten-sion in the duality of himself (a citizen of the world and a citizen of Wakanda).

McGregor used the absence of the Black Panther on Avengers-related duties to explore political unrest and a power vacuum in Wakanda, which acts as an ongoing subplot through much of the "Panther's Rage" storyline (it is also an idea revisited most notably by Ta-Nehisi Coates years later). In the first issue, T'Challa visits a village that had been recently attacked and is chided for not visiting the more isolated parts of the country, which have gradually been shifting apart. W'Kabi even questions his king's ability to bring the country back together. The perpetrator of the attack is revealed to be a man named Killmonger who has risen to fill the vacuum left behind by the Panther. The villain makes his first appearance in this issue as a gigantic bruiser with long hair wielding a spiked whip and wearing red spiked bracelets and white pants, the visual creation of the late artist Rich Buckler—McGregor would say in later years the straps and whip were intended to give "not just a sense of power, but a sense of the legacy of violence from slavery."[46] As the two tussle over the Warrior Falls, Killmonger's whip cracks and splinters the trees as the Panther dodges, as the larger man accuses the Panther of seeing Wakanda as a mere "toy" and throws him over the waterfalls (a scene that would be echoed later in the feature film).[47] The tension between T'Challa and Killmonger (who spends much of the saga off-panel and is referred to primarily by name and reputation) is both personal and ideological, with McGregor's script repeatedly challenging T'Challa's own morality and justifications—in one issue, while T'Challa laments Killmonger's desire to govern the land by his "own designs," his ally Taku asks if T'Challa's ambitions would have been any different.[48] It is a question that again evokes T'Challa's Western influence and his willingness to bring outsiders into the country, but McGregor digs more deeply into the idea than his predecessors and creates a blueprint for the tension that would become a defining part of the character.

Over the remainder of the series, Killmonger's plot takes shape—he has been stealing Wakandan technology to use it against T'Challa and his allies, plundering Wakanda's faunae and resources, and gathering followers from around the country to aid him in his quest to overthrow the king less for political reasons than for the naked pursuit of power. The plot largely moves T'Challa from one battle against Killmonger's lieutenants to another, but McGregor's words and the work of a rotating cast of artists truly turn Wakanda into a fleshed-out place. The Panther stalks across biomes ranging from primeval jungles full of prehistoric beasts to windswept tundra and snow-capped mountain ranges to secret underground caves and passages—far from the nondescript and often stereotyped jungle setting of other comics set in Africa (including previous Panther comics). Billy Graham's art in particular strikes a powerful chord in comparison to other artists' work then and since, breaking the standard panel arrangement, implementing thorough and occasionally horrific detail and working the title of his assigned chapters into the background and infrastructure of poster-quality splash pages. By the end of the journey, Wakanda feels like a real place worth fighting for, giving the finale—in which Killmonger attempts to once again throw the Panther over the Warrior Falls to his doom only to be pushed to his own death by Kantu, a young boy whose father had been killed by Killmonger—a powerful narrative symmetry echoing the Panther's own origin and demonstrating what the character could be used for when creators took him seriously.[49]

Much to Marvel editorial's dismay, McGregor refused to include white guest stars like the Avengers in his *Jungle Action* run, reasoning that the story's focus on a "hidden African culture" would make the inclusion of such characters unrealistic.[50] This is one of the other striking elements of the "Panther's Rage" arc—there is only one white character in it (the antagonist-turned-ally Venomm), and as such the unique themes of identity and isolation are reckoned with within the context of the specific African identity—though McGregor himself was still writing from the perspective of a white author. It is also clear evidence of McGregor's desire to subvert the *Jungle Action* name and challenge the white supremacy with which it was associated, as he put it in a 2018 interview:

> I felt that what we were doing was way too important to the medium and the audience for the Black hero to have the white heroes come in to save him. I stood ground on it fiercely. [. . .] Fortunately, so many readers really responded and took to heart many of those characters even though the stories themselves weren't that accepted in the hallowed halls.[51]

However, as Adilifu Nama suggests, this hyperfocus on Wakanda and isolation of the Panther from the rest of the Marvel Universe that allowed him to experiment with more in-depth and mature storytelling also served to make the character less relevant by separating the Panther from the context of civil rights issues in America.[52] McGregor's Panther grappled with the issues of identity and colonization, but at a marked distance from the readers who faced the legacy of those issues every day—and the modern *Jungle Action* run regularly reprinted the old jungle comics McGregor despised alongside the new Panther stories, an anachronism that only contributed to the dissonance. Discussing the sociopolitical reality of a fictional African nation from a Western perspective was one thing; exploring what the Panther represented in an America that was far from post-racial was quite another. It should be noted also that these comics existed at the height of the blaxploitation genre's popularity, and T'Challa's focus on domestic issues likely rang hollow in a post-1960s civil rights activism era where violent anti-heroes challenged white authority on screen in films like *Sweet Sweetback's Baadasssss Song* and *Super Fly*, offering what Joshua K. Wright called "symbols of power for many of the disenfranchised masses in the African American community"; while Wright contends this had the simultaneous effect of profitability and giving "the mainstream powers that be" justification to "[associate Black men] with deviance," it nonetheless spoke to a desire to see media that addressed these issues.[53]

The next *Jungle Action* story arc tried to get T'Challa out of his narrative bubble. The original plan was to follow up "Panther's Rage" with an apartheid story, but McGregor felt he could not do the proper research for it due to his personal life becoming more "emotionally turbulent."[54] Instead, the creative team decided to work closer to home and use the Black Panther to engage with issues of racism and extremism. And so, the cover for 1976's *Jungle Action* #19 and the start of the new story arc featured T'Challa doing battle with a horde of Klansmen.

Fighting the Ku Klux Klan was hardly new ground for comic book super-heroes—Superman had famously done it in a storyline on his 1940s radio show. In that instance, activist Stetson Kennedy had grown concerned about the Klan's growing resurgence and infiltrated rallies to learn more about the organization. Kennedy brought his findings to the writers of the *Superman* radio serial after being dismissed by local authorities and collaborated with them on a story arc called "The Clan of the Fiery Cross." Over the sixteen episodes, the show revealed the real Klan's secret codes and rituals, after which recruitment dropped precipitously and the Klan was largely ridi-culed by the public.[55] The story was later adapted to comics by writer Gene Luen Yang and artist team Gurihiru for the award-winning 2019 miniseries *Superman Smashes the Klan.*

The KKK provided an ideal comic book foil—with their arcane rituals, out-landish costumes and permeating hatred they were only a few steps removed from the likes of Marvel's own HYDRA. But the violence they perpetrated was all too real, and the toll of that hatred immediate and devastating—dur-ing the 1960s alone, the group was responsible for somewhere around 138 bombings including the infamous Birmingham church bombing that killed four young Black girls in 1963.[56] While the group's organization lapsed and waned after many of the group's most prominent leaders were arrested, by the mid-1970s they were primed for a comeback with former neo-Nazi David Duke leading the way. Duke, a master media manipulator, put a veneer of polite, articulate speech and nice suits over the festering malice and murder-ous bigotry that the organization represented. This more marketable form of hate—the same racism in a prettier package—had the desired effect, nearly doubling the active membership of the organization to 10,000 while reaching an estimated 75,000 more sympathizers.[57] A superhero fighting the forces of white supremacy and nationalism could not have been more relevant.

In the new story, the Panther accompanied Monica Lynne back to the United States to pay respects to her recently departed sister. While standing in front of her sister's grave, Monica is ambushed by members of the Ku Klux Klan—with help from the Panther and an investigative journalist named Kevin Trublood, she dispatches them and discovers that her sister was inves-tigating the Klan's infiltration into local real estate and politics when she was killed. The story becomes more complex when T'Challa reveals one of the attackers was Black. It is revealed that the attackers were from another group called the Dragon's Circle trying to borrow the Klan's imagery and rituals—the men then launch an attack on Monica and her parents at their home that is joined by actual Klan members.[58]

McGregor's verbose rhetoric and personal politics are on much starker display in this story arc. The aforementioned cover describes the "primitive power of the Clan," cleverly and subtly again jabbing at the notion of white supremacy and "savagery" that typified the earlier *Jungle Action* comics.[59] McGregor opens the second issue of the arc with a tangent about inflation and recession, following it up later with a joke about the inability of disposable paper towels to clean up the mess left behind by a brawl in a grocery store with the comment "But isn't everything disposable these days? Toys? Cars? Buildings? Human relationships?."[60] He once again subverts the "savage African" trope by reinforcing the Klansmen as something less than human via an aside about the Klansmen T'Challa fights later in the issue – "Through the slits in the white hoods, eyes express hatred and fear. It is the only sign of humanity about the figures."[61] But it is a monologue delivered by Trublood toward the end of the same issue #20 that makes McGregor's thesis on America and its legacy of hate clearer, with the reporter claiming that he believes in his country despite its history and believes in the "myths he was taught in school . . . the values this country was supposed to stand for."[62] Trublood continues saying that his character was questioned and he was warned not to "mess with the Klan," but he ultimately could not turn a blind eye or let fear of retaliation take away his freedom of speech.[63] Here McGregor lays out his case via the proxy of the white reporter surrogate, suggesting it is the duty of an American to challenge the ideology of white supremacy and racist oppression—a discussion timely then and timely now. In the next issue, T'Challa survives an attempt by the Klan to burn him alive, breaking free of the scene but carrying the burning cross his attackers set alight on his back—a potent visual metaphor evocative of the Panther's symbolic burden as one of the first prominent Black superheroes.[64]

More powerful yet is the following issue, wherein Monica's mother retells the story of her grandfather's cousin, who stood up to the Klan and was lynched—in Monica's picturing of the story, she imagines an alternate narrative, intercut with the real events of what happened, where T'Challa was there to protect him and battle their leader, the supernatural Soul Strangler. As the two return to the house, she confides in T'Challa her fantasy of him saving her ancestor, saying "I was conjuring my own mythology. How about that? Didn't you notice? Everything's so much simpler in fantasy. People can be such clear-cut symbols, know what I mean?"[65] With this, McGregor makes the subtext into overt text—the Black Panther in this case is a restorative symbol, a way to retroactively seek justice for the injustices of the past. Such a perspective, as the script implies, is somewhat romanticized and simplistic—if only this good and powerful person had been there, the horrible thing would not have happened—especially considering McGregor's role as sympathetic outsider in these issues.

In the real world, the Klan and the cruelty and hatred they espoused continued on—just a few years later, the Klan and members of the American Nazi

Party murdered five anti-Klan protestors in Greensboro, North Carolina on November 3rd, 1979.[66] Duke would parlay his association with the Klan into a semi-successful political career, as well. Just 15 years after he started with the KKK, he won an election for Louisiana's state legislature as a Republican after failed attempts to run for office as a Democrat; he also made unsuccessful bids for the U.S. Senate in 1990 and the Louisiana governor's office in 1991 as well as another failed attempt at the Senate in 2016. All these races were characterized by Duke's focus on what former police officer Ron Stallworth (who once famously infiltrated the KKK's ranks) called a "white supremacist/ethno-nationalist endorsement of a race-centered rhetoric and nativist populism."[67] Far from a bygone relic, Duke remains an active fringe voice in right-wing politics. Duke endorsed Donald Trump for president in 2016 and again in 2020 while encouraging the candidate to take on right-wing pundit Tucker Carlson as his vice president. He also appeared at the "Unite the Right" rally in Charlottesville, Virginia that led to the vehicular murder of protester Heather Heyer (Duke would end up paying a cash settlement to another man injured in the same car attack).[68]

As Lynne's closing monologue implies, fiction is a powerful balm. But it alone cannot end the specter of hatred that continues to haunt American politics and culture. There is even room to argue whether superhero characters are the right way to challenge such issues. As Chris Gavaler argues, there are parallels between Thomas Dixon Jr.'s "Grand Dragon" character from his novel *The Clansman* (later adapted into the film *Birth of a Nation*) and the costumed extrajudicial vigilantism of early superheroes (though his argument, while provocative and worth considering, makes broad assumptions about the insight and motivations of the early creators in the medium and gives entirely too much weight to narrative coincidences).[69] Still, there is rhetorical potency in a super powered African king battling domestic white supremacy, and wish fulfillment is often the role of the superhero—even and perhaps especially when the hurt is far from imagined.

RETURN OF THE KING (OF COMICS)

McGregor's run on *Jungle Action* would be unceremoniously cut short with issue #24, as the title was canceled during the Klan story to be replaced by a new Black Panther title from original co-creator Jack Kirby.[70] While sales were low and McGregor often had difficulty hitting the book's bi-monthly deadlines, he would state in later years that Marvel editorial was also never truly behind the series and viewed the Klan story in particular as "too political."[71] Kirby's new run on the character, for which he handled both art and writing duties, brought with it the dynamic art and high-concept oddity that characterized not only his earlier Marvel work but also his creation of the ambitious Fourth World mega-series at DC Comics; it also eschewed politics altogether and had essentially nothing to do with the work that McGregor, Graham, and others had put into the character.

This was unsurprising for Kirby, who also largely separated his Captain America work from then-current continuity when he took over the Captain America book in 1976. Kirby, still a pro-diversity, anti-fascism advocate, felt more conservative by comparison to his younger creative contemporaries and less interested in adapting to the changing political landscape, which had caused some friction with Captain America fans in the 1960s and furthered that disconnect with the readership, leading to rumored lower sales.[72] In addition to some growing hostility from Marvel editorial about his approach, Kirby's eye was bothering him and skewing his perspective, affecting his art—though Kirby at less than full ability was still the envy of most artists.[73] In comparison to what McGregor had done in *Jungle Action* or even Thomas' *Avengers* stories with the character, Panther seemed like a character out of time in Kirby's new series. Gone were the attempts to discuss imperialism, racism, and other issues relevant to a character from Africa in the 1970s, having been replaced with high-concept treasure hunt stories as the Panther ran afoul of mysterious artifact collectors and dangerous princesses, battling fantastical villains with preposterous technology (though Wakandan politics and another coup attempt against T'Challa's throne would show up again about midway through the series).

While the Kirby series was generally well-received, it did not add much more to the existing foundation of the character and had some strange idiosyncrasies that further complicated an already inconsistent narrative world—for instance, throughout his run Kirby refers to T'Challa as the leader of a "panther cult," which expanded on his spiritual elements but read as a diminishing of his more regal, statesman-like role and the complex depiction of Wakanda that had been established elsewhere.[74] Still, there were interesting ideas. Kirby gave T'Challa an extended family for the first time, several of whom don their own Panther masks and act as the "Black Musketeers" to help defend Wakanda from Jakarra, a former Wakandan general and T'Challa's half-brother who infused himself with vibranium and became a giant, hulking purple creature calling back to Kirby's earlier Marvel monster comics. All the while, T'Challa fights for survival in the desert following a helicopter crash (in a particularly odd sequence, he sabotages a movie shoot in the desert and steals a Jeep to get back to his city—apparently Kirby's Panther was not a man overly concerned with property damage or film insurance).[75] In another issue, after having prophetic and terrifying dreams of his own demise, T'Challa is revealed to have developed ESP, which he later uses to send a telepathic message to his cousin to direct him to free the captives of the villain Kiber the Cruel.[76] The idea of family being important to the Panther remained key to the character, though the "Black Musketeers" would fade into obscurity. The telepathic powers did not stick around for long, but Kirby's final *Panther* run was undeniably the master making his own signature style of comics. Unfortunately, Kirby burned out on making those comics late into the series and left with issue #11, eventually leaving the comics industry altogether for a late-career transition to the more lucrative field of television animation.[77] As we will see later, however, this odd detour nonetheless found a space within the Panther mythos through later writers—particularly in the Christopher Priest run, who used its ideas for high-level meditation on the character.

A new writer-artist team of Ed Hannigan and Jerry Bingham finished out the series' last few issues, bringing Kevin Trublood and Monica Lynne back into the fold and investigating the consequences of T'Challa bringing Wakanda out of isolation into the broader international community. The king is immediately beset by questions from American dignitaries about Wakanda's political loyalties, echoing again the strategic importance of Africa to the West during the Cold War.[78] T'Challa explains to Captain America that he is well aware the Americans are primarily interested in Wakanda's vibranium, and that his push to have Wakanda join the larger world is based on his newfound telepathic abilities and a belief that America and Wakanda will soon be at the center of a larger crisis. After Captain America expresses his concern about T'Challa's words, the king internally monologues to himself while on patrol, internalizing his ally's worries and reflecting once on the tension between being a political leader and superhero: "The danger posed by visionary leaders of great power is one of history's recurring lessons. For every Mohammed or Simon Bolivar, there's been a Hitler or Attila. Still, there's no way I can ignore my responsibilities or unique power."[79] Later writers, particularly Priest and Coates, would explore the thin lines between hero and villain (and leader and dictator) with the character, but Hannigan and Bingham's brief aside added further texture to the character and brought him back toward the complexity of McGregor's interpretation.

The Black Panther standalone series only ran for fifteen issues, and the tease of the return of Trublood and Lynne would finally be resolved as a limited feature in the *Marvel Premiere* series. Issue #51 of the series, emblazoned with the callout of "Marvel's #1 Black Super Hero!," ultimately served to resolve the loose threads of McGregor's earlier Klan story, though McGregor was uninvolved. Hannigan and Bingham, returning once more, mined the tension between T'Challa's connections to America and the broader Western world through Monica Lynne's reflections on the décor of T'Challa's consulate home, which she sees as a reflection of T'Challa's own status as "a study in contrasts—the old world clashing with the new."[80]

While McGregor was not involved in the ending, this "man of two worlds" notion of T'Challa caught between tradition and modernity is the logical endpoint to the story he told in *Jungle Action*. Hannigan and Bingham go out of their way to reconcile the gap in the story by explaining T'Challa's memory had been damaged and he had simply forgotten much of what happened. In #52, following an attempt on the Panther's life by the supervillain Windeagle, T'Challa and friends discover the Klan are behind a plot on the Wakandan king. T'Challa works in some commentary on the American justice system as he infiltrates the Klan hideout:

> For once I am grateful for this country's legal system—the men who attacked us were set free due to lack of evidence, enabling me to track them to their fellows—the Klan, as I suspected! No other regime in the world—including my own—allows such a degree of freedom to its dissidents! Perhaps I shall be able to determine the wisdom of such a liberal attitude this night![81]

The irony of "Marvel's #1 Black Super Hero" decrying the leniency of the criminal justice system and remarking upon the country's coddling of dissidents at a time where civil rights matters were far from settled is, of course, thick. Hannigan and Bingham's story refreshes the reader's memory of what happened half a decade prior to reintroduce a very real, reincarnated Soul Strangler as the ultimate villain of the piece and works in a jab at David Duke's attempt to make a more socially acceptable version of the Klan. As the Strangler smashes down the door to the meeting hall to rally the Klan to battle, one Klansman remarks that the Strangler is "overdoin' the scary spook routine," to which another replies "I thought it was part of our public relations to downplay that sort of thing!"[82] The Panther, doing battle with the Strangler, discovers that the Klan's leader is no mortal man but the embodiment of "hundreds of years of hate in a single being" as the Strangler drags him behind his horse on a noose.[83] However, he makes the realization that the Strangler, though powerful, is limited—by simply refusing to believe his lie or fear the Strangler's hate he manages to easily overcome him, a powerful if somewhat simplistic means of rejecting white supremacy and the lies that support it. Ultimately, the mystery of what happened to Lynne's sister is revealed and the men responsible are brought to justice, and McGregor's saga was finally concluded.

Through the innovations of *Jungle Action*, McGregor (and the writers who would conclude his story) had already made a mark on the character and laid the groundwork for the Black Panther to eventually become a transmedia presence as well as a prestige title at Marvel. Whether *Jungle Action* did not actually sell, or Marvel editorial chose to distance themselves from it is largely inside baseball. It still endured. Not only did Marvel editorial see fit to resolve the story well after its conclusion, the *Jungle Action* series inspired other creators as well—the late Dwayne McDuffie, the prominent Black comic creator of the Static Shock character and founder of the Black-owned Milestone Comics imprint, cited the series as one of his favorites, calling it "damn-near flawless" and praised its economy of storytelling, "seamlessly integrated words and pictures" and "beautifully developed character relationships."[84] McGregor's *Jungle Action stories define the hallmarks of the Black Panther character as stuck between two worlds and grappling with the burden of leadership as much as he grapples with his foes. Beyond that, however, the series* also opened the door for consideration of the metatextual burdens of the hero—what is the responsibility of a Black superhero in a world where that identity is under assault?

Ultimately this era of the Black Panther acted as one of the many forms of counter-narrative against the traditionally Eurocentric and colonialist visions of Africa and Black identity that permeated the pop culture of the era—the year after *Jungle Action* #24 heralded the unceremonious end of McGregor's work, the wildly successful television miniseries adaptation of Alex Haley's *Roots*, originally aired to fill time during a slow programming month, introduced millions of Americans to the long and tragic history of America's involvement in the slave trade and its enduring traumas and impact on generations of Black Americans.[85] The national conversation around these issues was expanding, and pop culture was doing its part. While Marvel and the Panther's contributions to these efforts were not always perfect—coming as they did from a mainly moderate white perspective and at least in the case of the *Avengers* stories taking a skeptical view of Black protest and liberation— the Black Panther was graduating to become a more significant character in his own right. However, that character was still largely confined to the printed page at a time where Marvel heroes were appearing in television programs, product tie-ins, and even in the nascent medium of video games. The lack of a transmedia presence for a character who was effectively Marvel's flagship Black hero—even if the presence of contemporaries like Luke Cage, Storm, Blade, Brother Voodoo and the Falcon (whose iconic wings were actually built and modified by the Black Panther over the years, in an intriguing bit of symbolism) meant he was no longer the only one—signified a lot about who Marvel felt was worth promoting at the time, as those heroes were also largely missing from these spaces.[86] For now, the Black Panther largely just added another splash of color to a comic book universe that was overwhelmingly white, but the die was cast for the character to gradually become one of Marvel's prestige intellectual properties—and for new voices to be heard.

NOTES

1. Hansler, "What Martin Luther King Jr.'s death did to civil rights."
2. Schwartz, "1960: The Year of Africa."
3. Myre, "The Day Nelson Mandela Walked Out of Prison"; Suttner, "The African National Congress."
4. Thomas et al., "Death Calls for the Arch-Heroes!"
5. Thomas et al., "In Battle Joined!," 11.
6. Thomas et al., "Death Be Not Proud!," 5; Thomas et al., "Some Say . . . ," 13.
7. Thomas et al., "The Name is . . . Yellowjacket!"
8. Thomas et al., "The Monarch and the Man-Ape!," 3.
9. Ibid.
10. Ibid.
11. Ibid, 10.
12. Ibid, 20.
13. Mahmoud, "Modernism in Africa."
14. Thomas et al., "When Strikes the Squadron Sinister!."
15. Thomas et al., "The Sting of the Serpent!," 4–5.
16. Ibid, 5.
17. Ibid, 14.
18. Ibid, 17.
19. Thomas et al., "Pursue the Panther!," 2.
20. Ibid, 17.
21. Thomas et al., "The Sting of the Serpent!," 15.
22. Thomas et al., "Pursue the Panther!," 7.
23. Thomas et al., " . . . And We Battle for the Earth!," 7.
24. Thomas et al., "The Sting of the Serpent!," 2.
25. Thomas et al., "A Life on the Line," 9–10.
26. Ibid, 18.
27. Silfer et al., "Conjure Night!."
28. Cronin, "Comic Book Legends Revealed #263."
29. Nyberg, "Comics Code History."
30. Kraft et al., "Voodoo & Valor!," 8.
31. Ibid, 12.
32. Ibid.
33. Nurnberger, "The United States and Idi Amin."
34. Klose, "Soviets, in Shift, Criticize Amin's Rule in Uganda."
35. Ibid, 20; Ellison et al., "The Summons of Psyklop."
36. Howe, *Marvel Comics.*
37. Dar, "Comics Writer Don McGregor Talks 'Black Panther.'"
38. Howe, *Marvel Comics,* 132–133.
39. McGregor, "Living Inside the Head of the King of Wakandans," xxi.
40. Dar, "Comics Writer."
41. Narcisse, personal interview.
42. McGregor et al., "Once You Slay the Dragon!," 1.

43. McGregor et al., "But Now the Spears are Broken," 6.

44. McGregor et al., "Once You Slay the Dragon!," 7.

45. Ibid, 8.

46. Riesman, "Untested Young Comics Writer."

47. McGregor et al., "Panther's Rage," 13.

48. McGregor et al., "King Cadaver is Dead," 5.

49. McGregor et al., "Of Shadows and Rages."

50. Howe, *Marvel Comics,* 133.

51. Dar, "Comics Writer."

52. Nama, *Super Black.*

53. Wright, "Black Outlaws and the Struggle for Empowerment," 82–83.

54. McGregor, "Living Inside the Head of the King of Wakandans," xxiv.

55. Juddery, "How Superman Defeated the Ku Klux Klan."

56. Southern Poverty Law Center, "Ku Klux Klan," 27.

57. Ibid, 35.

58. McGregor et al., "Blood and Sacrifices!"

59. Ibid.

60. McGregor et al., "They Told Me a Myth I Wanted to Believe," 1 & 5.

61. Ibid, 12.

62. Ibid, 15.

63. Ibid, 16.

64. McGregor et al., "A Cross Burning Darkly Blackening the Night!"

65. McGregor et al., "Death Riders on the Horizon," 16.

66. Fowler, "Nazis, Klansmen Killed 5 People in NC 40 Years Ago."

67. Margolin, "David Duke"; Stallworth, *Black Klansman,* 187.

68. Naughtie, "Former KKK Leader"; Welsh-Huggins & Associated Press, "David Duke."

69. Gavaler, "The Ku Klux Klan and the birth of the superhero."

70. Howe, *Marvel Comics.*

71. Cronin, "Comic Legends: Was Kirby Behind Black Panther's First Series Ending?"; McMillan, "'Black Panther' Creators."

72. Evanier, *Kirby*; Stevens, *Captain America, Masculinity, and Violence.*

73. Evanier, *Kirby.*

74. Kirby, "Black Musketeers," 1.

75. Ibid.

76. Kirby, "Kiber the Cruel."

77. Evanier, *Kirby.*

78. Hannigan et al., "The Beasts in the Jungle!"

79. Ibid, 6–7.

80. Hannigan et al., "The Killing of Windeagle!," 8–9.

81. Hannigan et al., "Journey Through the Past!," 13.

82. Ibid, 15.

83. Hannigan et al., "The Ending, in Anger!," 15.

84. McDuffie, "To Be Continued #3."

85. Butler, "Everyone was talking about 'Roots' in 1977"; Zoller Seitz, "Why *Roots* Is the Single Most Important Piece of Scripted Television in Broadcast History."
86. Englehart et al., "J'Accuse!"; Priest et al., "Snapped."

Chapter 5

The Panther in the 1980s–90s

A King for a New Age and a New Audience

The Black Panther was not the focus of the Marvel universe in the 1980s and 1990s—there were no Black Panther cartoons on television, no blockbuster film at the box office, and the character was rarely if ever represented in the merchandise and action figures on store shelves. But in a different context, the Black Panther represented a smaller niche of the Marvel output of that era—as the comic landscape continued shifting away from distribution on drugstore and grocery newsstands and toward a direct market aimed at enthusiasts buying their favorite titles from specialty stores, the content started evolving too. Marvel and other publishers, enticed by the new market that would allow near-complete sell through of their publications, started experimenting with more narrowly-focused titles, royalty systems, and longer-form arcs and graphic novels written and drawn by star creators.[1] The direct market, since it was able to largely bypass traditional retail and go directly to the audience, also allowed for more complex stories with higher levels of sexual content, violence, and occasionally even thoughtful political and philosophical takes—though this did little to challenge the deep-rooted dominance of the superhero genre in the industry, and many superhero tales simply became more grim and violent.[2] In practice, with the loosening grip of the Comics Code, the introduction of super-events like Marvel's *Secret Wars* and DC's *Crisis on Infinite Earths* and the overall increasing cost of single issues, they were just now increasingly being made for the adults who had grown up reading the books in the 1960s and 1970s.

The direct market started as a makeshift effort on the part of the underground comix scene, bypassing traditional retail to deliver counter-culture books to their audience through head shops and other alternative retailers. By the 1980s, it was in full swing for mainstream books with the advent of

Diamond Comics Distributors and a centralized distribution system.[3] Marvel
had experimented with niche books for the direct market in the past and found
success with some more esoteric concepts, and the success of DC's forays
into the graphic novel format—long-form, self-contained stories released in
single issues and collected in trade paperback later like Frank Miller's *The
Dark Knight Returns* and Alan Moore and Dave Gibbons' *Watchmen*—was
hard to ignore.

BLACK PANTHER VS. APARTHEID

Of course, Marvel had a superhero in their ranks that was already attuned
to this kind of long-term storytelling, and an author that had effectively pio-
neered it in the 1970s. That author had checked out of comics to focus on
films and other work, but Don McGregor took a meeting with Marvel editor
Michael Higgins in 1988 anyway about returning to the *Killraven* series—
eventually, as McGregor tells it, Higgins was able to convince him to come
back to Black Panther as well as a feature in the anthology series *Marvel
Comics Presents*. McGregor, who felt that the character worked best in a
serialized illustrated novel format, decided to return to his idea of telling a
story about apartheid in South Africa, while also answering the long-standing
question of what happened to T'Challa's mother.[4] The series, titled "Panther's
Quest," acted as an official sequel to his *Jungle Action* work and ran through
issue #13 to #37 in the book with Gene Colan handling art duties.

Apartheid was one of the most significant geopolitical issues of the late
1980s. The Carter administration placed sanctions on the South African
government and openly criticized their practices of legalized segregation and
systemic discrimination against non-white South Africans, but those sanctions were largely reversed when Ronald Reagan took office in 1981. The
Reagan administration saw the African National Congress, the most prominent anti-apartheid party in South Africa, as a "pro-communist movement"
and the openly racist South African government as a more corporate-friendly
ally and trading partner and took a moderate approach to dealing with them.[5]

Such a friendly relationship between the United States and the South
African government was far from unprecedented—in addition to pro-South
African policies put into place by the Nixon administration and then-National
Security Adviser Henry Kissinger, American comic artists collaborated with
the South African government on a series of propaganda titles aimed at rein-
forcing the apartheid government in an exercise of soft power.[6] The comics,
the brainchild of South African Department of Information Secretary Eschel
Roodie, were part of a larger propaganda effort by Roodie and sympathetic
American media to promote Western capitalist ideology among the Black

population of South Africa—and to defend the apartheid system against criticism and protest. In the case of *Afri-Comics*, law-and-order characters like "Mighty Man" failed to convince their target audience and publication ceased after widespread protests and attacks on newsstands carrying the comics. Joe Orlando, one of the artists who worked on the publications, later worked on *Superman* and became vice president at DC Comics.[7]

Nelson Mandela had attained global notoriety and admiration for the campaign he waged against the South African government's practice of legalized segregation and systemic discrimination against Black citizens from the jail cell he had occupied for over two decades. However, the Reagan administration and conservative entities like the Heritage Foundation rejected support for Mandela's release, believing he was a terrorist threat. Such a position echoed the infamous "Rubicon speech" made in 1985 by South Africa's then-president P.W. Botha in which he claimed Mandela and the ANC had plotted violent action against the government. In the same speech, Botha openly rejected "one man, one vote" unitary democracy, claiming it would lead to chaos and "domination of one race over another."[8] Just a year earlier, the U.S. had abstained from a United Nations Security Council vote condemning the policies of apartheid; meanwhile American citizen groups, academic scholars, and other entities engaged in a flurry of public anti-apartheid through the latter part of the 1980s.[9] From 1986 until 1992 (two years after his release from prison), South African intelligence interests collaborated with right-wing political operatives in the United States to delegitimize Mandela and the ANC through House committee hearings and newspaper ads. The social conservative adherence to the apartheid system ran deep—televangelist Jerry Falwell even jumped on board to defend the South African government and encourage US companies to invest in the country to support its anti-abortion policies.[10] In 1986, Congress overruled Reagan's veto of the Comprehensive Apartheid Act, which banned U.S. investment in South Africa and prohibited imports of South African goods and resources. This in turn put sanctions on the country once again and exerted economic pressure that would eventually lead to Mandela's release in 1990 and later his election as president.[11] All told, the apartheid government of South Africa had a willing partner in the American government for much of the 1980s, echoing America's own history of segregation and Jim Crow laws. America was not the only country that saw the apartheid South African government as an ally—the British government under Margaret Thatcher also accused Nelson Mandela of being a terrorist in the 1980s and opposed sanctions. While Thatcher would eventually advocate for Mandela's release from prison and told Mandela after his release that "apartheid must go," her government had also publicly condemned the ANC and anti-apartheid leaders as Communist enemies and she privately believed Mandela had "rather a closed mind."[12]

While the fall of apartheid was primarily the product of collective political action, entertainment and popular culture had their role to play as well. Musicians like Stevie Wonder, Steven Van Zandt, Bob Dylan, and U2 released anti-apartheid songs, participated in protests of the South African government, and boycotted the country's Sun City performance venue.[13] Many international sports associations also boycotted South Africa, which may have been more effective due to the importance of rugby and other athletic competitions to the South African identity—the boycott did make it "much more difficult for the international community to ignore the calls for the application of trade and financial sanctions."[14]

McGregor's story is, then, a small part of that larger effort, the use of a comic book superhero to fight a systemic injustice—and to his credit, he recognized that having the Panther punch the problem away was unrealistic and patronizing.[15] Instead, apartheid informs the situation in which the Panther finds himself, and McGregor found himself having to update parts of the story as the situation unfolded—for instance, after the pass laws requiring Black citizens over the age of 16 to carry a "pass" with them while traveling and to obtain housing and other necessities were repealed prior to the story's publication, McGregor set the story as taking place prior to that decision as the laws were necessary for the plot.[16] Working within the narrow format of eight pages an issue (with occasional negotiated increases in exchange for writing shorter stories about other characters), McGregor spun a yarn about a stranger in a strange land, battling not super-villainous forces but rather a more mundane, government-sponsored form of hatred.

Throughout the story's 25 chapters, T'Challa finds himself in the middle of a country ripped apart by systemic oppression and inequality, his only ally a miner by the name of Zanti who reluctantly aids the king on his quest. Rumors have surfaced that T'Challa's long-missing mother is alive in South Africa, and he goes on an unsanctioned personal mission to rescue her. The story was perhaps the deepest dive yet into the Panther's psyche—T'Challa's faint memories of his mother are woven throughout the narrative and his misled belief she does not actually want to see him is a major emotional beat—but it is also a very specific political polemic, with McGregor using the character as a philosophical proxy to challenge the apartheid government, his prose illustrating both the solitary brutality of the quest and the injustice of the setting. One section draws a line between the pleasurable gaudiness and beauty of the city of Johannesburg:

Johannesburg's edifices and striking spire scintillatingly ignore the dirt and sweat and blood that it took to rip the precious ore from the earth. [. . .] The electronic elegance of the golden city thrusts up from the flatlands, almost in furious denial of the arid stretches that surround it. More subtly, also a denial of those Black townships surrounding it.[17]

At the time, McGregor was aware of the exploitation and inequality of the Black people of South Africa and how that inequality was illustrated in the country's largest city—but he could not have known that same systemic inequality would continue decades later. Today, few if any white citizens fall below the middle class stratum in South African's socioeconomic standings, and citizens in Black neighborhoods and townships often bear the worst of a lack of resources and infrastructure and a startling 25 percent unemployment rate (as of 2019).[18] "Panther's Quest" is by purpose and design a story set in a specific moment in time, but the issues that informed the narrative still persist, apartheid in all but policy. This sentiment is echoed when McGregor pauses the action of the Panther's final assault on the mansion of his mother's captor, Anton Pretorius, to reflect on the building's symbolism—"It is also a manifest symbol of a way of life, imposed as law, not centuries old, but started a mere 40 years ago. The first statutes of apartheid are newer than the mansion itself, yet its directives stubbornly swear such places will endure."[19]

The rhetorical comparison between the recency of apartheid and the enduring power of the mansion edifice makes McGregor's stance on the injustice of not only the system but the American power that served to uphold it clear. He also uses the story to comment on the divisions among those who stood against apartheid—a subplot focuses on the battle between rival Black factions the Comrads and the Fathers, both of whom resent and wish to overthrow the oppressive South African central government but use it as justification to torture and kill those they feel support it. Their conflict turns deadly after T'Challa intervenes to save a man from "necklacing," a common form of extrajudicial torture and murder used by South African revolutionaries and ANC supporters at the time. "Necklacing" involved the filling of a tire with gasoline, which was then ignited around a person's neck (the ANC leadership disavowed the practice, though Winnie Mandela once famously said that "our boxes of matches and our necklaces" would "liberate" South Africa, seen by many as an endorsement of the practice).[20] McGregor's use of a such a horrific action and his portrayal of the Comrads and Fathers flirts with political paternalism, as T'Challa scolds the men shortly before he is necklaced himself—"You are positive your solution to apartheid is right . . . and that being right allows you to act as inhumanely as your oppressors . . . that being right gives one the right to murder!"[21]

A young boy who attempts to free T'Challa is burned by the gasoline and flames, ultimately dying despite T'Challa's attempt to get him treatment at the nearest whites-only hospital. The senselessness of the death further underscores McGregor's depiction of an arbitrarily cruel system that pits a government against its people and those people against each other. Zanti, acting as an audience surrogate but also the representative of those who would be directly affected by apartheid's grasp, reflects the belief that change in the system cannot come from those outside it (such as T'Challa) but instead from within and from the bottom up:

> But many voices will have to be heard . . . will have to be raised . . . before any of them can or will listen. [. . .] Too many people positive they are right, and because of that—are convinced that it gives them the right to imprison, assault, tear apart families, maim . . . and kill! [. . .] You made me realize my voice must be heard. I do not want you to die, you can be certain—but I will no longer live silent.[22]

As discussed previously, "Panther's Quest" was not the first time the Black Panther came into conflict with systems of apartheid. In addition to the storyline resulting in the ill-advised "Black Leopard" name change, Peter Gillis and Denys Cowan's 1988 four-issue *Black Panther* limited series saw T'Challa travel to Anzania, an apartheid government with its own team of white supremacist superheroes. Yet McGregor's work eschewed the political safety of setting its tale in an abstract fictional country and instead faced the reality of the issue as directly as a superhero comic could. The narrative mixes grounded political reality (a TV news report states that Wakanda has dismissed accusations that it is sympathetic to Communism) and a level of brutal violence that was surprising for a mainstream Marvel book both then and now—dogs and children die, the Panther himself is subject to numerous graphic injuries, a mercenary's hand is caught in an escalator at a Johannesburg mall, and the antagonist mercenary Gore is dispatched when the Panther dodges his attack and the man stabs himself in the throat.[23] When the Panther is finally reunited with his mother Ramonda, she reveals that she has been held captive by Pretorius ever since she joined a protest against the South African police. Pretorius had become obsessed with her and used his wealth and influence to simply make her disappear into his home, where he imprisoned and raped her. T'Challa and his mother return to Wakanda after she talks T'Challa into sparing Pretorius' life (though she strikes him in anger before they go).[24] It can be argued that Ramonda symbolizes the country of South Africa itself, held captive by abusive and exploitative white influences and ultimately overthrowing its cruel and exploitative captors through non-violent means.

In 1991, McGregor would finish out his quadrilogy of stories by teaming with artist Dwayne Turner on *Panther's Prey*, released in a series of four "prestige format" volumes with higher page counts, better quality paper and cover stock, and no advertisements—and that were not subject to the content restrictions of the Comics Code Authority. It was a return to form for McGregor, who had with his independent work *Sabre* published one of the first graphic novels to be sold through the direct market in 1978.[25] While not the first graphic novels Marvel had released, it was certainly new territory for the Black Panther and arguably the ultimate product of what McGregor intended to achieve with the character. The original release copies of the *Panther's Prey* story evoked mass market paperbacks, with dramatic text teasing the story between the covers and ancillary materials like creator biographies, photos, and essays. The prestige format also allowed for breaking of artistic convention (Turner experiments with a variety of panel layouts and sketchy art styles, even flipping panels upside down and bending the narrative text boxes around T'Challa's leaping arcs to convey motion) and content that would have been unable to see print in a traditional newsstand book. The story confirms without ever outright stating a homosexual relationship between the reformed villain Venomm and T'Challa's advisor Taku; it also engages in frank depictions of sexual intercourse. Monica Lynne is often portrayed in various stages of undress and nudity—the latter unusual for a Marvel book then or now, and reflective of McGregor's more sexually-tinged work outside of the company.

Like "Panther vs. the Klan" and "Panther's Quest," the story also deals with a then-contemporary political issue, in this case drug abuse. The villain, Solomon Prey, is smuggling drugs into Wakanda with fatal results for Kantu, the boy who rescued T'Challa from Killmonger at the end of "Panther's Rage." While the trafficking of drugs through African nations to meet European demand through the 1980s and 1990s is well-documented, it is more likely given McGregor's comments in the ancillary materials for the comics that the story was primarily aligned with the ideological and political "war on drugs" of the Reagan and Bush years. At one point, Marvel apparently discussed donating proceeds from the comics to drug rehab programs, though it is unclear if they ever did.[26] Yet for most of the four issues, the drug storyline takes a backseat to a love story as T'Challa's confidant W'Kabi encourages him to find a bride—effectively a means of reuniting T'Challa and Monica Lynne. In fact, much of the story exists to draw all of McGregor's prior threads together, including the return of Tanzika (who had committed the murder for which Monica was framed in "Panther's Rage") as Prey's love interest.

Ultimately, the series is ended without a great deal of closure on any front—while Prey and Tanzika's plot to destroy Wakanda is foiled, T'Challa and Lynne are not yet married, and the threat of drug use and mistrust between the king's inner circle still exists in Wakanda, as evidenced by the volume's closing shot of a young Wakandan woman smoking a crack pipe. A column written by McGregor bookending the volume hints at another series, "Panther's Vows," that would have likely included the wedding.[27] Unfortunately, that series never materialized, and readers were left wondering what might have been given the new flexibility the prestige format offered. Yet it would be in the traditional periodical that the Panther would return, providing arguably one of the single most definitive takes and the first Panther ongoing series written by an African American writer.

THROUGH NEW EYES: CHRISTOPHER PRIEST AND THE MODERN PANTHER

Prior to 1998, the Black Panther had been a character primarily written by white authors. While Black artists like Billy Graham, Denys Cowan, and Dwayne Turner had put indelible creative stamps on the character, most of the writers who handled stories about the character treated him as largely superfluous or expressed their own implicit bias toward Africa and limited knowledge of the character in their stories.[28] It took nearly three decades for the Panther to be written by a Black writer. Dwayne McDuffie, the trailblazing writer who would go on to found Milestone comics and play a pivotal role in rival DC's television output, wrote the Panther into his 1993 *Deathlok* series and as such holds the honor of being the first Black creator to write T'Challa. McDuffie, who was open about his affection for the character and the formative impact of McGregor's run in the years following, explained what the character meant to him in an essay years later: "[. . .] the Black Panther was king of a mythical African country where black people were visible in every position in society, soldier, doctor, philosopher, street sweeper—suddenly everything was possible. In the space of 15 pages, black people moved from invisible to inevitable."[29]

McDuffie's enthusiasm for the character is evident in the short arc, in which the Black cyborg Deathlok visits Wakanda to help T'Challa solve a computer system breach orchestrated by the supervillain Phreak—but the story is secondary to the subtext, wherein McDuffie seems to be waxing poetic about his own feelings for the character through the words of Deathlok, wherein the cyborg encourages T'Challa as the king worries about whether Wakanda's technology comes at the cost of its humanity: "My humanity can't be destroyed. Not by this metal shell I'm in, nor by anything else. The same's true of your people. [. . .] When you became an Avenger, it was a matter of pride for a whole generation of African-Americans. You see me as a metaphor. I see you as a personal hero."[30]

McDuffie's generational perspective and personal connection to the character is a significant moment in the character's history, as it is one of the first to reify the symbolic power of the Black Panther metaphor outside of the constraints of the comics narrative. The series explores themes of humanity and Black identity with the assassin Killjoy claiming that the now-cyborg Deathlok "used to be" Black and the supervillain Moses Magnum offering up the neighboring country of Canaan as a "homeland of African-Americans" only for Deathlok to reject the invitation by reasserting his identity as an American and saying that "too much of my ancestors's [sic] sweat was invested in building America . . . too much of their blood has been spilled defending it."[31] McDuffie's rhetoric positions Magnum's offer as a sort of inverse of Wakanda, wherein the power comes at the expense of others (Deathlok chastises Magnum for trying to advance his station at the expense of other Black people). Simultaneously, his script casts the Panther as an aspirational figure for Deathlok and by proxy the reader with Deathlok assuring T'Challa he will "try to live up to the example you've set."[32] McDuffie's story, by introducing a mechanism for the reader to see the Black Panther through the eyes of another character, introduces a powerful rhetorical device to recontextualize what the reader themselves thinks of the character.

That same device became pivotal to the 1998 Christopher Priest run, one of the most definitive takes on the character and the focus of the bulk of this chapter. Priest, the first full-time Black writer at Marvel, was born James Owsley and grew up reading comics, eventually landing a position at Marvel and working his way up to a full-fledged editor by 1984 while also writing occasional one-off titles and a miniseries about The Falcon, Marvel's first African-American hero.[33] Priest was eventually fired amid racial and professional friction at the Marvel offices, briefly finding work at DC Comics before leaving over another editorial dispute; he later co-created the superhero comedy series *Quantum and Woody* (about an interracial superhero team) at Acclaim Comics in the late 1990s.[34]

In 1998, Marvel approached Priest about writing a new book for the "edgier" Marvel Knights imprint and suggested Black Panther. Priest was not enthusiastic, as he felt the Panther had been reduced to a largely ineffectual secondary character in many Marvel titles (in Priest's words, Panther was "the colorless cypher who sort of stood in the back row for the Avengers class picture").[35] He also had his own concerns about being pigeonholed as a "Black" writer and long-standing concerns about the commercial viability of books with Black protagonists.[36] Priest eventually acquiesced when the imprint's editors, Joe Quesada and Jimmy Palmiotti, allowed him to reintroduce the character in a manner closer to his more mysterious and capable form in the original Lee and Kirby comics and include a white "point of view character." This would become Everett K. Ross, a State Department attaché who over time came to in Priest's words represent a more "deconstructionist" view of the Marvel universe and "giddily [make] salad of all of the anxiety of the adult super-hero fan, kicking over many a sacred cow in the process."[37]

Here it is worth noting that Priest catalogued many of this thoughts and experiences from working on the series on his personal website—they offer an insightful look at the construction of the character and the mindset behind the series, and are invaluable documents in decoding Priest's role in the transmedia mythology of the character.

Priest's run began, appropriately enough for an imprint aimed at telling darker stories aimed at an older audience, with the Panther running afoul of the demon Mephisto while investigating the death of a young girl.[38] Instead of writing from the perspective of the Panther's internal monologue as McGregor had done, Priest and artist Mark Texeira made the character alien to the reader. Priest's script positioned the reader outside T'Challa's head, using Ross's reactions as an audience surrogate to paint a picture of an unfamiliar character they themselves were trying to figure out. In later essays on his website, Priest wrote at length about how this decision alleviated his initial concerns regarding the character:

> I feel the most profound statement I can make about race is to make Panther so cool he transcends the racial divide here in America. Rather than try and force the readers to identify with a black character, I accepted the fact a great many readers would not be able to overcome the race thing, and withdrew Panther from the reader entirely.[39]

In effect, Ross became a vehicle through which the audience could come to understand the character as well as break what Priest saw as inherent tension between the writer and reader. Ross, who Priest based on a combination of Michael J. Fox and Matthew Perry, was portrayed simultaneously throughout the series as a competent lawyer and attaché and as a bumbling fool who repeatedly underestimated the Panther with a tendency to get into bizarre situations, like making a deal with the devil to get a pair of pants or accidentally becoming the acting regent of Wakanda, complete with traipsing around in the ill-fitting Panther habit.[40] To Priest, Ross—who repeatedly made off-color jokes about Black stereotypes in his stream of consciousness narration—"[gave voice] to the [white male] audience's misgivings or apprehensions or assumptions about this character and this book." Yet, Priest was careful in interviews to say that his intent was not for Ross to actually be racist, but rather offer "a window into things I imagine many whites say or at least think when no Blacks are around; myths about Black culture and behavior."[41] Such a statement opens up a metaphorical can of worms about Priest's read of the audience—though, given his lengthy experience in the industry, that read was probably not without merit—and some of Ross's comments probably stretch the boundaries of what the reader may be comfortable with. It should also be said that Priest saw Ross as a metaphor not only for Marvel's "disrespect of

Panther but of Stan Lee," whose original vision was one of Priest's guiding creative principles.[42] However, as a narrative device, Ross solves a significant problem in the transmedia construction of the Panther—like Ross, we are being reintroduced to the character, *tabula rasa*, allowing for the character's identifying fictive elements to shine through unfettered.

This effectively recalibrated the depiction of Black Panther—without stating the rationale behind his actions, he became enigmatic—and re-instilled some gravitas to a character he felt had been largely marginalized and forgotten rather than simply trying to integrate the Panther seamlessly into the existing Marvel Universe. To emphasize the "coolness" of the character, Priest drew inspiration from Denny O'Neil's Batman villain Ra's Al Ghul, a similarly mysterious character Priest admired. He and artist Mark Texeira also gave the Panther expensive cars, brought back his cape and cowl, and added gadgets like the proto-smartphone Kimoyo card. Ironically, despite drawing inspiration from his villain at first, Priest's version of the Panther was often referred to as Marvel's equivalent of Batman (a critique artist Sal Velluto would reference in issue #22 with a cheeky homage "nightmare" wherein Panther and Ross are dressed as Batman and Robin).[43] Such a move was not without creative risk, and while Priest's run is now considered essential to the current depiction of the Black Panther not all readers were on board. As Priest wrote in a retrospective about his time on the series [emphasis the original author's]:

> What was even odder, for me, was the uproar of fans outraged by our evolution of the character into an extremely capable and not always clearly heroic figure, a man of uncertainty and mystery who used all of the vast resources at his disposal to accomplish his goals. [. . .] Again and again I was asked, "How dare you change Panther!", to which I replied, "I didn't change Panther—other writers over the years changed Panther, losing sight of FF #52. *I* changed him *back*."[44]

While Priest was initially skeptical about taking over the character's baggage, time has shown the decision to reimagine the character as something other than the Avengers' token Black friend was prudent and closer to the original intent. As Priest wrote through Ross's perspective in issue #11 of his run: "The thing people keep forgetting about my client is, well, he's a KING. He's not just another nut job in tights. He's a full-bird monarch from one of the most technologically advanced nations on the planet. And, somehow, we keep forgetting that."[45] In short, as later *Panther* writer Ta-Nehisi Coates would argue, "[Priest] had the classic run on Black Panther, period, and that's gonna be true for a long time [. . .] People had not put as much thought into who and what Black Panther was before Christopher started writing the book."[46]

Effectively, Priest's work served to take the character—and his representation of Africa and Blackness—into a new era by paying tribute to the past.

Priest's first issue opens early on that note, with a scene where a car full of gang members mock T'Challa for his costume and "carrying the other Avengers' bags."[47] After T'Challa and his Dora Milaje bodyguards dispatch the men, the king emerges from a nearby alleyway, cloaked in shadow with glowing gold eyes—unlike the sunny and noble vision of Panthers past, this one was at first glance mysterious and terrifying, signifying a new version of the old standby.

A brief note on the Dora Milaje, which Priest and Texeira created, here—in Priest's run, the Dora Milaje are the Panther's elite female bodyguards, presented per Wakandan tradition as women who were "promised" brides to the king, a tradition T'Challa rejects. Later writers Reginald Hudlin and Ta-Nehisi Coates would continually downplay this aspect of the Dora Milaje. The 2018 film does not include it at all, in favor of making the Dora Milaje and specifically their leader Okoye more pivotal to the narrative. The Dora Milaje are a significant part of Priest's interpretation of the character—building on what he called the "brilliant work" of Don McGregor, who introduced the idea of Wakanda as a nation comprised of many tribes that did not all get along. Priest introduced the Dora as an army of women sent from each of Wakanda's tribes as a means of dealing with internecine Wakandan strife as well as to "[give] us a foot in both of the worlds the Panther struggled to maintain peace between—the modern and tribal."[48] Priest and Texeira, both students of popular culture, based the appearance of the two primary Dora Milaje (Nakia and Okoye) in the series on supermodels Tyra Banks and Naomi Campbell.[49]

As fans and scholars have noted, the idea of deadly female bodyguards is not exclusive to Priest's work but in fact a long-standing one in African history. While historical accounts vary, the former West African kingdom of Dahomey appears to have recruited women as palace guards in the 1720s, with the king forming a bodyguard regiment out of women "who had not borne children" and were "insufficiently beautiful to share his bed"—the women were formally married to the king and pledged their lives to defend him.[50] These so-called "Dahomey Amazons" (a name given by Europeans on the continent) defended the kingdom and its king until the nineteenth century, when the kingdom was colonized and eventually became what is the Republic of Benin.[51] It is unclear whether Priest based his Dora Milaje directly on this bit of history, but it nonetheless significantly contributed to one of the recurring themes McGregor introduced and other writers would expand upon—the importance of women and matriarchal influence in T'Challa's life and the history of Wakanda.

In the first arc of the series, Wakanda is in a state of unrest after T'Challa opened the country's borders to refugees, and T'Challa is in the United States investigating the death of a young girl associated with a Wakandan charity fund. Priest works through his own issues with the character by juxtaposing the gravitas of the quest and the intent with which Panther pursues it with the lack of respect given to him by the other characters in the story—at one point Ross waves off the challenge of acting as T'Challa's attaché due to the king's lack of powers.[52] In this way, Black Panther in this story acts as a loose metaphor for the overall dismissal of the character (and in a vaguer sense Africa) in the white American mainstream—a dismissal repeatedly proven false by the king's advanced technological prowess and his grimly efficient detective work. Said work ultimately ties the young girl's death (and many others) to an American charity acting as a front for money laundering and trafficking activities orchestrated using Wakandan funds by a political usurper named Achebe. T'Challa brings the girl's murderer to justice, only to be fooled by an illusion from the demon Mephisto that tricks him into accidentally kissing Nakia—and in Wakanda culture, declaring his intent to marry her. That most of the above happened in a single issue is a testament to how dense Priest's plotting and intrigue can be.[53] T'Challa even manages to outwit Mephisto (the Marvel equivalent of the Christian Devil) using advanced technology and strategy. He lures the demon to the Ancestral Plane, where the Panther allows him to consume his soul—which is bound to all other souls of his ancestors, and their purity and number overwhelm and nearly kill the demon.[54] Again, T'Challa uses the ignorance and disdain the outside world has for Wakanda/ Africa and its traditions and beliefs to overcome a powerful adversary—this continual underestimation is a common downfall among Priest's antagonists, and the country and the character reflect real-world underestimation of the continent and its people.

Priest's first story arc on the character also explores the role colonization played in T'Challa's origin, once again through the villain Klaw. Unlike previous iterations, however, Priest carefully uses analogies taken from American Westward expansion, comparing Klaw's slaughter of T'Chaka and the Wakandan people to the Wounded Knee massacre in which U.S. soldiers killed over three hundred Lakota Indians.[55] In this way, he draws a clear connecting line between European colonialism on the African continent and the North American one, making the subtext of the original Lee and Kirby origin story more overt. Throughout the first arc, Priest also pokes at the Eurocentrism of American politics at the time—a fancy dress ball put on by the White House as a means of honoring T'Challa and reaching out to the African-American committee is described by Ross this way: "Outside of the king and his entourage, there wasn't another Black person at the ball who wasn't carrying a tray."[56]

As Priest expands on McGregor's exploration of the disdain and mistrust Wakandans have for the outside world, he also explores the friction of Panther's split membership between Wakanda and the West. A recurring aspect of the Black Panther mythos is T'Challa's presence in both the Western world as well as his own home—in one issue, Priest elects to illustrate this through a flashback to T'Challa's time at university where a group of black students attack him for dating a white woman (revealed later to be Ross's boss, Nikki). However, the division between T'Challa's background and the West is explored differently here by Priest as a function of Wakandan isolationism, with T'Challa's bodyguard Zuri explaining it is a "division not of race but of character" and that T'Challa's father would disapprove "not because the girl is white—but because she is not of the realm."[57] Later, as T'Challa addresses a gathered throng of Black citizens who have gathered outside the ball, insisting that he has "always been among you," a man in the crowd replies "You were with them—the Avengers, the Fantastic Four. They don't care nothin' about us. They not our heroes—they their heroes. You're our hero—you know how *we* feel!"[58] In this scene, Priest maps a rather loose interpretation of W. E. B. Du Bois' "double consciousness" concept onto the superhero by illustrating how T'Challa struggles to reconcile his responsibility to those who have a common heritage with the perception of privilege afforded by his education and royal standing. Yet, it is an imperfect example because unlike Du Bois and so many others, T'Challa is both not an American citizen and is in the country by choice.[59] In short, Panther tries to be an international hero to all, but he is still defined by his African heritage and his Blackness and the implicit positioning and responsibility that comes with it.

This is further illustrated during a tense moment where T'Challa discovers his old college rival, now a Senator, orchestrated the crowds to put them at risk when the NYPD shows up with helicopters and guns. After an incident in which a sniper—revealed to be the Panther's lost love Monica Lynne in a remotely-controlled exoskeleton controlled by Achebe—fires a shot at the gathered crowd and incites mass panic, Achebe taunts Panther via video, asking why he left the throne to play hero: "Why, in every photograph, these 'Avengers' have the King of the Realm standing in back. They do not even honor you by addressing you as king."[60] Given Priest's interest in trying to make the Black Panther a more vital character, it is hard not to read Achebe's taunt as a metatextual critique of how Marvel had handled him—less as a wholly self-sufficient character and more as a token pal for white heroes. Earlier in that same issue (#8), Ross's retelling of the history between the Black Panther and Captain America loosely adapts both the story and Jack Kirby art of *Captain America* #100, culminating with the Panther being given honorary membership in the Avengers.[61] This metatextual nod to the reader's assumed perception that being an Avenger would be the highest possible honor for an African king—complete with Ross, like Lee and Kirby before him telling the story from a white standpoint—is challenged by Priest when Ross refers to the Avengers as "gaudily dressed borderline fascists."[62] While disabling a bomb set by Achebe, T'Challa explains that he joined the Avengers to spy on them, causing friction with Captain America and the rest of the Avengers as the two investigate whether the American government incited the coup in Wakanda—an investigation that results in T'Challa virtually declaring war on the United States in front of the United Nations (T'Challa nearly starting global crises to serve Wakanda's needs is a recurring theme in Priest's run).[63]

In this storyline, Priest draws upon real-world history to inform his vision of the character—the revelation that elements of the U.S. intelligence community worked in concert with the Russian mob and a giant tech company to destabilize the neighboring country of Ghudaza to flood Wakanda with refugees and bring down T'Challa's rule is not terribly dissimilar from real-world incidents where American intelligence has interfered in African countries.[64] Consider the CIA's plans to attempt to assassinate Patrice Lumumba in the Congo and alleged backing of Hissene Habre in Chad as an attempt to counter Muammar Gaddafi in the region, as a start.[65] It is likely events like these inspired Priest's story or were at least on his mind. In Priest's version of the character—one influential to the contemporary vision of the Black Panther—T'Challa acts as a symbol of the inherent tensions in Blackness and African identity through a Western lens as well as part of the counter-narrative to challenge white American hegemony on the continent. While McGregor had opened this door, Priest walked through it confidently and started a few fires on his way through for good measure—in his own words, he saw his run on the character as "equal parts social commentary and political satire."[66]

It is not hyperbole to say that Priest's run went a long way to rehabilitate a character Marvel had largely overlooked for many years. In the second year, with the book's future in doubt and Priest's contract with the Marvel Knights imprint renewed, new editor Ruben Diaz stepped in with a directive to bring the book "more into the mainstream of the Marvel Universe"—which meant more traditional superhero action and cameos as well as a team-up with the company's "blaxploitation heroes" like Black Goliath and Power to fight a cadre of inner-city villains.[67] The out-of-sequence storytelling that had led to so many of the first year's best moments and comedic beats became too much to handle with the necessities of tying into the larger publishing line, so Priest gradually retired that too.[68]

What was not lost, however, was the creative chip on Priest's shoulder. His Panther remained every bit the strategic and scientific mastermind demonstrated in the first year, going toe-to-toe with the Marvel Universe's greatest leaders and intellects (and usually coming out on top) throughout.[69] Priest also took this opportunity, backed by the eye-catching visuals of Sal Velluto (who gave the Panther a bigger, more flowing cape and more tribal-styled accoutrements on the costume), to explore the character's legacy to the other Black heroes and villains of the Marvel Universe—in a battle with the deadly poison-user and expert geneticist Nightshade, she expresses her admiration for him and honor in fighting a legitimate African king.[70] Small moments like this underscore Priest's central thesis—that the Panther really should be a more important character in the Marvel Universe than he had been up to that point—and in-text creates an image of the character that helps to convince even skeptical readers of his importance.

Priest's run, while not afraid to jab at previous editorial handling of the character, also sought to expand the world of Wakanda and build on the work of previous Panther writers, particularly Don McGregor. Priest brought back elements from McGregor's run, particularly his recurring romantic interest Monica Lynne (who repeatedly points out throughout his run how tired she is of being kidnapped and assailed by T'Challa's foes) and expanded on Killmonger, the hero's greatest canonical foe and the one he had never actually defeated. Where McGregor had written Killmonger as a power-seeking brute who was primarily a physical match for T'Challa, Priest re-imagined the character as a ruthless capitalist channeling his hatred for T'Challa into manipulation of the stock market. At one point, as the acting regent of Wakanda, Everett Ross visits Killmonger's N'Jadaka Village (an "evil, corporate-sponsored Disneyland" that acts as a "mirror" of Wakanda) and likens him to Michael Milkin or Donald Trump, referring to him as "Erik Killmonger: Agent of Pepsi."[71] Killmonger, seemingly friendly to the Wakandan envoy, reveals his true plan to Monica Lynne (who he had taken in after she was lost in the jungle) as gaming the global economic system to destroy the value of vibranium, Wakanda's sole economic export—and in so doing introduces more of Priest's political commentary. The structure of the global economy, Priest-through-Killmonger states, is not based on tangible assets or real currency but rather blind faith and the encouragement of hiding assets through investments and shell companies like his iFruit tech enterprise: "The money keeps moving—but it's electric money. It's play dough. [. . .] It's there because we think it is. [. . .] The money is real only as long as the market holds—so the time to leverage it—to use it for some practical or constructive purpose—has a limited window."[72]

That practical purpose, as he alludes to in the explanation, can involve overthrowing governments. As he explains, T'Challa is responsible for all vibranium sales as king, making him one of the richest men in the world, but if the value of vibranium decreases by Killmonger's companies refusing to purchase it, the worth of the king and Wakanda alike goes down with it. As Priest-through-Killmonger states, "Your lover has fought off the CIA, the

LCL, the Russians—but he's about to lose it all to Dow Jones"—suggesting a belief that it is capitalism, not the world's governments or intelligence agencies, that holds true global power.[73] To counter this, T'Challa dissolves the Wakandan parliament and nationalizes all of the companies Killmonger made deals with, crashing the stock market and creating a global recession that foils Killmonger's plans. Killmonger, stunned, tells T'Challa "The planet is in an uproar—markets across the globe are crashing, panic is spreading—armies are going on alert. And—why? Because of the madman ruling Wakanda!"[74]

Here, Priest deftly raises the narrative stakes and demonstrates the true power and responsibility the character faces while needling the artifice of the global economy. The critique is all but Marxist in nature: if two extremely wealthy men who controlled important global economic centers simply decided to, they could cause untold economic disruption and devastation—and "[sentence children] to hunger, poverty, or death," in Killmonger's words.[75] Such words read as prescient in a contemporary time of unfathomable wealth being concentrated in the hands of a few unaccountable billionaires. However, complicating it further, the two men battling with the global economy as a proxy for their personal feud are Black men of African descent rather than Tony Stark or a Doctor Doom—both an inversion of narrative tropes and in its own way a funhouse mirror of the counter-narrative role of the character speculating a world in which a historically marginalized group can amass enough power to cause global financial meltdown.

Ultimately, T'Challa agrees to Killmonger's challenge at Warrior Falls in accordance with tribal custom, knowing that to do otherwise would make the villain a martyr. T'Challa's eventual defeat only relegates Killmonger to the ceremonial Black Panther role while leaving ruling power in T'Challa's hands.[76] The role does not suit Killmonger—he expresses open frustration with the Avengers, who he calls "calcified, hand-wringing bureaucrats" and calls out their tokenism for including the Black speedster Triathalon among their ranks—"I'm not sure who I respect less—you for wanting a token, or him for accepting."[77] Priest's metatextual efforts appear to shine through here again, as Killmonger's words about Triathalon could just as easily be about T'Challa and the broader problem of tokenism in superhero comics more generally. Ultimately, Killmonger succumbs to side effects from the heart-shaped herb as part of his ascension ritual and is placed in suspended animation. T'Challa undoes his plot by reverting the monetary standard of Wakanda to the U.S. dollar and de-nationalizing the foreign companies in Wakanda. Notably, Priest never did explain exactly why Killmonger went into his coma, explaining later that he lost the plot thread in the middle of writing a Marvel-mandated crossover story.[78]

But while Priest's run paid homage to what had worked in the past, he and his co-creators also added characters to the mix. One of Priest's other most enduring contributions to the Panther canon is T'Challa's adopted brother Hunter, AKA the White Wolf. Hunter acts as the de facto head of the now-decommissioned Hatut Zeraze, better understood as the Wakandan secret police. Hunter had been taken in as an orphan by T'Chaka and welcomed into the family despite his white identity.[79] Hunter acts as an inverse mirror of T'Challa's experiences. Once T'Challa is born, Hunter is pushed aside and finds comfort only in fellow outsider Queen Ramonda, who similarly was never fully embraced into Wakandan culture by virtue of her South African heritage.[80] Even though T'Challa disbanded the Hatut Zeraze, Hunter appears to show unblinking loyalty to his adopted brother and Wakanda throughout, but his actions often also intentionally weaken T'Challa's standing and cause diplomatic and personal difficulties. Priest again skillfully shows the reader another angle on Wakanda from the perspective of an outsider and creates a situation in which a white character is the minority representation in a super-hero group while also using the character to build out the complexities and contradictions of Wakandan society. In Priest's imagining—largely building on the text already present elsewhere—Wakandans are not only xenophobic but disdainful of other cultures. Such a position builds on ideas introduced in McGregor's run, but Priest made Wakanda's opinion of the rest of the world crystal clear in an FAQ on his personal site:

> Wakandans are not nice people. By and large, they are aware of the outside world, they are reasonably free to visit the outside world, but they do not like or respect the outside world [. . .] Their culture is hundreds of years older than ours and is largely undiluted, an unconquered race that has, until very recently, lived in total isolation. We, and I include African Americans in this, are mongrels to the Wakandans. Uneducated and barbaric.[81]

As Priest elaborates, Hunter shows "rabid loyalty to the throne" as a means of "overcompensating" for the lack of respect and inclusion into Wakandan society because of that cultural disdain.[82] Through the character of Hunter, Priest shows a fallible side to the unflappable master scientist and diplomat that is T'Challa and complicates the counter-narrative potential of the Wakanda metaphor. As Michael Hoskin points out in an essay on white privilege in the series for the Sequart Organization website, Hunter is a riff on the Tarzan myth, "a white boy, orphaned in Africa, adopted by a different culture he considers himself one with"; Hoskin argues that like Tarzan, Hunter also came to see himself as above the members of the culture he joined and resents T'Challa for denying his self-perceived right to be a "white man raised in Africa who assumes a noble lineage." He also notes that Hunter's loyalty is primarily to his own idea of Wakanda, rather than T'Challa or its people.[83] In short, Hunter adopts a pseudo-colonialist mindset of entitlement—wrapped in loyalty to the nation on his own terms—that makes him a curious inversion of T'Challa, the oft-reluctant ruler.

Similarly, the character of Queen Divine Justice, a teenage girl from New York who is revealed over the course of the series to be of Wakandan ancestry and becomes a new Dora Milaje following Nakia's excommunication (she had attempted to kill Monica Lynne out of jealousy) offers an alternative perspective on the culture of Wakanda and what it has to offer to outsiders. To discuss one of these characters is to discuss the other, as they illustrate both sides of the significant but complex role women play in Priest's run. Queen Divine Justice, a politically active young woman who bristles against the ceremonial and cultural expectations of Wakanda, represents a brash and unapologetic form of Black feminism that openly challenges the tradition of being betrothed to the king (she ends up in a relationship with Vibraxas, another young Wakandan hero) and modernizes the role of the Dora Milaje by showing open independence and defiance of the Panther's edicts. In her debut, she talks down a rampaging Hulk and convinces him to hit T'Challa with a police cruiser rather than a neighborhood resident's car, convincing him that the "downtrodden, disenfranchised minority class" has it hard enough already— "Look around you—this is the ugly by-product of the American Dream, Hulk—for every Lexus they sell uptown, there's 25 hungry minority kids just trying to survive an institutionalized degenerative economic system." The Hulk acquiesces and the two go to a nightclub as friends.[84] When she begins her training, she points out the problem with an old man ("way over 30!") having "rights" to teenage girls, and expresses skepticism when her attendant D'Won says that the arrangement is an act of "mercy"; she also steadfastly refuses to marry M'Baku when it is revealed she is part of the Jabari tribe.[85] By comparison, Nakia—who later adopts the moniker Malice after being conditioned and abused by Killmonger and Achebe and uses toxins to control the minds of men—acts as a different consequence of the role of women in Wakandan culture. Nakia reflects the inherent tension between tradition and progress in the Black Panther character but also acts as a stereotyped "crazy woman" villain using sexual wiles and coercion to solve for unrequited affection and who is unafraid to attempt to murder her romantic rivals. Even accounting for the fact that the men in Nakia's life ultimately led her down this path, it is an unfortunate blemish on an otherwise foundational creative interpretation to terms of expanding the importance of women and femininity to the Black Panther.[86]

One of Priest's other most enduring contributions to the canon would not come from an original character, but rather expanding on an existing one. For the story arc "Stürm und Drang," in which T'Challa and Wakanda nearly start a world war to protect a child, none other than the X-Man Storm, a fellow orphan of African origin with the ability to control the weather, reappears in his life. The idea of Storm and T'Challa's relationship is an extension of 1980's *Marvel Team-Up* #100, which recounted the pair's adventures as they fell in love as children and were then reunited as adults after a failed attempt on her life. After working together to stop the man who hired the assassin, the two part as friends, each wondering what could have been.[87] Capitalizing on that story's open assertion that the two "traveled together for a time," Priest posited that the relationship was more important and formative than previously alluded to, and in Storm the king finds warning about the aggressiveness of Wakanda's posturing and T'Challa's certainty in the outcome of that posturing:

> There was once a great man of sound mind and temperament who had great dreams of protecting his people from evil—and building a great society that would enlighten all mankind. His fatal flaw was his crippling inability to admit he didn't know everything . . . that he was afraid. That man's name was Magnus. One of the most tortured souls I have ever encountered. You, my friend, are in grave danger of becoming just like him.[88]

To a long-time reader, familiar with the fact that the "Magnus" Storm refers to is Magneto, the recurring X-Men antagonist whose understandable goals became zealotry over time, the rebuke is stern. But rather than showing anger, T'Challa confesses his uncertainty and shame to her, stating that he is unworthy of his father's legacy—"I martyr him afresh with my weakness . . . my accursed humanity."[89]

T'Challa's grappling with his patrilineal legacy is nothing new at this point in the series, but what is important is how much the character admits to Storm in this moment and the degree to which he blames himself for his situation. As historian Todd Steven Burroughs suggests, the scene is "reminiscent of a priest confessing his sins to an oracle, or to a goddess in her temple [. . .] She is powerful enough for him to humble himself in front of her, to confide in her"; he notes that Reginald Hudlin would pay close attention to this scene and expand upon it for a crucial arc in his narrative (as discussed in the next chapter).[90] Priest's encyclopedic approach to respecting what other writers had done before him mined a potentially rich vein of meaning in the characters' relationship with Storm, and despite the unfortunate outcome of Nakia it can be argued that Priest expanded the importance of women to the Black Panther mythos that would become so pivotal to the modern incarnations of the character.

In one of the final major arcs Priest wrote for the character, that attention to previous story arcs paid off as the Panther faced two of his greatest antagonists yet—fellow Avenger Iron Man and, through the magic of comic book contrivances, himself. Shortly before the events of "Enemy of the State II"

(Priest, at this point the longest continuous author on a single Black Panther series, had the luxury of being able to write numbered sequels to his own stories), M'Baku revealed that the "true" Black Panther had been frozen in the mountains of Wakanda. That "true" Black Panther happened to look a lot like the Black Panther from the somewhat controversial late 70s Kirby run that ignored much of the serious overtones of McGregor's *Jungle Action* story in favor of making him a more traditional pulp hero. The Kirby Panther is portrayed in Priest's story as constantly dancing and singing and speaking in a clever approximation of Kirby's bombastic and over-the-top style of dialogue while also maintaining his ESP powers. The difference extended visually, as well, with the character represented in a Kirby-aping style with broader cartoon features and flat shading compared to Velluto's more realistic style and coloring on the contemporary Panther. Many of Kirby's additional creations, like Princess Zanda and Mister Little, also showed up, with the former working at a fast-food chicken restaurant before being called to adventure by the Kirby Panther.[91] Throughout the run, the relationship between the current Panther and the Kirby Panther is complex—they mutually identify the other as king and show each other respectful deference, but the Kirby Panther surmises that the current Panther is less than pleased he has returned:

> You are the world's greatest liar, T'Challa. A missing piece of myself that leaves me a bit vulnerable. You don't care for me, you were glad to be rid of me, and my return horrifies you. [. . .] You desire love. Laughter. Family. All that you have denied yourself. T'Challa—I am the best part of you! I am that which you now wholly deny yourself! [92]

Priest, never one to shy away from metatext, placed a gentlemen's battle for the soul of Black Panther within the pages of his own book, arguing against his own interpretation and grappling with the very version of the character he had been so skeptical toward. Kirby Panther's quest was to once again find the magical frog artifacts that were the subject of Kirby's run—but this was an interrogation, not a throwback.

Running concurrently with the Kirby Panther plot was a continuation of the long-simmering feud Priest had set up earlier in his run with the Avengers, specifically Iron Man. The white billionaire industrialist with the suit full of gadgets and an ego to match seemed like a natural foil for the Black Panther—in his commentary for the arc, Priest identified both men as "cunning, ruthless, and willing to bend the rules to win the game: the game being more important than actually who wins (as such things are subjective designations, after all)."[93] The story, which fully kicks off when T'Challa acquires a small island on Lake Superior (Anishinabe Island, technically a Canadian territory) using an old and obscure treaty in order to root out the intelligence coalition "XCON" that was responsible for the coup attempt in Wakanda.[94] Fearing an international incident and concerned that XCON may be operating within the United States government, Panther's new handler Henry Peter Gyrich contacts Tony Stark with information proving that T'Challa owned the company that made all the wire and cable for Avengers Mansion and rigged it with nanomachines that allowed him to spy on the team. T'Challa and Stark meet over a game of poker on XCON's casino yacht, where Stark demands T'Challa understand that the world is changing and to drop his crusade. T'Challa demonstrates skepticism: "In the years we've known one another, this is the longest conversation we've ever had. [. . .] The truth is, you've never pursued my friendship and never considered me your equal. You obsess not over some vitiation of amity so much as hollow, jingoistic entitlement."[95]

T'Challa's repudiation of Iron Man is borne as much out of the narrative as it is Priest's long-standing frustration with the way the character was treated as an afterthought in the 1970s Avengers books. Learning from his old nemesis Killmonger, T'Challa even goes after the seat of Stark's power by acquiring the bank funding Stark Enterprises' European expansion, effectively gaining control of Stark's company with a "single phone call."[96] Once again, the Panther's economic resourcefulness provides the tools necessary to overcome his adversary—those who have the money, make the rules.

Priest's social commentary extends also to the obvious sociopolitical ramifications of Panther acquiring First Nations land. He claims to simply wish to use the treaty that had been signed with his grandfather by a "drunken French nobleman" to return the land to its rightful owners, but the Canadian superhero Guardian accuses him of seeking to "polarize the government" and get back at the CIA in the process.[97] Complicating matters further, Nightshade (again, an "expert geneticist") reveals to Ross that the Kirby Panther is genetically the "real" Panther, begging the question of who the current Panther truly is and also revealing that Kirby Panther is suffering from a debilitating brain aneurysm.[98]

Later, Stark reveals that he has been a step ahead of Panther the entire time, stating that he owned the wire and cable company and staged the rigged cables and knew that T'Challa had a larger plan—and that XCON and most of its operatives had been destroyed by Hunter and the Hatut Zeraze long before any of this had happened. The American coup T'Challa was trying to prevent had also already happened—the company used the aforementioned magical frogs, which have time travel properties, to bring in perfect but pliable duplicates from just before the future to install as the U.S. President and the Canadian Prime Minister.[99] Hunter and Stark fight, and in a fit of rage Hunter reminds Stark that Wakanda built the Avengers' quinjets and improved their security—"We have befriended you—and all America has done is take, kill, and exploit our brothers . . . spit on the throne of T'Chaka, the great king.

And you . . . in your hubristic conceit—drape yourself in a flag . . . call yourself hero . . . "[100] Hunter's open anger at the perceived imperialism of the United States as represented by one of its pre-eminent superheroes is one of the rare times Priest's run openly engages with the anti-colonialist themes of the broader Panther mythos—but it is ironic that it comes from the mouth of the Tarzan allegory, still as much in love with his own vision of Wakandan supremacy as anything else.

T'Challa reveals that this labyrinthine plot was necessary to work around Hunter and send Stark a message, as he feared for Stark's safety given Hunter's objective of wiping out anyone associated with XCON; the two stories finally intersect when Panther and Kirby Panther incapacitate Stark, only for a future version of Stark to show up and reveal that Stark had never truly trusted Panther and built a suit of armor to negate his powers—a threat reserved only for the most dangerous, otherworldly threats like Hulk and Thor (once again adding to Priest's rehabilitation project for the character) but ultimately negated by T'Challa's quick thinking.[101] It is ultimately revealed that the Kirby Panther had passed himself off as the current Panther during the battle, and the two duplicates lay unconscious and nearly dead after their fight. The political leader duplicates and the future Stark are sent back to their proper time, and Stark and Panther share a moment in which T'Challa admits it is "vaguely insulting" that Stark thinks he could not figure out a way to develop countermeasures against the Iron Man armor the way Stark countered him, later telling the billionaire "We will never truly be friends until you stop thinking you are better than me—explaining this 'Good' and 'Evil' to a king. I am he who my father ordained."[102]

Here, once and for all, is Priest—via T'Challa—stating that the Black Panther is not a superhero for his own sake, but rather something more powerful and serving different interests than his costumed brethren. The complexities Priest introduces into the character—as Stark suggests, many of his actions are less than heroic and more about proving a point in this arc—provide a more nuanced and detailed vision of T'Challa than other writers had offered to this point as Priest reflexively challenges his own interpretation. The postscript to Priest's final arc with T'Challa comes in issue #49, where it is revealed that T'Challa knew about the Kirby Panther eighteen months before Ross arrived, and that the Kirby Panther was actually him from the future, suffering from the after-effects of the brain injury he sustained during a battle with a mind-controlled Iron Fist earlier in Priest's run.[103] Through the metaphor of the superhero and the fantastical if somewhat contrived elements of comic book storytelling, Priest engineered a way for his main character to come face to face with his own legacy and his mortality simultaneously while also resolving another writer's dangling plot thread.

In issue #49, the Kirby Panther speaks with a previous version of the character designed to look like the *Jungle Action* panther, presumably shortly after the events of "Panther's Prey," and it is implied that this is what canceled their nuptials.[104] In the previous issue T'Challa revealed to Monica Lynne, who had fallen in love again with the Kirby Panther, why he broke off their engagement all that time ago—after meeting his future self, he realized "A man who has no future . . . has nothing to give."[105] The two leave on amicable terms, finally understanding one another, and while not the romantic ending long-time fans might have hoped for it provided closure to a long-standing arc, reconciling the narrative gap left by the lack of McGregor's planned "Panther's Vow" storyline years earlier. Ultimately, after hallucinations caused by his injury cause him to inadvertently hurt Queen Divine Justice, he realizes that Storm was right and he is becoming the thing he feared—as such, T'Challa leaves the Panther habit and the throne behind.[106]

Priest, a Christian minister, references St. Paul when he talked in his series commentary about the aneurysm as a "thorn in my flesh" for Panther, a "damningly human vulnerability that grounds T'Challa somewhat and keeps him keenly aware of his own limitations and the consequences of his constant scheming."[107] This, coupled with the admonishment from Kirby Panther not to worry about that which is the domain of the Panther God, arguably leaves the character in a more spiritual place than first imagined in Priest's run— the cool, calculating strategist at the beginning is a defense mechanism and the character is recognizably human. As Burroughs argues, Panther's goal throughout Priest's series to that point is to "control the present because he knows he has no future," but his humanity is realized when he understands there are things beyond his control and consequences for his actions.[108] In thematic terms, this was a mic drop—the successful creative culmination of years of careful plotting and keen narrative insight that resulted in a years-long story that not only resolved itself but also arranged years of editorial musical chairs into one cohesive vision. Unfortunately, there is a postscript.

After years of cancellation fears and a brief public dispute between Marvel editorial and its writers about increasing the cost of certain books (*Black Panther* being one of them), Priest was given another attempt, with the mandate that the series had to be retooled to streamline the book's "over-complexity and the weight of 35 years of continuity."[109] The solution was to replace T'Challa as the man behind the habit in favor of Kevin "Kasper" Cole, a biracial NYPD narcotics officer who idolized his cop father and, after finding T'Challa's discarded uniform, uses it to fight crime and hide his identity as he works to bust the crooked officers in his division. Simultaneously, Cole also navigated turbulent relationships with his mother and pregnant girlfriend—a setting Priest described as a sort of cross between Denzel Washington's performance in the 2001 film *Training Day* and a "dark satire of Spider-Man."[110] Cole echoed many of his forebear's themes—the Panther's paternal anxiety played out in Cole's relationship with his father's legacy and concern for his own unborn son, as did the tension of being caught between different identities and worlds, and the idea of Cole as the outsider and audience surrogate reacting to T'Challa when he appears again later in the arc. Priest even brought back Ross, Queen Divine Justice, Killmonger, and other beloved characters from his earlier run, including an appearance from Falcon, who dresses Cole down for wearing the Panther habit without understanding its importance (an interesting bit of symbolism considering the character's long-standing relationship with the Panther and a homecoming for Priest, whose first Marvel series starred the character).[111]

Ultimately, T'Challa returns and reclaims the Panther habit, saying that while Cole can be recognized by the Wakandan council he cannot be the Black Panther—instead, he gets a new identity and a color-inverted version of T'Challa's habit as the White Tiger.[112] While these are bold moves, reading the series now it feels like the product of diminishing returns—Cole's story is interesting enough, but it feels like a focus-grouped attempt to tap into the zeitgeist of edgy crime dramas, a letdown after Priest's skillful deconstruction and reconstruction of a symbolic hero. Priest brought the character back shortly after the series concluded as part of *The Crew*, a series casting Cole as part of a ragtag group of heroes of color fighting criminal conspiracies—while acclaimed and ultimately a better fit for Cole's character, it met an early end after seven issues.

In later years, Priest would say he was unsure who made the decision to change the identity of the man in the Panther suit and create a "new, hip-hop relevant Panther," suggesting frustration with the cultural differences on the creative side that failed to convey the intended ideas about hip-hop and urban identity in the character's design and adventures, as well as the perception that he had made the change out of desperation rather than as part of an editorial mandate on a limited one-year time frame.[113] He would also suggest that Marvel editorial's direction to make the character more "street" in order to improve sales showed a lack of foresight and cultural ignorance—"T'Challa was not African American. He was *African*"—and that Marvel's decision to cancel *The Crew*, which had been aimed specifically at the Latino and African-American markets, before the first issue shipped was what made him ultimately quit comics:

> The development process was so difficult, the bar set so high, the hill so steep, weeks and months of agonizing rewrites and redos and begging, pleading, only to cancel the book before it ever had a chance to earn an audience. It's worth stressing none of this was the fault of Marvel editorial, it was a bean counter thing, but for me it was an enormous punch in the face.[114]

In short, Priest's Panther run elevated the character and the series into one of Marvel's most acclaimed, even if its last year is largely forgettable and marred by questionable editorial decisions. Priest concluded the run with both T'Challa and Cole in his new White Tiger guise leaping into action with a brief editorial note of thanks to those who had come before—specifically Don McGregor, Stan Lee, and Jack Kirby—but in analyzing the transmedia brand that the Black Panther has become, he deserves to be in that conversation himself.[115]

Priest's "Black Panther" run not only added many of the elements that have become iconic and essential to the Panther brand, it also served as a five-year referendum on the character, the fandom, and the broader superhero industrial complex from the perspective of a man who had been one of only a small group of prominent Black creatives in the world of the Big Two's superhero comics. The Panther was no longer simply swashbuckling, reluctant royalty dealing exclusively with problems in Wakanda or a third-string Avenger—rather, he was now a fully-realized, competent, and often flawed hero with recognizable and celebrated continuity and all the contrasts that came with it. Priest's series poked at the concept of the Panther as a perfect utopian hero and Wakanda as an unspoiled paradise while at the same time celebrating the significance of what it truly meant to have African royalty in the pages of American superhero comics—Ta-Nehisi Coates' take on the character would pick up on many of these threads he so admired from Priest's run. Many of the editorial and sales problems Priest predicted came to pass, demonstrating the inherent systemic hurdles in the predominantly white mainstream superhero comics industry—and the writer would arguably channel some of those frustrations into his later *Deathstroke* series at DC, where he introduced the Red Lion, the amoral, villainous leader of a war-torn African nation who wears a cat-themed suit of armor made of a rare metal—an inverted version of one of his most enduring characters.[116] Yet, despite these setbacks, Priest showed what five years of a consistent voice on the page and a steady creative hand that took the character seriously could do.

NOTES

1. Wright, *Comic Book Nation.*
2. Ibid.
3. Ibid.
4. McGregor et al., *Black Panther: Panther's Quest.*
5. Elliott, "Reagan's embrace of apartheid South Africa."
6. Culverson, "The Politics of the Anti-Apartheid Movement"; Worger, "Afri-Comics, South Africa, 1970s."

7. Worger, ibid.

8. Kleiner, "Apartheid Amnesia"; Laurence, "Defiant Botha."

9. Culverson, "The Politics of the Anti-Apartheid Movement."

10. Kleiner, "Apartheid Amnesia."

11. Glass, "House overrides Reagan apartheid veto."

12. Little, "Why Nelson Mandela"; Bowcott, "Thatcher Dismissive."

13. Barker, "Stevie Wonder Arrested"; Amorosi, "Little Steven."

14. Keech & Houlihan, "Sport and the End of Apartheid," 120.

15. McGregor, *Panther's Quest.*

16. Andrews, "ICE Raids"; McGregor, *Black Panther: Panther's Quest*, 6–7

17. McGregor et al., *Panther's Quest*, 160–61.

18. Anna, "Post-apartheid South Africa is world's most unequal country."

19. McGregor et al., *Panther's Quest*, 205.

20. Beresford, "Row over 'mother of the nation' Winnie Mandela"; Fihlani, "Is necklacing returning to South Africa?"

21. McGregor et al., *Panther's Quest*, 118.

22. Ibid, 185.

23. McGregor et al., *Panther's Quest.*

24. Ibid.

25. Gough, "Interview with Don McGregor."

26. McGregor, "Panther's Spoor"; Syvertsen et al., "An ethnographic exploration of drug markets."

27. McGregor et al., "Panther's Prey" vol. 4.

28. Hoskin, "Panther's Range."

29. McDuffie, "To Be Continued #3."

30. McDuffie et al., "And We Are Not Saved!" 11.

31. Ibid; McDuffie et al., "Vices Pass for Virtues," 20.

32. McDuffie et al., "Protect and Defend," 36.

33. Riesman, "The Man Who Made Black Panther Cool."

34. Ibid.

35. Smith, "PRIEST on BLACK PANTHER PT. 1."

36. Priest, "The last time priest discussed the viability of black characters."

37. Culver, *Black Panther*; Priest, "black panther series commentary"; Smith, "PRIEST, PT. 1."

38. Wiacek, *Black Panther.*

39. Priest, "black panther series commentary."

40. Smith, "PRIEST PT. 1."

41. Smith, "PRIEST on BLACK PANTHER, PT. 2."

42. Smith, "PRIEST, PT. 1."

43. Priest, "black panther series commentary"; Priest, "year one." Priest et al., "Nightmare," p. 10.

44. Priest, "the death of the black panther."

45. Priest et al., "Enemy of the State: Book Three," 8.

46. Riesman, "The Man."

47. Priest et al., "The Client," 6.

48. Joyner, "Who Are the Dora Milaje?"; Priest, "black panther series commentary."

49. Priest, "black panther series commentary."

50. Dash, "Dahomey's Women Warriors."

51. Kai, "Digging the Dora Milaje?"

52. Priest et al., "The Client," 15.

53. Priest et al., "Original Sin."

54. Priest et al., "The Price."

55. Cole, "Remember the Massacre"; Priest et al., "Lord of the Damned."

56. Priest et al., "Hunted," 10.

57. Ibid, 15.

58. Ibid, 19. Emphasis original author's.

59. Du Bois, *The Souls of Black Folk.*

60. Priest et al., "That Business," 17.

61. Ibid; It is worth nothing that Amanda Connor, a comics legend in her own right, was the artist who imitated Kirby's style for the first five pages of this issue.

62. Ibid, 10.

63. Priest et al., "That Business"; Priest et al., "Enemy of the State."

64. Priest et al., "Enemy of the State"; Priest et al., "Enemy of the State Book Two"; Priest et al., "Enemy of the State Book Three."

65. British Broadcasting Corporation, "Four More Ways the CIA Has Meddled in Africa."

66. Priest, "black panther series commentary: year one."

67. Priest, "black panther series commentary: year two."

68. Ibid.

69. Priest, et al., "Turbulence."

70. Priest, "year two"; Priest et al., "Local Hero."

71. Priest et al., "Local Hero," 15–17.

72. Priest et al., "Legacy," 13–15.

73. Ibid, 16.

74. Priest et al., "Freefall," 6.

75. Priest, et al., "Retribution," 7.

76. Priest et al., "Freefall"; Priest et al., "Retribution."

77. Priest et al., "More of that Business with the Avengers," 13.

78. Priest, "black panther series commentary: year three"; Priest et al., "Passage."

79. Priest et al., "Enemy of the State: Book Two."

80. Priest et al., "Enemy of the State: Book Four—The Taking of Wakanda 1–2–3."

81. Priest, "black panther faq."

82. Ibid.

83. Hoskin, "Exploring White Privilege."

84. Priest et al., "Smash," 5–6.

85. Priest et al., "Beloved," 4.; Priest et al., "Hell(O)," 4; Priest et al., "Gorilla Warfare Book Two: Masks."

86. Priest et al., "Enemy of the State: Book Three."

87. Claremont et al., "Cry . . . Vengeance!"

88. Claremont et al., "Cry . . . Vengeance!" 36; Priest, Velluto, & Almond, "An Epidemic Insanity," 15.

89. Priest et al., "An Epidemic Insanity," 18.

90. Burroughs, "Black Panther, Black Writers, White Audience," 70.

91. Priest et al., "Mirror"; Priest, Velluto, & Almond, "Alliance."

92. Priest et al., "Mirror," 14–15.

93. Priest, "black panther series commentary: year four."

94. Priest et al., "Enemy of the State II—Book One: Mirror."

95. Priest et al., "Enemy of the State II—Book Two: Alliance," 13.

96. Priest et al., "Enemy of the State II—Book Three: The Kiber Chronicles," 10–11.

97. Ibid, 17.

98. Ibid, 7–9.

99. Priest et al., "Enemy of the State II—Book Four: 60 Minutes"; Priest's plots are again very intricate and dense, and I have endeavored to explain the relevant parts as concisely as possible.

100. Ibid, 16.

101. Ibid; Priest, et al., "Enemy of the State II—Conclusion: All the President's Men."

102. Ibid, 21.

103. Priest et al., "The Death of the Black Panther Book Two of Two: The King is Dead."

104. Ibid.

105. Priest et al., "The Death of the Black Panther Book One of Two: The King is Dead," 20.

106. Ibid.

107. Priest, "the death of the black panther."

108. Burroughs, "Black Writers," 72.

109. Priest, "black & white: a crime novel."

110. Ibid.

111. Priest et al., "Ascension: Part 1 of 4."

112. Priest et al., "Ascension: Part 4."

113. Priest, "What I Forgot to Mention."

114. Smith, "PRIEST, Pt. 3."

115. Priest et al., "Ascension: Part 4," 25.

116. Corley, "Who is DC's Version of Black Panther, the Red Lion?"

Chapter 6

The Panther in the 2000s–10s

A Rise to Prominence and Growing Pains

Priest's run on the Black Panther established the Black Panther as one of Marvel's crown jewel characters—perhaps not pulling down the numbers of a Spider-Man or Incredible Hulk, but certainly a prestige character who had the focal point of one masterful run after another by writers operating at the top of the form. With renewed creative and corporate interest in the character, the most recent two decades of the Panther's existence are also the busiest, as he not only appeared in his own regular ongoing books but was a fixture in several major publishing events. More significantly, however, it is crucial to recognize that Black Panther's current "A-list" prominence would not be possible without the work of Black writers and artists looking to use the character to tell more personal, representative stories. This chapter explores the intertwined nature of these two trends, first by focusing on Reginald Hudlin, one of the most significant writers of this era and who brought defiant Blackness and a Hollywood eye to the character, proving the Panther's transmedia potential. It also delves into the work of white writers like David Liss and Jonathan Hickman, who navigated the character through a challenging transition to the modern era and integrated him further into the larger Marvel universe.

HUDLIN ASKS THE QUESTION

Reginald Hudlin didn't need to write for Marvel Comics. Hudlin, a Hollywood veteran, had directed the smash-hit Eddie Murphy romantic comedy *Boomerang* and worked on other 1990s favorites like *House Party*, *The Great White Hype*, and the first Black animated film *Bebe's Kids*. He would even end up serving as the President of Entertainment for the BET Network, among countless other achievements, and could make a case for having one of the strongest resumes of any writer hired to work at the company.[1] Yet, comics were a passion project for the multi-hyphenate, who told *Vulture*'s Victoria Johnson that he had even gotten a Marvel rejection letter after submitting a comics pitch as a child.[2] After making it big in multiple creative industries, Hudlin took a meeting with Marvel that culminated in the company offering him the chance to write whatever book he wanted—Hudlin suggested Black Panther and was given a deal to write a six-issue miniseries on the spot, a luxury afforded to few writers.[3] At the time, Hudlin was in good company, becoming the latest in what historian Todd Steven Burroughs called "the celebrity novelist/playwright clique that, by the earliest 21st century, had begun writing American superhero comics [. . .] doing this completely out of a love for comics, not to make a living or pursue a career with a comic book company."[4] That freedom also gave him carte blanche to do what he wanted with the character.

Hudlin pulled no punches in his initial pitch letter to Marvel, reprinted in the trade paperback collection of his first arc. Taken as a whole, the three-page letter is as much manifesto as it is mission statement. Like Priest before him, Hudlin lauded the creative vision of Jack Kirby and Stan Lee and spoke effusively that "no black super hero before or after the Black Panther is as cool as the Black Panther"; he also specifically praised Priest's run, particularly the addition of the Dora Milaje, the tensions between Panther and the Avengers, and the character's place among Marvel royalty like Namor and Doctor Doom.[5] The praise was not universal, however—Hudlin criticized the character's 1970s *Avengers* appearances ("he never made much of an impression on me") and he bemoaned the "morose characters that endlessly droned on with overflowing captions" of McGregor's run.[6] His Panther represented, in his words, a shift toward the essence of a Spike Lee or Sean Combs, "the artist/businessman hero who profits from his own cultural integrity. In other words, the man who has it all—the money, the politics, and the cool and style of black culture."[7] Drawing a sketch of his intent by name-dropping Malcolm X, Miles Davis, and Muhammad Ali, all of whom had in Hudlin's mind "the knowledge that the act of being a black man in white America is an inherent act of rebellion," he envisioned a Panther who envisioned the hip-hop spirit of "being a bad@$$" and suggested "the harder the Panther is, the more appealing he is to both black and white audiences"—easily a more coherent vision of a hip-hop friendly Panther than Marvel editorial's earlier fumbling attempts.[8]

In Wakanda, Hudlin saw a country whose existence and independence was "galling to the rest of the world" and whose "cultural evolution had gone unchecked for centuries [. . .] no one has colonized them, burned their books,

erased their language or broken their spirits."[9] Rather than an origin characterized by the incursion of the white Fantastic Four, Hudlin, writing about
fifteen years ahead of his time, wanted to reimagine the Panther's origin with
an eye toward creating a easily-digestible trade paperback that would be his
vision of a possible Black Panther movie.[10] In short, Hudlin foresaw the transmedia potential of the character, arguably before anyone else did, and used
the opportunity to tell a version of the character that was unapologetically
his own, unburdened by decades of continuity. Christopher Priest, a friend of
Hudlin's, summed up his successor's approach:

> [. . .] as he explained it, he realized we'd tried every trick in the book to broaden
> the appeal in an attempt to woo more readers and it failed. So Reginald didn't
> see the point of doing that, and from the start simply chose to write a good book
> and invest himself in the work rather than constantly worry over sales figures.
> And you know what? His book vastly outsold mine because the investment was
> in doing good work and not constantly struggling to win people over.[11]

Todd Steven Burroughs, in his indispensable recounting of the Panther's
comic history, suggested that Hudlin's approach (and the freedom granted by
his resumé) delivered on the character's long-standing potential: "Reginald
Hudlin [. . .] created a racially and culturally *de-colonized* Panther that
appealed to the African-American imagination [. . .] it did not hold back its
Blackness; not unlike hip-hop music or Black-oriented television and feature
films, it was not afraid to demand that *all* readers accept its terms."[12]

Such ambitions were grand, but there was work to be done. The title of
Hudlin's first arc, "Who is the Black Panther?" may as well have been the
question on the mind of a new reader. It was treated like a prestige collaboration, with superstar artist John Romita Jr. lending his artistic talents at
Hudlin's request. Where Priest paid tribute to what had come before, Hudlin's
first arc did a soft reset of the Panther's comics history without completely
ignoring it. His writing offered a looser and less verbose style and a hipper,
less stoic protagonist than Priest imagined. Hudlin also delved further into
Wakanda's history, opening his story with brief vignettes of the country as it
fends off rival tribes and the de Boers' attempts to colonize the region over
the centuries. Hudlin clarified and modernized the often muddy cultural and
social structures of Wakanda via a brief explanation of the Black Panther
title as being the head of a "spiritually-based warrior cult" that is "sort of
like being Pope, President, and the head of the Joint Chiefs of Staff all at
once," a hereditary title that must be earned pending an annual challenge to
the throne—"So as royal lineages go, it's a lot more of a meritocracy, than
say, England."[13] Right away, Hudlin tosses aside colonized viewpoints of rule
and leadership, casting Wakanda as a comparatively more enlightened and

merit-based society of which T'Challa becomes the de facto political and spiritual leader through honorable defeat of his uncle—though Wakanda is treated by administration officials in the room as a potentially destabilized rogue state due to the transition.

Like Priest, Hudlin also poked at sensitive topics, but did not hide behind subtlety. Much of Hudlin's run, especially the first six issues, are a direct response to and critique of the political doctrines of the George W. Bush administration, from thinly-veiled parodies of Condoleezza Rice (Dondi Reese in Hudlin's story) to references to Halliburton in the first issue; the administration officials also present significantly heightened interest in the country when Everett Ross (still the resident Wakanda expert in the room but no longer having the history with T'Challa he did in Priest's run) reveals its massive oil deposits.[14] The Bush administration's reliance on pre-emptive invasion in dealing with hostile nations, ostensibly to keep rogue actors in check but in practice to achieve questionable nation-building goals, is identified directly and with a critical eye in the debate over how to handle the Wakanda situation in Hudlin's work.[15] When Reese presses for military action by suggesting Wakanda is both highly militaristic and has no allegiances or ties to the U.S. and that T'Challa's ascension may change the nation's non-intervention policy, Ross (likely Hudlin's stand-in here) suggests that the military is already adventuring across the Middle East and is stretched too thin to attack Wakanda.[16] With Wakanda possessing two valuable resources—oil and vibranium—it is hard not to see Reese's push as a contemporary form of colonization, and Hudlin's introduction of a secret plot to overthrow Wakanda and its government using supervillains only cements this thematic conceit.

Hudlin's arc criticizes the justifications for colonization across the years, from the economic to the political to the religious, through the twin efforts of this supervillain team and the U.S. government. Exploitation of Wakanda and its resources is not a new villainous motivator in Panther lore, but rarely had the U.S. government and other world leaders been implicated by name as actors wishing to destroy the sovereignty of an African state. Hudlin also sought to make Klaw's metaphor of colonization more explicit, revamping his origin and giving him a definitive white South African ancestry that would come to define the character going forward and a racist worldview to match; in one issue, he complains about the United Nations as "a place for the powerless to whine about the white man."[17] As Burroughs suggests, Hudlin's choice of villains for the clandestine destabilization unit also evokes the multinational history of colonization on the African continent, with representatives from America (the Spider-Man villain Rhino), France (Captain America antagonist Batroc the Leaper), and most intriguingly the British Catholic super soldier the Black Knight.[18]

This last character bears mentioning, as he represents an underexplored aspect of colonialism rarely seen in Panther stories to this point. In Hudlin's story, the Black Knight acts as a metaphor for the long history of Africa as a proxy locale for the soft war of religious ideological power throughout history—Christianity and Islam have both taken significant root on the continent, with religious scholar Jacob Olupona stating in a 2015 interview that nearly 40 percent of the continent belongs to one of the two religions, both of which have begun to supplant traditional indigenous faith. More recently, Africa has been revealed to have the fastest-growing Catholic population on the planet.[19] Historian Elizabeth Foster argues that the rising prominence of Catholicism on the continent has resulted in a much more decolonized and Africa-centric version of Catholicism; however, as historian Michael Gomez contends, that change in Church diversity was about more than converting new adherents:

> Colonialism was to a minor degree a response to missionaries' lobbying for the imposition of European political authority in order to overcome resistance on the part of indigenous rulers, but with the establishment of colonialism, catechizing Africans was also seen as a means of facilitating political control, which in the end was all about promoting European economic interests. [. . .] As such, the movement of monotheism throughout much of Africa cannot be easily separated from the objectives of imperialism; the extent to which Africans were really free to choose, and what they would have chosen, remains an open question.[20]

Hudlin's view is cynical and more aligned with Gomez, casting the Black Knight as a tool of conversion and colonial influence with a healthy disregard for Wakandan and African beliefs and traditions. In issue #3, Cannibal, a villain with the ability to take over the bodies of others through touch, arrives at the Vatican in the form of an attractive woman and is shown the Ebony Blade, a former weapon of the Templar. A cardinal at the Vatican tells Cannibal that Africa is "the front line of religious warfare in the 21st century"; when Cannibal asks if Wakanda is Muslim, the cardinal responds "No, they're worse! They're a bunch of animal-worshipping pagans! All that technology and they still pray to the 'Panther God'! That's why we have to convert Wakanda, no matter what it takes!"[21] Hudlin's intertwining of white colonialist imperatives with religious conversion is made more explicit with a sermon delivered by the Black Knight to the gathered insurrection forces, casting their coup attempt as a holy crusade for the betterment of the people with a speech right out of the colonizer's handbook: "Centuries ago, we brought civilization, commerce, and God to Africa. We dragged them into the 20th century [. . .] Now at the dawn of a new century, Africa needs our help more than ever. [. . .] The people of Africa want God in their lives, and this ebony blade shall grant them their wish."[22]

Hudlin's twin critiques of colonizing attitudes and American imperialism come to a head as the first arc concludes with a reveal that the U.S. government sent forces to "assist" Wakanda in repelling the coup attempt (in truth to shore up U.S. military presence in the region in advance of a possible resource grab). In one of the most gruesome and nakedly political turns in Hudlin's run, the forces are revealed to be undead cyborgs reanimated from the corpses of dead American service members. As the commanding officer of the mission explains to Everett Ross: "These brave men and women died for their country. All that training and manpower wasted. The military hates waste. We've found a solution to our manpower problem. They're tougher, stronger, fearless, take orders exactly and don't do interviews or write sad letters back home."[23]

Hudlin's script highlights on the transactional nature of U.S. foreign policy (expending resources toward receiving greater gains) and what he argues is the expendability of the human element in service of U.S. imperialism—the idea of reanimating dead soldiers so they cannot undermine the war effort is ghastly but a direct extrapolation of criticism of the second Iraq War, which is believed to have killed (based on 2018 estimates) as many as 600,000 people.[24] It also underscores the unique storytelling possibilities of the Black Panther, who as a head of state dealing with issues of military engagement and diplomacy can be used to make these critiques and observations in a way that a Spider-Man or Incredible Hulk cannot.

Such critiques were not limited to foreign policy. As part of the next major storyline, Hudlin sent T'Challa, fresh off his coronation and successful defense of his country, out into the world to find a queen. Along the way, he runs into fellow Black superheroes Luke Cage, Brother Voodoo, Monica Rambeau, and Blade while on a charity mission to help New Orleans residents displaced by Hurricane Katrina. Katrina, which made landfall on August 29, 2005, was easily the most significant domestic policy failure of the Bush Administration, a powerful storm turned devastating via a combination of the federal government's poor engineering on the city's levees and a meager and tardy emergency response—all told, over 1800 people died, with New Orleans' poorer Black and minority communities hit the hardest.[25] T'Challa tells Cage he wants to help those being exploited during the tragedy and protect them from threats ranging from "marauding gangs to real estate speculators looking to permanently displace poor people forced from their homes"; meanwhile, a coterie of the city's old money white Southerners led by a well-heeled man named the Colonel is looking to remake New Orleans "as our forefathers intended it" now that "[the] flood has washed away many of our city's undesirables."[26]

That those forefathers turn out to be Confederate vampires looking to raise an army and feed on the city's displaced residents is a neat if somewhat ham-fisted metaphor for social stratification and exploitation of Black Americans and the lingering legacy of the Confederate South that arguably helps perpetuate these issues. To really drive the point home, Hudlin has Monica Rambeau's father express his doubt that the government will be able to help—"Hell, F.E.M.A. couldn't fix the levees in time. How they gonna handle this?"[27] In a dramatic splash page in issue #12, the Panther and Luke Cage are shown rescuing the people of New Orleans and inspiring everyday individuals to follow suit—again, the character acts as a restorative counter-narrative to real-world systemic racism and inequity as well as a metaphorical champion of community uplift. The short series concludes with the Panther and his allies defeating the vampires, with another cheeky political reference that the vampire hunter Blade has moved on to his next targets—Brother Voodoo speculates they are in Washington, D.C.[28]

Given the time and era, Hudlin's commentary was not always welcomed by fans, with one complaining about the U.S. government being portrayed as "little more than a bigger, more evil form of Hydra or something."[29] One particular moment, in which Storm's grandfather, a former Black radical, bemoans Bush appearing at the wedding between Storm and T'Challa ("If it were my country, I'd say get on 'fore you get spit on. But that's just me.") seemed to particularly provoke fans.[30] Two issues later, one reader asked, "Why don't you leave your political agenda out of comics and just tell good stories [. . .] Give me a call when Hudlin leaves the book and I'll probably jump back on."[31] Other fans were more open to the critique. A fan named Dereck Allen Philips pointed out in issue #21's letters column that the Panther should not trust anyone outside of Wakanda due to "a simple deduction of how the world powers, especially the American 'leadership,' betrays, lies, and misuses other nations, people, etc. for political gain" and that readers do not have to "blindly follow" Bush as president; another reader named Jordan Hofer appreciated the comments because "The Bush administration cares nothing for African-Americans. They let my hometown of New Orleans get destroyed and stay devastated [. . .] thanks for giving us one superhero who specifically gives a damn for black people."[32] These comments illustrate not only the contentious political debates of the day but also illustrate a key aspect of Hudlin's development of the Black Panther mythos—like most superheroes, the Panther is political, but unlike most superheroes he can be used expressly as a means to interrogate and debate social, racial, and historical issues his contemporaries cannot, reflecting the anxieties and concerns of the time and acting as a means of catharsis for writer and reader alike.

Beyond the Panther as a pathway for political commentary, Hudlin also expanded the rhetorical significance of the hero both to the reader and to

Marvel's superhero community. Where Priest was somewhat detached in his feelings toward the character, Hudlin wrote as a fan, particularly using Luke Cage as his proxy to explain what the character meant to him. This idea is represented first in a monologue Cage delivers while reflecting on his time in prison, where he had a Daily Bugle clipping of the Black Panther on his cell wall: "He's the only man I've ever looked up to in my life. A Black man, king of his own kingdom, never been conquered, free to speak the truth to the white man and got the muscle to back it up. Not pimping his people, but parlaying and making power moves. There aren't a lot of Black men that free."[33]

T'Challa and Cage eventually cross paths and travel together for a while as T'Challa looks across the world to find a bride. After battling a dragon together, T'Challa gifts Cage a set of Wakandan robes, which Cage accepts with enthusiasm, saying "Wait 'til the old heads at the Hue Man bookstore up town check these out!"[34] Here, Hudlin rhetorically ties the Black Panther again to the Black community in a typically referential aside, this time regarding the now-defunct Hue-Man Bookstore in Harlem, which was especially known for carrying works and hosting appearances by Black authors. The store closed its physical location several years after this reference in 2012 but exists as an online store today.[35] The symbolic importance of T'Challa and Wakanda is also illustrated in a brief one-panel conversation where Luke suggests to his wife Jessica Jones that they could leave with their baby and live in Wakanda where their child could be unbothered about her race or potential powers and suggests that Falcon and Monica Rambeau could also come. Jessica replies with a bemused "You've been on this 'Black Avengers' thing since New Orleans, but you've got to let it go."[36] On a metatextual level this could be seen as Hudlin reflecting on the canceled series *The Crew* or just angling for a spin-off, but by connecting the characters in a close-knit manner it also calls attention to Marvel's long-standing hesitance to showcase its Black heroes.

After decades of marginalization, the Black Panther was finally becoming a more significant star in the Marvel constellation. His profile was raised even higher yet by a marriage to Marvel's (arguably) other most significant Black character at the time, the X-Men's Ororo "Storm" Munroe. Like the Panther, Storm was herself a character caught between two worlds, in this case her split Kenyan and American heritage and her place as a mutant. Hudlin did not create the connection between the two heroes—Priest's run built on *Marvel Team-Up* #100 and the two had even ended up together in the alternate universe "Earth X" storyline—but Hudlin made the relationship official and treated it like a massive event.[37] The countdown to the couple's wedding took place over several issues, a dedicated special edition in the main series dedicated to the couple's courtship and wedding, and a spin-off *Storm* series by the best-selling author Eric Jerome Dickey chronicling the younger years of

T'Challa and Ororo's relationship that had only been suggested in the original Marvel Team-Up story and the Priest run. The event (billed as "The Wedding of the Century") was big enough to merit both extensive retailer support and a joint press conference with Hudlin, Dickey, and Marvel editorial executives, where Hudlin explained the characters, both of whom were "regal, powerful, their roots in Africa, but they're international and interstellar travelers," made sense together.[38]

Hudlin's comment acts as a rather clear mission statement for how the series unfolded from there on—after some initial friction, the characters' engagement led to a new narrative dimension in which T'Challa was challenged to grow as a leader and Storm was challenged to become a diplomat, which made for compelling stories and a rare high-profile Black romance in comics. Like Priest before him, Hudlin laid out the significance of Storm to T'Challa's personal and royal evolution—in issue #14, T'Challa recalls his father's words about the importance of a strong marriage with a beloved partner: "Romantic love is the highest ideal. The family is the foundation of the nation. Without love in your heart, the weight of responsibility will crush you, turn you into a tyrant."[39] When Storm visits Wakanda, Ramonda takes her aside and explains that T'Challa never stopped loving her and that the two should be married: "Wakanda is a warrior culture. It takes a strong woman to lead and breed these strong men. And here you are. A princess. Street-tough. A warrior on a galactic scale. I have followed your adventures closely. You are a hero worthy of my son."[40]

The in-text reification of Storm as T'Challa's equal and confidant moved the relationship between the two characters forward—no longer just the pep talk or vessel into which he pours his anxieties in the Priest run, Storm became a significant part of the cast and mythology under Hudlin as well as bringing many of the inherent tensions in Wakandan society to the forefront. Issue #16 opens with intercutting between different groups across Wakanda talking about the wedding—elders in a barber shop worry their king has "been so corrupted by foreign influence that he does not recognize the beauty of our women" and fret about the message he is sending to the youth while Wakandan women in the beauty salon wonder if their genes will match and why they are rushing into a marriage.[41] Unlike previous incarnations of the Black Panther that were largely isolated from ongoing events in the Marvel Universe, Hudlin's Panther was an active and major citizen of the universe and his actions affected characters outside of it—a key point in the transmedia evolution of the character.

The official wedding happened in issue #18 of the series, marketed as a "Cease-Fire" tie-in to the then-ongoing *Civil War* event. Hudlin, at this point President of Entertainment for Black Entertainment Television, turned the wedding of T'Challa and Storm a major media and social event covered by the network (including guest appearances by BET reporters and personalities Touré and Ananda Lewis, both of whom were drawn into the comic by artist Scot Eaton) as well as a destination for politicians like George W. Bush, Fidel Castro, and Nelson Mandela.[42] In another nod to Hudlin and Marvel's Hollywood connections, *Guiding Light* costume designer Shawn Dudley created Storm's gown for the wedding, which was then interpreted by Eaton and cover artist Frank Cho for the book.[43] Hudlin pulls off several neat narrative tricks in the issue, balancing the worldbuilding of Wakanda (in another key contribution to the mythos, the Panther God Bast appears in tangible spiritual form to judge T'Challa and Storm's union as the two journey across the Ancestral Plane) with the current collaborative storytelling in the Marvel Universe (T'Challa invites Iron Man and Captain America to the wedding in a failed attempt to broker peace between the two on a neutral site) as well as laying the groundwork for the remainder of his tenure on the series by establishing a global diplomatic mission for the new couple—effectively combining together many of the different thematic strands of his approach to the character and bringing new readers into the fold.[44] One reader, Bali White from New York, proclaimed her long-time fandom for Storm and belief that the two were perfect for each other despite her prior lack of knowledge of the Panther while celebrating what the union represented:

> I have wanted Storm to have a relationship and partner like this for decades. [. . .] An earnest reader will not deny their commonalities—background, animist spiritual beliefs, personalities, strength of character and principle. It is a perfect fit. I cried reading both STORM #2 and PANTHER #14—the combo of great comic writing with African/American realities overwhelmed me.[45]

Storm and T'Challa spend the next several issues visiting allies and enemies alike around the world to establish the groundwork for diplomatic relationships, giving Hudlin another avenue to use the character to comment upon real-world sociopolitical trends. On their trip to Latveria, Doctor Doom lectures T'Challa about trust and his allegiances to his Avenger allies, but T'Challa quickly deduces that Doom has sent a robot doppelganger to speak with them. Doom applauds his deduction and gets straight into eugenics territory with minimal prompting, stating his belief that "the African is a superior *physical* specimen" and that this physical ability generally compensates for what he sees as a lack of intellect—"But clearly the Wakandan is exceptional! Perhaps a low-grade mutant strain in your peoples' DNA." T'Challa rejects the dictator's armchair eugenics with a retort of his own—"Or perhaps because we had the military might to maintain our cultural integrity, and our technological superiority over Europeans such as yourself. When you were in caves, we were charting the stars."[46] Doom's words, a strawman for Hudlin to challenge with his script, echo the common stereotype that Black individuals (especially men) are somehow more physically gifted at the expense of their intelligence; a stereotype with its roots in long-standing racial prejudices that still rears its head in venues like sportscasting, where Black athletes are portrayed by reporters and commentators as less intellectually prepared but more physically gifted than their white counterparts.[47] Doom's ethnocentrism and backhanded cultural bigotry again reflect the prejudice of lowered expectations that is often central to Panther antagonists, but Hudlin's approach makes the covert significantly more overt, even going so far as to have Doom invoke a different racial media stereotype by calling Panther the "Tonto" to Captain America's Lone Ranger.[48]

Hudlin's tenure on Black Panther saw the character play a significant role in several of Marvel's biggest crossover events, but none were bigger (or tied together more of Hudlin's thematic elements) than the *Civil War* tie-ins. Through the conflict over government surveillance and oversight on superhuman activities (itself a pointedly obvious metaphor for the weakening of civil liberties under Bush), Hudlin's ideas about Blackness, international diplomacy and foreign policy, and the role of the Black Panther as a leader and pivotal figure in these communities came together. T'Challa, who had been neutral in the conflict and was afforded a degree of protection due to his status as a political leader in a foreign nation, eventually is coaxed into it by the sea prince Namor, who sees T'Challa, "a man of unshakable moral fiber" and one of the most respected and powerful men in the world, as the ideal leader of a coalition against potential U.S. aggression.[49] T'Challa is hesitant to violate Wakanda's non-aggression doctrine, fearing a loss in this conflict would result in him being imprisoned and losing control of Wakanda. Ultimately, however, he agrees to Namor's proposal—"Then let foes of freedom beware . . . the Black Panther will defend the oppressed!"[50]

The following issue, #22, opens with a monologue from James "War Machine" Rhodes, a Black hero put in charge of the government's new Sentinel program to track down and apprehend unregistered heroes. Rhodes muses on the complexity of the Superhuman Registration Act and what it represents:

Historically speaking, Uncle Sam has always kept an eye on the populace. Sometimes with the intent of protecting the vulnerable minority from vigilantes with a skewed idea of justice. Sometimes with the intent of monitoring the minority itself. Were the Black Panthers of the '60s terrorists . . . or merely citizens practicing self-defense? That depends on who you ask. The bigger question is: WHO do you trust to tell the difference?[51]

Rhodes' words are superimposed over crucial moments in history, rendered by artist Manuel Garcia—KKK cross burnings under the "skewed idea of justice" caption and FBI COINTELPRO spying operations against civil rights leaders and revolutionaries under the "monitoring the minority" caption.[52] The page represents a key moment—rather than running from the association, Hudlin is the first Panther writer to actively and directly engage with the legacy of Black activism, the real-world Black Panthers, and their accidental relationship with Marvel's hero. By comparing Black Panther (the superhero) with the Black Panther Party, he is creating analogy via fantasy metaphor—specifically, how both entities had motivations and goals that were considered ambiguous if not dangerous to white audiences and just and righteous to others. More importantly, through the actions taken by the Black Panther in this section of Hudlin's series, T'Challa represents the idea that Black revolutionaries have often run afoul of world governments, contextualizing the fictional metaphor of the character into real-world history in a way with which other writers had not fully engaged.

That implicit association is made explicit when a white soldier asks Rhodes what he thinks of the Black Panther as he prepares to drive a Sentinel out for crowd control in front of the White House. Rhodes, annoyed, asks if the Black Panther is the "new litmus test question" asked by whites of Black people. The soldier asks Rhodes to relax—"To be honest, if I was tasked to take down Captain America, I don't know if I could do it."[53] Hudlin packs a lot of meaning into this brief exchange, specifically the white assumption that Black political and cultural beliefs are monolithic in nature (a brief glance at electoral politics would show the opposite), but also the idea that Captain America (the star-spangled embodiment of the American ideal) represents white identity in the same way that Black Panther represents Black identity. This is not accidental on Hudlin's part. The conflation of whiteness and American values by the soldier—and, by extension, much of the comics industry, where patriotic-themed heroes of color are few and far between—is a common refrain to anyone who has ever been asked "where are you really from?" based on the color of their skin. Even a charitable read based on the representation of nationality (Wakanda is, after all, a sovereign Black nation) results in the same ethnocentric concept of white centrality in American nationalism.

Another pivotal moment in the *Civil War* storyline involves the death of Bill "Goliath" Foster, a Black scientist able to grow exponentially in size at will and who fights on the side of the anti-registration heroes. He is killed by a robotic clone of Thor and laid to rest, but where the main series glosses over the funeral, Hudlin's *Panther* series deals with the aftermath of the event and its symbolism. As T'Challa stands with Foster's family over his enormous gravesite, he and the reader are brought face-to-face with the inequitable treatment of Black bodies in America as Foster's mother weeps over his grave: "They wrapped my boy in a tarp. A tarp. Like a dead dog. And then they lowered him with a crane."[54] T'Challa offers the family a hero's burial in a real coffin in Wakanda, but Foster's sister asks if he knows how to shrink him down because "I don't know that they even tried. It's like, okay, we get the message, if you use an Aryan thunder god to blow a hole in big ol' *Black Goliath* . . . "[55] Meanwhile, representatives of the U.S. government meet to see what dirt they have on Foster to tarnish his name to prepare for the family's pending wrongful death suit, which they are convinced T'Challa is orchestrating (the script makes it clear he is not). When an official says it doesn't matter because "the Black vote won't mean that much in the next election anyway," another says that if Bill Foster becomes the new Emmett Till, "it will be bigger than a Black issue," to which the official replies "Who's Emmett Till?"[56]

Again, the fact that the government's first effort was to attempt to smear Foster's character and justify his death is not an unfamiliar refrain, as media coverage of Black victims of state-sanctioned violence and murder by law enforcement often seek to dehumanize and discredit them. As CalvinJohn Smiley and David Fakunle wrote in their 2016 analysis, said media coverage focuses less on the individual and more on their behavior, appearance, location, and lifestyle, all of which often serve to create criminal doubt in the mind of the audience and the assumption that their deaths were understandable and inevitable if not outright warranted—for instance, coverage of the shooting death of Michael Brown focused on his sizable physical stature and strength, while coverage of Freddie Gray's death focused on his prior police record.[57] As Smiley and Fakunle argue, "media depictions of Black bodies have remained compliant to White supremacist structures" even if individual reporters are not consciously racist.[58] The long history of media slander against Black male victims of state violence was undoubtedly on Hudlin's mind in this brief aside, and it further uses the fantastical nature of Black Panther and the Marvel Universe to have genuine conversations about systemic racism in the real world.

Ultimately, as the *Civil War* event came to an end and tensions cooled, T'Challa and Storm took over temporary positions as part of a new *Fantastic Four* team. Hudlin shifts from sly activist and commentator to more traditional superhero author at this point, writing enjoyable if not altogether challenging stories involving interdimensional travel and zombified versions of Marvel heroes. It is worth mentioning here one of Hudlin's last story arcs for the series, a tale where the new Fantastic Four travels to a planet seemingly run by 1920s gangsters (in reality, shape-shifting Skrull aliens) with futuristic sci-fi weaponry. This would not be otherwise noteworthy except said gangsters are being fought by a resistance effort comprised of other Skrulls who have adopted new permanent identities and called themselves the "Black Panthers," led by Skrull doppelgangers of Martin Luther King Jr. and Malcolm X.

The Skrull Panthers looked to the Civil Rights movement of Earth as a model and inspiration for their movement that emphasizes "morality and self-worth," and the Skrull versions of King and X are portrayed as respectful allies who disagree on how violent their resistance should be.[59] The heroes help the Panthers fight back against their mobster oppressors, and T'Challa tells Skrull X and Skrull King that they have a long task ahead of them. King says they must "move beyond anger over the past and create a fair and pluralistic society where Black and white, human and alien, can all live together in peace"; X adds they "can only do that if there is justice" where "the prime movers and collaborators of these evil regimes have their crimes exposed to the world and proper punishment is applied."[60] As Burroughs points out, Hudlin's story explores "an idea Blacks have had for 50 years: what if Martin and Malcolm had joined forces?" and also casts Storm as "a kind of Angela Davis figure" to boot, complete with a cover featuring the character wearing a white Afro and paramilitary gear.[61] In his excellent analysis of the story arc, Brian Yates reads the story as Hudlin portraying King and X "as a moiety, intractably linked parts of the same whole" while also acknowledging a moral justification for violence in defense of Black freedom.[62] Implicitly, the issue uses the Black Panther's high-concept super heroics in the service of a utopian vision of Black liberation, reconciling the challenges of the past with visions of a better possible future. Once again, a Black Panther story offers a restorative counter-narrative to the pain of real-world history in the form of a world where America's greatest civil rights leaders had the chance to build the society they sought.

It is impossible to move on from Hudlin's contributions to the character without also recognizing the introduction of his most significant original character, T'Challa's sister Shuri. Shuri, who Hudlin and artist John Romita Jr. created in the first arc of the run, was introduced first as an ambitious young woman looking to challenge for the throne and later grew into a confidant and trusted warrior alongside her brother; she is also one of the first other characters to take over the Panther identity following her brother's incapacitation by Doctor Doom. Hudlin returned after a brief hiatus from the series to start a new volume chronicling Shuri's exploits as the Panther that served both to flesh out her character and to explore the meaning of the Panther legacy. At first, after ingesting the heart-shaped herb to gain the Panther's powers, Shuri is rejected by Bast, who says the mantle of the Panther is about sacrifice for the greater good and Shuri does not understand: "Jealousy has festered in your heart since your brother took up the mantle of Panther. Of all the enemies you've faced, hubris is the one you have never defeated. You are NOT worthy to be the Black Panther. It is not your burden. It is not your destiny."[63]

It is only later, as the vampire Morlun rampages through Wakanda, that Shuri realizes her overconfidence in her scientific training and fighting tactics manifested as a belief that she had the sole right "to become Wakanda's weapon in her hour of need. Just as all of us trust too much in bombs and bullets and the advanced toys of war that only Wakanda can create. How like a daughter of modern Wakanda I have become."[64] This interpretation of Shuri is interesting considering the forward-thinking scientist who chafes against tradition that defines the modern interpretation of the character, but her willingness to potentially sacrifice her own life for that of the nation by fighting Morlun nonetheless illustrates the common themes of sacrifice for the good of the nation that drive the various Panthers. With the importance of Storm as a counterpart and source of support and strength, the promotion of Ramonda from stepmother to biological mother and advisor, and Shuri's gradual assumption of the mantle, Hudlin also greatly expanded the role, importance, and strength of women to the Black Panther mythos.

Hudlin's final Black Panther series would come in 2011, partnering with Panther veteran artist Denys Cowan for the four-issue Captain America team-up *Flags of Our Fathers*. The plot involves Captain America, Nick Fury, and the Howling Commandos team going on a mission to Wakanda to prevent the Nazis, led by HYDRA commander Baron Strucker, from getting vibranium for their weapons program. There, they meet Azzuri, T'Challa's grandfather and the then-current Black Panther. Young Black soldier Gabe Jones (seemingly no relation to the *Young Allies* character from the 1940s) is the de facto lead and perspective character of the piece, having been personally recruited by Fury to act as the first Black soldier to fight alongside white soldiers.

During the mission, Fury asks Jones to get intelligence from the Wakandans on vibranium and the Panther (nominally because Fury trusts him, implicitly because he too is Black), and Jones grapples with his own conscience and emotions about what Wakanda represents compared to the segregation back home throughout the series—"I find myself in a Black man's paradise, only to be asked to spy on another Negro to see if he's a Nazi puppet, an overconfident fool, or if he's the truth. Am I scared to find out he's not real?"[65] Meanwhile, Captain America, representing well-intentioned if naïve white liberal idealism, tries to convince Azzuri that the war will change race relations in America—"You can't go to war with a bunch of jerks who call themselves the Master Race and turn around and do the same thing back home"—but Azzuri is unconvinced: "Evil is only allowed to flourish when good men do nothing to stop it. [. . .] A nation at war has an enemy to unify them. A nation with *no* enemy . . . often looks for one within its own borders."[66]

Any student of real-world history, of course, knows that Azzuri's statements are prescient—integration was still slow to come after soldiers returned home from the Second World War, many soldiers were denied employment and financial opportunities, and faced brutal violence and lynching despite their veteran status.[67] Nonetheless, Azzuri and the Americans strike an alliance that is cemented when Jones saves a young T'Chaka and his brother from a Nazi super soldier. Azzuri tells Strucker to go back to Germany and inform Hitler of his failure, "And if I ever see a Nazi jackboot anywhere near my country again, I will rescind our non-interventionist policy, invade Germany myself and kill you all. Am I clear?"[68] But it is Jones, ultimately, who the story is about—and Azzuri offers him and his family Wakandan citizenship in gratitude for his actions. While briefly tempted by the offer, Jones declines saying that he needs to finish the fight abroad and at home and can't leave anyone behind; he smuggles a small amount of vibranium out of the country but decides not to inform Fury out of respect for Azzuri. Fury momentarily questions whether Jones would rather stay in Wakanda but ultimately accepts his loyalty.[69] Like Luke Cage and Marvel's other Black heroes, Jones acts as a reflective metaphor of Hudlin's own valuation of the Black Panther and a means of exploring the lived experiences of Black GIs; the conflict between Jones' temptation to stay in the Black utopia of Wakanda or fighting an unjust system at home also provides significant narrative and historical tension, initiating a difficult conversation in a broadly accessible fashion.

Ultimately, Hudlin's tenure on the Black Panther may not be rougher and not as critically renowned as his contemporaries, but his impact on the character and his transmedia evolution is undeniable. In addition to his comics work, Hudlin also wrote and oversaw an adaptation of his *Black Panther* series that aired on BET at the same time he was president. This prompted some concerns over the ethics of such a move and how Hudlin would be compensated (neither Hudlin nor the network commented at the time).[70] Nonetheless, the series—which lasted six episodes and utilized an advanced form of the "motion comic" style that animated art and panels directly from the first six issues of Hudlin's run with an all-star cast including Kerry Washington and Djimon Hounsou—was extremely popular and sold well on DVD, bringing the character to audiences well beyond the comic space.[71] Hudlin also pushed to use African-inspired music in the adaptation, and composer Stephen James Taylor went so far as to develop a Wakandan language for the lyrics of the show's theme song based on several trips to Africa.[72] The adaptation is undeniably and thoroughly Hudlin's work—with only a few small alterations and the addition of content from Dickey's *Storm* series, it is otherwise nearly a panel-for-panel adaptation of the "Who is the Black Panther?" arc to the point where one can more or less hold the comic up to the screen and follow along (hence why it is discussed here and not in the later chapter on the Panther's televised appearances). The visibility of this series raised interest and awareness in the character, but also importantly illustrated Hudlin's status as something of a futurist for the transmedia complex the superhero industry would ultimately become. By pitching his vision as one easy to adapt into film and proving the validity of the Panther in the moving image as well as demonstrating what he can represent to the larger audience, Hudlin had his finger on the pulse of the character and the marketplace by seeing the Panther as an extendable brand across media forms. The very idea of the Black Panther as a uniquely Black transmedia character owes a great deal to him.

TRANSITIONS AND GROWING PAINS

The increased profile Hudlin's work brought to the Black Panther led to greater representation across Marvel's publishing line to varying degrees of success. New adaptations of the character ranged from the insightful to the puzzling as Hudlin stepped away and the character's importance to the nascent MCU started to come into focus. In 2008, near the end of Hudlin's run, star Marvel writer Brian Michael Bendis introduced an alternate-universe version of T'Challa into Marvel's *Ultimate* line of comics, originally introduced as a streamlined and modernized version of continuity for new readers that was quickly becoming top-heavy and only a few more years away from obsolescence itself.

The Ultimate T'Challa was a "man-made mutant" discovered at a Weapon X facility in Canada, a headstrong young man who attempted to undertake the Panther trial himself but had his throat slashed by a panther for his efforts. His father T'Chaka was duped into sending him to the Weapon X program, which gave him mutant powers like enhanced speed and vision as well as claws that come out of his knuckles—but it could not cure his throat injury, leaving him mute.[73] Why Marvel editorial decided to make the Ultimate version of their most historically significant Black superhero an imitation of the white hero Wolverine with no ability to speak for himself, I will leave to the reader to speculate. The slight is worsened by its eventual irrelevance, as it is revealed that the Black Panther that joins the Ultimates team (that universe's version of the Avengers) is actually Captain America in disguise, who took pity on the boy and let him return home.[74] The rest of the character's tenure is largely uneventful—when the real T'Challa appears as part of the team, he does not speak or have much impact on the overall series. The Ultimate universe incarnation of the character is ultimately best forgotten, but it is included here for the sake of thoroughness. It also offers a reminder that in the creation of a transmedia mythology this sprawling in nature, not all incarnations leave a mark, and some are even particularly ill-advised.

More significant as a bridge to the contemporary comics depiction of the Black Panther is Jonathan Maberry's later *Doomwar* event in 2010. Maberry, who had taken over the *Black Panther* title when Hudlin left, wrote the event as an extension of themes explored in the main series, leading into the next few years of Black Panther material. The story picks up when Doctor Doom, having funded and supplied the Desturi, a group of traditionalist Wakandan fanatics, has effectively removed Shuri and the royal family from power in Wakanda and cut off the outside world. Meanwhile, Storm, who has been arrested and charged with attempted murder for accidentally electrocuting a villager she thought was attacking her, warns the Desturi at her trial that T'Challa will come back, to which the judge snorts "Let him come. Or have you forgotten, Wakanda has never been conquered." "It is YOU who are forgetting something," she replies. "You are not Wakanda. He is."[75] This line underscores a key concept throughout the Panther canon—the idea that the Black Panther, whoever they might be, and the nation of Wakanda are one and the same. In Priest and Hudlin's runs, the country's fortunes rise and fall based on how the Panther is doing, and the rhetorical significance of tying the well-being of an entire sovereign nation to its ruler is worth considering. It could be argued that Wakanda and what it represents as a liberating and equalizing force being tied to one person downplays the historical need for collective action to inspire meaningful change (indeed, Coates would make this conflict a central part of his take on the character). Moreover, the traditions and shortcomings of Wakanda are echoed in the Panther's own feet of clay—frequently, he is as hamstrung by the status quo he tries to uphold as he is empowered.

Doom's plot, ultimately, is not dissimilar from the colonialist and imperialist ambitions of other villains throughout the series—destroying Wakanda's resources and sovereignty is easily the most common motive for Black Panther antagonists, apart from personal antipathy—but Shuri's more aggressive and hot-tempered approach changes the dynamic somewhat. She leads a coalition of Wakandans, the Fantastic Four, and some willing X-Men against Doom with more than a little invective against her own as she states her intent to defeat those who "betrayed their own heritage" and "take back my country. By *any* means necessary."[76] Shuri's invocation of one of Malcolm X's most famous rhetorical flourishes is likely not by accident, though a white writer placing it in the mouth of a character defined in the storyline by her short fuse and bloodlust is questionable. Shuri sees herself as the "claws of the Panther God on Earth" and reminds the pacifist X-Man Nightcrawler that Wakanda "is a tiny nation in the midst of a vast continent that has never known true peace" and it would not exist "were we not willing to defend it, fiercely and decisively."[77] Shuri speaks the words of Black liberation and self-defense framed in a story that often sees her as recalcitrant and even violent, creating an equivalency between the two in the reader's mind and leaving one to wonder how a different writer may have approached the subject.

As part of his plot, Doom takes the entire supply of Wakanda's vibranium by presenting himself to Bast and stating his intent to create a safer, more just world without crime or poverty where he rules over all (which Bast acknowledges he does out of a genuine concern for humanity, despite the fact it would result in the deaths of millions and his tyrannical rule—a strange narrative choice, to say the least). He unlocks its magical properties and utilizes his science and sorcery to gain control over everything that has vibranium particles in it—which turns out to be most of the world, due to fallout from the vibranium asteroid that hit Earth millions of years ago. T'Challa, realizing the human cost of the fight against Doom and Wakanda's seeming overdependence on vibranium ("Honor does not come from a thing. Honor comes from within. From courage and from the strength to make hard choices") triggers a device that deactivates the mineral all over the world. This defeats Doom but also leaves Wakanda without its primary economic resource—hardly the first or last time T'Challa has put his country into economic jeopardy.[78] The erasure of vibranium and uncertainty of Wakanda's place on the world stage stripped away much of the resources and political influence that made him unique among his contemporaries, and it is here that one of the more controversial runs on the character began.

A depowered, resource-poor T'Challa next appeared in a rebranding of the ongoing Daredevil series later in 2010, offering the character as a street-level vigilante substituting for the absentee titular hero in his Hell's Kitchen neighborhood. Writer David Liss, along with primary series artist Francesco Francavilla, crafted a moody neo-noir immigrant story in the *Black Panther: The Man Without Fear* and *Black Panther: The Most Dangerous Man Alive!* series, and while this status quo was relatively short-lived it is worth considering in terms of the character's rhetorical potential. Living amongst the denizens of Hell's Kitchen in the guise of "Devil's Kitchen" diner owner and Congo immigrant Mr. Okonkwo, T'Challa's primary motivation is to come to terms with the events of the *Doomwar* series by rediscovering who he is and wants to be. Matt Murdock, Daredevil's civilian alter ego, suggests the Kitchen is the ideal place for T'Challa's purposes—"If you want to find out who you really are, what you're made of, how far you can bend and stretch without breaking, then learn by protecting these people."[79] T'Challa takes these words to heart, protecting both the spiritual and the physical needs of the citizens of Hell's Kitchen by giving opportunities to marginalized immigrants at the diner while also battling mobsters and other threats to the neighborhood.

T'Challa also runs afoul of larger-scale threats, such as a racist office drone named Josh Glenn who becomes a host for the spirit of the villain Hate-Monger because of the events of the largely-unrelated *Fear Itself* miniseries, using his new powers of mind control and persuasion to drum up anti-immigrant hysteria in Hell's Kitchen. Jacobs, overtaken by Hate-Monger's energy, starts slowly turning the white citizens of the area against their neighbors, encouraging mob violence against the makeshift clinic and camp for displaced people T'Challa and his staff operated out of the diner and introducing his own champion, the American Panther. The American Panther, wearing a version of T'Challa's modified street-level Panther costume bedecked in red, white, and blue, served as the new Hate-Monger's enforcer and acolyte. When the American Panther shrugs off an uppercut from T'Challa he responds with what can only be described as arrogant white nationalism: "Nice punch, African. That might have even hurt an ordinary man. But Hate-Monger has taught me to believe in my own strength. The strength of America!"[80]

Liss' usage of the racist rhetorical device of "America" as a white country and ideal in opposition to immigration and people of color for his villains' motivation is unfortunately all too familiar today, as is Glenn's gradual radicalization through online forums and social media prior to receiving the Hate-Monger's powers of mind control and persuasion. Online radicalization of young white men via racist ideology is a major concern as domestic terrorism and violence has been on the increase in the United States over the last few years, with FBI Director Christopher Wray identifying racist extremism as a significant source of focus for the organization in 2021 testimony in front of the Senate Judiciary Committee.[81] Glenn-as-Hate-Monger's appeal to the crowd even reads like something that would not be out of place in the writings of an online malcontent or right-wing political candidate today: "Do you see how the immigrant strikes out in fear and desperation? Do you see how the American strikes with purpose and resolve? The time is coming when America will no longer give away what is rightfully ours."[82]

T'Challa, realizing that he can no longer think like or be Daredevil in this situation, performs a sort of high-tech exorcism on Glenn and removes the Hate-Monger's spirit from him, and he and the man in the American Panther suit are both arrested. Liss, writing in 2011, seems prescient about the dangers of populist appeals to racism and hate online and in-person, though it is foolish to pretend these problems are new or began only with the election of certain world leaders. More importantly, the status of T'Challa and his staff as immigrants is crucial to the story being told. The Black Panther is inherently a character that speaks to the Diaspora, and his heroism is uniquely tailored to a world wherein members of that Diaspora are marginalized, ridiculed, or violated for those differences—and his relationship as a fellow member of that Diaspora to the rest of his immigrant neighbors and allies differs from that of his white contemporaries.

The *Man Without Fear/Most Dangerous Man Alive* era, like those that came before it, also drew upon the works of prior authors and artists to flesh out its narrative, remixing and reheating returning characters and plot devices in the new context of a deposed king. In one issue, meant as a jumping-on point for new readers, T'Challa's adopted brother Hunter was revealed as the perpetrator of a series of murders of Hell's Kitchen residents, with the intent of drawing T'Challa out to stake a claim as the rightful Black Panther. T'Challa disposes of him handily and with finality. Liss brought years of relationship between the two to the forefront, with T'Challa telling Hunter his murderous acts against the innocent in the name of Wakanda served himself rather than the nation—"Wakanda is too great a nation to allow you to use it as an excuse to engage in petty brutality"—a loaded scene given the checkered past of the country, and the larger question later authors would explore of whether the Wakandan ideal is a genuine one.[83]

Liss also adds more fuel to the "Marvel's Batman" qualifier/pejorative for Black Panther started under Priest's run by giving him a sidekick in the form of Sofija, a young Serbian woman who sleuths out his identity and helps him in his crimefighting quest, even wryly calling herself the "girl wonder."[84] Toward the end of the series, T'Challa also does battle with recurring Daredevil nemesis Wilson "Kingpin" Fisk, a powerful crime lord who attempts to take advantage of economic instability in Wakanda to own the majority of the country and its resources by assassinating and coercing members of the country's national bank. Again, T'Challa defends his homeland not just from supervillains or aliens but the rapacious and overlooked greed of white colonizer mentalities—arguably his single most consistent foe.[85]

The decision to de-power T'Challa and leave him as a street-level hero was not without controversy—reader Michael Anyanwu was typical of reactions to the new direction, as he wrote in to express his "disillusionment" with the post-*Doomwar* handling of the character in issue #520. To Anyanwu, the current story was "not really the kind of story that makes much sense to anyone familiar with T'Challa's true origins or motivations," and he signed off with the phrase "T'Challa R.I.P."[86] Liss, in a somewhat unusual move, replied, offered up a defense of the choice in the column, saying that T'Challa appearing in Hell's Kitchen was consistent with the character's history of taking on "challenges to test himself" and concluded that "characters who grow and change and evolve and experiment with who they are" are one of the best parts of the comics medium.[87] As Liss wrote in an essay in his final issue, acting as the final word on the matter, his goal was to take T'Challa, "a brilliant and powerful man, knock him down to his lowest point, and figure out how he builds himself back."[88]

While brief, the Hell's Kitchen detour is an interesting fragment of the transmedia mosaic of the Black Panther character. Liss and a rotating crew of artists crafted an interesting neo-noir story with something to say about the immigrant experience in America and further expanding the character's political dimensions by forcing him to deal with the ramifications of his choices. However, while there is localized narrative power in asserting that the Black Panther does not need the trappings of resources and power afforded by kingship to be a hero, removing him from that context also strips him in part of what makes him significant and historically important as a counter-narrative. Rather than a regal leader, warrior, diplomat, and spy, the Black Panther becomes not only another street-level vigilante, but also a temporary fill-in for a white hero. It is not hard to see why it was controversial. Yet, that it worked at all when similar efforts under other writers floundered is a testament primarily to the high quality of Liss, Francavilla, and the other creatives' work. If nothing else, it proved the character's malleability to different time periods and situations, a crucial testing point for the character's transmedia viability.

At this point, the Black Panther was a significantly more visible part of the Marvel publishing pantheon. Simultaneously, the Marvel Cinematic Universe was running at full speed and early plans were being put in motion for the character to make an appearance on the big screen. In that light, it is significant that star writer Jonathan Hickman made the Black Panther an important part of a years-long, status quo-destroying storyline that not only served as editorial housekeeping for an unruly Marvel continuity but also explored the more existential aspects of the Black Panther character along the way. Hickman first brought the character in on his tenure on the main *Fantastic Four* series in 2012, fittingly returning the hero to the series in which he originated and playing off his long history with the team.

After his stint in Hell's Kitchen, T'Challa returned to Wakanda where he summoned his long-time friends, the Fantastic Four, to visit. Reed Richards offers his help in rebuilding Wakanda's vibranium supply, but T'Challa, in a reminder to Richards and the audience of his nation's abilities and rejection of his white paternalism, declines: "We are not peasants who fell backwards into wealth, Reed. We were the first around the world. We preceded the immortals. We stood while Rome burned . . . Wakanda has always been a city on the horizon."[89] T'Challa reveals that he had been slowly liquidating Wakanda's vibranium stockpiles and diversifying the raised capital into other emerging economies, including buying American debt—as a result, Wakanda is as prosperous as ever (again, T'Challa's economic power as head of a sovereign nation answers some narrative questions). Instead, T'Challa asked Reed for help to deal with recurring assaults from undead spirits and reanimated skeletons from the underworld. His plan is to go into the Necropolis, an older, underground part of the city where the Black Panthers of the past are laid to rest, to speak with the panther goddess Bast (again represented in corporeal form, albeit a more humanoid one than in Hudlin's run) who gave Wakanda her blessing millennia ago.[90] As Shuri, Storm, and Susan Storm-Richards do battle with Anubis, Richards and T'Challa make their way to Bast's inner sanctum. Bast quickly surmises that T'Challa is truly there to become the Black Panther again and gets him to admit as much. Bast, showing visions of fire in the sky and great waves destroying Wakanda (both of which are foreshadowing for stories to come) states she has higher needs for him and makes him the King of the Dead, with power over the Necropolis of Wakanda while Shuri rules over the city of the living. In addition, she gives him the power to commune with all previous Black Panthers—"Every Panther that has ever lived, their strength, their knowledge is now yours. Every battle fought . . . every battle won. Unbeaten. Unbroken. A crown of the unconquered. A king of kings."[91] A surface-level analysis would find Biblical parallels to a "king of kings" with power over death, but such ideas are also deeply woven into African and Egyptian animism and faith as well. The formalization of T'Challa's connection to his ancestors is both a reflection of African belief and became a consistent part of his abilities. With that, the Black Panther was in power again, a neat narrative trick preserving Hudlin's contribution of Shuri to the mythology while also making the Black Panther a significant and empowered part of the universe in time for his on-screen appearance.

Unfortunately, a return to power came at a cost, as Marvel's editorial staff decided to dissolve the marriage between the Black Panther and Storm in the 2012 *Avengers vs. X-Men* series. The basic premise of the plot—the X-Men are protecting a young mutant who appears to be a channel for the Phoenix Force, one of the most powerful destructive entities in the galaxy, while the Avengers are looking to stop it—is largely an excuse for the heroes to fight each other, and the schism between the formerly ostensibly friendly factions naturally ran down the middle of the union of the two most important Black characters in comics. The marriage had always been controversial, with skepticism about the characters being romantically involved and married just because they were both of African descent as well as how long it could last in a genre perpetually reverting to a previous salable status quo. Chris Claremont, one of the longest-tenured writers on the X-Men series in the history of the franchise (and one of the writers who introduced the idea of a romantic connection between the two in the first place), said in a 2018 interview the fundamental problem with "a marriage of leading characters in comics" is who gets top billing, as well as where to go next in a medium where the characters cannot get older.[92]

The two battle each other early in the series as well as in its companion *Vs.* series that consisted primarily of semi-out-of-context battles, but it is in issue #9 of the event that the marriage officially comes to an end. Namor, empowered and made more ruthless by the Phoenix Force, summons a gigantic tidal wave (the one alluded to in Hickman's Fantastic Four series) that destroys much of Wakanda to drown out an Avengers stronghold. After the event, Storm approaches T'Challa offering help, saying that she wants to help her people rebuild. T'Challa tells her "they're not your people anymore," and that the high priest of the Panther Clan annulled their marriage. As long-time readers know and Storm sadly points out, T'Challa is said high priest—a cold ending to the highest-profile Black romance in comics.[93]

Once again, T'Challa puts his loyalty to the kingdom of Wakanda ahead of his personal needs—not an uncommon sacrifice in the genre but one emblematic of his unique role. In the accompanying "Vs." issue, Storm realizes that T'Challa had plans in place to neutralize her powers if it came to it—implicitly stripping her of her agency. The two muse about their relationship during the battle in intercutting internal monologues representing opposing but complementary interpretations of the situation ("I will always love this man."/"I will always regret what could have been."), ultimately ending with Storm punching T'Challa and returning her wedding ring.[94] The marriage of Storm and T'Challa was a significant if controversial event, but its revocation as the background of a superhero punch-fest feels like an aggressive and somewhat cruel pruning of a narrative branch editorial did not want to be stuck with; it is also worth noting that it involved Storm, a character Marvel did not own film rights to at the time and was less interested in promoting in comics stories. Even in service of the larger arc about the rebuilding of the Black Panther, it feels like a somewhat unnecessary diversion and a regression to a baseline status quo.

Hickman brought the Black Panther back as a key character in his run on the *New Avengers* series, leading up to the universe-altering *Secret Wars*. The arc starts off with T'Challa bringing together the Illuminati, a group of super heroic elder statesmen consisting of luminaries like Tony Stark, Professor X, Namor, and Reed Richards that he had once refused to join, over concerns about incursions of other worlds into the main Marvel universe. One such incursion happens as T'Challa speaks with a group of young Wakandans and tasks them with rebuilding Wakanda's space program—"Great societies are crumbling around us, and the old men who run them are out of ideas. So all eyes turn to you, our children—to build us something better"—and the ensuing battle with the mysterious woman Black Swan who leads the incursion results in the deaths of the young Wakandans.[95] T'Challa recalls the prophecy given to him by Bast:

Once the goddess spoke, and I was given a prophecy. A word spoken in fire and flood, a word of dead kings and hopeless causes. Of the future lost and of worlds dying. Of fallen angels and lost souls. When facing the end . . . when everything around you crumbles—when everything withers and dies . . . who answers the call of desperate men?[96]

This dialogue sets up much of T'Challa's arc and motivation for the remainder of the series—gifted with knowledge of what is to come, what is the role of a leader to stop it and at what cost? T'Challa and the Illuminati work together to develop a solution that results in the destruction of incurring worlds—at great cost to T'Challa's moral fiber and his relationship with Shuri, who bans him from Wakanda when she realizes he has been working with Namor. Namor, seeing the interaction, shows his gratitude and taunts his long-time rival while referencing what he sees as the ultimate futility of such matters in the grander cosmic scheme: "You could have told her many things [. . .] But you did not. Because you know . . . what we used to call life has very little worth these days. Welcome to the very edge. For it is the perfect place . . . for kings who have lost their kingdoms."[97]

Namor's words also echo the narrative scaffolding Hickman builds onto T'Challa's character—can one who has seen as much as T'Challa truly have empathy for all or must the utilitarian view of the greater good win out despite sacrifice? The new Illuminati discover that the next incursion world is defended by heroes much like them (in a metatextual nod, the heroes are analogues to DC's Justice League team, an idealistic force compared to the morally compromised Illuminati) and Panther grapples with the morality of destroying their world to save his own. He convenes the previous Black Panthers for guidance on the ancestral plane, who are dismissive of his moral concerns about committing mass murder to save his people: "Are you a king? Have you sat on the throne? Then you have done evil. It is impossible to place yourself—or be placed—above man and not act as a god."[98] Hickman's rejection of kingship as an inherent virtue is a significant departure for the character that would become a vital part of the Panther's existence—and T'Chaka's insistence that Wakandan inaction being best for the nation despite its human cost begins to break down the mythologizing of the nation as an inherent good.[99] Hickman challenges the idea of kingship and implicitly the idea of the Black Panther itself in a monologue about kings by the villain Maximus:

You can't think of them as normal men [. . .] they are larger than that, bigger than that . . . they exist above other men because they were born that way. [. . .] The people—their people—expect them to do violence to ensure a certain amount of peace and prosperity. And like gods, they are also expected to commit murder . . . so the people can sleep at night, knowing they are protected.[100]

This idea—of the cruelty afforded to the leaders of nations in the guise of protecting their people—is a core tenet of T'Challa's development and one echoed throughout his transmedia existence; his ultimate rejection of the idea reclaims him as a hero despite the moral ambiguity of his actions in Hickman's series. The team ultimately fights the other earth's heroes—Hickman again pokes at the "Marvel's Batman" idea by pitting T'Challa against the Rider, a grim hero in a black cape—and after defeating them return to their earth with the understanding that destroying the other heroes' world would save their own. T'Challa volunteers to push the button to destroy the other world when the other heroes balk, but he too is overtaken by remorse and throws the device aside (leading to T'Chaka's apparition to deny him as his son in the afterlife).[101] Namor picks it up and activates it, destroying the other world and leading to a brawl wherein he reveals that he had sent Thanos' generals to Wakanda earlier in the series looking for the Infinity Stones, an action that resulted in scores of dead Wakandans—"Do you know what I regret, king of the dead? That so many were left alive. But I want you to know one thing: of those that remain . . . every breath they take . . . is mercy from me."[102]

Namor's utilitarian cruelty—and his vengeance against Wakanda—puts him in line with the idealism of Maximus and the previous Black Panthers, with T'Challa on the opposing side of the ideological spectrum. Here, Hickman truly digs into what the Black Panther represents as a study of leadership and kinghood and his reluctance to compromise his morals for his royal obligations—can a good man truly be king? T'Challa's rejection of his apparent kingly duty alienates him from Wakanda's legacy and drifts him further away from that role. At the same time, it reunites him with his humanity—later work by Coates and the character's presence in the Marvel Cinematic Universe would pick up on these themes in the years to come.

Eventually, as another incursion looms, the heroes realize they can no longer justify destroying other worlds to save their own. Each hero goes their separate ways believing the end of their world is imminent. T'Challa spends the night with Storm, revealing his feelings for her and his desire to be with her rather than spend his last day on earth as king of Wakanda. Storm sends him away, believing their dalliance to be a mistake; however, the incursion fails to happen due to Namor making a secret deal with Thanos and other villains to create a Cabal to kill and pillage other worlds to spare their own.[103] The Cabal overtakes the world and destroys most of Wakanda, and it is revealed that the mastermind of all the incursions is Doctor Doom, who has been systematically eliminating all other universes in the hopes of making one in his own image (evoking his motivation from *Doomwar* years prior) and resulting in Hickman's *Secret Wars* event. The *Secret Wars* event was simultaneously a conclusion to Hickman's story that went through *New Avengers*, but it served the primary purpose of cleaning editorial house by erasing the Ultimate Universe (now apparently unsalvageable due to flagging sales and overly complex continuity) and rolling its most lucrative character, the new Spider-Man Miles Morales, into the mainline universe. Effectively *Secret Wars* acted as a "reset button" for Marvel's continuity, illustrating the problem with decades-long episodic storylines in which characters are not allowed to age—when every story "counts," the infrastructure starts to buckle under the weight.

Doom erases both universes and all their prior history, creating one world where he rules as a god. T'Challa and Namor, realizing the futility of holding a grudge when the past has been erased, work together to lead an army of the Marvel Zombies (because he is king of the dead, after all) against Doom's forces. Knowing he is about to be defeated, Doom offers T'Challa a rebuilt Wakanda on the new world—everything as it was, with T'Challa once again the king. T'Challa, with new clarity granted by his recent experiences, refuses: "And what good would that be? A fake kingdom, on a manufactured world, subjected to the whims of a vain fraud . . . you may have the power, Victor, but raising up a new Wakanda would require a vision you just don't possess."[104]

Doom is defeated and Battleworld is destroyed and replaced with a new and rebuilt Earth, and T'Challa is brought back to the same place in a new Wakanda where he spoke to the group of young Wakandans about the space program and a plan to send a ship to the stars at the beginning of *New Avengers* a neat narrative bookend and conclusion to Hickman's longer-form story as well as a metaphorical victory for the hero, who rejected the offers and demands of others to create his own vision of leadership. At the same time, it also created a fresh start for Disney's transmedia marketing slate—it is not coincidental that the end of *Secret Wars* happened not long before the release of the character's first cinematic appearance, which demanded less continuity-heavy stories for a new audience brought in by the film. Such is the power of the narrative device of superhero comics, and such is the demand of multimedia synergy—entire fictional worlds can be rebuilt and destroyed just to supplement a more economically viable product.

Yet, there is a common through line in this decade-long span of the Black Panther's history. Hudlin started it off by asking "Who is the Black Panther," and he and the other authors in this chapter spent a lot of time trying to answer that question. The Black Panther, depending on who you ask and at what time is an aspirational figure, a heroic icon, a symbol of the importance of immigration to the American story, a cautionary tale about the cost of power, and the man next door. In this way, he offers the potential for insight and philosophical argument on the heady issues of our time that few other heroes could. In the final major era of the character's comics history, one of the country's most insightful Black writers would embrace these questions head-on, contextualizing the character inextricably and powerfully into real lived experiences at the same time he became an iconic household name.

NOTES

1. Internet Movie Database, "Hudlin"; Johnson, "Black Panther Writer Reginald Hudlin"; Kempley, "Bebe's Kids."
2. Johnson, "Hudlin."
3. Ibid.
4. Burroughs, *Marvel's Black Panther,* 1641.
5. Hudlin, "A Historical Overview."
6. Ibid.
7. Ibid.
8. Ibid, censoring is that of the original author.
9. Ibid.
10. Ibid.
11. Smith, "PRIEST, Pt. 1."
12. Burroughs, *Marvel's Black Panther,* 1695.
13. Hudlin et al., "Who is the Black Panther?" 3–5.
14. Ibid.
15. Tunç, "Preemption."
16. Hudlin et al., "Who is the Black Panther? Part Two."
17. Hudlin et al., "Who is the Black Panther? Part Three," 7.
18. Burroughs, *Black Panther,* 1710.
19. Chiorazzi, "The spirituality of Africa"; Foster, "How Africa is transforming the Catholic Church."
20. Foster, "How Africa"; Gomez, "Africans, Religion, and African Religion," 84.
21. Hudlin et al., "Who is the Black Panther? Part 3," 20.
22. Hudlin et al., "Who is the Black Panther? Part 4," 8–11.
23. Hudlin et al., "Who is the Black Panther? Part 5," 17–18.
24. Bump, "15 years after."
25. Lopez, "Hurricane Katrina."
26. Hudlin et al., "Black Steel," 11 & 15.
27. Ibid, 14.
28. Hudlin et al., "Black Steel"; Hudlin et al., "White Light."
29. Hudlin et al., "Wild Kingdom (Part 2)," 25.
30. Hudlin et al., "Here Come a Storm," 16.
31. Hudlin et al., "World Tour Part Two," 26.
32. Hudlin et al., "Aqua-Boogie," 25; Hudlin et al., "Inside Man," 25.
33. Hudlin et al., "Two the Hard Way Part One," 3.
34. Hudlin et al., "Black Steel," 11.
35. Feeny, "Harlem's Hue-Man bookstore."
36. Hudlin et al., "Bride of the Panther, Part Two," 24.
37. Hudlin et al., "Here Come a Storm," 29.

38. CBR Staff, "Hudlin & Dickey."
39. Hudlin et al., "Bride of the Panther Part One," 13.
40. Hudlin et al., "Bride of the Panther Part Two," 21.
41. Hudlin et al., "Bride of the Panther Part Three," 3–8.
42. Hudlin et al., "Here Come a Storm."
43. Ibid.
44. Ibid.
45. Ibid, 26.
46. Hudlin et al., "World Tour Part 1," 11.
47. Mercurio & Filak, "Roughing the Passer."
48. Hudlin et al., "World Tour Part 1," 11.
49. Hudlin et al., "Aqua-Boogie," 19.
50. Ibid, 23.
51. Hudlin et al., "Inside Man," 4.
52. Ibid, 4.
53. bid, 11.
54. Hudlin et al., "War Crimes Part 1," 3.
55. Ibid, 4.
56. Ibid, 6.
57. Smiley & Fakunle, "From 'brute' to 'thug.'"
58. Ibid, 17.
59. Hudlin et al., "Ready to Die (Part 3)," 13.
60. Hudlin et al., "Endgame—Conclusion," 20.
61. Burroughs, *Marvel's Black Panther,* 1790.
62. Yates, "Twenty-First-Century Race Man," 112.
63. Hudlin et al., "Deadliest of the Species, Part 4," 20.
64. Hudlin et al., "Deadliest of the Species, Part 5," 16.
65. Hudlin et al., "Part II," 6.
66. Ibid, 7.
67. Clark, "Returning from War, Returning to Racism."
68. Hudlin et al., "Part 4," 19.
69. Ibid.
70. Braxton, "Black Panther battles ethics."
71. Burroughs, *Marvel's Black Panther*.
72. Hudlin, "Looking Back."
73. Bendis et al., "Ultimate Origins (Part V)"; Loeb et al., "Favorite Son."
74. Loeb et al., "Robots in Disguise"; Loeb et al., "Training Day."
75. Maberry et al., "Doomwar Part 1," 5.
76. Ibid, 28.
77. Maberry et al., "Doomwar Part 2," 18.
78. Maberry et al., "Doomwar Part 6," 19.
79. Liss & Francavilla, "Urban Jungle," 6.
80. Liss & Francavilla, "Fear and Loathing in Hell's Kitchen Part 1," 19.
81. Bump, "FBI Director Wray"; Bullington, "White supremacy in America."
82. Liss & Francavilla, "Fear and Loathing in Hell's Kitchen part 1," 19.

83. Liss et al., "True Sons," 20.

84. Ibid, 11.

85. Liss et al., "Kingpin of Wakanda (Part 1)."

86. Liss et al., "Storm Hunter Part 2," 23.

87. Ibid.

88. Liss et al., "The Kingpin of Wakanda: Conclusion," 23.

89. Hickman et al., "Inert," 10.

90. Ibid; Hickman et al., "City of the Dead."

91. Hickman et al., "City of the Dead," 20.

92. Pulliam-Moore, "Chris Claremont."

93. Aaron et al., "Avengers vs. X-Men (Part Nine)," 10.

94. Aaron et al., "Black Panther vs. Storm," 19.

95. Hickman et al., "Memento Mori," 7.

96. Ibid, 20.

97. Hickman et al., "Builders," 15–16.

98. Hickman et al., "Into the Breach," 11.

99. Ibid, 11–12.

100. Hickman et al., "The Bomb," 14–15.

101. Ibid.

102. Hickman et al., "We Are Not Brothers," 19.

103. Hickman et al., "All the Angels Have Fallen."

104. Hickman et al., "Beyond," 2.

Chapter 7

The Panther Today

Meditations on Kinghood

By 2016, the Black Panther had become a household name thanks to his appearance in the *Captain America: Civil War* film. Marvel, after decades of mostly pretending their first Black superhero didn't exist outside of comics, had finally started expanding the character's presence into a variety of animated television projects, video games, merchandise, and more, all of which had a significant role to play in the broader cultural understanding of the character. However, as argued elsewhere in this book, while these portrayals of the character may have the largest popular audience they are indebted to the work of artists and writers working in the comics medium—and those creators were now turning out more Black Panther comics than ever. Not only did the character appear in major Marvel events, from 2016 onward he and the larger Wakandan cast were at the center of his own recurring monthly series, made appearances throughout the broader Marvel publishing line, and received multiple spinoffs and miniseries. In many ways, these last five or so years as of this writing have been some of the busiest for the character, packing a significant amount of important material for the character's history and acting as a primary conduit for prominent Black authors and creators to shape the notional idea of the Black Panther at the same time the character was reaching full bloom in the public consciousness.

Once again, Marvel put a writer from outside the comics industry at the center of the new era of the Black Panther—this time the acclaimed essayist, journalist, and MacArthur award winner Ta-Nehisi Coates, who brought extensive experience and fame from outside the comics industry to bear, creating mainstream interest and increased sales for a character that was finally enjoying a meaningful spotlight. But while Coates is important and a focal point of this chapter, it is important to note up front that he did not do this alone—writers like Roxane Gay, Evan Narcisse, Nnedi Okorafor, and many others brought fresh perspectives and cultural significance to their work on the character and his ever-expanding prominence in the Marvel publishing line as the world fully realized what had been hiding in Wakanda all along.

COATES AND THE PHILOSOPHER-KING PANTHER

On paper, Ta-Nehisi Coates was an unusual choice to take over the job of writing a new vision for Black Panther to simultaneously coordinate with his Marvel Cinematic Universe debut and wrap up the complex web of narrative decisions—good, bad, and otherwise—that characterized the post-Hudlin era of the character. Coates, an established correspondent for *The Atlantic* whose work focused on systemic racism and grappled with America's history of discrimination, had also received worldwide acclaim and a MacArthur "genius" grant for the 2015 release of *Between the World and Me,* a memoir-slash-statement of principles presented as a discussion between a father and his son. There is no question to those who have read his work that it is singular in quality and impact, but little in his output to that point signaled his suitability to write an ongoing superhero comic—he had published no fiction to that point and would not publish his first novel, *The Water Dancer*, until well after he started the *Panther* series.[1] Yet, in a 2016 interview with NPR's Audie Cornish, Coates saw comics as both a formative influence and natural transition:

> When I was a young person, my introduction frankly into the world of literature and the beauty of words and the beauty of language, occurred through three things. It occurred through the magic of hip-hop, it occurred through the magic of Dungeons and Dragons, and it occurred through the magic of Marvel comic books, so I feel back at home.[2]

Coates, who had blogged about his love of Spider-Man and other Marvel characters in the past, appeared on the company's radar after leading a May 2015 interview and discussion with Marvel editor Sana Amanat about diversity in comics; the company approached him shortly after the event and he was announced as the ongoing *Panther* writer in September of that year.[3] But where Hudlin approached the Black Panther as a fan, Coates came in as a relative neophyte (by his own admission) due to the lack of an ongoing Panther series or appearances in other books during his childhood, though he had been a fan of Priest's run when he came back to comics as an adult.

Coates nonetheless placed his own take on the character in the context of what had come before, telling *Kotaku* reporter (and later *Panther* writer) Evan Narcisse that he credited Priest with there being a Panther movie at all by "getting a mostly white readership to take the guy seriously" while also championing Hudlin's attempt to "write this character for black folks" where he "was just like the dream we wish we had" as well as Hickman's more deconstructionist work.[4] It is not unusual for writers on a superhero book to pay homage to that which has come before, but where Hudlin and Priest largely started from scratch and wove continuity in where necessary, Coates focused on a Wakanda and a Panther that was shaped by the "trauma" of the narrative arcs that had come before rather than starting *tabula rasa*.[5] At the same time, Coates also wanted to continue deconstructing the mythology of Wakanda, starting with creating his own map of the country that replaced the outdated animal-based names of cities and regions in the country dating back to McGregor's run with names adapted from real African language and fictional Wakandan history. He also positioned the country in an identifiable part of the African continent—specifically in Eastern Africa on the coast of Lake Victoria and surrounded by fellow fictitious nations like Niganda—due to his interest in making Wakanda a "real" and "lived-in" place.[6] Coates also made it clear that his version of the Black Panther mythology would take full advantage of the stories the character could tell not only about the Black experience and the Diaspora but also more fundamental questions of political and social reality:

> I made most of my career analyzing the forces of racism and white supremacy as an idea in America. But what you begin to realize after you do that long enough—you aren't talking about anything specific. In other words, you aren't really talking about whether some people have lighter skin or some people have blonde hair or some people have blue eyes or some people have kinky hair. You're talking about power. [. . .] And [race] is just a label that we've put on who has access to certain aspects of power and who will not.[7]

Coates' approach synthesized his writing style and personal and philosophical interests in a manner that both synthesized his predecessors and carved out a new path for the character. It would be somewhat reductionist but not inaccurate to say Coates adapted his style in part from the writers who came before, with some of Priest's taciturn and occasionally morally-compromised take on the character as well as Hudlin's more socially conscious and Black identity-centric approach and McGregor's predilection for long internal monologues. Yet Coates' run is undeniably his own, using the character as a canvas to explore questions of leadership, politics, and even whether the popular conception of Wakanda as a nation ruled by a benevolent and monolithic kingship could square at all in an age of social and political upheaval. Deconstructionist approaches in comics are a dime a dozen and often not as insightful as they claim to be, but Coates' work explored a fundamental and yet underexamined question at the heart of the character:

[. . .] what occurred to me was the distinct possibility that a) maybe T'Challa does not like being a king and b) maybe Wakandans have come to believe they don't need a king. [. . .] Wakanda has this mythology of having never been conquered. But in fact, there have been several comic books where in one case it does get conquered and really in other cases it really just suffers a terrible fate. [. . .] So if a monarch can no longer ensure the security of its people, what good is he then? Why would the people not then decide to take their safety and security and the fate of the nation into their own hands?[8]

The first arc of the series, "A Nation Under Our Feet," seeks to answer those questions and is an intentional and direct homage to the work of Steven Hahn and his Pulitzer prize-winning book of the same name. Hahn's work focused less on the major names and figures that characterize a "Great Man theory"-centric approach to history and more on the smaller popular movements and actions that characterized Black political engagement and power in the Civil War and Reconstruction era—a concept that feeds directly into the series and speaks to the question of democracy and popular power it addresses.[9] It is also an example of how Coates brings his personal interests and philosophical quandaries to the page.

I argue here that to truly understand Coates' approach to these questions—and indeed, why he asks them—it is instructive to read his run in the context of his other works. Echoes of *Between the World and Me* and his other pieces like the seminal "A Case for Reparations" (many of which are collected and given new context in the essential volume *We Were Eight Years in Power*) move throughout his *Black Panther* run. A key part of my thesis is that the context in which Black Panther operates is crucial to understanding the character—and by cross-applying Coates' nonfiction work to the fictional world of Wakanda a powerful rhetorical lens is developed that shows exactly how Coates interrogates these notions of race, diaspora, and power throughout his run on the character.

It is also crucial to note that Coates, unlike previous writers, was a sort of *de facto* architect of a semi-self-contained Panther mythos, writing not only the main series but also consulting on and co-writing books written by other prominent authors of color.[10] Read as a collective whole, the five years in which Coates and other creators crafted a new direction for the Black Panther are unique in their depth and impact and represent a vital evolution in the transmedia depiction of the character—as *Hollywood Reporter* contributor Graeme McMillan pointed out, the Coates era represented a "shared sensibility that built on the sparse framework already present to create a Wakanda, and a Black Panther, that properly spoke to something beyond the white fantasy of the black experience after decades."[11] In fact, as much as Coates gave credit to Priest for the character reaching the cinematic mainstream, former

Disney CEO Bob Iger credited Coates' run on the character with inspiring him to "green light" a cinematic treatment in his 2019 memoir.[12]

It would be an incomplete analysis of Coates' work to not mention that—even by his own admission—Coates was not immediately a natural comics writer. He learned much on the job, crediting his fellow writers and collaborators, most notably artist Brian Stelfreeze, with helping him learn how to tell stories and build the world.[13] The first several issues of the run are often criticized as being heavy on dialogue and exposition, with minimal action apart from a few fight scenes Coates seemingly felt obligated to include, telling NPR that the expected fighting in superhero comics "probably is not the thing that moved my soul."[14] By the end of his five-year stint on the character, Coates struck a clearer balance between philosophical dialogue and superhero action, making his run on the character a fascinating portrait of his development as a writer in the medium.

If there is a primary focus and theme to much of Coates' long arc on *Black Panther*, it is the interrogation of the myth and meaning of Wakanda. For a long time, Wakanda had been an idealized nation in the comics—technologically and politically advanced, unconquered, and unbent. The popular conception of Wakanda almost feels akin to Coates' discussion of his time at Howard University in *Between the World and Me*, where he described the culture at the university as the Mecca, "a machine, crafted to capture and concentrate the dark energy of all African peoples and inject it directly into the student body."[15] Coates writes of the "Mecca" as an idealized place key to his growth as a person and an intellectual, the dream of which is punctured by the murder of one of his fellow students, Prince Jones, at the hands of police—a key recurring point in his book is the notion of brutal American reality puncturing the stories told among Black people and their institutions.[16] Indeed, Coates was an ideal choice to deliver on the potential for the Black Panther as a counter-narrative, turning his own experiences toward challenging dominant societal narratives and collective mythology. As he put it in *We Were Eight Years in Power*:

> What I wanted most was to shine an unblinking light on the entire stage, to tell my people with all the authority I could muster that they were right, that they were not crazy, that it really was all a trick [. . .] I didn't feel like my aims were original or pathbreaking but part of something; I aspired to join a long-line of dream-breakers.[17]

Throughout the "A Nation Under Our Feet" arc, Coates breaks apart the dream of Wakanda and the Black Panther as the natural product of a continuous, unbroken string of tragedy starting with the events of *Doomwar*, showing the cracks forming in the idea of Wakandan inevitability. This question of what

Wakanda is and where it should be hangs over the head and motivations of the entire dramatis personae in the arc. Each character has their own approach and perspective on the truth of Wakanda, from the revolutionary scholar Changamire; his former student Tetu, a metahuman who took Changamire's teachings about revolution and the role of the state to their logical conclusion to foment a rebellion; Zenzi, a young woman with the ability to manipulate and control emotions who acts as Tetu's second-in-command; and most importantly Ayo and Aneka, a pair of renegade Dora Milaje questioning their continued service to a king they see as uninterested in protecting the nation.

Rather than taking advantage of the status quo-destroying events of the Secret Wars storyline to start fresh, Coates' Wakanda picked up right where it left off, with a populist uprising against the Wakandan monarchy owing to the public's perception that T'Challa had largely abandoned them to their own devices. T'Challa, no longer the untouchable king seen before, is first shown in Coates' run on his knees and bleeding, the result of an altercation with a crowd of angry miners whipped into a frenzy by Zenzi's powers.[18] Later, reflecting on the unrest, he likens Wakanda to his own child dying in front of him.[19] Coates spends a great deal interrogating the political and social fallout of the last several years of Wakandan history, and gives the nation a pair of new vigilante heroes in the form of Ayo and Aneka, who steal prototype weapons suits and become known as the Midnight Angels, seeking to protect Wakanda where they felt the royals no longer could.[20] While disputes over the future of Wakanda and how it should be ruled were nothing new, here Coates adds a level of unrest and upheaval, not the product of a supervillain but indirectly the result of T'Challa's own contradictory motivations.

That interrogation, particularly in the first twelve issues of the arc, plays out to a significant degree through the character of Changamire. Changamire, a scholar who teaches at a university in Birnin Azzaria after being exiled from the Wakandan capital for "exhortation against the monarchy," professes a doctrine of Westernized political thought.[21] He cites the works of John Locke (as Coates does in his "A Case for Reparations" piece) to discuss the notion of power and who truly has it. But his student Tetu, the leader of the uprising against T'Challa, accuses him of discussing these ideas primarily in the abstract from the comfort of an academic ivory tower. Tetu turns the words of Locke against his former teacher to justify his actions against the monarchy— "How long will they plunder our people while we stand aside and look? What is my remedy against the robber, who so broke into my house?"[22]

That Coates evokes Locke here is significant to the story he is building. Locke's work specifically lays out that in a state of nature people have unalienable rights but may also enter conflict with one another when those rights are violated; in Locke's view the role of government is to protect the rights of the governed and mediate such disputes when they arise. However, as Locke also is quick to point out, a criminal act conducted by the state is no less criminal than if it were perpetuated by a thief or brigand—except that "great robbers," as he refers to those in power who profit from or exploit those who are not in power, are rewarded rather than punished as they are effectively above the law.[23] Yet, in the passage Changamire quotes, Locke goes on to say "he who conquers in an unjust war can thereby have no title to the subjection and obedience of the conquered"—implying that the people can hold those in power accountable.[24] Therefore, it is not a stretch in Tetu's eyes to argue that the Wakandan government has failed in its duties and the people are no longer obliged to show fealty. Later, after wounding Changamire, Tetu answers the question both Locke and his former teacher posed: "What is our remedy against the robber, who so broke into our house? We burn down the house—with the robber inside."[25] Through Tetu, Coates offers a unique ideological foil to T'Challa that challenges Wakandan inevitability and rightness—at least on a surface level.

Yet, if he is not the revolutionary he educated Tetu to be, Changamire plays a significant role in reassessing Wakanda and the role of the king. He tells Ramonda, his former student, that "Wakanda is science and wonder, all of it achieved by ensuring your subjects do not ask too many questions. Wakanda has all the intelligence any advanced society would want and none of the wisdom any free society needs."[26] After their meeting, Ramonda speaks with T'Challa as he seeks her counsel. When her son says that he has done battle with "world-breakers, death cultists, and men who make themselves gods" and that he sacrificed his relationship with Storm, "the only woman I ever truly loved" for his people and he can give no more, she replies:

> No, T'Challa. Let us not mince words here—you have never given willingly. You feel the weight of the crown, but you have never felt the great honor of being king. Your people are a burden to you, and you have never let them forget this. You say you have given it all. You are wrong. You have never truly given yourself to your country.[27]

This notion—that T'Challa has seen the kingship as a burden rather than a calling—speaks to one of the core ideas that Coates identified as a tension within the character, simply by observing his long publishing history. A superhero and a ruler exist at cross purposes—one tasked with adventuring and reactionary defense, the other tasked with governing and proactive efforts for the good of the people and the nation—and it has historically been challenging for writers to strike this balance. By directly leaning into the contradiction, Coates adds new texture to the character, demanding the reader to reconcile the two drives.

T'Challa also flirts with autocracy to a degree in Coates' run in a manner that is surprising but not wholly out of character. He convenes a secret meeting of different nations' security and secret police specializing in counter-revolutionary tactics to help with the unrest. Alexi Sablinova, the head of internal defense in fictional Marvel autocracy Symkaria, challenges T'Challa's own view of his role:

> You think yourselves men of honor, lowered to the company of repressive thugs. [. . .] In fact there is only one great tradition in Wakanda, and it is the same tradition among us all—the tradition of holding a nation under our feet. You asked for my counsel: Here it is: you lack the will to follow your own mores. Return to your true nature, and your country will be as peaceful as any of ours.[28]

Video of the meeting, in which one of the advisors tells T'Challa to execute people to create a sense of ordered chaos—"Only in terror can a wise man rule"—is leaked by Tetu and Zenzi with the backing of the villain Zeke Stane, who is supporting Wakandan unrest in hopes of obtaining vibranium for his weapons company.[29] Of course, such video would not exist had T'Challa sought to soothe the populace through less oppressive means—a fact Coates points out as a consequence of flirting with the forces of autocracy and fascism, continuing Hickman's flirtation with the Panther's moral ambiguity. However, he was also quick to point out in the letters section (Coates responded to readers himself, which is unusual for a comics author) that he saw T'Challa not as "corrupt" but "wrestling with superhuman powers"—this seems a charitable but fair read of the character's role in the story at this point as trying to apply superhero-style force to a political problem and the problems thereof.[30] Again, the challenge of applying the superhero genre to fundamental issues of equity and justice is raised—and Coates argues such solutions do not necessarily solve the problem.

Throughout Coates' work on *Black Panther*, he challenges the idea of inherent nobility in kinghood. Late in the "A Nation Under Our Feet" storyline, T'Challa seeks counsel with Changamire himself. The two discuss the Edmund Morgan book *American Slavery, American Freedom*, a book on the legacy of slavery in seventeenth-century America Changamire sees as applicable to Wakanda's current state:

> "Can you imagine it? Whole generations brought up with the daily weight of turning their fellow man into slaves. It drove them mad, you understand. [. . .] Whole generations turned to dust. All for the right to live as kings."
>
> "What happened to the slaves?"
>
> "The slaves? It was the slaves who started the war. Their country merely joined in."
>
> "But the slaves are free now, are they not?"

"It is too soon to tell, my king."[31]

Outside of comics, Coates addresses the rhetorical potency and allure of king-ship to the oppressed in an essay entitled "This is How We Lost to the White Man," a critique and challenge to a specific brand of Black conservatism and respectability politics like that espoused by disgraced comedian and activist Bill Cosby that also addressed the Black nationalist sentiment:

> What both visions share is a sense that black culture in its present form is bastardized and pathological. What they also share is a foundation in myth. Black people are not the descendants of kings. We are—and I say this with big pride—the progeny of slaves. If there's any majesty in our struggle, it lies not in fairy tales but in those humble origins and the great distance we've traveled since. Ditto for the dreams of a separate but noble past.[32]

Here neither I, nor I am assuming Coates, intend to suggest that the experi-ence of Black Americans and fictional Wakandans are equal or easily trans-ferred. Yet the foundation of myth—the very force of a fictional collective story to which Coates casts himself as challenger—is crucial in both narra-tives. The justification of subjugation in the name of a myth of Wakandan exceptionalism and the justification of subjugation of Black individuals dur-ing the slave trade in name of a myth of white supremacy are both post-hoc justification for the exertion of power. And, as Coates suggests, the notion of "power" is the center point of his vision of the Black Panther. If T'Challa is given great power, is it right for him to use it with abandon as he does because the notion of Wakanda allows or requires it? T'Challa admits to Changamire that he is the "lesser evil" between himself and the bloody revolution of Tetu, arguing that he has battled numerous godlike foes and even remade entire galaxies and survived universal death —"Do you think I faced the terrors for my own good?" Changamire challenges him. "Of course you did. You have said it yourself. You are not a king, at your heart. You are a hero."[33] While Changamire ultimately agrees to help, Coates' point is largely made—the line between self-gratification and popular benefit has historically been blurry for many rulers.

Throughout the series, the Midnight Angels Ayo and Aneka play a signifi-cant role as agents of change—but the recurring rhetorical rally cry they use is "no one man," the idea that unilateral power should not be concentrated in a single person. Changamire invokes that sentiment when he acts as the spokesperson for a renewed Wakanda and implores the citizens of the nation via a broadcast on the Kimoyo network to join up and reject Tetu in favor of democracy: "The old ways have failed us, this is true. And for a new time we will need new traditions. No one man can possess all the wisdom. No one man can have all the power. But the path to our new country cannot be written in blood and fire. Come back to the house of your ancestors. Let us speak as brothers should."[34]

This new focus for Wakanda is cemented when T'Challa, joined by Shuri and his allies as well as the Midnight Angels and the ancestral spirits of past Black Panthers, faces Tetu once more. Tetu says "No one man can stand against the people!" but T'Challa, his allies and the spirits in unison rejoinder "You are not the people, Jambazi. And we are no man. We are a nation."[35] T'Challa has finally centered himself as a representative of his people, rather than simply a king onto himself—a significant move away from the unquestioned monarchy and nobility previous writers had afforded the character. Coates had reimagined the domain of Wakanda as one not of kings but of a democratized people.

Not all readers agreed with this move. One, Marcus Dennis, wrote to Coates in issue #14 to express his dissatisfaction with the introduction of Western democracy to Wakanda. "I think it's a mistake to 'modernize' the values of the most advanced culture on Earth and a disservice to the core material of what makes Black Panther both entertaining and empowering," Dennis said. "I implore you to stop writing the book as an American, and to write it instead, as a Wakandan," suggesting that the idea of rebelling Dora Milaje and nascent democracy pushed a Westernized mindset.[36] Coates disagreed, citing real-world history:

I'd dispute the idea that a people asking for the right to determine their own, as a people, is culturally "Western". That right was at the heart of many of the great anti-colonial struggles in Africa, and was at the heart of black struggles throughout the Diaspora. Indeed, many of the people who've given democracy its lived meaning were people who were left out of it. There is no history of democracy worth writing that excludes Nelson Mandela.[37]

Coates used Wakanda as a proxy metaphor to comment on American and world history and the struggle for self-representation and democracy. Yet his response is consistent and in keeping with what appears to be his general ongoing internal debate about Black nationalism and what it represents, as he writes in *We Were Eight Years in Power*:

Later I came to feel that nationalism was, ultimately, its own kind of dream. But it was nationalism that gave me a sense of politics separate from the whims of white people. [. . .] If there is a power that has ever surrendered itself purely out of some altruistic sense of justice, I have yet to come across it. Nationalism had its flights of fancy—the vision of a separate state outside America or a separate society within it. Neither could work.[38]

To Coates, the introduction of democracy into Wakanda—in many ways, the closest thing to a Black nationalist state in fiction—is not kowtowing to the demands of Western readers and publishers, but rather a natural and inevitable outcome. Eventually, power must be questioned—and those in power are not always willing to give it up for the greater good but rather must be challenged to do so. For the Black Panther, a character whose political power is every bit the equal if not the superior to his superpowers, this too is a natural philosophical route.

Coates' work on the Black Panther series can really be best thought of as challenging Wakandan myth—and in many ways, the myths it represents by proxy—in three major ways. The first arc, as discussed, challenges the very idea of kingship and centralized power. The second, however, is a more personal one. Coates is open throughout his works and interviews about his atheism, informed largely by both his growing up in an atheist household and his own experiences as a youth seeing the death and destruction of his friends and neighbors at the hands of the legal system in Baltimore. He wrote in *Between the World and Me* that he could not imagine a God on his side and that "my understanding of the universe was physical, and its moral arc bent toward chaos then concluded in a box"; though in *We Were Eight Years in Power* he acknowledged that as important as his atheism was, "my sense of ancestry is its equal."[39]

Yet at the same time, even a writer so focused on challenging societal narratives and mythology could not wholly ignore or devalue religion and the idea of a god or gods watching, as evidenced by his 2017 interview with Michael Eric Dyson for the *Washington Post*:

> I don't know how you grow up black in this country and not have tremendous respect for the church, even though I was raised outside of it. [. . .] Am I drawing some sort of conclusion, or some sort of feeling, that folks get in church anyway, regardless of their belief in Jesus Christ as their savior? Is there a route that they're traveling in their religion that leads to a similar place that I go, even with my lack of religion?[40]

It is not hard to see why such a perspective is an interesting challenge for writing the Black Panther, a character who is not only the ruler of a nation but also its religious and spiritual figurehead and convenes regularly with spirits on the ancestral plane and metaphysical manifestations of his god. Coates' respectful atheism makes for another interesting way in which the very notions of Wakandan myth—and the larger social myths for which it acts as allegory—is explored and challenged.

The second arc, "Avengers of the New World," sees T'Challa posing a simple question as he looks at destructive weather patterns and encroaching supernatural creatures besetting his country—why did the Orisha, the pan-theon of gods to which Wakandans pray, not come to assist Wakanda in their various times of need? It should be noted here that, like much of the rest of Wakandan lore, the concept of "Orisha" is borrowed and altered from real-world cultural traditions—specifically, that of the Yoruba people of south-western Nigeria as well as many members of the larger African Diaspora. Where actual Orisha is described a supernatural force "linking people, objects, and powers" that and incorporates many ideas seen across African cultures, including the importance of ancestors, for the purposes of Marvel Comics lore it is used as the name for a pantheon of gods led by Bast.[41] T'Challa convenes with Storm, with whom he is once again on friendly terms, and asks if she, as someone who was worshipped as a goddess, knows. Hinting that T'Challa's question should be whether such beings exist, she says that in her experience "is that the more the people believed, the stronger I grew. If I was not divine, the strength I drew from their belief made me feel as though I was."[42]

Coates' inclusion of the last line indicates a critical perspective in which gods too act as a sort of myth given power by their adherents, not unlike the American Dream or democracy or even Wakanda in text. Yet, he also acknowledges the power of those stories. Earlier in his run on the character, Shuri is revealed to be in suspended animation, as a means of keeping her alive following the grievous injuries she sustained in the defense of Wakanda during the attack by Thanos and the Black Order. During her unconscious-ness, she travels across the Djalia, the Wakandan ancestral plane of memory, and trains under the Griot, a manifestation of the concept of memories and story from Wakanda's past. The Griot, which takes the form of her mother Ramonda (and appears in different forms to other characters based largely on the parental figure most important to them) informs her that on the Djalia, she will be armed "not with the spear, but with the drum, for it is the drum that carries the greatest power of all [. . .] the power of memory, daughter, the power of our song."[43] When she returns to consciousness, she is effectively reborn as what the Griot refers to as "Aja-Adanna, keeper of Wakandan lore. The bearer of what was . . . what is . . . and again shall be."[44]

The move is significant, as it makes Shuri a more important standalone character and operationalizes the importance of story to Wakanda in the form of literal empowerment, giving Shuri abilities reflective of the lore and his-tory of Wakanda, such as the ability to turn her skin to stone and fly as a flock of birds. Shuri also acts as a spiritual anchor and link to the "deep past" of Wakanda, manifested as the written history and oral story of the land and its people as a "past so deep it's not even the past."[45] The importance of ancestry, history, and story echo through much of Coates' work—in fact, as he often suggests, the current reality cannot exist separate of it. It is significant that

Shuri is given her own ability and direction tied to these ideas, as they serve to interrogate many of Coates' own about the importance of myth and story and how they become meaningful reality.

Storm too plays a significant role in this narrative, as Coates' run is characterized much like the *Black Panther* film as a celebration and recognition of the importance of women and femininity to African culture as well as the history of the character. Storm's perception as a goddess by people across the continent has been well-established in the character's history, with her ability to control weather serving both as a means of protecting the innocent as well as helping the environment. In this arc, she is given the name "Hadari Yao," or the "walker of clouds," by the people who see her as a goddess—a title and recognition for which she is grateful but hesitant—" . . . this power that I glimpsed today. The power of faith and divinity . . . what of those who gleefully embrace that divinity, who lust after it? What of those who are not wary of power . . . but consumed by it?"[46]

Storm's question appears to be answered when T'Challa suspects that the creatures harassing Wakanda are related to the efforts of a returning Klaw, who has thrown his lot in with Zenzi, Tetu, Ezekiel Stane, and Doctor Faustus as a group with a mutual goal of defeating and overthrowing T'Challa using counterfeit vibranium (known as "reverbium"). More importantly, the Griot reveals that the very notion of Wakanda as an unconquered, uncolonized land is itself a lie—the first Wakandans had come into contact with a race of creatures known as the Originators, the indigenous inhabitants of the land, who were defeated by the Wakandans after the Orisha gave their blessing and aid in exchange for the Wakandans' faith—"And upon the land of the Originators, upon the land seized by the pilgrims and their young gods . . . we built the most advanced society ever known to man."[47] In perhaps his most radical departure from the dogma of what had come before in the Panther mythos, Coates made the Wakandans—the long-standing symbol of an anti-colonialist mindset—colonizers themselves, their prosperity earned through the subjugation of others. The Griot underscores Coates' approach to myth and faith in their entreaty to T'Challa:

> [D]id you truly believe that a great nation could be built without another under-foot? [. . .] Every man is the hero of his own story, the champion of his chosen myth. But you are a king, and while the people can afford to live in myth, you cannot. [. . .] Your burden is to act, my king, knowing that to be human is to be ignoble and fallen.[48]

As if to set aside the more mundane concerns of the Panther's existence, Coates writes a scene in which T'Challa uses a destabilizing device to dismantle Klaw's new reverbium body, turning his long-time adversary and

primary antagonistic metaphor into chunks of inert matter and, metaphorically destroying a part of the Panther mythology perhaps used too often by
writers in an effort to move onto larger matters. With this, the Panther
reunites the country under a common banner once and for all, only for
the supposed Originator god Sefako to appear, revealing himself to be the
long-standing X-Men nemesis The Adversary. The Adversary, who had freed
the Originators that were causing havoc across Wakanda, proves to be too
much for the heroes to handle and traps Storm—the only person capable of
fighting him—under a pile of rubble, triggering her claustrophobia. In a message that encapsulates the arc's primary themes, T'Challa sends a message
of encouragement to his former wife that underscores the idea that whatever
power religion has comes from the faithful: "I am the king of Wakanda. I am
the nation incarnate. And on behalf of that nation, I say: let the faith of all of
Wakanda power you. That faith is more than any mutation. It is a gift of godhead, passed down from your ancestors. Claim the gift. Let this be the hour
when gods again stalk the land."[49] With the faith of the nation, Storm easily
defeats the Adversary. In the end, Coates' skepticism about godhood is outweighed by his recognition of the power of faith and belief—an extension of
his larger idea that breaking myth and having faith are far from incompatible.

The question of the Orisha and their whereabouts remained unanswered
until Coates' third and final arc—"The Intergalactic Empire of Wakanda."
Here, Coates ties together all the themes introduced so far into his longest
and most challenging story, which interrogates both the legacy of Wakanda's
unknown colonialist past and the natural outcome of its policies. The
twenty-five-issue arc—far longer than a normal single superhero story—
begins with the premise that a group of Wakandans far into the future have
established a colony in the far reaches of space that takes the Wakandan ethos
of self-defense to its logical and radical conclusion by destroying and conquering all potential foes and threats. This new empire, Coates' introduction
warns, has "set their acquisitive eyes on a new galaxy—our own" and that
only one man can stop them—"A king who was reduced to a slave, a slave
who advanced into legend."[50]

The idea of a Wakanda that uses its advantages and resources to exert its
will across the galaxy gave Coates opportunity to challenge the notion of
empire and where it comes from—as well as extend his cynicism about the
idea of gods and goddesses, as it is revealed that Bast and the Orisha left the
earthbound Wakandans in search of finding a more devoted people, and the
imperialist space Wakandans fit the bill as fanatics.[51] Those who speak of
empire, Coates seems to argue, see themselves as favored by the gods—and
from the perspective of one who sees no comfort in the idea of a supernatural
Other, it is not a stretch to imagine the gods implicitly validating those acts.
Bast has chosen as her new avatar N'Jadaka (as is explained in the series,

most members of the new Wakandan empire take names from Wakandans throughout history, and it is no accident that he took Killmonger's Wakandan name), who explains to her the necessity of his actions:

> I razed whole star systems, imposed order where there was none, brought the purifying light of your gospel. They called me a monster. But I knew that the weak crumble, while the strong endure. Only among the strong can a durable peace be made. [. . .] I knew then the folly of my ancestors, who sought to avoid war through defense. Conquest was the only defense.[52]

N'Jadaka, who used the power of the Klyntar (for those not immersed in Marvel lore, the Klyntar are the name of a race of symbiotic alien creatures that bond with other living beings to give them immense power and ability, the most notable of which is the Spider-Man antagonist Venom) to overthrow the previous king, sees his power challenged by a slave from one of the empire's vibranium mining outposts—our T'Challa, though bereft of his name and his memories. The effect of removing T'Challa from his support network and rebuilding him as a different hero is not unlike what Liss did in the Hell's Kitchen-era series, but where those felt like diversions from the character's central thesis, the "Intergalactic Empire" series feels like an essential part of it. In this story, Coates explores another theme common in his work, and not for the first time in the pages of a Black Panther comic—the connection between name, body, and identity. The recasting of T'Challa as a nameless slave—a man out of time and out of place—echoes Coates' ideas about disembodiment. Coates opines on the role of the body to the Black identity and concept of self as a recurring theme in *Between the World and Me*, and remarks upon how disembodiment and destruction of that body by destructive white supremacist structures is a "a kind of terrorism, and the threat of it alters the orbit of all our lives and, like terrorism, this distortion is intentional."[53] Here, T'Challa's body is not broken but his name and heritage are, and in Coates' view the heritage and the body are linked and must be reclaimed when taken or destroyed.

Coates explores this idea first in the previous "Avengers of the New World" arc, where T'Challa and a team of Wakandan heroes investigate the disappearance of the Wakandan woman Asiri (known to long-time readers as Queen Divine Justice from the Priest run), doing battle with a team of supervillains including Eliot "Thunderball" Franklin. After dispatching the villains, T'Challa speaks with Franklin to remind him he had another role before—that of a genius scientist in the field of gamma radiation whose work the king admired. Scoffing, Franklin says he was referred to as "the Black Bruce Banner," to which T'Challa admonishes him:

No, Dr. Franklin. Dr. Eliot Augustus Franklin. The names these people give us—as though they know us better than our fathers, or our own deeds. [. . .] To them, we are only shadows of their glory, never our beautiful, original selves. [. . .] I believe that you are a brilliant man. But more, I believe you were a good man once. And that you might well be again. [. . .] It is not too late to recover your own name.[54]

Not only does this scene reify the idea of a reclamation of self and identity as the first step toward actualization—echoing Coates' negotiations with his own identity—it also reinforces a long-running notion of the Black Panther as an elder Black statesman of the Marvel universe. Coates, in a letter column, indicated that he found Hudlin's idea that T'Challa was "not just revered in Wakanda, but by other black meta humans" interesting and felt that T'Challa's "great power isn't in his suit, it's in his power as an inspirational figure."[55]

Yet, in the "Intergalactic Empire" arc, that knowledge and ability is stripped and T'Challa must again find it. In one scene a fellow slave chastises him to not let the Empire steal his humanity and mind after he gets into a fight with another slave.[56] T'Challa is rescued from his predicament by a group of rebels known as the Maroons led by the alien Captain N'Yami (in a significant nod, she shares her name with T'Challa's birth mother), who informs him that he is considered one of the Nameless, a slave caste from whom the Empire has stolen their names and memory in order to assure their compliance. This acts as a clear allegory to the practice of giving slaves in the Atlantic slave trade era new names to erase their cultural identity and rebrand them as property.[57] T'Challa accompanies them on their ship, the *Mackendal*, where they give him his name once more as "T'Challa, whose name in Old Wakandan translates to 'he who put the knife where it belonged'" and suggesting the name is often adopted by those hoping for a reincarnation of the great king.[58] Eventually, following N'Yami's death at the hands of the Empire, T'Challa consults with Nakia, another Maroon who was part of the Empire before turning against it, who gives him a video recording of N'Yami where she confirms her knowledge of his real identity. He comes around to who he is and joins the fight officially, crossing his arms over his chest in the traditional Wakandan salute—a gesture used in an example of transmedia borrowing from the films but also carrying significance as reference to the pharaohs of Egypt and West African sculpture where kings would be posed or buried with their arms over the chest (in addition, it is also very similar to the ASL symbol for "hug" or "love," representing affection and community).[59] I propose that this scene in context acts not only as a cinematic reference but also as a continuation of the theme of reclamation of identity and heritage—a celebration of those ancestors that had come before. Coates riddles his intergalactic Wakandan culture with allusions to the history of the Diaspora—the rebel Maroons are named for the fugitive slaves who fought for Haitian independence in the 1700s, and N'Yan's ship is named for their leader, François Makandal.[60] Coates is interested in challenging myth at the same time he pays homage to the reality of the ancestors he so admires.

Such ideas are directly in line with Coates' stated goal of writing T'Challa and Wakanda as a product of the Diaspora "or the Atlantic world," a concept not without its challenges.[61] Coates often used *Black Panther*'s monthly letter column as a space for public musings about his beliefs in what the character should be. While recognizing that while he tried to have the character and his homeland reflect "many of the traditions of the black Diaspora, from the continent to the Caribbean," he also added the Black Panther "somewhat problematically, is a creation of the Western imagination. I've tried to write in such a way that doesn't infantilize the continent from which he hails."[62] Beyond decolonizing the map of Wakanda itself, Coates thought perhaps more than any other Panther author of Wakanda as a place with resources and history beyond the magic catch-all of vibranium, with the Alkama fields and their historical value as a significant part of the conflict between Wakanda and Niganda, the latter of which felt the former stole them unlawfully centuries ago.[63] Wakanda, in Coates' view, exists as the sum of fictional and real-world geopolitical and social forces, and by the end of the "Intergalactic Empire of Wakanda" arc T'Challa has returned with his new Maroon allies to his homeland (Wakanda Prime, as Coates calls it) pursued by a thought-dead emperor who reanimates the body of Killmonger to battle T'Challa one last time.

More important, however, is the internal battle between T'Challa, his nation's legacy, and his own responsibilities. It is revealed in issue #12 that T'Challa became obsessed with the question of where the Great Mound of vibranium originated from, primarily out of concern for what Wakanda's enemies would do if they found a ready source of the material—an obsession, it turns out, that he shared with his birth mother and which provided the basis for Wakanda's early space program. T'Challa sends a ship out to find where the vibranium came from and travels with his ally Eden to find it after it disappears, but the two travel through a time fold that sends them two thousand years into the future just as the explorers that came before had—making T'Challa himself indirectly responsible for the rise of the brutal Wakandan Empire. As he mused in a later issue, "so attractive was their war-making that our gods deserted us for them. Is that our future? Is that who we are fated to become?"[64]

It is at this juncture that Coates' other writings become important to understanding how he utilizes the Black Panther to explore the restorative power of a nation coming to terms with who it is and righting past wrongs. Shuri and T'Challa speak with the Griot, who suggests that it is necessary to destroy the Djalia plane to restore the names and memories of the Nameless and in so doing enlist their aid to stop the Empire. T'Challa balks, saying it is too much upon Wakanda (and arguably, himself), to which the Griot replies "No, T'Challa. It is life. It is Wakanda as it has always been," suggesting that this is their responsibility to make up for their ancestors' "folly" in taking the land from the Originators.[65] T'Challa comes to realize that he is ultimately responsible for the Empire's actions, and that he initially "indulged in a dream" when forced to confront it "until I was expelled from it . . . and forced to see the truth."[66] Bast even takes him to task for blaming her for leaving for a new society of followers:

> Was it Bast who sent those Wakandans out into the stars? Was it Bast who hunted the five galaxies for your precious vibranium? It is the circle. The child who is the mother. [. . .] It is a burden, I know. But you birthed it, and now you will carry it. [. . .] Curse your god, if you wish. I've seen it in every age. But in this matter, curse your kings first.[67]

Not only does Coates put the lie to the idea that colonialism is a divine mandate by suggesting the gods would simply align themselves with those they saw as the most powerful, but he also digs into the collective myths a nation tells itself about its rightness, in which it sees past atrocities as history irrelevant to the present. This was one of the fundamental underpinnings in Coates' 2014 "A Case for Reparations" article, where he argued that the forces of white supremacy that have held Black Americans back for centuries are "a force so fundamental to America that it is difficult to imagine the country without it" and that reparations go beyond the financial:

> Reparations—by which I mean the full acceptance of our collective biography and its consequences—is the price we must pay to see ourselves squarely. [. . .] What I'm talking about is a national reckoning that would lead to spiritual renewal. [. . .] Reparations would mean a revolution of the American consciousness, a reconciling of our self-image as the great democratizer with the facts of our history.[68]

Coates adds that such intellectual honesty "would represent America's maturation out of the childhood myth of its innocence into a wisdom worthy of its founders."[69] But, as Coates acknowledges in his essay, the necessity of such a thing does not make it easy or simple for the public to accept. Nor does it guarantee they would recognize it. Coates illustrates this point in a conversation between T'Challa and Storm in issue #18, as Storm recounts her trips to Harlem in her youth and her puzzlement over seeing anger in the "land of opportunity": "What I know now is that empires built on slavery are very good at concealing that fact. That the concealing, the lie, is part of the enslaving. And there I was in a country that had four hundred years to perfect that lie."⁷⁰

And so, it is important that Wakanda acts here as the source of historical colonialism and opportunism, a chance for a reader to open their minds to considering the fallacy of such myth when they may be hesitant to do so with their own myths. I argue that Wakanda is seen here as a metaphor for America, historically and innately convinced of its own rightness, and T'Challa's arc not just in this story but since Coates' first issue was to challenge and mature out of that idea. It is Ramonda who offers the most explicit statement of Coates' reparations thesis as she offers the Originators just that to seek their help against the encroaching Empire:

> I come not in service of mockery, Originator . . . but reparation. We cannot heal what we have done. We cannot return to you what was taken. [. . .] But we also need not act as though that plunder did not happen. Nor pretend that our beloved Wakanda is without stain. It has taken time to see ourselves fully, to understand our faults. To accept. To remember.⁷¹

The united forces of the Originators, the Maroons, the restored Nameless, the Wakandan Prime armies, and (in an important symbolic gesture) other Black heroes including Luke Cage, Monica Rambeau, Miles Morales, and Riri "Ironheart" Williams help defeat N'Jadaka and his Empire, leading to a new unified Wakanda bringing together both the intergalactic colonies as well as the indigenous Originators and all other people seeking a new home. T'Challa, a reluctant king, has now become an emperor, anxious about his new role. Once again, Storm counsels him and ties Coates' themes together:

> But in the eyes of all the assembled worlds, you are something much more. And there is not just pain but also beauty in that. Think of all the outcasts— shunned, beaten down, told to go back to some strange land they never knew. But they have found it now, and it is not so strange. You did this, you opened Wakanda, and then you transformed it from a name that inspires fear, to one that gives hope.⁷²

Coates' run, apart from its longevity—at fifty issues of a main series as well as consulting and co-writing work on other titles, he acts as one of the longest-serving *Panther* writers perhaps behind only Christopher Priest—is notable for the degree to which it challenges the very foundation of the character. Where other Panther writers challenge Wakanda's innate sense of superiority and isolationist tendencies or present them as a background in a different tale, Coates engages with it head on and rejects it. In Coates' view, Wakanda is not a geographic location but the locus of myth, story, pain, and reparation, an ideal to live up to even when reality falls short.

In the final issue, T'Challa utters the line "the miracle is Wakanda," meant to represent the collective action of Wakanda and its diasporic allies and family as well as a nation that may have been attacked and beaten physically but is also as Narcisse suggests, "the spirit of the people that remains unconquered."[73] He engages with similar themes in his *Captain America* run—his title character there spends much of his time ruminating via internal monologue on what it means to be a symbol of an American Dream that few believe in—but it is Wakanda, existing between the physical and the metaphysical; the present, the future, and the past; and the intersection between legacy and self-determination that creates a volume which speaks to the unique experiences of America and the Diaspora.

THE "IMPRINT"

In a piece for *The Hollywood Reporter,* writer Graeme McMillan suggests that Marvel Comics had historically shied away from the creator-led "imprint" idea, in which a single creator curates a line of comics, but that Coates' time with the Black Panther "was the closest Marvel came to the idea."[74] As McMillan points out, Coates's run on the flagship brought in many new writers of color, many of whom were also new to the medium, and together they created a consistent collaborative vision for the Wakandan corner of the Marvel Universe. It is not unusual for a domain of characters to fall under the auspices of a single editor for continuity reasons—historically, Spider-Man, the X-Men, and other big brands have had their own dedicated offices. It was, however, the first time the Black Panther had an entire set of coordinating titles in service of one larger story spanning multiple authors and perspectives—many of which Coates co-authored or consulted on to create a cohesive narrative whole and which ranged from lighthearted adventure to new audience onboarding to insight into the American socioeconomic reality.

One such series, on which Coates traded writing duties with poet and college professor Yona Harvey, was the short-lived 2016 reinvention of Christopher Priest's equally short-lived *Black Panther* spin-off *The Crew.* Entitled *Black Panther & The Crew* to signify its status as a companion piece to the main storyline, the series ran around the first year of Coates' Panther book, unofficially starting off with a tie-in appearance from the title heroes in issue #7 of the main series. Harvey, like her friend Coates, had never written a comic book before but Coates recommended her for the job due to her poetry experience and ability to say a great deal in a small amount of space.[75] *Black Panther & The Crew* maintained a similar structure to its predecessor, with each issue focused on and narrated by a different member of the titular Crew, including T'Challa, Misty Knight, Luke Cage, Storm, and the mutant

Manifold as they worked together to find out why an old man named Ezra Keith has died in police custody and why that death brought them all to Harlem. If the main book was where Coates interrogated the higher-minded, nebulous ideas of faith, leadership, the body, and history, *The Crew* is where those ideas became street-level, speaking to the American Black experience with depictions of police brutality, the Black liberation movement, systemic racism, and gentrification.

But fundamentally it too is a story about legacy, as Keith is revealed to have been the Lynx, the leader of a Harlem-based team of Black costumed vigilantes known as the Crusade in the 1950s. To each member of the Crew, he meant something different—to police detective Misty Knight, he was an anti-cop rabble-rouser, to Storm a welcoming friend and confidant in America, to Luke a mentor, and to T'Challa the apparent beneficiary of stolen Wakandan biotechnology. Misty, the police officer, maintains a level of skepticism about Keith that her compatriots do not share, bristling at the idea of intersectionality when Storm mentions being both Black and a mutant despite her own complex intersectional identity as a Black woman and police officer. Knight also brushes up against systemic racism her own badge cannot shield her from, running afoul of the private cybernetic police force known as the Americops, whose programming does not recognize Knight's badge and beat her and Keith's niece Hazel into submission while shouting "STOP RESISTING!"[76] While the idea of a robotic police force existing at the intersection of police, military, private industry, and patriotism owes its material form to the realm of science fiction, the post-9/11 intertwining of supposed national security interests intertwined with a system that encourages militarization of the police is all too real. As Howard Bryant notes in his crucial volume on sports activism *The Heritage*, this is nothing new in culture, popular or otherwise:

> To the public, cops and military were interchangeable, even though the two occupations were markedly different. One did very little on domestic soil, the other no business on foreign land [. . .] In the new world of fighting terror, police and military fell under one giant 9/11 umbrella: heroes. [. . .] Except that the conflation wasn't harmless, nor was it merely semantics. [. . .] If in the minds of the public, police and military served the same function in a time of terror, it only stood to reason they should be able to use the same equipment, employ the same tactics, wear the same gear.[77]

Indeed, as police departments continue using surplus military equipment in the name of "urban pacification," utilize artificial intelligence disproportionately biased against people of color, and create databases of supposed predictive criminal tendencies to prevent "future crime," the idea of a robotic police force programmed to excessively and selectively exercise authority against people of color in the name of patriotism seems almost quaint.[78] Misty and Luke Cage visit Paul Keane, the head of Paragon Industries—the company that built the Americops—and he offers a profuse apology for the attack and that the Americops offer "not just law, but justice—blind and inconsiderate of any . . . extenuating factors."[79] Understanding the elephant in the room at the end of the sentence, Luke and Misty call him out, wondering why the Americops responded to attack "two girls literally just strolling through a park" but not a bombing at Luke Cage's apartment earlier. When Keane protests the insinuation that the Americops do not protect all of New York equally, Misty replies "I'm saying I don't think you protect people at all. You protect interests. You protect property"—a line that cuts deeply when one reflects on the violent tactics taken by real-world police to attack protestors in the name of private property.[80] At the same time, the mysterious Paragon Properties is building a new set of luxury condominiums threatening to gentrify much of Harlem's population out of the neighborhood. Here, the metaphor becomes a pointed one as T'Challa likens Harlem's situation to his own back home over images of white faces gawking at Harlem natives and asking for extra kale at restaurants: "For centuries, Wakanda held empire at bay. Cloistered behind our walls, we rained death upon all invaders. But Wakanda is not what it was. And empire is a plague—insidious and relentless. And could it be that empire anywhere . . . meant empire everywhere?"[81] In the modern era, *The Crew* seems to argue, colonization happens at multiple levels of culture.

Storm and T'Challa go undercover as a young couple looking to purchase one of the new condominiums, where their realtor claims to have been a Black Studies major at Empire State University and raves about Frank Ocean and that "as more creatives and Millennials move in, we're taking Harlem back to its glory days. It's the Renaissance, you know?"[82] Invoking and appropriating the Harlem Renaissance—an explosion of Black talent, creativity, and art—and suggesting that gentrification would recreate it seems like the sort of empire T'Challa lamented, and the cultural takeover quickly becomes something more tangible as it is revealed that both Paragon outfits are part of a shell company for Nazi splinter group and supervillain faction HYDRA, who is seeking to foment a riot by using Zenzi's powers to whip the anti-gentrification crowd into a frenzy and justify the destruction of the neighborhood and its people. The plot is foiled but not before it is revealed that Ezra's nephew Malik had been working with HYDRA the entire time and was in fact his uncle's killer. The reader discovers that the Wakandan emissary who had given Ezra and his compatriots their powers in the 1950s was a HYDRA plant too and the pursuit of power aided by their technology led to a violent schism in the group as his ally Frank turned to more criminal acts under the guise of liberation and revolution. Ezra had tried to bring all the heroes together to form a new crew, unburdened but educated by that legacy—unfortunately, the series ended too early because of low sales to see what would have come next. While a small part of the overall legacy of the Coates years, *The Crew* arguably surpassed its source material and acts as a small-scale but powerful interrogation of how the intersection of race, class, and resources determines power in America.

Roxane Gay, another author known for her focus on feminist essays, most notably the *Bad Feminist* collection, was enlisted to write *Black Panther: World of Wakanda*, a companion series focused on the Midnight Angels, Ayo and Aneka. Gay, who Coates became familiar with after attending a reading of her zombie short story, jumped at the chance to write "black women and queer black women into the Marvel Universe" and to help combat the underrepresentation of people of color in the industry.[83] In World of Wakanda, the motives of the two women are given more time to unspool—they are distressed by their king's seeming lack of interest in protecting the country and chafe against their burden of loyalty to him at the same time they fall in love—an act that is implicitly forbidden, as the Dora Milaje are intended only as potential wives for the king despite T'Challa's disapproval of the tradition. The Dora Milaje are also given greater complexity, as they gradually start to push away from the kingship and go into the business of protecting Wakanda unmoored by the responsibility—and the focus on these characters underscores the significance of Black women and femininity to the Panther mythos. Gay's words are beautiful and the relationship powerful, but the series abruptly and unceremoniously ends not with Gay's contribution but a standalone issue reintroducing Kasper Cole into modern continuity to little meaningful effect.

Africanfuturist author of *Who Fears Death* and *The Binti Trilogy* Nnedi Okorafor was perhaps one of the most prolific writers in the ersatz Black Panther "imprint," contributing two series and a brief trilogy of one-shots. 2017's *Long Live the King*, a relatively light sci-fi adventure tale in which T'Challa traces to the origins of apparent giant monsters attacking Wakanda to decades-old experiments attempting to create sentient vibranium, was nonetheless evocative of her Nigerian-American background. Okorafor's characters, from T'Challa to the surrounding cast, adopt Nigerian slang in their dialogue—particularly the onomatopoeia "mscheew." Sometimes spelled "mtcheew," the term is used as a sigh of disapproval in Nigeria and West Africa, meant to signify the sound of inhaling and hissing through one's teeth.[84] Similarly, the series explores differing systems of government within Wakanda as T'Challa involves himself with one of the Mute Zones, small democracies operating just outside of the golden city's sphere of influence. Okorafor, who is Igbo, writes in an essay concluding her series that there is a saying, "Igbo enwe eze" that translates to "The Igbo have no king," a state-ment reflective of their popular democracy. In the essay, she wrote of how writing a king coming from this background gave her pause, but concluded:

> What I feel I was able to give to T'Challa and Wakanda, I think I also took from it. I'll always have a strained relationship with any type of monarchy, but I've learned this one is struggling with its own success, structure, and evolution. And I've also learned that there are many different types of freedom in the country of Wakanda.[85]

Okorafor's statement echoes Coates' own interest in making the Black Panther part of the Atlantic and African Diaspora, a perspective that naturally requires the inclusion and negotiation of a myriad of different perspectives and backgrounds—some of which may brush up harshly against the source material. That connection also appears to have been a personal one. Okorafor, who considers herself an Africanfuturist rather than an Afrofuturist author because her work is specifically "rooted in the history and traditions of the continent, without a desire to look toward Western culture," was also once a star athlete who was paralyzed following an attempt to correct her scolio-sis and had to relearn how to walk.[86] Okorafor channeled that story into the creation of Ngozi (who shares a name with one of her sisters), a Nigerian teenager first appearing in 2017's *Venomverse: War Stories* and returning for a solo story in the final issue of *Long Live the King.* Ngozi is confined to a wheelchair until she encounters a Venom symbiote that allows her to walk again, which leads her to becoming the new interim Black Panther after her universe's T'Challa dies.[87]

Okorafor also contributed two more female-centric series—the first, *Wakanda Forever*, was really an anthology of "one-shot" issues that told a cohesive story of a group of Dora Milaje teaming up with Spider-Man, the Avengers, and the X-Men to track down Malice on behalf of the king. The second, *Shuri*, expands on the title character's role and power set from the main series, running roughly concurrent with the early parts of the "Intergalactic Empire" storyline and interweaving not only Shuri's adven-tures with the larger Marvel universe (she collaborates with Tony Stark and her consciousness inhabits the tree creature Groot for a time) but also con-textualizes Wakanda within greater Africa. In issue #4, General Okoye of the Dora Milaje discovers that Ramonda has been convening a secret council of female representatives from across Africa called the Egungun as part of an effort T'Challa had made earlier to reach out to Wakanda's neighbors. When Okoye asks what Wakanda could need from them, one replies "Do you Dora Milaje not speak Hausa? The language of 30% of my country? Or maybe you think you all made it up."[88] Drawing upon Okorafor's Africanfuturist style and interests, *Shuri* attempted to reconcile the more scientifically-minded version of the character from the film with the spiritually-minded one of Coates' series, which Okorafor noted as a challenge until the first cover showed character that was a fusion of both and was "strong, beautiful, and African."[89] If Coates tried to reconcile Wakanda with America, Okorafor brought out its connection to the continent that served as its inspiration.

Coates also brought Evan Narcisse, a well-known and regarded journalist and critic specializing in popular articles on comic books and video games, into the fold to take primary writing duties on *Rise of the Black Panther*, a six-issue miniseries intended to act as a gateway for fans of the film to access the Panther's comic adventures. Narcisse had conducted in-depth interviews with Coates on the character as well as written extensively on the Panther's legacy and history, leading Marvel editor Will Moss to reach out to Coates to recruit him.[90] *Rise* was both an introduction to and reconciliation of the character's nearly six decades of continuity, implementing additions both obscure (Jakarra, the energy monster from Kirby's 1970s run) and well-known (Hunter, T'Challa's adopted brother from the Priest run) from the pantheon of writers that helped shape the character. It contextualized him in the twin domains of international politics and familial relationships as the hero negotiated Wakanda's presence on the world stage and battled familiar adversaries like Doctor Doom, Killmonger, and Klaw. At the same time, the series introduced quirky new wrinkles like the Panther's ability to sense vibranium energy signatures as the product of the mineral's impact on the flora and faunae of Wakanda including the heart-shaped herb that granted his powers and heightened senses, which Narcisse saw as a "neat feedback loop" on vibranium's importance to the character.[91] But it is in an essay published in the final issue of this run that Narcisse sums up the appeal of the Black Panther as well—and maybe better—than any other writer:

> He was a king of a hidden land learning to fit in with Earth's Mightiest Heroes. As the shy kid of Haitian immigrants growing up in New York City, I knew that struggle on a smaller scale. [. . .] I've always loved how the Black Panther stands at the crossroads of tradition and modernity, with the fate of a whole country resting on his shoulders. [. . .] T'Challa's a hero who moves through history and makes it at the same time.[92]

In many ways, this statement summarizes the mission statement of this volume—to identify the Black Panther as a fictional character existing and operating in larger real-world contexts, forever shaped by global and social history. Narcisse saw the theme of the story as "what do we do with what we inherit" both for himself and for the character, and made an effort to write his story in a way that would fit into the continuity established by the previous authors.[93] When I asked him what he thought about what the different creatives and eras of the character contributed, his response spoke to another fundamental aspect of the character:

> So, one of my main theses about Black Panther's publishing history is that I think first and foremost, every time somebody Black touches the character, the character takes a big evolutionary leap, right? [. . .] Yeah, it may have been the creation of two middle-aged Jewish guys, but ultimately the Black creators and the Black fanbase I think largely co-authored the iteration of Wakanda that became so popular. You think about somebody like Dwayne Turner, that *Panther's Prey* series, it's gorgeous! And you don't do that unless you love that character. You don't put in all that work unless you're like okay, let's really blow this all the way out.[94]

In the Coates era, a super-staff of writers and artists of color ultimately made good on the long-standing promise and potential of the Black Panther character and what had come before—and in so doing used the character to speak to issues both mundane and spiritual in the Black community and the broader African Diaspora, inspiring a new and growing fanbase. That these stories come not through investigative journalism, but high-concept fiction is intentional. In a 2021 interview about the reactionary backlash to the New York Times' *1619 Project*, Coates (who had recently been announced as the writer behind a new Superman movie for Warner Bros.) explained what he saw as the value of fiction in changing the ideological imagination:

> And I just think so much of our rhetoric about what we think is quote unquote "politics" actually displays our imagination. [. . .] I'm not done with opinion journalism yet, but it really, really occurred to me that there's a generation that is being formed right now that's deciding what they will allow to be possible. What they will be capable of imagining. And the root of that isn't necessarily the kind of journalism that I love that I was doing, the root of that is the stories we tell. And I just I wanted to be a part of that fight.[95]

It is not overmuch a stretch to imagine that the stories told on the comics page and on screen about the Black Panther will resonate in ways both small and perhaps bigger in the mind of the readers who enjoy them and go on to become active in their communities and the world at large. Certainly, the news that *12 Years a Slave* screenwriter John Ridley and artist Juann Cabal have taken on writing and art duties for the *Black Panther* series going forward is exciting, with Ridley's promise that it would focus on the political intrigue, espionage, and action surrounding the character as well as embracing the contemporary Black experience and the emotions of "love and caring and hope and regret."[96] But those impacts and the future of the character will be even more significant because of what Coates, Gay, Okorafor, Harvey, Narcisse, and others have done with Panther in his most modern incarnations—not only to challenge and add new texture and dimension to a long-standing comics hero and what he represents, but also to imagine that hero as part of an ongoing conversation about who we are and who we can be.

NOTES

1. Narcisse, "'The miracle is Wakanda."
2. NPR Staff, "Ta-Nehisi Coates."
3. Gustines, "Ta-Nehisi Coates."
4. Narcisse, "Ta-Nehisi Coates Is Trying to Do Right."
5. Ibid.
6. Opam, "Wakanda Reborn."
7. Ibid.
8. NPR Staff, "Ta-Nehisi Coates."
9. Yarm, "Ta-Nehisi Coates Fights the Power."
10. Narcisse, "The miracle is Wakanda."
11. McMillan, "Ta-Nehisi Coates Leaving Marvel's 'Black Panther.'"
12. Ibid.
13. Narcisse, "Ta-Nehisi Coates Is Trying to Do Right."
14. NPR Staff, "Ta-Nehisi Coates."
15. Coates, *Between the World and Me*, 40.
16. Coates, *Between the World and Me.*
17. Coates, *We Were Eight Years in Power*, 212.
18. Coates et al., "A Nation Under Our Feet Part 1."
19. Coates et al., "A Nation Under Our Feet Part 3."
20. Coates et al., "A Nation Under Our Feet Part 1."
21. Coates et al., "A Nation Under Our Feet Part 4," 4.
22. Coates et al., "A Nation Under Our Feet Part 2," 18.
23. Locke, "Second Treatise."
24. Locke, "Second Treatise," 55–56.
25. Coates et al., "A Nation Under Our Feet Part 7," 23.
26. Coates et al., "A Nation Under Our Feet Part 4," 10; "A Nation Under Our Feet Part 5."
27. Coates et al., "A Nation Under Our Feet Part 4," 16.
28. Coates et al., "A Nation Under Our Feet Part 5," 11.
29. Ibid, 23.
30. Coates et al., "A Nation Under Our Feet Part 7," 24.
31. Coates et al., "A Nation Under Our Feet Part 10," 15.
32. Coates, *We Were Eight Years in Power*, 26.
33. Coates et al., "A Nation Under Our Feet Part 10," 16.
34. Coates et al., "A Nation Under Our Feet Part 11," 14–15.

35. Ibid, 22–23.

36. Coates et al., "Avengers of the New World Part 2," 24.

37. Ibid, 24.

38. Coates, *We Were Eight Years in Power*, 212–13.

39. Coates, *Between the World and Me,* 28; Coates, *We Were Eight Years in Power,* 212.

40. Dyson, "Ta-Nehisi Coates on education, religion, and Obama."

41. Brandon, "Orisha."

42. Coates et al., "Avengers of the New World Part 1," 13.

43. Coates et al., "A Nation Under Our Feet Part 3," 14.

44. Coates et al., "A Nation Under Our Feet Part 8," 21.

45. Coates et al., "Avengers of the New World Part 1," 15.

46. Coates et al., "Avengers of the New World Part 5," 25.

47. Coates et al., "Avengers of the New World Part 7," 21.

48. Coates et al., "Avengers of the New World Part 8," 22–23.

49. Coates et al., "Avengers of the New World Part 13," 19–20.

50. Coates et al., "Many Thousands Gone Issue #1," 2.

51. Coates et al., "Many Thousands Gone Issue #6," 9.

52. Coates et al., "Many Thousands Gone Issue #4," 9 & 15.

53. Coates, *Between the World and Me*, 114.

54. Coates et al., "Avengers of the New World Part 4," 22–23.

55. Coates et al., "Avengers of the New World Part 6," 24.

56. Coates et al., "Many Thousands Gone Issue #1."

57. Holligan, "I'll be at front of queue to change my slave name."

58. Coates et al., "Many Thousands Gone Issue #3," 3 & 4.

59. Bradley, "How Chadwick Boseman."

60. Shen, "French Rule and Tensions."

61. Coates et al., "A Nation Under Our Feet Part 7," 24.

62. Coates et al., "A Nation Under Our Feet Part 8," 24.

63. Coates et al., "A Nation Under Our Feet Part 9," 24.

64. Coates et al., "Two Thousand Seasons, Issue #15," 12.

65. Coates et al., "Two Thousand Seasons, Issue #16," 15.

66. Coates et al., "Two Thousand Seasons, Issue #18," 19.

67. Coates et al., "Wakanda Unbound, Issue #25," 35–37.

68. Coates, *We Were Eight Years in Power*, 201.

69. Ibid, 207.

70. Coates et al., "Two Thousand Seasons, Issue #18," 21.

71. Coates et al., "Wakanda Unbound, Issue #23," 16.

72. Coates et al., "Wakanda Unbound, Issue #25," 38–39.

73. Narcisse, "The miracle is Wakanda."

74. McMillan, "Ta-Nehisi Coates Leaving Marvel's 'Black Panther.'"

75. Wells, "Roxane Gay and Yona Harvey."

76. Coates et al., "We Are the Streets—Part 1: Double Consciousness," 21.

77. Bryant, *The Heritage*, 149–50.

78. Guariglia, "Senators Demand Answers"; Metz, "Who Is Making Sure the A.I. Machines Aren't Racist?"

79. Coates et al., "We Are the Streets—Part 4: Nothing but A Man," 17.

80. Ibid, 19–20.

81. Coates et al., "We Are the Streets Part 3 – Black Against the Empire," 12.

82. Ibid, 15.

83. Gustines, "Marvel's World of Wakanda."

84. "Mtcheew."

85. Okorafor et al., "Obinna's Folly," 24.

86. Borrelli, "How Nnedi Okorafor is building the future of sci-fi."

87. Ibid; Pulliam-Moore, "The New Black Panther."

88. Okorafor et al., "Timbuktu," 10.

89. Okorafor et al., "Godhead," 25.

90. Narcisse, in conversation with the author.

91. Narcisse, et al., "Coffin for Head of State"; Narcisse, in conversation.

92. Narcisse et al., "Underground Spiritual Game," 24.

93. Narcisse, in conversation with the author.

94. Ibid.

95. The Ezra Klein Show, "What's Really Behind the 1619 Backlash?"

96. Gustines, "Marvel Announces a New Black Panther Series."

Chapter 8

A King in Many Forms

*Black Panther in TV,
Games, and Elsewhere*

This chapter focuses on three distinct transmedia depictions of the Black Panther and his surrounding mythology—the animated television series in which the character appears, the video games in which he is playable, and Kendrick Lamar's concept album released in conjunction with the film. These depictions are worth discussing on their own merits as they are reflections of the character's status within the comics and the larger Marvel brand in their respective timeframes, as well as unique experiential means of forwarding the transmedia brand and concept. It is also important to understand that these other media depictions happened concurrently with the arc of the Black Panther in comics and reflect the character's broader publication history in microcosm—and that notably, most of the appearances happen late into the character's existence. These performances are also worth noting as they are likely to reach far wider audiences than a comic would; as such they can be a significant venue through which Marvel has expanded the transmedia brand of the Black Panther.

T'CHALLA, TELEVISION STAR

It is noteworthy that the Black Panther was nowhere to be seen in the spate of live-action and animated Marvel programming for decades after the "Marvel Age" of comics began. Cartoons starring various configurations of Spider-Man, the Incredible Hulk, and the X-Men littered the television landscape from the late 1960s onward, starting with 1967's animated *Spider-Man* series, known largely today for its catchy theme song and as the inspiration of countless Internet memes.[1] In the 1980s, Marvel expanded

163

into television animation with the launch of Marvel Productions, which led to the well-regarded *Spider-Man and his Amazing Friends* series and a less successful take on the *Incredible Hulk*. Marvel Productions also worked on series outside of the Marvel pantheon, including *Muppet Babies*, *GI Joe*, and *The Transformers*, each of which had a tie-in comic series published by the Marvel Comics imprint in an early prototype of Marvel's approach to synergy across platforms.[2] A 1990s partnership with Fox Television and their Fox Kids network brand also led to influential takes on *Spider-Man* and the *X-Men*.[3] In fact, it is the latter series in which the Black Panther makes his animated debut, albeit in an extremely brief, unvoiced and uncredited cameo in the 1995 episode "Sanctuary, Part 1." As the story goes, the script had simply called for an anonymous "African Mutant Refugee," but Larry Houston, the first Black storyboard artist on a Saturday morning cartoon and a life-long Marvel fan, thought differently. Houston had a reputation for inserting quick cameos and references to other Marvel characters in the *X-Men* series and decided that the anonymous character should in fact be the king of Wakanda, in his full black suit and cowl watching the scene's action unfold from a mountaintop vantage point.[4]

The *X-Men* appearance was inauspicious, but a harbinger of things to come. A series based on the *Fantastic Four* debuted after the success of Marvel's other animated shows but never quite found the same audience or critical reception as its contemporaries. Yet it is in this series, nearly three decades after some of the first Marvel animation hit the airwaves, that the Black Panther made his first non-comics appearance in the 1995 episode "Prey of the Black Panther." Houston, who had left *X-Men* for *Fantastic Four* on the promise of adapting the Panther character to the screen, pushed the studio to adapt *Fantastic Four* #52 and #53 to introduce the character to television and personally drew some of Kirby's original panels into the storyboard for the episode.[5] "Prey" is therefore an extremely condensed retelling of those two issues—T'Challa travels to New York and commanders the Fantastic Four's craft to lead them to Wakanda, battles them and then arrives at a truce, and Klaw is introduced, transformed into his supervillain form and wholly defeated—all in the span of about twenty-two minutes.[6] Much like the comics, the episode focuses on T'Challa's intellect and technical prowess as he dispatches the Fantastic Four, though it is clear that he is primarily a "guest of the week"-type character and the Four are the main attraction.

In a nod to the show's more modern sensibilities and the cultural literacy of its assumed younger audience, the Thing upgrades his Tarzan jokes from 1966 as he responds to the discovery of T'Challa's royal identity by quipping "You mean I've been clobberin' the Lion King?"[7] The quip, while more reflective of contemporary popular culture, still comes across as patronizing and implicitly labels the Panther as something animal rather than human. Yet at the same time, in a surprising move for a mid-1990s children's cartoon, the episode leans into the representation of Klaw as a colonizing force. The character's pre-supervillain design in the series re-creates the coded iconography of his pith helmet from the comics, and he insults the Wakandan defenders as "pathetic savages" during their final battle.[8] Ultimately, little came of this appearance and the Panther did not show up again outside of a brief flashback scene in another episode before the series was canceled.

However, as the first genuine transmedia appearance of the Panther, "Prey of the Black Panther" deserves consideration. While elements of the series seem dated by contemporary standards and it still carries the residue of some regressive attitudes from the original 1966 incarnation of the Panther's origin story, it nonetheless is a significant moment in the character's history. Moreover, the episode further solidified the transmedia parameters of the character, reinforcing Wakanda's alien isolation from the world and T'Challa's dual-identity status, adding a level of complexity that many contemporary superhero characters on children's television did not have. It is also worth noting the stellar performance of actor Keith David, who was cast for the role by Houston and holds the distinction of being the first actor to play the character.[9] David's signature baritone imbues the character with regal authority and demands the viewer's attention, making the Panther a memorable part of the series.

Had things gone differently, that memorable character would have gone beyond the *Fantastic Four* series. According to David, he and legendary comics writer and animation showrunner writer Dwayne McDuffie had a meeting about a standalone Black Panther series, but McDuffie felt "the world wasn't ready for that at that time."[10] McDuffie would go on to co-found the Milestone Media comics company and developed one of the characters he co-created there, Static, into the popular *Static Shock* TV series. He also later served as a writer and director on the animated *Justice League* series, leaving an indelible mark on the industry by mainstreaming Black voices and heroes and turning out an impressive body of work until his death in 2011.[11] As discussed in chapter 5, McDuffie was a long-time Panther fan and was the first Black writer to write the character, and it is easy to imagine how a series with him at the helm could have launched the character as a transmedia superstar much earlier. Sadly, it was not to be, and the cancellation of *Fantastic Four* meant Panther appearances would be scarce for a long time.

In fact, Panther's next appearance on television would come 15 years later, well after the successful runs of Priest and Hudlin had raised his profile on the publishing side, in an episode of Marvel's *Super Hero Squad Show* (a children's toy line tie-in). The comedy series, which aired on Cartoon Network, cycled through different Marvel heroes as guest stars fighting alongside a core team of Iron Man, Thor, Hulk, Wolverine, Falcon, and Silver Surfer.

The Panther appears in the first season of the show in the episode "Tremble at The Might of . . . M.O.D.O.K.!" Directed by Patty Shinagawa and written by Mark Hoffmeier, the episode sees the titular team of heroes depowered as the result of a newly powered M.O.D.O.K. gaining the ability to sap their energy, requiring them to reach out to their friends for help. Black Panther and his girlfriend, the X-Man Storm (an homage to Hudlin's then-recent series), appear because the team needs someone to replace the unpowered Wolverine's "animal factor."[12]

What this "animal factor" is exactly is never explained in the episode—but it serves as an illustration of an odd trope that appears in several television incarnations of the character wherein the Panther runs on all fours or exhibits other animalistic behaviors, actions without basis in the source material that echo toxic racist stereotypes.[13] It is also, notably, a trope that appears a great deal in current Marvel parent company Disney's output, which commonly either transforms non-white characters into animals as in *The Princess and the Frog* or *The Emperor's New Groove* or projects racial stereotypes onto animal characters, as in *Dumbo* and *The Lion King*—while this series was developed prior to Disney's acquisition of Marvel, such trends still permeated not only through Disney's output but also throughout the industry.[14] The problem with projecting animalistic characteristics onto Black people and characters is obvious, as it represents a process of systemic and media-assisted dehumanization that has served to justify police brutality and murder as well as harsher legal punishments and discrimination more broadly. A 2008 study in the *Journal of Personality and Social Psychology* found that one of the more pernicious and long-standing stereotypes of likening Black individuals to primates not only led to participants primed with the stereotype being more likely to believe that violence against Black suspects was justified, but language related to the stereotype appeared more often in news articles written about Black suspects "convicted of capital crimes."[15] While the Black Panther takes on an animal-inspired garb paying homage to actual African gods and goddesses, portraying him as actually behaving like an animal is a very strange and counter-intuitive decision that undercuts the credibility of the character as a counter-narrative. Adding to the stereotyping, the episode also goes out of its way to characterize T'Challa as aggressive and spoiling for a fight (as Storm puts it while watching T'Challa show off his abilities, "My boyfriend, always sparring.").[16] The entire appearance is largely unremarkable in the grander scheme apart from this, and his few lines come from American actor Taye Diggs, who speaks in his normal voice and does not attempt to reflect the character's African identity. If nothing else, this episode illustrates the growing pains Marvel's transmedia arms had adapting the character despite the plethora of available source material.

Running somewhat concurrently with the *Super Hero Squad Show* but mer-
iting its own discussion is the character's appearance in *Iron Man: Armored
Adventures*, which reimagined Tony Stark and his friends Pepper Potts and
James Rhodes as high schoolers. Here, T'Challa appears in multiple episodes
in an interpretation that feels at least somewhat closer to the comics, drawing
particularly on the more stoic, less trusting Panther of the Priest run and offering a more kid-friendly versions of that run's social and political critiques.
The costume echoes this, carrying forth the golden accoutrements of that
costume but eschewing the cowl and cape. He is also a more significant character in this series, appearing in four episodes—the first of which, "Panther's
Prey," aired August 28, 2009. In the episode, T'Challa is presented as a young
college student—older than the other characters but similarly aged down
compared to his comics appearance. He is also the new king of Wakanda after
the villain Moses Magnum initiated a coup and hired mercenaries to kill his
father T'Chaka, making off with vibranium in the process.[17] Recasting the
death of T'Chaka as the product of political insurrection as opposed to direct
colonialist interference is an intriguing choice. It effectively serves to shift
somewhat the blame for the act away from European exploitation to a more
generic sort of geographical tumult, something the show—surprisingly, for a
children's program—does explore to a degree as the Panther's arc unfolds. It
is also worth noting that, for the first time in an animated series, the Panther
speaks with a noticeable African accent.

What this incarnation of the character does, rather than portraying T'Challa
as largely an inscrutable force, is go out of its way to draw parallels between
him and the other heroes, specifically Iron Man. Initially, he refuses the latter
hero's help, despite the fact that A.I.M. had found a way to disable vibranium
in a way that would render his armor ineffective, and actively threatens to
reveal Stark's secret identity if he interferes.[18] However, through Stark's
explanations in the show, the writers illustrate that the two are more similar
than they are different—they are both the young scions of legacies beyond the
ones they are making, entrusted at a young age with taking over their father's
legacies and the responsibilities that come with them (though one could argue
running a secretive country with sole control over one of the world's most
sought-after elements is a bit different than running a business). Stark sees
a kindred spirit in T'Challa, offering his help once again as Panther battles
Magnum and his A.I.M. allies toward the end of the episode. Believing the
vibranium to be lost, he remarks that he is "not worthy of Wakanda's crown"
and that he has "brought dishonor to the mantle of the Panther."[19] In a move
that would have perhaps been helpful before the young king soliloquized his
troubles, Stark reveals that he had picked up the vibranium, telling T'Challa
he understands what it means to lose a father and take on his responsibilities,
but that he could not have done it without help from his friends. The Panther

seems to accept this, adding that the experience has made him re-evaluate his role: "Perhaps keeping Wakanda isolated from the world has hurt us more than it protected us. Perhaps had Wakanda called for help, my father would not have perished in the attack. Perhaps this king needs to change the way Wakanda thinks about outsiders. Do not get excited, Stark. I said 'perhaps.'"[20]

T'Challa again returns to the role of a nascent reformer at odds with tradition and the forces of modernity in the second season episode "Line of Fire," which opens with the Panther assaulting a Hammer Multinational manufacturing facility. The character, again portrayed in an animalized fashion, runs on all fours and even lands like a cat. It is unclear if this was simply a misunderstanding of what the character does or a deliberate stylistic choice, but when combined with his sniffing of the air to track his foes in the first episode it again creates a depiction of him as more animal than human (though the latter is at least a slightly more canonically-accurate action due to his heightened senses and tracking ability).[21] It is revealed that the Panther is after Hammer for smuggling vibranium to use in his Titanium Man project, and he labels Stark an "enemy of Wakanda" when the latter interferes, invoking Wakandan law, tradition, and antipathy to the outside world—"I come from a line of Wakandan kings. If outsiders cause us harm, this is how we act."[22]

Yet, this mistrust is earned, and the episode takes a surprising turn into territory not well-explored by children's animation. When T'Challa gives a speech at a university, he mentions that vibranium smuggling is causing civil war between Wakanda and its neighboring country of Niganda (borrowed from Hudlin's run), identifying his associate Nakia as the peace envoy trying to broker a ceasefire. Later, Panther tells Stark that money earned from black market sales of vibranium and other precious metals is funding that civil war—and that Stark Industries representatives were among those buying it, making Hammer and Stark equally complicit in Wakandan strife.[23] An angered Stark realizes that Obadiah Stane, the current Stark Industries CEO, was buying "blood vibranium" and pledges to help.[24]

This phrase is powerful and intentional. Many minerals used in technology and products around the world come from African sources, and the sale and importation of such goods can be used to illegally fund the training and deployment of military forces that lead to destabilization, environmental destruction, and endangerment of lives on the continent. Congo in particular holds vast quantities of tin, tungsten, and coltan, all of which are found in products from laptops to light bulbs, and the mines that produce these minerals are often taken over and exploited by militias who use the profit to extend their power, leading to pillaging and the murder and rape of Congo citizens.[25] Research published in the journal *American Economic Review* suggests that rising mineral prices can potentially explain at least one-fourth of violence across Africa between the years of 1997 and 2010, and that annexation of one mine can triple the fighting activities of an armed group; the authors also warned in an accompanying editorial that the political instability caused by these actions "can escalate into more widespread conflict."[26] In 2010, the U.S. government passed a law as part of the Dodd-Frank Act that requires companies to disclose if their materials came from Congo or its neighboring countries and to take steps to ensure the purchase of those materials does not fund militant groups; despite this, militias have still grown and the boycott policies instituted by the U.S. and many other countries have led to unintended economic hardships for the region by cutting off trade.[27] Invoking such problems by using vibranium as a proxy for real-life conflict minerals is an illustration again of the Panther as a small-"a" avenger of the crimes inflicted on the African continent by capitalism and colonialism, though it is fairly quickly glossed over beyond motivation for the rest of the episode's plot.

This version of the Panther is also a more violent and ruthless version of the character, largely as a direct comparison to the textually more benevolent and patient Stark—he begins the episode by blowing up the Hammer facility and later upon discovering that Nakia had actually been arranging the vibranium smuggling threatens her with a "fate worse than banishment."[28] Presenting T'Challa as a more aggressive and violent reactionary compared to Stark's levelheadedness unfortunately brings with it unfortunate racial coding, but the episode nonetheless invokes the political realities of African exploitation when Nick Fury reveals that Stane and Hammer will both be let off the hook with a fine for smuggling the vibranium. An irritated Panther suggests the reason is that "SHIELD does not want to cripple their biggest weapons suppliers."[29] Here again the *Armored Adventures* incarnation of the Panther echoes the geopolitical espionage narratives of Priest's version, acknowledging the tangled role of the U.S. government and foreign policy in promoting and encouraging certain conflicts and outcomes in Africa to serve their own purposes—yet when the Panther appears again in the two-part season finale, he has largely put these concerns aside and still arrives to help the heroes fend off an alien invasion.

From this point on, the Panther's appearances in televised animation grew in prominence, with the character taking on a major role in *Avengers: Earth's Mightiest Heroes,* a series debuting in 2010 to again capitalize on the growing popularity of the Marvel Cinematic Universe and the then-upcoming *Avengers* film. Unlike the guest role he played in many prior series, here the Panther eventually becomes a core member of the Avengers team, appearing in many episodes and having multi-episode arcs. He and Wakanda first appear in "The Man in the Ant Hill," an episode made up of several shorts edited together that aired on Disney XD in October of 2010. Two of the shorts specifically focus on Wakanda and the Panther—the first is a brief encounter in which Hank "Ant-Man" Pym dispatches a group of smugglers led by Ulysses

Klaw (voiced by Mark Hamill and wearing his colonizer-coded pith helmet and safari gear) attempting to steal the vibranium sample on which Pym is experimenting.[30] The second is a retelling of the Panther's origin, where M'Baku (in full Man-Ape regalia and referred to as such, in a very strange move for a 2010 Marvel show) challenges T'Chaka for the Wakandan throne. T'Chaka shuts down his son's pleas to reject the challenge with a stern "This is how the kings of Wakanda have chosen to rule. This is how it is written, and we will respect it."[31] M'Baku kills T'Chaka with assistance from Klaw, who uses his sonic disruptor cannon to incapacitate T'Chaka, allowing M'Baku to deliver the killing blows. This line and moment set up a character arc for T'Challa in the remainder of the series, putting the younger man at odds with Wakandan tradition and revealing that Klaw and M'Baku were working together to give the former access to the Great Mound of vibranium.[32] The forces of colonizing exploitation again result in the death of T'Chaka, though the means are different—and the direct association with M'Baku evokes the conflict mineral dynamic discussed earlier.

In a later episode, "Living Legend," T'Challa silently stalks around the Avengers compound seeking information, only to help a recently defrosted Captain America defeat the villainous Baron Zemo.[33] The fallout of this act is explored in a later episode, "Panther's Quest." While borrowing the title from McGregor's apartheid-era saga, this episode largely invokes the same dynamic from his debut in the pages of *Fantastic Four* as he arrives on the grounds of Avengers Mansion and uses his vibranium technology and fighting skills to assess whether the Avengers are worthy allies to retake Wakanda. Upon hearing of Panther's plan, Captain America asserts his support for liberal democracy, stating that if the people follow M'Baku, it is their choice. The Panther is not terribly convinced by Captain America's faith in populism, saying "The people are the problem. They follow the old ways. Man-Ape won the throne in combat. They feel they must follow him, even if he destroys everything."[34]

Here again the Panther is shown as something of an insurgent force challenging the established order of Wakanda, which is implicitly suggested to be backward in its adherence to tradition at the same time its technology has advanced, as well as implicitly the vessel for which liberal Western democracy and modernity can and should replace existing indigenous societal structures (indeed, at the end of the episode, T'Challa signals his intent to install a "council of the people" to lead the kingdom while he is away on Avengers business).[35] Such attitudes would not be out of place in the 1970s *Avengers* comics; they were also more deftly explored in Coates' run. Similarly, the American heroes show skepticism and surprise at Wakanda's capabilities, with Iron Man being shocked that his advanced cloaking technology did not work on their flight into the country (as the Panther reminds him, "Wakandan defense tech is better") to the soft colonialist views of Hank Pym, who remarks that for an "uncharted African nation, they've got tech that's decades ahead of anything we've got."[36] While the writers undoubtedly intended these moments to showcase the technical prowess of the country to an unaware viewer, they still read of the same worldviews that had defined that "uncharted African nation" with the lowered expectations of internalized ethnocentric ideology since the character's inception. Ultimately, this version of T'Challa—a sort of middle ground between the more traditional acrobatic warrior of McGregor and the gadget-focused super-intellect of the Priest run—triumphs over M'Baku's rejection of modernity, once again echoing the same ideological struggle that has played out in multiple incarnations of the character.

While the Panther remains a fixture on the team throughout the series, there are only a handful of episodes where he plays a primary role in the narrative. Following an invasion of Earth by the shape-shifting Skrulls, the Panther leaves the team to prepare Wakanda's defenses, stating that he cannot truly trust anyone on the Avengers team.[37] The Panther eventually crosses paths with the Avengers again when Captain America arrives and refuses another offer to re-join the Avengers. Hawkeye, angry at Panther for leaving, picks up the Ugly American ball for this episode, calling Wakanda a "mud pit" and threatening to challenge T'Challa for the throne—a threat the Panther shrugs off, ultimately made moot by a Dora Milaje knocking the archer out when he draws on the king.[38] The android Vision shows up in Wakanda to collect vibranium for his boss and creator Ultron (Panther quickly surmises this with a wry "Whenever there is trouble in Wakanda, it is always about the vibranium," a meta-textual nod at the motivation of so many of his adversaries), but is ultimately defeated by the coordinated efforts of the Avengers, whose ranks T'Challa once again agrees to join.[39]

Again, the narrative themes—mistrust of outsiders, Wakandan advancement in the fate of White racism, and exploitation of indigenous resources by outside interests—are brought back to the forefront, but the series deserves recognition for portraying the scientific intellect of the character as well—in a later episode, he is even able to learn how to fly and operate a Kree starship after a few moments of studying the controls.[40] This aspect of the character is often left out of many incarnations, including the MCU one, and harkens back to the earlier depictions of the character as a scientist and engineer. Moreover, it gives the character and Wakanda by proxy a meaningful arc, culminating in the Panther informing the other Avengers as he is about to make a sacrificial trip into the sun to give them an opportunity to stop the invading Kree army "I only do now as my father did. I protect Wakanda. But unlike any other Black Panther, I have had the privilege of doing it by your sides, as an Avenger." He ultimately survives due to using the ship's teleporter at the last minute, but the themes of embracing collectivism and team membership are nonetheless there.[41]

As the Panther became a more significant part of the Marvel Cinematic Universe, he also became a more significant part of the transmedia branding at Marvel, appearing again as a pivotal character in the 2013 *Avengers Assemble* series and acting as the focal point of the series' fifth and final season following the 2018 release of the *Black Panther* film. The character is introduced first in the third season episode "Panther's Rage," which makes subtext that had been bubbling under the surface of the character more explicit. Speaking at the United Nations, T'Challa explains that the world is getting smaller and bringing people together, but Wakanda's future "will be on our terms, not yours"—signaling a more aggressive version of Wakandan foreign policy.[42] T'Challa arrives to back up Captain America in a fight with the supervillain Crossbones, but leaves with the Avenger's famous shield, declaring it property of Wakanda due to the vibranium it contains. The material resource of vibranium is both plot-central and given monetary value— T'Challa estimates a small chunk of the metal at about $20 million—but also the focus of colonialist exploitation. T'Challa accuses Iron Man's father Howard Stark of stealing vibranium from Wakanda to build the shield, an accusation implicit in several threads of the Marvel transmedia franchise—in comics incarnations, the shield and the vibranium in it are generally seen as a gift from a grateful king, but in others the question of whether the symbol of America is the product of colonialist theft is evaded.

For instance, in the Marvel Cinematic Universe, it is never explained how the vibranium used to build Captain America's shield is obtained. Given the moral ambiguity of SHIELD and the U.S. government in the Marvel Universe, it is a question worth asking. In an episode of the Marvel Cinematic Universe streaming series *The Falcon and the Winter Soldier*, it is revealed that Isaiah Bradley, a former Black U.S. soldier, was illegally experimented upon with a revamped version of Captain America's super soldier serum. As in Robert Morales and Kyle Baker's *Truth: Red, White, and Black*, the source material in which Bradley debuted, the use of Black bodies as test subjects is meant to parallel the real-life tragedy of the Tuskegee Experiments, and it is not a stretch to imagine that a government capable of exploiting Black soldiers without their consent would not balk at the idea of smuggling essential resources out of an African country in the name of the war effort.[43] "Panther's Rage" avoids the narrative side-stepping around this issue by directly accusing a representative of the U.S. government of stealing another country's resources and heritage just long enough to induce reasonable motivation for Wakandan suspicion. Ultimately, however, it salvages the heroes' reputation by having Captain America eventually reveal the vibranium was a gift from T'Chaka for stopping a HYDRA invasion in World War II. By the end of the episode, the Panther simply tells him the Wakandan people would be proud for him to wield it.[44] Apart from this too-neat ideological out (largely necessary to maintain the profitability and goodwill of the characters), the series also complicates the geopolitical and sociohistorical dimensions of the character by having the Panther lead a government-sanctioned team of Avengers to bring in the main Avengers team when they refuse to round up superpowered individuals. As the two sides fight in the inevitable superhero punch-up, Black Widow tells T'Challa he does not know what it is like to have to fight for his freedom—while technically true in that Wakanda was never conquered, it is an odd statement to make to an African king whose entire country is founded on keeping outsiders out to ensure their continued existence and liberation.[45]

Avengers Assemble is primarily important to this chapter because it builds an entire series around the character in its fifth season, appropriately named "Black Panther's Quest." The tone of the season, focused primarily on a threat from within to overthrow T'Challa and the existing Wakandan government from a group of villains and politicians known as the Shadow Council, borrows heavily from the espionage-influenced narratives of the Priest run, casting the Black Panther as a technologically advanced spy character and political actor not unlike James Bond. The Bond parallels involve gadgets—it is revealed that the Panther habit can generate rebreathers and flippers to assist in underwater missions—as well as a Q in the form of Shuri, who acts both as diplomat and designer of the Panther's technology. The season's focus is placed on T'Challa after a conflict between Wakanda and the underwater civilization of Atlantis threatens global investment markets, causing T'Challa to take a leave of absence from the Avengers for political reasons.[46] The renewed focus on the Panther as the main character, seeking answers in Wakandan history to address the threat of the Shadow Council, allows for *Assemble* to go deeper into the Panther lore and roster than other televised incarnations to this point. His adopted brother Hunter appears for the first time on screen in this series as an exile rather than the head of the Hatut Zeraze, as does a re-imagined version of M'Baku as a modernized crime boss that eschews the problematic Man-Ape persona and costume in favor of a white "force enhancer" suit, and in one episode the Panther dons a white camouflage suit for a mission in the Alps that evokes the Kasper Cole White Tiger.[47]

More importantly, the expanded running time offers deeper thematic exploration into many of the ideas that have constituted the transmedia character of the Panther. The conflict between the traditionalist idealism of the Panther and the self-serving outward expansion of the Shadow Council remains a through line of the series, as does familial and paternal legacy. Parallels to T'Challa's journey to live up to the throne and to his father's legacy are found

in an inverted fashion in the villain-turned-temporary ally Baron Zemo, who
resents his father and his role as part of the original Shadow Council—even
going so far as to ally himself with T'Challa before inevitably betraying him
later in the season—and Princess Elanna of Atlantis, who rejects her father's
hostile approach to Wakanda only to swear vengeance and lead an invasion
of Wakanda after T'Challa brings Killmonger back to his home country following Killmonger's murder of her father.[48] Echoes of Priest's interpretation
of T'Challa as an uneasy ally with the Avengers while in secrecy seeking
his own agenda also run throughout the series, with T'Challa even being
pursued by the Avengers when they mistakenly accuse him of killing Captain
America—at one point, he retreats to Wakanda and makes his separation from
the Avengers literal by closing off the country's physical borders.[49]

At the center of the plot is a mysterious artifact called The Crown, the
search for which leads T'Challa and Shuri to an ancient temple where they
experience the memories of their ancestors. It is here that "Black Panther's
Quest" goes into new territory for televised depictions of the Black Panther,
basing a three-episode arc around previous rulers of Wakanda at different time
periods throughout history. Each of these incarnations approaches the crux of
the Wakandan paradox in different ways—T'Chanda, T'Challa's grandfather,
reluctantly partners with Captain America and Peggy Carter to protect the
Crown from HYDRA during World War II while Carter chastises him for
hiding in his "perfect utopia" and avoiding the conflict.[50] Again, Wakanda
is criticized by the outside for not participating in global conflagrations—a
position of historical privilege—and criticism of understandable Wakandan
caution is shown as the admirable and ethically correct point of view.
Yemandi, another ancestor, is shown to have fought the sorceress Morgan Le
Fay alongside a temporarily amphibian Thor while searching for the spear of
Bashenga, the original Black Panther and the first king of Wakanda.[51] But it
is the story of Bashenga and his sister Bask—the latter of whom had been
forgotten in Wakandan history—that is the most important. In this continuity
they were the first to discover vibranium and use it to ward off an Atlantean
attack, but where Bashenga wished to use it solely as a means of protection
Bask sought to take a more proactive and violent approach. Using the power
of what would later be called Bashenga's Core—a mysterious orb of energy
at the center of the vibranium asteroid that had struck Wakanda that later
becomes the energy source for the Crown—she lays waste to an Atlantean
city and pushes them into the ocean, only to reawaken in the modern day.[52]

It is Bask, not Killmonger or M'Baku or Tiger Shark, that is written as
posing the greatest ideological threat to T'Challa—where T'Challa has
largely sought to keep Wakanda protected while strategically seeking alliances with the outside world, Bask sees him and his father T'Chaka as
rulers that have weakened Wakanda by seeking peace rather than conquest,

ultimately defeating him in ritual combat for the throne.[53] No longer king and sentenced to death, T'Challa is rescued by his brother the White Wolf amidst the Atlantean invasion, but it is Shuri who foils an attempt by the Shadow Council to turn the Crown's energy against the city to stop the Atlanteans using her words: "Wakanda, Atlantis—they're not things. They're not chess pieces to take or defend. They're people who only want to protect themselves. Force will be met with more force because you have given them no choice."[54] While these episodes aired before the relevant parts of Coates' run, the thematic similarity of the Wakandan myth coming back to pose a material threat feels familiar—the inevitable question to be asked.

After Bask ceases her attack, Killmonger turns on her and reveals that she—as someone of royal blood—was a necessary figurehead for his plan. While T'Challa defeats Killmonger in hand-to-hand combat at the foot of Bashenga's monument in a symbolic final battle ("his weakness has brought you here," Killmonger snarls) it is Shuri who ultimately overcomes Bask and helps her to see the error of her ways through words alone, giving Bask peace and crossing her arms in the Wakandan salute as she disappears into the ether (another example of the film's lasting impact on the transmedia depictions of these characters as well as the gesture's link to African ancestry). Ultimately, T'Challa's growth is in the passing of the crown to his sister, secure in the belief that the progressive vision they share for Wakanda is safe in her hands.[55] Again, the Black Panther (whether T'Challa or as would now be implied, Shuri) is represented as a spiritually pure vision of Wakanda and its ideals, a rejection of colonialist conquest and celebration of ancestral legacy; what makes this interpretation unique is that said legacy is more complex and evolves over the course of the season's narrative to provide context for how that vision has developed and the costs of adhering to it—that the path forward runs through female leadership also feels in keeping with the modern feminist overtones of the transmedia character.

The Panther's history in animation is not without some curios that have added interesting wrinkles to the character's transmedia presence, including a series of shorts ("Marvel Super Hero Adventures") aimed at teaching basic moral lessons to young children, appearances in a 2017 anime series, and an original Lego film.[56] While most of these tread similar ground to other productions in terms of the character's depiction and development, there is one oddity briefly worth mentioning as part of how far the character has come. In 2006, Black Panther was the subject of a feature-length animated film released direct-to-DVD as *Ultimate Avengers 2: Rise of the Panther*. The film is largely dull and forgettable, noteworthy primarily for being the second animated appearance of the Black Panther and the second film based on the Ultimates version of the Avengers (though not the Ultimate version of Black Panther, confusingly enough). Once again, the Panther meets the

Avengers in combat and once again their misunderstanding is resolved as a common purpose is revealed, this time avenging the death of T'Chaka and battling the extraterrestrial menace responsible. T'Challa brings the Avengers into Wakanda and the modernity-tradition tension is again a plot point, with the council of elders stripping T'Challa of his role as king as a result and blaming the "Western philosophies" for corrupting him.[57] The film also portrays a more primitive version of Wakanda than contemporary depictions, with the Wakandan soldiers appearing as stereotyped Zulu-esque warriors and using spears, bows and arrows, and trebuchets (albeit vibranium-infused ones). This is regressive, but the most bizarre choice the film makes is to give T'Challa and all Black Panthers the ability to shapeshift into a human/panther hybrid monster—a power with no precedent in the comics that also provides perhaps the most severely animalistic and dehumanized depiction of the hero in animation and ultimately makes the film an unfortunate curiosity in the character's transmedia legacy that has largely been ignored.[58]

In short, the Panther's history in animation is an exemplar of the larger growing pains the character has faced in other media—unlike many other Marvel heroes like Spider-Man or the Hulk, who are largely well-defined in the public eye by appearances in other media and popular comics, the Black Panther was largely an unknown quantity not only to the audiences but to many of the people making the shows. This led to decisions that ranged from baffling oversights—the lack of a defined African accent for the character in several interpretations—to outright problematic ones, like the transposing of animal characteristics onto the character. Yet at the same time there are stories worth telling—Larry Houston's push to tell the Panther origin story at a time when Black superheroes were not common on television is an important part of the Panther's development, and actors like Keith David and James C. Mathis III have played definitive roles in the transmedia creation of the character for man audiences. Despite a host of flaws and questionable decisions, the animated legacy of the Black Panther is an important part of this story and reinforces the unique narrative role the character can play.

BLACK PANTHER AS VIDEO GAME HERO

If one is looking for an indicator of how much the Black Panther was an afterthought for Marvel until well into the twenty-first century, one needs to look no further than the video game industry. The world of Marvel Comics is a lucrative and effective backdrop against which to set fantasies of player empowerment and active engagement that the medium often requires. As such, characters like Spider-Man, Captain America, the Incredible Hulk, and the X-Men have multiple video games to their credit from a variety of different companies around the globe. However, despite the fact Black Panther has been around since nearly the inception of the contemporary age of Marvel Comics and was an Avengers mainstay for years, he did not appear in a video game until 2006, four decades after his debut in the comics and fifteen years after his arch-nemesis Klaw appeared in the 1991 arcade game *Captain America and the Avengers* as a boss character.[59] Even the massive 1990s crossover rosters of Capcom's "Vs." fighting game franchise, which plucked obscurities like Shuma-Gorath and X-Men villain Omega Red from the comics, could not find room for the king of Wakanda (though this could have been Marvel's licensing restrictions at the time, as characters like Thor and The Thing also were off-limits for the developers—which also raises the question of why Marvel put Black Panther on that restricted list).[60]

Black Panther's appearance—or lack thereof—in video games poses a unique issue to consider in our discussion of the character and his transmedia impact. Video games, it must be said, are a special case in media criticism because they need to be understood as one of the only media in which audiences control the outcome. Players are empowered with at least some degree of choice and influence over the way their experience progresses in a way not seen in film, television, and comics. To this end, it is helpful to consider the work of Lev Manovich, whose "narrative database" model is a framework to understand the rhetorical and narrative capability of video games, the Internet, and other interactive communication forms.

The basic premise of the "narrative database" theory is simple—interactive media consists of databases of information that are accessed and utilized via an interface, such as pressing buttons on a controller or clicking links in a web browser. These aspects theoretically allow the user to actively control what they see, unlike other inherently more passive forms of media. I could not control the way the way the animated series involving the Black Panther mentioned earlier in this chapter played out, but I could choose to select him in a fighting game and employ his unique style and abilities or change those abilities in a role-playing game that features the character—if he is available to select. Video games also include art, coding, sound effects, and other elements that compose this database. In Manovich's parlance, the database acts as a "paradigm," or a collection of choices and points of data, and the interface allows users to create a "syntagm," or a unique narrative trajectory through that database not unlike choosing words to create a meaningful sentence.[61]

So, in a game like the 2020 online action title *Marvel's Avengers* (which received a delayed Black Panther-themed expansion in which the Avengers aid T'Challa in battling the forces of Klaw and A.I.M. in Wakanda nearly a year after its initial release) I could choose my preferred hero from the roster the game provides (the paradigm), and then allocate skill points and gear to build out the skills and abilities that I prefer to use to accomplish the missions I wish to undertake (the syntagm).[62] However, as Manovich informs us, the paradigm is "real" and the syntagm is "virtual"—the options in a database are concrete but what we do with them is by comparison a more intangible notion, a "set of links" between elements in the database that we create.[63] In this view, the selection of the hero and how I play as that character is based on the concrete options in the game but does not exist as an entity onto itself the way the game code and audiovisual assets of the game do. This is helpful to understanding the unique rhetorical power of interactive media to inspire transmedia meta-branding, but we must also grapple with what this arrangement implies.

If the database is in fact "real," the options located within it become deterministic of what the "virtual" narrative can accomplish. Put another way, the options included in the paradigm can severely impact what narrative the player can create and more importantly represent concepts beyond the game itself. For instance, games that include female characters but makes them physically weaker than their male counterparts or casts them in primarily supporting roles reinforce existing heteronormative gender essentialism.[64] Because games made using licensed characters like the Marvel heroes must pass approval by the license-holders before release—and indeed Marvel has historically exercised that approval to dictate which characters appear and do not—the inclusion (or lack thereof) of characters in a game creates part of the paradigm and can tell us a lot about what that company values and in which direction their transmedia interests lie.

So once again, we return to the fact—rather, the conscious choice—that the first Black superhero in mainstream comics and media does not appear as a playable character in a video game until 2006's *Marvel: Ultimate Alliance,* an action role-playing game starring an expansive roster of Marvel heroes. However, players could simply miss the character altogether—to unlock him as a playable hero, the player must discover five Black Panther action figures hidden throughout the game worlds.[65] Despite the massive number of heroes present in the game, Marvel's pioneering Black superhero could only make the cut as a secret. Things improved slightly in the game's sequel, *Marvel: Ultimate Alliance 2*, which featured an extended story sequence in Wakanda and greater prominence for T'Challa in the game's narrative, which borrowed heavily from the *Civil War* storyline. In the game, Wakanda is once again identified as a "highly-advanced country" and the world's only source of vibranium as well as a target for the incursion of nanite-controlled villains and heroes. The Black Panther himself, as well as the Dora Milaje, are simply supporting characters in this sequence, helping the player fight their way through Wakanda's capital city.[66] Those looking to actually take direct control of the character had to pay for the privilege, once again relegating

Black Panther to optional status—and despite his marriage to Storm and narrative split with her on opposing sides of the Act, no special dialogue or story content was included in the downloadable content.[67] Unfortunately, due to licensing agreements, both games and their downloadable add-ons are now no longer accessible for purchase through traditional retail venues. Despite a brief re-release, the expiration of publisher Activision's licensing rights once again rendered them unplayable, meaning the first two *Ultimate Alliance* games an important but ultimately ephemeral part of the character's transmedia legacy—and one that speaks more broadly to the need for greater preservation of the medium.[68]

It was not until 2019's *Marvel: Ultimate Alliance 3* that the character would actually appear both as a core part of the roster and play a significant role in the game's story. Unlike the first two games, *Ultimate Alliance 3* was published by Nintendo and released well into the character's transmedia popularity. Where *Ultimate Alliance 2* borrowed from the *Civil War* storyline, the third game in the franchise created its own rough take on the *Infinity Gauntlet* storyline, in which an assemblage of Marvel's heroes come together to thwart the efforts of the intergalactic tyrant Thanos and his Black Order lieutenants to collect the six Infinity Gems—a storyline tailor-made for a video game due to the sequential MacGuffins at its core.[69] When the heroes arrive in Wakanda, the Panther rescues them from an ambush by A.I.M. forces, his introduction culminating in a "splash screen" with the identifying text "Proud King. Fierce Protector. Wakanda Forever!"[70] The text not only reifies T'Challa's primary identity as "king" but also references the costume and "Wakanda Forever" rallying cry from the 2018 film, showing once more its outsized importance in the transmedia depiction of the hero (but the casting of James Mathis, the Panther voice actor from *Earth's Mightiest Heroes* and *Avengers Assemble*, suggest a synergistic relationship with Marvel's animation arm as well).[71] The storyline also adapts the Hickman-era idea of the Panther as the King of the Dead, with Wakanda's Necropolis playing a significant role in the narrative. M.O.D.O.K., one of the villains attacking Wakanda, scoffs at the nation's ancient culture in one scene, suggesting that what they called "magic" was in actuality science—it is unclear if this was simply meant to illustrate the character's arrogance or it is actually a misunderstanding of how scientifically advanced Wakanda is traditionally supposed to be, but it is likely the former due to the fact that T'Challa's ancestors appear as he suggests there are powers greater than science and the walls of the Necropolis predict Thanos' plot.[72] In terms of his in-game ability, much of his attacks are close-ranged and based around slashing and attacking with his claws—at a paradigmatic level, his baseline stats suggest he is one of the game's stronger heroes but less powerful in terms of his energy attacks (though the player can equip stat-altering ISO-8 crystals to retrofit the character as they wish, emblematic of the syntagmatic elements of the design), and players can get special stat bonuses for teaming him up with relevant heroes and teammates. Most notably, however, Black Panther is part of the "shipped" roster of the game and does not require an additional purchase, meaning that players who wish to use him only need to advance to the Wakanda section of the game to unlock him—a literal paradigm shift from previous games in the series and again a representation of the fact that the Panther, at that point, would be a character fans expected to be present.[73]

Alongside these appearances, the Panther also appeared (alongside hundreds of other characters) as a playable character in the *Lego Marvel* series, appearing first as a cameo at the end of 2013's *Lego Marvel Super Heroes* and again getting his own separate downloadable content campaign focused on the original incarnation of the character as part of the 2016 Marvel Cinematic Universe-centered spinoff *Lego Marvel's Avengers*. He took greater prominence in 2017's *Lego Marvel Super Heroes 2*, with a section of that game's campaign devoted to the character as well as a downloadable add-on pack based on the 2018 film.[74] The Lego games are relatively simple puzzle-based action games aimed at a younger audience, but the gameplay choices made within and what abilities are assigned to which characters reflect how the narrative database constructs the transmedia character. For instance, in the game Black Panther is given the ability to "track" (meaning he can use his heightened senses to find hidden secrets) as well as dig and climb walls—all powers within his purview but also again the more animalistic ones in his arsenal. These skills are used to solve rudimentary puzzles within the framework of the game's narrative, where the Panther is portrayed as a wise mentor dispensing philosophical advice from which younger heroes like Ms. Marvel and Spider-Man learn. He plays a significant role in the game's narrative, joining with the Avengers to help foil the time-traveler Kang and his villain associates, and his main story level takes place within Wakanda and its vibranium mines, with the main gameplay puzzle centered on pushing a minecart through them to unlock the next level. At the end of the main story level, players do battle with M'Baku in his Man-Ape form (it is surprising that a children's game in 2017 would still use a name the comics had long since abandoned).[75] While limited, the Lego games nonetheless illustrated a clear operationalized outline of the character in interactive form based on his broadest fictive elements.

Finally correcting the long-standing omission of the king of Wakanda in its flagship crossover fighting series in 2017, developer Capcom finally added Black Panther to the roster of the long-awaited *Marvel vs Capcom: Infinite*—albeit, again, as a downloadable character despite his role in the game's story mode. T'Challa had previously appeared in *Marvel vs. Capcom 3* as part of Storm's ending, but here he was a full-fledged character with a complete move set, victory quotes, and more. In a nod to the popular trans-media perception of the character, T'Challa plays with a focus on speedy, close-up melee attacks. His in-game appearance draws from several artistic interpretations, most notably a variation on the gold-and-black Panther habit for his default costume. Narratively, while the main plot of the game centers around the villains "mashing up" the Marvel and Capcom worlds together (Wakanda is combined with the town of Val Habar from Capcom's *Monster Hunter* franchise to create the portmanteau Valkanda), Panther's role is again as the isolationist king of a hidden country, refusing to give over the item that lends his nation protection despite the needs of the outside world. In this case, it is the Time Stone, one of the Infinity Stones that keeps Valkanda outside of the villains' view, and this refusal leads to brief friction between the heroes before an attack by Ultron's drones forces cooperation.[76] The character's dialogue also reinforces these monomythic qualities, dispensing such philosophical musings on leadership as "If a king cannot see when he must change, then he is not fit to lead his people" alongside post-fight victory quotes confirming he sees himself as the "aegis" between the world and his new homeland of Valkanda and his belief that "T'Chaka would be proud" of his victory, a signal to the character's patrilineal aspects.[77]

While Panther's part in the story is brief, it is worth noting that *Infinite* reflects many recurring elements of the Panther's transmedia character. Wakanda crossed over with one of the less technologically advanced and more "savage" locales in the game, an unfortunate thematic implication, and the character was once again not part of the base roster, meaning other characters took priority. It is also potentially an example of Marvel's licensing interference at work—the game was poorly received by fans, who bemoaned the simplified structure of the game and lamented that the popular X-Men characters, who had been such a significant part of the franchise's history, were left out of the game in favor of a roster more heavily influenced by the Marvel Cinematic Universe (Black Panther, in particular, mirrors much of Wolverine's move set from the earlier games). While the developers have not said publicly, speculation based on comments from *X-Men* writer Chris Claremont and others suggests that Marvel's reluctance to use the mutant characters in media outside of the comics stemmed from a desire not to promote or create new characters to which they did not own the film rights (the game came out a few years before Disney acquired Fox and gained those rights).[78] If nothing else, *Marvel vs. Capcom: Infinite* acts as a near-perfect microcosm of the pitfalls of synergistic transmedia branding as well as the very specific ways in which the Panther mythology is adapted to new media situations.

In December of 2020, the wildly popular game *Fortnite* added the Black Panther to its expanding roster of Marvel heroes, resulting in arguably his most prominent video game appearance to date. *Fortnite*, like other "Battle Royale" games, drops 100 players, either on their own or in teams, onto an island beset by an incoming energy storm. Players use their combat skills, a variety of guns, and hastily built structures to be the last player standing as the storm shrinks the available space to a series of smaller geographic circles. Despite (or perhaps because of) its premise and whimsical cartoon visuals, the game became a cultural phenomenon, at one point boasting over 350 million registered accounts as of May 2020 and millions of active players.[79] The question for IP holders, then, is not *whether* to get involved with *Fortnite* but *when* and *how*—the NFL, Star Wars, DC Comics, Adult Swim, Netflix, and other massive brands looking to reach youth markets have all shared their lucrative IP with the game in the forms of costumes, items, and special events. A concert put on by rapper Travis Scott within the world of the game supposedly grossed $20 million, and Christopher Nolan's film *Inception* was shown on a massive movie screen in the game as part of a promotional effort for his film *Tenet*, which had been beset by marketing woes as a result of the COVID-19 pandemic.[80] In an unusual piece of transmedia storytelling, an integral plot point to the 2019 film *Star Wars Episode IX: The Rise of Skywalker* was exclusively broadcast in the game and only briefly referenced in the film's opening crawl.[81] *Fortnite*, for many brands, is just another part of their multimedia marketing rollout—and its ongoing, years-long narrative positions the game's island location as a "nexus" that can intersect with multiple fiction worlds as a common point, presenting nearly endless potential synergistic crossovers.[82]

Marvel, for their part, has had one of the longest-running partnerships with the game, at one point culminating in a battle where players around the world worked together to defeat the planet-devouring cosmic force Galactus.[83] The event was even made canonical in the then-current *Thor* comics storyline. Rival DC Comics also published a standalone series chronicling Batman's attempt to escape the island; each issue came with unlockable in-game elements. Important landmarks and characters to that story were also accessible in the game, meaning that Fortnite is not only a layer within the transmedia matryoshka doll of both companies but also a rare place where the two transmedia empires can unofficially intersect[84] Black Panther's debut came as a surprise release, with the character arriving as part of a package deal of in-game "skins" (or costumes) including Captain Marvel and the villain Taskmaster that players could purchase with real-world money.[85] While the Panther shared the spotlight, the announcement trailer made it clear who the star of the package was. The trailer, which featured the in-game Marvel roster and Fortnite's original heroes gathering outside of the giant panther statue in Wakanda, lifted heavily from Coogler's film and other Panther media. As

Wolverine, Iron Man, Captain America, Storm, and other heroes gaze upward, the Panther walks to the edge of the statue to the ending chorus of Vince Staples' "Bagbak." The gathered heroes cross their arms across their chests in the now-iconic cross-armed "Wakanda Forever" salute as the king returns the gesture.[86] After the announcement, players could also engage in a series of short quests to unlock the salute as an animation for their in-game avatar.

For a brief thirty-second promotional trailer, the video is rich with meaning, and it does a lot of heavy lifting as part of a transmedia construct by implicitly acknowledging multiple strands of the Black Panther meta-brand. The characters involved—all of them original *Fortnite* characters or stylized versions of established Marvel heroes redrawn in the game's house style, making them video game characters as well as comic heroes—gather to exchange a salute specifically tied to the cinematic incarnation of the Black Panther. The in-game Black Panther model is an amalgamation of several designs, echoing the mask piping, tribal textures, and overall look of the cinematic version with the gold accents and cowl seen in Priest and Hudlin's incarnations. However, this is less important than the salute from the upward-looking characters—clearly meant as a tribute not just to the prominence of the character in the comic and game worlds but also to Chadwick Boseman, who had passed away only a few months prior to the character's release. The tacit meaning of the Black Panther standing atop a giant monument as the characters look heavenward toward him is hard to miss.[87] In short, in thirty seconds we have seen a video game adapt characters from a comic book medium to pay tribute to a cinematic interpretation of a character and the actor who plays him in service of promoting the appearance of that character within the game. If any interpretation in this chapter embodies the ethos and spirit of transmedia meta-branding, it is *Fortnite*'s approach to making the Black Panther part of its narrative tapestry not just in function, but in spirit.

The implementation of the character in the game shows the limitations of this approach, however. *Fortnite* character costumes are generally only cosmetic in nature and do not afford the player any special abilities, but rather just more stylish or iconographic approaches to the same gameplay mechanics. To put it in Manovich's terms, they are additional options in the database and expand the paradigm but wearing the Black Panther habit does not meaningfully change the gameplay any more than dressing like an Xenomorph from the *Alien* franchise or a Detroit Lions football player would. The player gets access to an aesthetically pleasing costume (proclaiming T'Challa as "the rightful king of Wakanda") and cape ("Dark as night and woven with Vibranium thread") for the character, and a "Wakandan Skyrider" ("A kingly ride") to glide across the map—but it is not functionally different from other such gliders in the game.[88] Most interesting are the Vibranium daggers ("Old school tool meets new school tech") that act as a replacement for the game's standard harvesting tools of axes and hammers, which are used to gather resources from breaking down rocks and structures on the island to build walls and other structures. This is a key part of the game's gameplay loop, but feels somewhat strange considering the source material's explicit coding of mining and harvesting as a goal of colonization—the Black Panther landing on another island and harvesting its resources when he has so often fought against outsiders doing the same to Wakanda feels vaguely hypocritical.[89] A charitable read of all of these criticisms is that the game treats these choices as "Outfits," meaning that they are simply costumes worn by faceless avatars and not the actual characters themselves, though this seems at odds with the transmedia symbolism of the associated marketing material.

The Panther also appeared in the short-lived online role-playing games *Marvel Heroes* and *Marvel Super Hero Squad Online,* both of which have been deactivated, as well as making an appearance as a playable character (with associated interactive figurine) in the "toys to life" game *Disney Infinity 3.0* as a tie-in with his appearance in the "Captain America: Civil War" film. Players who purchased the NFC-enabled figurine could simply place him on the base and use him in the game's building and exploration modes as well as a multiplayer battle arena.[90] The Panther also appears in several mobile games, such as the action-RPG *Marvel Future Fight* (where many of his abilities center on creating status effect changes for enemies), the color-matching puzzle game *Marvel Puzzle Quest* (where he has abilities emphasizing his strategic mind and Wakandan technology), the squad-based tactical RPG *Marvel Strike Force* (where he is labeled as an "agile, relentless hunter who shreds his enemies with rapid attacks" similar to other in-game appearances), and countless others.[91] While these games are less narratively complex than many of the others listed in this section, they nonetheless reinforce the paradigmatic definition of the Black Panther from an interactive media standpoint and in so doing also contribute to the larger transmedia understanding of the character.

This paradigmatic and syntagmatic construction of a transmedia identity within the larger transmedia brand of the character also tells us about the implicit perspectives and values assigned to the character—and the lack of in-game appearances until recently suggests that the developers (and more importantly Marvel as licensor) of these games simply did not see the Black Panther as a priority until the marketing requirements of the films forced their hand. That Marvel's first Black did not appear outside of comics and the occasional cartoon until there was a blockbuster film to attach the appearance to, all the while countless other heroes got their shot first, says something about what these companies feel about Black characters in terms of their marketability and beyond. Williams et al. suggested in their landmark "virtual census" study that the broad history of Black characters in video games is defined by the twin forces of underrepresentation and stereotyping, and Evan Narcisse pointed that the problem with avatar creation options and a perceived risk in the industry associated with portraying Black characters is a direct function of an overwhelmingly white developer population.[92] Yet, as Rico Norwood argues in his historiography of Black game characters for *Wired*, including such characters can be a "politically radical act that can combat the default of whiteness and, arguably, provoke systemic change in the industry."[93] While it is unreasonable to suggest that earlier appearances from Black Panther would have changed the course of the industry alone, the hesitance to include the character has often been a symptom of a much larger problem that is only now being rectified in a meaningful way with the character appearing in major releases. The historical reluctance to do so is both an indictment of larger systemic issues of race and representation in the gaming space and Marvel licensing, and this narrative too is a significant part of the Black Panther's transmedia legacy. As such, an interrogation of said legacy must account for the areas in which these transmedia industries remain hesitant to embrace non-white characters and perspectives.

KING'S DEAD: THE *BLACK PANTHER* CONCEPT ALBUM

In 2017, "Black Panther" director Ryan Coogler invited rapper Kendrick Lamar to view an early screening of a rough cut of his film. Coogler, who had long been a fan of Lamar's music, had originally asked the Pulitzer Prize-winning artist to contribute a few songs to the film. However, as the story goes, Lamar was so enamored with what he saw those few songs turned into a full concept album he worked on concurrently with his 2017 tour in support of his Pulitzer Prize-winning album *DAMN.*[94] The album released a week before the film did, and acts as an interesting sonic companion piece to the film and the larger legacy of the Black Panther—and while fully explicating the density of its themes and resonance to the character as well as the larger climate of Black identity and Lamar's own career would require more space than the current project allows, this chapter would not be complete without at least hitting some of the highlights.

One of the most striking things about the album is that while it has its origins as a piece of tie-in media to the *Black Panther* film and acts as a response to and interrogation of its themes, it is also indelibly a full-fledged Kendrick Lamar album and acts as an exploration of his own narrative interests. Part of that narrative is inspired by Lamar's 2015 visit to Africa after the success of his *good kid, m.A.A.d city* album, a point in his life where, in his own words, "The world around me kind've opened up."[95] While Lamar had rapped about his experiences in Africa before on his *To Pimp a Butterfly* album, for *Black Panther* he actively sought out to include African and African-descended voices from around the world, including several South African artists who contributed verses in their native Zulu language, to create a project that National Public Radio's Rodney Carmichel and Sidney Madden called "Pan-African in scope" in their review.[96] The result is a fascinating piece of work that serves as a sort of public forum for Lamar to work out the ideas in his head while also echoing some of the key themes present in so many other entrée points of the Panther transmedia franchise.

Lamar uses the Marvel material as a metaphor to explore his own thoughts on fame, legacy, and identity, with each track roughly aligning with different points in the film's narrative. Sonja Foss argues that criticism of metaphor consists of recognizing two parts of the metaphor—the tenor, which is the subject addressed by the speaker, and the vehicle, which is the "mechanism or lens through which the topic is viewed"—the drawing out of similarities between the two sets the rules for determining the system of meaning involved and changes how we view the tenor.[97] Consider how you might describe a difficult or tense situation as a "ticking time bomb"—something that can cause great harm and destruction in an impending timeframe—and the implicit fear generated by the use of such a vehicle may reflect a preference to avoid the situation or be overly cautious in handling it. In this way, the metaphor constructs our reality and filters our experiences through it.[98] In the case of Lamar's album, the story of T'Challa, Killmonger, Nakia, and other characters that implicitly weaves through the album's 13 tracks serves as the vehicle for Lamar and his collaborators to explore the tenor of larger themes of Diaspora and professional and personal struggle.

A recurring motif in the album is the dichotomy between T'Challa and Killmonger specifically, with Lamar identifying himself as both characters not only to clarify the narrative for the listener but also almost as a means of conflating warring aspects of himself with the characters. The first track, "Black Panther," naturally comes from T'Challa's perspective and echoes Lamar's exploration of themes of royalty and duality of the self in his other work, as he introduces himself as a king to all. He also fully rejects this idea of royal magnanimity in the ninth track "King's Dead," as he rattles off in a fast, aggressive flow "Fuck integrity, fuck your pedigree, fuck your feelings, fuck your culture, fuck your moral, fuck your family, fuck your tribe" and ends the verse with a defiant "all hail King Killmonger."[99] The album sympathizes with Killmonger's situation and upbringing, as seen later on the seventh track, "Paramedic!," a collaboration with Northern California hip-hop collective SOB x RBE. The song features a verse from artist Yhung T.O. which is, as explained in annotations by the group and other contributors on the lyrics analysis website *Genius,* about the violence and poverty he experienced growing up in his Bay Area neighborhood of North Vallejo (not dissimilar from Killmonger's orphaned Oakland upbringing), which brings a personal tenor to bear through the vehicle.[100] After all, what good is utopian tradition to someone who has never benefited from it?

Throughout the album, Lamar battles with himself as the two rivals do in the film, yet as Killmonger and T'Challa share a moment of commonality on screen toward the end of the film, so too does Lamar reconcile these disparate parts of himself at the end of the twelfth track, "Seasons" as he raps the chorus "I am T'Challa / I am Killmonger / One world, one god, one family." This continues the real empathy for Killmonger and those like him demonstrated throughout the album as Lamar and his collaborators compare their own life experiences and upbringing to his own, but also recognizing the T'Challa within as someone looking to bridge a gap and move forward.[101] As Slate's Carl Wilson identifies, this is the great rhetorical trick of Lamar's narrative— that he empathizes both with the "noble hero and [. . .] the hellbent dispossessed street fighter" and identifies a place where the vehicle truly explores the tenor's meaning and relates back to the film's thesis as well:

> [. . .] Lamar's signature, Shakespearean feat of negative capability is always to find the unities in the contradictions, to hold them in spiritual suspension. [. . .] Like the movie, this album follows from early on this arc of an ongoing confrontation between forces that really shouldn't have to be opposed at all, were it not for the distorting influence of injustice.[102]

And yet, in the end, Lamar also recognizes the limits of framing the complexity of Black liberation, African Diaspora, and identity in a protagonist/antagonist framework as the tenor starts to push up against the inherent challenges in the vehicle. In the final track, "Pray for Me," Lamar caps off several lines portraying the weary resignation of a man with the world on his shoulders and cleverly critiques the premise of both the film and the album with the line "Who need a hero? / You need a hero, look in a mirror, there go your hero."[103] While the Black Panther is a heroic figure, Lamar seems to be arguing that waiting for a government or a benevolent or supernatural individual to step in is a fool's errand, and that one should take on their own responsibility at the same time he suggests perhaps casting oneself as the hero or a king in their own story perpetuates these myths. Yet it is in that myth that Lamar's art found power and success—the album went platinum a few months after release—and Lamar himself suggests that the myth has power so long as we do not lose sight of reality the metaphor seeks to help us understand.[104]

Fundamentally, Lamar's album—and the other media in this chapter—act as a representation of that metaphor, allowing the audience to experience it and approach the vehicle and how it reflects the tenor of the situation in different ways. Whether it is reimagining the Black Panther for new audiences in the context of animation and children's programming or giving players the chance to inhabit the role of the character pursuant to the assets and rules of a video game, one of the most important aspects of the transmedia legacy of the character is how it acts as a parallel to explore and explain ideas beyond the page or the screen. How the transmedia character of Black Panther does this for different audiences and creators is dependent on the medium. Particular interpretations can therefore have a more outsized impact on that relationship based on how many people have access to them—say, for instance, the character's first feature film.

NOTES

1. Kendall, "Don't Look for These Spider-Man Shows."
2. Riesman, *True Believer*.
3. Howe, *Marvel Comics: The Untold Story*.
4. Couch, "Why Didn't 'Black Panther' Get A TV Show 20 Years Ago?"
5. Ibid.
6. Leopold & McLaughlin, "Prey of the Black Panther."
7. Ibid.
8. Ibid.
9. Couch, "Why Didn't 'Black Panther.'"
10. Simmons & Langley, "The First Panther."
11. McLellan, "Dwayne McDuffie."
12. Hoffmeier & Shinagawa, "Tremble at the Might."
13. Staples, "The Racist Trope That Won't Die."
14. Tejada, "Representation Without Transformation."
15. Goff et al., "Not Yet Human."
16. Hoffmeier & Shinagawa, "Tremble at the Might."
17. Juffé, Robinson, & Kyle, "Panther's Prey."
18. Ibid.
19. Ibid.
20. Ibid.
21. Juffé, Guyenne, Henry, & Constantine, "Line of Fire"; Juffé, Robinson, & Kyle, "Panther's Prey."
22. Juffe, Guyenne, Henry, & Constantine, "Line of Fire."
23. Ibid.
24. Ibid.
25. Kasinof, "An ugly truth."
26. Berman et al., "How minerals fuel conflicts in Africa"; Berman et al., "This Mine is Mine."
27. Bloem, "The Unintended Consequences"; Kasinof, "An ugly truth."

28. Juffe, Guyenne, Henry, & Constantine, "Line of Fire
29. Ibid.
30. Yost & Heuck, "The Man in the Ant Hill."
31. Ibid.
32. Ibid.
33. Heuck, Burke, & Wyatt, "Living Legend."
34. Montes & Giacoppo, "Panther's Quest.
35. Ibid.
36. Ibid.
37. Reed & Hartle, "Who Do You Trust?"
38. Ryan & Burdine, "Behold . . . The Vision!
39. Ibid.
40. Ibid; Yost & Kirkland, "Operation: Galactic Storm.
41. Yost & Kirkland, "Operation: Galactic Storm"; Yost & Gordon, "Live Kree or Die."
42. Son & Gunnell, "Panther's Rage."
43. Newby, "'Falcon and the Winter Soldier.'"
44. Son & Gunnell, "Panther's Rage."
45. Casey & Eldred, "Civil War Part 2."
46. Son & Gunnell, "Into the Deep."
47. Cooper & Gunnell, "The Zemo Sanction"; Son & Eldred, "The Panther and the Wolf."
48. Cooper & Gunnell, "The Zemo Sanction"; Devall & Eldred, "Atlantis Attacks"; Dunlap & Eldred, "Descent of the Shadow"; Easton & Eldred, "King Breaker, Part 2."
49. Craley & Lee, "The Last Avenger."
50. Son & Eldred, "T'Chanda."
51. Downer & Lee, "Yemandi."
52. Thorne & Eldred, "Bashenga."
53. Cooper & Lee, "Widowmaker."
54. Devall & Eldred, "Atlantis Attacks."
55. Ibid.
56. Gregori, "Family Friendly"; Hoffmeier & Black, Lego Marvel. King & Satō, "Black Panther." King & Satō, "The Final Fateful Battle."
57. Meuginot & Sebast, Ultimate Avengers 2.
58. Ibid.
59. Panels to Pixels, "History of Black Panther in Video Games."
60. Leone, "X-Men: Children of the Atom: An oral history."
61. Manovich, "Database as a Symbolic Form"; Manovich, *The Language of New Media*.
62. Ibid; Crystal Dynamics, *Marvel's Avengers*.
63. Manovich, "Database as a Symbolic Form," 89–90.
64. Carr, "Playing Like a Girl."
65. *Marvel: Ultimate Alliance*; Panels to Pixels, "History."
66. *Marvel: Ultimate Alliance 2*; RandomBlackGamer, "Marvel Ultimate Alliance 2."

67. Sung, "Marvel Ultimate Alliance 2 DLC."

68. Khan, "Marvel Ultimate Alliance Games Delisted."

69. *Marvel: Ultimate Alliance 3.*

70. Gamer's Little Playground, "Marvel: Ultimate Alliance 3 Movie"; *Marvel: Ultimate Alliance 3.*

71. *Marvel: Ultimate Alliance 3.*

72. Gamer's Little Playground, "Marvel: Ultimate Alliance 3 Movie"; *Marvel: Ultimate Alliance 3.*

73. *Marvel: Ultimate Alliance 3.*

74. *Lego Marvel Super Heroes*; *Lego Marvel's Avengers*; *Lego Marvel Super Heroes 2*; Panels to Pixels, "History."

75. *Lego Marvel Super Heroes 2.*

76. *Marvel vs. Capcom: Infinite.*

77. GenericGaming, "Marvel vs. Capcom: Infinite"; *Marvel vs. Capcom: Infinite.*

78. Johnston, "Chris Claremont"; Lawson, "Marvel vs. Capcom: Infinite."

79. Hurley, "Here's how many people play Fortnite."

80. Molly & Kelion, "Fortnite Movie Nite."

81. Good, "The Rise of Skywalker."

82. Phillips, "Fortnite storyline."

83. Webster, "Fortnite's Galactus event."

84. Whitbrook, "Batman's in Fortnite"; Whitbrook, "Marvel made Fortnite canon."

85. The Fortnite Team, "Black Panther."

86. Fortnite, "Marvel's Greatest Warriors."

87. Ibid.

88. *Fortnite.*

89. Ibid.

90. Panels to Pixels, "History."

91. *Marvel Future Fight*; *Marvel Puzzle Quest*; *Marvel Strike Force.*

92. Narcisse, "The Natural"; Williams et al., "The virtual census."

93. Norwood, "Coding Blackness."

94. Flanagan, "Kendrick Lamar's 'DAMN.'"

95. Lamar, "Position of Power."

96. Carmichael & Madden, "'Black Panther: The Album.'"

97. Foss, "Metaphor Criticism," 267.

98. Ibid, 268–69.

99. Lamar, *Black Panther: The Album.*

100. SOB x RBE & Contributors, "Paramedic"; Lamar, *Black Panther: The Album.*

101. Lamar, *Black Panther: The Album.*

102. Wilson, "Kendrick Lamar's *Black Panther* album."

103. Lamar, *Black Panther: The Album.*

104. Jefferson, "Wakanda Forever."

Chapter 9

A King Goes Hollywood

Black Panther and the Marvel Cinematic Universe

As the twentieth century wound down and the twenty-first century loomed, it was increasingly clear that the true value of the superhero genre was less in the comics that birthed it and more in adapting those characters to other media. Richard Donner's *Superman* proved there was a market for films based on superhero material, becoming a box office smash in 1978 and spawning several increasingly lesser sequels with which Donner was not involved. By 1984, Warner Bros. was scraping the bottom of the barrel with an ill-advised *Supergirl* movie that refused to take the character seriously and featured the heroine doing battle with her nemesis over the affections of a man.[1] 1989's *Batman* righted the ship again, setting eccentric lead performances from Michael Keaton as the title character and Jack Nicholson as the Joker against the stylized visuals for which director Tim Burton was quickly becoming famous. The movie became a major cultural phenomenon, shattering box office records with a then-unheard of $40.4 million opening weekend take that ultimately served to refocus the blockbuster film industry on short-term profitability in the first weekend of a film's release. The movie also underscored the vital importance of tie-in merchandising for superhero cinema, with Batman logo T-shirts, toys, and other consumer goods flooding the market.[2] The film's sequel, *Batman Returns*, played further into Burton's darker sensibilities and alienated much of the audience that had been captivated by the first film—its grim violence and queasy sexual overtones were seen as inappropriate for kids. This led many of Warner Bros.' marketing partners to reevaluate their relationship with the film. McDonald's, working from a rough cut of the film and assuming it was family friendly, covered their restaurants with Batman tie-ins but after backlash from parents and conservative groups went so far as to openly distance themselves from the movie and claim they were trying to capitalize on the concurrent *Batman: The Animated Series* instead. Action figure manufacturer Kenner made tie-in toys that had nothing to do with the movie.[3] As a result of the backlash (and the movie's lower overall box office revenue), Warner replaced Burton with Joel Schumacher for significantly campier, more merchandising-friendly sequels that eschewed the darker material altogether; the first cinematic Batman experiment ultimately ended with *Batman and Robin*, a movie that has since been lauded for its subversive homoeroticism but which failed at the box office in part to a new class of online critics who loudly and angrily rejected its extremely silly interpretation of the character.[4] The *Batman* films of the 1980s and 1990s, indirectly, are crucial to the narrative of understanding the Black Panther's long and difficult road to the big screen—and also demonstrate the cultural and economic forces of often toxic fandom, conflict between art and commerce, and need for immediate profitability that complicate the transmedia ecosystem.

Marvel itself had attempted to turn its characters into bankable movie stars in the 1980s as well, though the Black Panther was nowhere to be seen. Considering their output, that may have been for the best. Box-office bombs like 1986's *Howard the Duck*, which turned creator Steve Gerber's brilliantly subversive series into a bizarrely raunchy story featuring duck nudity and ill-advised puppets, was a spectacular failure, making back only $16 million of its astronomical-for-the-time $36 million budget. Later projects like a 1989 Dolph Lundgren *Punisher* film and a bizarre low-budget 1990 take on *Captain America* starring Matt Salinger (son of J. D. Salinger) both skipped theaters entirely in favor of direct-to-video releases.[5] Marvel's propensity to sell off the film rights to their characters also resulted in several abortive attempts at a big-budget film for the incredibly lucrative *Spider-Man* franchise and a 1994 *Fantastic Four* movie rushed into production by German producer Bernd Eichinger to keep his rights to the material from expiring. The latter project's budget varies depending on which accounts one reads, but it was likely not much more than $1.5 million. This bought a cast that looked less like superheroes than four friends in an awkward group Halloween costume and unintentionally hilarious special effects like attaching a fake arm to a camera and running it into actors to illustrate Mr. Fantastic's stretching ability. Reportedly, Marvel was so horrified by the project that Avi Arad, then the head of Marvel Entertainment, bought the film back from the producers so it could never be released—though bootlegs of the movie remain a hot commodity on the convention circuit.[6] If nothing else, Marvel's output at the time illustrates the lack of a clear and concise vision on the part of the company's owners and partners that would ultimately lead to financial difficulties to come over the next couple decades.

As a point of fact, there is a strong likelihood that Marvel would have never made any of the Avengers movies at all had the company still retained the rights to perennial favorites like Spider-Man, Hulk, and the X-Men. In 1993, Marvel acquired a significant ownership stake in the Toy Biz toy company, which held many of its licenses—the deal brought exclusivity to the Marvel brand for Toy Biz but also led to a change in leadership in the form of designer Avi Arad, who took over Marvel Films from Stan Lee (whose own power was dwindling after countless Hollywood meetings failed to result in any concrete productions).[7] Arad signed a deal later that year to make an *X-Men* film with 20th Century Fox, but the investment group that owned both Toy Biz and Marvel moved its money elsewhere after the comics industry bubble burst. As it turns out, endless collector's covers and first-issue re-releases were good for temporary profits, but the lack of scarcity resulted in little return for the comics speculator looking to make a profit on their purchase. Arad, determined, continued pushing Marvel's properties to anyone who would listen and was rewarded with a leadership position alongside Toy Biz president Ike Perlmutter for his efforts when Marvel finally came out of bankruptcy, but the company had already sold off the film rights to most of its characters to clear its debts.[8]

For years, the question of "which studio owned what?" was as convoluted as the plots that filled the publisher's pages—Universal owned the Hulk and Namor, but maybe only in solo movies for the former and only at the producer level for the latter.[9] Fox had the Fantastic Four and Daredevil and the X-Men, but Spider-Man and Ghost Rider were Sony's domain. Marvel's enviable pantheon of characters were divided throughout Hollywood without much rhyme or reason beyond who was willing to pay the most for each property, but they were all making money. Marvel flops happened, but they were rare, and even films of questionable quality like 2005's *Fantastic Four* tended to have impressive box office hauls. The superhero boom that started in the early 2000s was at a fever pitch, and Marvel—specifically Perlmutter and Arad—were trying to figure out how the company could cash in on its own characters. Once again, it should be noted the Black Panther was curiously missing in action during this corporate maneuvering.

This is not to say the king of Wakanda went wholly unnoticed by Hollywood in those times. In 1996, a financially floundering Marvel took a meeting with Wesley Snipes, then the wildly popular actor who had starred in films like *New Jack City*, *Demolition Man*, and *Passenger 57* to pitch him on a Black Panther film. As the story goes, Snipes was enthusiastic—in an interview years later with *The Hollywood Reporter*, he identified the Black Panther as "the antithesis of the stereotypes presented and portrayed about Africans, African history and the great kingdoms of Africa."[10] To Snipes, the movie would be an opportunity to celebrate both a character that meant a great deal to himself and "the communities that I grew up in" as well as promote Africa's heritage, but the project quickly ran into an issue that would plague the character for years to come—trying to explain the difference between the Black Panther (the superhero) and the Black Panthers (the revolutionary movement). *Boyz n' the Hood* director John Singleton pitched a version of the story where T'Challa, in this version a former member of the Black Panthers, tried to get his son to join him in the organization. Snipes felt it was too far from the vision of a technologically-advanced Africa that initially attracted him to the character.[11] While a later pitch from screenwriter Terry Hayes inspired some excitement, the film ultimately never got off the ground despite Snipes' efforts—though he would later ultimately serve to start the long tradition of successful Marvel adaptations with 1998's wildly popular *Blade*.[12] Not only was that movie a wildly successful vehicle for Snipes, who would reprise the role twice more, it also shored up Marvel's film brand at a critical time. Though most of the film's grosses went to the studio rather than Marvel itself, it sketched out the basic formula for success that later adaptations would follow and, as Richard Newby suggests, created a "successful business model that helped lead to the Marvel Cinematic Universe today."[13] Such a statement may seem like hyperbole, but consider: without the success of *Blade*, the case for making 2000's *X-Men* is much weaker, and without that film's success 2002's *Spider-Man* becomes less likely, and without that film sparking another wave of superhero cinema it is possible that Marvel Studios would not have had the drive to salvage what remaining cast-off characters they could to build a wildly profitable connected franchise. Marvel Studios president and Chief Creative Officer at the company Kevin Feige confirmed this in a 2017 interview with the movie fan site *Jo Blo*:

> But a few years before that, there was *Blade*. A character nobody had heard of at all, had only appeared in a few issues of *Tomb of Dracula* or something, turned into a big franchise. That was always a great lesson for me, where you go, "It doesn't matter how well known the character is, it matters how cool the movie is." Which, many years later, would be the reason we do *Guardians of the Galaxy, Doctor Strange*.[14]

Snipes may have never had the chance to play the Black Panther, but it is inarguable that he had a hand, however indirect, in the character finally reaching the screen. Still, it would be a long time—and only after Marvel Studios had proven its ability to take nearly any concept from its intellectual property holdings and turn it into a multimillion-dollar franchise—that they would finally take a chance on the company's original Black superhero.

The mid-2000s into the 2010s saw a rapid pace of expansion into transmedia discourse for Marvel. By 2007, the industry was starting to cool—superhero movies were still omnipresent but starting to wear on audiences, leading to lower box office takes and less critical enthusiasm. Marvel decided to take one last shot by attracting foreign investment with the rights to their remaining characters (of which Black Panther was one) as collateral.[15] Arad and Feige, then a new producer, began hiring directors to develop films. Jon Favreau was assigned to *Iron Man*, Edgar Wright was to develop *Ant-Man*, and Louis Leterrier would develop a take on *The Incredible Hulk*, who Marvel was able to reacquire from Universal Studios.[16] But it was Iron Man, the former arms dealer turned superhero, that would be the unlikely linchpin of the new cinematic franchise—allegedly because Perlmutter, ever the toy executive, felt he would be the best action figure.[17] As odd as it is to say now, an Iron Man film was far from a sure thing (though perhaps not an unreasonable risk)—the character was far from a household name and lead actor Robert Downey Jr. was attempting a career comeback after a long history of personal and legal issues. The movie, as the reader no doubt knows, turned out to be a massive success, encouraging Marvel to move forward with its ambitious cinematic universe plans that would allow the characters to cross over with each other across films—an innovation in film, though old hat on the comics page.

Feige oversaw a new slate of superhero films starring the Marvel heroes. While the plan started off cautiously—2008's *Iron Man* keeps its worldbuilding to a minimum save for the first of what would become a mandatory post-credits tag scene in which SHIELD director Nick Fury invites Tony Stark into "the Avengers Initiative"—it grew as frothing fan demand (and Marvel's own confidence in the products) grew. Disney, seeing an opportunity, acquired Marvel a year later for $4 billion—a miniscule investment compared to the transmedia juggernaut Marvel would eventually become.[18] The "Marvel Cinematic Universe," separated into distinct narrative "phases," went beyond merely adapting characters and plots and adapted the serialized nature of comics itself. Semi-annual (at minimum) releases rewarded fans who saw every movie with running gags, plot points, and insider knowledge they could debate with their friends and share with family and coworkers—and it opened the door for Marvel to use the relatively small stable of lesser-known heroes they had left to turn out massively-earning films with generally consistent critical success.

It also further solidified Disney's stranglehold on entertainment—in 2019, Disney and its subsidiaries accounted for nearly 40 percent of the year's box office, in no small part because of *Avengers: Endgame,* the final film in the decade-plus "Infinity Saga."[19] Disney's influence—and ownership of an unrivaled selection of intellectual property including not only Marvel but Star Wars, 20th Century Fox films, and its own legacy content—gives the company unmatched power in the theatrical exhibition space. In 2017, Disney forced theatrical exhibitors to hand over 65 percent of box office revenue for showings of *Star Wars: The Last Jedi*, an unheard of percentage—and their stunningly consistent box office takes means the studio releases fewer films, making theaters even more willing to accept Disney's unfavorable terms to protect their own profitability.[20] So significant is the role that Disney plays in theatrical exhibition that the 2020 announcement of a reorganization shifting the company's focus to streaming and direct-to-consumer distribution resulted in a jump in the company's stock price and immediate angst among theater chains, many of which were already facing significantly lower box office takes and even outright closure in the wake of the COVID-19 pandemic.[21] Disney's relative lack of competition in the space has also resulted in mass layoffs following the acquisition of 21st Century Fox's film and television libraries and production businesses and the closure of high-profile studios like animation house Blue Sky Studios on top of the consolidation.[22] In many ways, Marvel's success led to a more consolidated and less competitive entertainment industry. This crucial part of the transmedia legacy of Marvel—and by association the Black Panther—ultimately exists as a product of corporate short-sightedness made good, a happy accident made to capitalize on market trends that provided rocket fuel for an intellectual property conglomerate already taking up an inordinate amount of the cultural landscape. Given this context—and Disney as a company that acts as an industry onto and competing only with itself, who can take on nearly any risk and write off any loss—it is astounding that it would still take nearly a decade after Iron Man first suited up for Marvel's pre-eminent Black superhero to hit the silver screen.

THE PANTHER GOES MAINSTREAM

This is not to say T'Challa was not totally invisible—as seen in the previous chapters, the comics were critically acclaimed, and he was showing up more often in cartoons, games, and merchandise. But his long-awaited Marvel Cinematic Universe debut finally pushed the character into a new stratosphere. The Panther had in fact been considered in early plans for what would become the Marvel Cinematic Universe, both as that initial list of ten potential film franchises as well as a more actively developed project. Snipes was still attached to the character well into the early days of Marvel Studios, though his legal troubles (he had been charged with eight counts of tax fraud and failure to file tax returns for several years and would serve a three-year prison term starting in 2010) kept him out of contention to take on the role. He was released in 2013, a year before Feige would officially announce that a Black Panther film was in active development and the character would also appear in 2016's *Captain America: Civil War* played by up-and-coming actor Chadwick Boseman.[23]

As would become custom for Marvel projects, the studio laid the groundwork for his eventual appearance early, with a brief background reference to Wakanda in 2010's *Iron Man 2* and a direct mention of vibranium in 2011's *Captain America: The First Avenger.*[24] As Marvel's futures solidified from successful experiment to box office certainty, the second Avengers team film, *Age of Ultron*, served to introduce many of the upcoming narrative threads to be explored in subsequent films. While this focus on synergy made a mess of the film's narrative, plot elements related to the eventual inclusion of Wakanda and the Black Panther are nonetheless pivotal to the story. The villainous android Ultron and his heroic counterpart Vision are both made from vibranium, and Panther arch-nemesis Ulysses Klaw/Klaue debuts— once again prior to his heroic foil—as the film's secondary antagonist.[25] Hints aimed at long-time fans are one thing, though—it was quite another to develop who the MCU version of the Black Panther was.

Boseman, for his part, only began conversations with Marvel about taking on the role about a month before his involvement was announced; in his words, the meeting was less an audition and more of a mutual "feeling out" of what both parties wanted to do.[26] Boseman had already starred as Black luminaries like Jackie Robinson, Thurgood Marshall, and James Brown in well-received films like *42*, *Get On Up*, and *Marshall* (in an interesting side note, the last of which was directed by former Black Panther writer Reginald Hudlin). In Boseman's telling on a 2016 episode of *Live with Kelly and Michael*, the character had first crossed his path thanks to Charles Carter, an Australian bodyguard working as security for one of Boseman's co-stars in the film *Gods of Egypt*, who passed him his personal copy of an early *Black Panther* comic in early 2014 (well before Marvel made the announcement) with a note saying Boseman was going to get the role—Boseman also supposedly took the fateful Marvel call in front of an antique store window display of panther statues.[27]

Of course, Panther did not debut in his own film—rather, his grand reveal was saved for part of the quasi-Avengers team up film *Captain America: Civil War* in 2016.[28] In *Civil War*, audiences were introduced to Boseman's T'Challa as a reluctant young man seeking revenge for the murder of his father T'Chaka. The origin of the Panther as a response to Klaw's attempt at colonization and exploitation is curiously excised in the Marvel Cinematic Universe version of the character; instead T'Chaka is murdered as collateral damage in a plot to discredit and fracture the Avengers. Yet, *Civil War* functions well as a narrative construction of the Black Panther character within the framework of the larger Marvel Cinematic Universe structure—it reads best, perhaps, as the first act of a multi-film narrative arc in which T'Challa grows into the role of leadership.

Civil War's T'Challa is portrayed as someone who is capable and well-versed in the niceties of global politics, but chafes at the posturing and diplomacy necessary to participate in the role of king and ambassador to the outside world.[29] Such a position is not surprising for the Black Panther, a character more traditionally interested in adventuring than governing. The film also begins to position Wakanda into the larger world, with the country actively supporting the Sokovia Accords that would require superheroes to register with the United Nations after Wakandan citizens are killed during an Avengers battle as well as the fact that stolen vibranium was used to create the villainous android Ultron. T'Chaka's address to the United Nations also underscores Wakanda's isolationist nature, offering an overture for Wakanda to join the rest of the world before it is cut short by an explosion supposedly set off by the Winter Soldier, also known as Captain America's old friend Bucky Barnes. T'Challa takes it upon himself to bring the Soldier to Wakandan justice, casting his lot with the pro-registration side led by Iron Man.[30]

While T'Challa is a secondary character in *Civil War*, his story is nonetheless a thematic mirror to the main storyline. It also serves to set forth an identifiable African culture for Wakanda, with Boseman and Kani sharing a brief, unsubtitled scene in the Xhosa language. The language, spoken by millions of African people, is also Kani's native language, which he taught Boseman.[31] It also builds upon and introduces the Wakandan belief system. Following the death of T'Chaka, Black Widow expresses her sympathies. Holding his father's ring in his hand, T'Challa pontificates: "In my culture, death . . . is not the end. It's more of a stepping-off point. You reach out with both hands and Bast and Sekhmet, they lead you into a green veld where . . . you can run forever."[32]

As Harvard theology professor Jacob Olupona explains, many African cultures view ancestors as wise and powerful beings that live not only beyond in the afterlife but also through the lives of their descendants, offering advice and good fortune if properly honored—though he adds that this is far from a "fixed creed" and many cultures have different interpretations.[33] While the later solo Panther film would make the Ancestral Plane an actual inhabitable space, this is the first hint that the cinematic interpretation of the character would bring forward what had become from the Christopher Priest run onward a significant part of the character's relationship to African culture—and also a clear sign that patrilineal legacy would be a primary theme. Most importantly, however, *Civil War* lays the groundwork for the ongoing evolution of T'Challa as a character. Throughout the film, T'Challa is motivated primarily by vengeance for his father, framing his pursuit of Barnes not only as a wronged son but as a categorical imperative in his new role as he confronts Captain America: "The Black Panther has been a protector of Wakanda for generations. A mantle passed from warrior to warrior. Now because your friend murdered my father, I also wear the mantle of king. So, I ask you, as both warrior and king, how long do you think you can keep your friend safe from me?"[34]

The pretenses of diplomacy cast aside and one massive CGI superhero fight later, T'Challa secretly follows Tony Stark to a secret facility where it is revealed that the murder of King T'Chaka was part of a larger plot orchestrated by Helmut Zemo, a Sokovian intelligence agent whose family was killed as collateral damage during the Avengers' battle with Ultron—by pinning the explosion on the Winter Soldier and exploiting the tensions over the Sokovian Accords, Zemo successfully drove a spiritual wedge between the heroes, throwing their reason for existence into question. It is T'Challa who ultimately apprehends Zemo in a scene demonstrating that he has begun to grow into the role of king. After Zemo calmly explains his plan and motivation, he apologizes to the young king for murdering his father. A weary T'Challa retracts his claws and tells Zemo "Vengeance has consumed you. It's consuming them. I'm done letting it consume me.'" shortly before foiling Zemo's plan to commit suicide ("The living are not done with you yet").[35] By sparing the man's life and allowing an international system of justice to process him, T'Challa demonstrates both personal growth and the ability to make the first of many hard choices on the path to opening Wakanda up to the rest of the world, followed shortly by his later invitation to Barnes to stay in Wakanda for deprogramming. In this way, he perhaps respects the precedent set by his father's desire to go to the UN in the first place, but more importantly he internalizes his own personal code of ethics that carries forward into future depictions of the character—and opens up a world of other problems, per the character's transmedia traditions.

HIS OWN HERO

Shortly before the release of *Civil War* in 2016, Marvel confirmed that Ryan Coogler would helm the *Black Panther* solo film. The director, who confessed a love for comic books, stated that the Marvel job was "just as personal to me as the last couple of films I was able to make."[36] While *Panther* would only be Coogler's third feature film, his track record in both independent and large-scale blockbuster films was impeccable. An Oakland native and graduate of the USC School of Cinematic Arts, Coogler's feature film debut was 2013's *Fruitvale Station*. That film offered a dramatized depiction of the day in the life of Oscar Grant III, a young man who was detained and killed on the Fruitvale Station BART platform by a police officer. It starred Michael B. Jordan, who soon became a recurring collaborator for Coogler and again took the lead role in 2015's *Creed*, a sequel to the *Rocky* franchise focused on Adonis Johnson, the son of Rocky's rival Apollo Creed.

Both films, in their own way, echo the complex realities of the Black experience in America and would inform Coogler's *Panther*. *Fruitvale Station* offers a look at the mundanity and lived experiences of a victim of police brutality, looking at the innate humanity of someone beyond the headlines or protest slogans. Not much happens in the film, which is arguably the point—the act that ended Grant's life is part of the day, but not the sum of his life or his value to others. In an interview with the Washington Post, Coogler suggested that the film was deeply personal for him:

> I was in the Bay Area, on Christmas break from film school when it happened [. . .] I realized that Oscar could have been me. We were the same age, his friends looked like my friends and we wore the same type of clothes. [. . .] Oscar was a real person with real struggles and personal conflicts, but also with real hopes, real dreams, goals and a family.[37]

In this way, the film acts as its own necessary counter-narrative to decades of popular culture and entertainment that, in the words of critic Steven Boone, trafficked in stereotypes that treated Black men generally as "loud, imbecilic thugs" and created a "dehumanization circus" that served only to support racist attitudes. Boone suggests that Jordan's portrayal and Coogler's direction illustrate "how aware Oscar was that his freedom and even his life could depend on overturning a superficial, unfair impression."[38] Boone's comments hit at the core of what makes *Fruitvale Station* so resonant—the film simply rejects the idea that there is not a life or meaning behind the statistics and stereotypes and asks the viewer to consider the entire person instead.

By comparison, 2015's *Creed* was a more straightforward film, a sports drama drawing on Coogler's own affinity for athletics that helped prove his bona fides as an action director. While not as heavy or insightful into the Black human condition as its sister film, *Creed* nonetheless tries to address these issues in its own way. The film starts with Adonis Johnson's stint in juvenile hall as a young boy after his mother's death—analogous to Grant's brush with the adult carceral system explored in a flashback in *Station*. Despite him being the product of her husband's extramarital affair, the late Apollo Creed's wife takes the young man in and raises him as her own. While an impactful and well-acted scene, this is merely a moment of table-setting before the main story of the film. More important to the construction of Coogler's "Panther" is how *Creed* grapples with parental legacy. Johnson idolizes his late father and quits his white-collar job to pursue boxing full time, ultimately tracking down Rocky Balboa to train under him. The older man is hesitant, wondering why Johnson, who had advantages he and his father never did, would go into boxing and insisting that Apollo would tell him not to fight if he didn't have a choice, though he ultimately takes Adonis in and trains him.[39] Throughout the film, Johnson struggles to overcome his father's name and hides it to make one of his own but by the end of the film ultimately embraces it, going by the Creed name after a promoter requires him to in the film's climactic title bout. As Johnson comes out to the ring in the iconic red, white, and blue trunks his father wore, his story becomes part of the legacy rather than something he must live up to—as Balboa encourages him, "You're doing it for your-self—not me, or your father's memory."[40] That frequent collaborator Michael B. Jordan plays both of these characters as well as the antagonist in *Black Panther* is not an accident—not only is Jordan a stellar actor in his own right, Coogler puts these themes into the vessel of Erik Killmonger. One could argue Jordan is the transmedia connection between Coogler's sensibilities and the larger world of the Black Panther—his performances act as spiritual connections between the films, manifesting thematic resonance.

The *Black Panther* film is set shortly after *Civil War* and expands on the groundwork for the character established in the latter film, opening with a brief explanation of the lore of Wakanda presented as a story from father to son in a minimalist animated sequence. The opening sequence echoes much of the symbolism of the rest of the Black Panther mythology, exploring specifically how Wakanda chose to specifically isolate itself from the war and strife of the outside world, segueing into 1992 Oakland and demonstrating the potential cost of that choice as then-king T'Chaka confronts his brother and an associate for smuggling vibranium out of Wakanda.[41] Here, Coogler makes the rhetorical choice to juxtapose the mythic quality of Wakanda's history—presented in dreamlike purple hues and abstract animated physical forms as a story of "home" from T'Chaka's brother N'Jobu to his son N'Jadaka—with the harsh reality of a city and people indirectly harmed by Wakandan isolationism. It is revealed in 1992 N'Jobu had gone against the king's wishes and worked to arm Black revolutionaries by selling vibranium to the arms dealer Ulysses Klaue. N'Jobu's partner is revealed to be Zuri, another Wakandan who is working undercover at T'Chaka's behest to keep track of his brother—the disagreement results in T'Chaka killing his brother with his Panther claws, a metaphor for the needs of Wakanda outweighing the life of a man. On a nearby basketball court, the young N'Jadaka watches the Wakandan ships fly off into the night, unaware of what has happened to his father. From the beginning, the tension of Wakanda as idealistic home and the nation's political agenda are at the core of how N'Jadaka sees the world—he both loves what Wakanda represents and hates what it (or the people in charge) have done to him to keep the nation a secret. The opening scenes of the film explore the promise and the lie of Wakanda—asking the viewer to consider the "rightness" of the space and carrying forth the complex legacy that other creators had explored in their work.

However, as this is primarily a comic book film, Coogler is quick to follow this philosophical table-setting up with an action scene of the Panther, his bodyguard and general Okoye, and love interest Nakia rescuing a group of women from an insurgent group clearly meant to evoke Boko Haram. The film references the group's practice of conscripting child soldiers when Nakia stops Black Panther from incapacitating a militant by identifying him as a child.[42] Here the Panther acts again as a "corrective" or "recuperative" influence—much as he metaphorically saved a man's life from the Ku Klux Klan in McGregor's stories, fought back against imperialist interests in Priest's tales, and evacuated citizens in Louisiana after Katrina in Hudlin's run, Coogler imagines a hero for Africa that does battle with a proxy for one of the continent's real-world social ills. Indeed, many other elements present in other Black Panther media that critique the real-world exploitation of the African continent appear in this film. The MCU's reimagined Klaue remains the embodiment of white colonialism and exploitation, trading the coded pith hat for a more disheveled gangster look but still maintaining the colonialist language and attitude he uses in other versions, referring to Wakandans as "savages" and likening Wakanda and its resources to the "lost city of gold" El Dorado—implying a sort of colonialist Manifest Destiny for exploration and exploitation.[43] While many aspects of his character are changed for the film, his role as white plunderer of African culture and resources remains consistent, further casting the Panther as a character existing in direct opposition to these ideas.

The concept of T'Challa as a reluctant leader caught between worlds appears in this film as well, exacerbated by the nominally anti-colonialist threat of Killmonger. T'Challa's rule and right to lead are questioned throughout the film, both by Killmonger and T'Challa's rival M'Baku—who loudly proclaims T'Challa lacks the strength to lead and fight without his powers before losing his challenge to the throne. T'Challa's early conversations with his deceased father echo his own concerns about his readiness, to which his father speaks on the inherent compromises of leadership—"You are a good man, with a good heart. And it's hard for a good man to be king."[44] With this line, T'Chaka alludes to his own failure—killing his own brother in service of protecting his country—but also to the compromises a king must make. T'Challa, at this point, is aware of the need for compromise, having handed Zemo over to international justice rather than Wakanda's own, but if *Civil War* was the incipient days of T'Challa as leader, *Black Panther* represents the infinitely more complex growing pains of governing a nation and upholding potentially contradictory sets of ideals in a culture that rejects outside authority. Yet it is this liberal engagement and diplomatic outreach to the rest of the colonizing world that positions T'Challa, at least in this narrative, as the representative of potentially compromised systems of order.

Where Coogler truly sets his vision of the character apart is the sympathy his direction and script show for the antagonist. Killmonger has often been portrayed as T'Challa's intellectual and physical equal if not his superior, but Coogler and co-writer Joe Robert Cole position him in the film as a philosophical and ideological threat to Wakandan dogma and legacy as well. From an early scene in an exhibit of West African artifacts, Killmonger is positioned in the film as an anti-colonialist voice. After threatening to take one of the artifacts and being rebuked by the curator who says they are not for sale, Killmonger asks "How do you think your ancestors got these? Did they pay a fair price? Or did they take it, like they took everything else?"[45] The ensuing theft of the artifacts—and the death and destruction left behind by Killmonger, Klaue, and their associates—is justified at least in Killmonger's mind as a reparative act, a means of reclaiming that which was stolen from him and others.

Working with Klaue, Killmonger and his team rob the exhibit and take a vibranium artifact to sell for their own purposes, but not before Killmonger takes a tribal mask from a display, effectively reclaiming it as his own identity and wearing it throughout the film. This is an important rhetorical moment, as the antagonist acts as both an inversion of the protagonist but also representing a similar "double consciousness"—like T'Challa he is Wakandan by birth and brings his knowledge of the outside world to the walled garden of the country. Unlike T'Challa, his bona fides are questioned—in one scene CIA agent Everett Ross corrects Shuri by saying Killmonger isn't Wakandan, but "one of ours," an American.[46] This identification complicates the character further, both by associating the antagonist with the forces of American empire as well as underscoring his lack of acceptance in Wakandan culture.

Killmonger's goal is revealed over the course of the film as entering Wakanda and gaining access to its technology and power to overthrow white power structures around the world—carrying forth what he saw as his father's legacy just as T'Challa grapples with T'Chaka's. In part, this is a revenge play, but again he justifies it (to the viewer, and to himself) as an attempt to help those Wakanda has ignored over the years: "You know, where I'm from . . . when Black folks started revolutions, they never had the firepower . . . or the resources to fight their oppressors. Where was Wakanda? Hmm? Yeah, all that ends today. [. . .] The world's gonna start over, and this time we're on top. The sun will never set on the Wakandan empire."[47]

The concept of an inverted vision of Wakanda driven by imperialist goals of conquest, echoed later in Coates' "Intergalactic Empire of Wakanda storyline," serves again both as a rhetorical interrogation of the concept but also pulls the character back from being fully sympathetic. The film invokes some clever critique of U.S. foreign policy even as it ultimately reassures the viewer that Killmonger is in fact the bad guy, though never losing sight of the fact that the reason he is a threat because he internalized and inverted American colonizing attitudes. Killmonger's means are ruthless and utilize the training he received in the U.S. military—effectively appropriating the role of imperialism for his own ends—and his willingness to toss aside female life (he sacrifices his lover and slits the throat of a Dora Milaje in the final battle of the film) show him as a clear opposite to T'Challa's more measured exercise of power, guided and tempered by matriarchal respect. Killmonger's actions echo the "by any means necessary" philosophy of Malcolm X while ignoring X's caveat against being the aggressor and pursuing his own version of an "equitable" outcome where he happens to be on top. In one scene, he speaks of training and killing across the world just to get to T'Challa and overthrow him—"I took life from my own brothers and sisters right here on this continent! And all this death just so I could kill you."[48] Killmonger is held up rhetorically as both aggressor and victim, representing the threatening force of colonization to Wakanda but also the tragic product of that force on his worldview and his own status as a victim of colonization and subjugation. Shortly after he defeats T'Challa in the trial by combat and undergoes the ritual to become the new Panther, he meets with his late father on the Ancestral Plane just as T'Challa had conversed with T'Chaka. When N'Jobu asks why his son does not shed tears for his father's death, Killmonger explains it by saying death is simply a part of his life, though Jordan's performance and his tears suggest this is a lie he tells himself to avoid confronting his genuine pain.[49]

Yet for all the ink spilled over the prominence of Killmonger and his role as a revolutionary anti-colonizing force in the film, it is arguably Lupita Nyong'o's Nakia who advances much of the same ideology without accompanying imperialism. From the beginning, she challenges Wakanda's isolationism just as Killmonger did but without the implicit belief that militarism is a necessary restorative for the ills of Wakanda's past: "I've seen too many in need just to turn a blind eye. I can't be happy here, knowing that there's people out there who have nothing. [. . .] Wakanda is strong enough to help others and protect ourselves at the same time."[50] Nakia's role of seeking equity and justice for the victims of Wakandan isolationism and non-intervention rather than vengeance often goes overlooked in most critiques of the film. I argue it is a key ideological force in what the movie asks us to consider. Is Killmonger truly revolutionary, or simply redirecting the same imperialist mindset away from his people and toward the rest of the world? As Ross points out, Killmonger was part of a unit that was trained to destabilize governments by striking during moments of transition or strife, interfering at a pivotal moment to gain access of the military, government, and resources of the country.[51] This seems to be a conscious choice on the part of the filmmakers to illustrate the ultimate ill effects of colonization by drawing clear allegories to real-world history. Yet the fact that it comes from the mouth of a CIA agent is ironic, considering the agency's long history of interventionism and interference in African politics and war.

The issue of Everett Ross's role in the MCU is one of the stickier, if less-considered aspects of the MCU discourse. Rather than being the hyper-verbal, comically ignorant State Department attaché of Priest's run, Ross is presented here as a more competent ex-fighter pilot and CIA agent. Given real-world history and the traditional role of the character, this change is one of the more difficult aspects of the film. It could be argued that much of this change is driven by plot convenience—he must be a representative of some form of internationally recognized agency, law enforcement or otherwise, to explain his appearance in South Korea tracking down Ulysses Klaue. The most logical solution would have been to make him an emissary of SHIELD, but due to the events of *Captain America & the Winter Soldier*, that spy agency is gone. Moreover, since he had been established as CIA in *Civil War*, it would require additional explanation to change—and it is unlikely Marvel would care to. This misstep suggests a problem with Marvel's approach to plot secrecy and its proven impact on creative collaboration and cohesion. Winston Duke, who played M'Baku in *Black Panther* and *Avengers: Infinity War* and is as of this writing slated to return for the *Panther* sequel *Wakanda Forever*, claimed that he had no idea he was auditioning for the original film at first because the studio would not tell him. In addition, because *Black Panther* and *Infinity War* were in production at the same time the latter film's directors had little to no idea of what Wakandan culture was like—so the Wakandan actors were ultimately responsible for improvising the chants, language, and dialogue used in the action sequences set in the country.[52] Regardless of reason, the fact that Ross takes on a heroic role in the film's ultimate confrontation by shooting down aircraft carrying Wakandan soldiers as they attempt to bring the country's weapons and resources outside of the nation's borders further complicates the film's politics. These choices, well-intentioned as they may have been, explain some of the criticism leveled against the film and explored later in this chapter.

Coogler's interest in patrilineal legacy is explored elsewhere in the film via the recurring motif of the Ancestral Plane, which is used in the film by both T'Challa and Killmonger to grapple with their respective questions of legacy and identity. On this alternate plane of existence, drenched again in purple hues of royalty, those undergoing the process of gaining the Black Panther's powers seek counsel from their ancestors in accordance with many traditional African belief structures. Late in the film, the purple motif goes away as T'Challa—resurrected after nearly falling to his death after his battle with Killmonger—recognizes the truth of what his father did and the real cost of Wakandan isolation, meeting his father's spirit with a heartbroken declaration that the ancestors and Wakanda "let the fear of our discovery stop us from doing what was right" and that Killmonger is "a monster of our own making."[53] T'Challa's statement here neatly serves both to recognize the complicity of Wakandan dogma in the current situation and more broadly as a source of injustice in the larger scope of history while also neatly reminding the viewer that Killmonger's neo-imperialist position cannot be abided, regardless of stated justification.

Yet in the end, this represents the ultimate revolutionary act of the film as an example of the superhero genre—the antagonist sparks a situation that ultimately changes the hero's mind. As T'Challa and Killmonger face off for a final time, T'Challa calls his rival out for what he views as inherent hypocrisy. When Killmonger says he is just learning from his enemies to "beat them at their own game," T'Challa yells back that he has become them, and he will "destroy the world, Wakanda included."[54] The message is clear: in his quest for both personal and historical retribution, T'Challa sees Killmonger as becoming the very thing he despised. The final struggle between the two rivals becomes something of a ham-fisted metaphor as the battle for the soul of Wakanda (and Black liberation) takes place on the subterranean tracks of the rapid transit system of cars ferrying vibranium out of the mines of the Great Mound—a literal underground railroad.

T'Challa then mortally wounds Killmonger—a clear callback to *Fruitvale Station* as both Oscar and Killmonger, young men from Coogler's home in the Bay Area, meet their ends on a train platform. Yet, where the dread of impending loss hangs over *Fruitvale*—as critic Mohit Priyadarshi put it, "we are constantly thinking about the inevitable tragedy that is due to unfold and feel our fists clench tighter because of it"—Killmonger's unfortunate and shocking death nonetheless seems to restore the genre's implicit order.[55] We grieve for what might have been and the circumstances that led him there, but the language of superhero films suggests the villain—or at least the ideological opposition—must be vanquished or defeated. As Priyadarshi suggests, it gives the audience "an end which leaves everyone satisfied."[56] At their best— and it is hard to argue that Coogler's *Black Panther* is not among the best— superhero stories can be complex and challenging and speak to fundamental truths, yet the genre struggles to engage with these issues because of its need to offer resolution and karmic balance. That Killmonger—represented both in his own words and on a metatextual level as a rare Black revolutionary in blockbuster film—pays the ultimate price for his beliefs suggests that the film still has that audience-pleasing imperative on its mind and less interest in interrogating why such an event creates that satisfaction.

Yet this read also leaves out the more thoughtful way in which this moment—the end of a complex life that could have gone differently had Wakanda embraced him and his father rather than leaving him and the Black community he represents to their own devices—provides sympathy and sorrow and ultimately results in a fundamental paradigm shift for Wakanda and the Black Panther. It is not victory, but a bittersweet tragedy to inspire a quiet revolution. After being stabbed by his cousin, Killmonger uses his final moments to reflect on how he got to this point: "My pop said Wakanda was the most beautiful thing he ever seen. He promised he was gonna show it to me one day. You believe that? Kid from Oakland, runnin' around, believing in fairy tales."[57] This line serves to illustrate again the idea of Wakanda as a corrective and healing metaphor for the pain of colonization and black exploitation—but also to recognize it as fictive, a dream of promise and potential harshly out of step with real, lived experiences. As an act of kindness, T'Challa takes Killmonger to the cliffs overlooking Wakanda as the sun sets so he may see it for himself (he is, once again, done letting vengeance consume him). He offers to heal Killmonger's wound, to which Killmonger offers one final renunciation as he pulls the blade out himself and ends his own life: "Why, so you can lock me up? Nah. Just bury me in the ocean with my ancestors who jumped from ships, 'cause they knew death was better than bondage."[58]

This line, one of the most famous in the film, was not in the original script, and evidence of how much influence Boseman had on the production. Per Coogler, Boseman had not only pressed for Xhosa to be the "native language" of Wakanda, he also had insisted that the Wakandan representatives dance during the coronation ceremony scenes in the film and that T'Challa speak English dialogue with an African accent "so that he could present T'Challa to audiences as an African king, whose dialect had not been conquered by the West."[58] In an interview with *CNet*, Boseman went further:

> Colonialism in Africa would have it that, in order to be a ruler, [T'Challa's] education comes from Europe [. . .] that would be counter to everything that Wakanda is about. [. . .] If it's supposed to not have been conquered—which means that advancement has happened without colonialism tainting it, poisoning the well of it, without stopping it or disrupting it—then there's no way he would speak with a European accent. If I did that, I would be conveying a white supremacist idea of what being educated is and what being royal or presidential is.[59]

Per Coogler, the original draft of the script had Killmonger requesting to be buried in Wakanda, but "Chad challenged that and asked, what if Killmonger asked to be buried somewhere else?"[60] The result is one of the more powerful and challenging moments in the film and arguably the entire genre, a scene of brutal clarity for its characters and the audience about how the Wakandan metaphor butts up against the real world legacies of colonialism and slavery.

Moved by Killmonger's words and guilt over what his father did, T'Challa ultimately follows Nakia's wishes and opens Wakanda up to the rest of the world, investing in housing, education, and technology in Killmonger's home city of Oakland and elsewhere. In the film's first post-credits scene, T'Challa addresses the United Nations and informs them of Wakanda's intent to share its knowledge and technology with the outside world, with his words serving as a summary of the film's themes: "Now more than ever, the illusions of division threaten our very existence. [. . .] More connects us than separates us. But in times of crisis, the wise build bridges, while the foolish build barriers. We must find a way to look after one another as if we were one, single tribe."[61]

Ultimately, while Killmonger's presence in the country puts the lie to the legacy of the royal line of Wakanda, it is Nakia's vision of Wakanda's future that wins out—through the creation of a Wakanda open to all, perhaps the circumstances that led to the fall of one of its sons would not happen again. Yet this comes after an action set piece representing what is effectively a civil war in which many Wakandans die as the heroes attempt to stop Killmonger's export of weapons and soldiers from the country. Africa has a long history of internal conflicts—the conflict and later cold war between Ethiopia and Eritrea and the conflicts in Sierra Leone and the Congo to name a few—resulting in long-lasting instability and pain for the people of these regions.[62] The film does not remark upon this or stop to lament the bloodshed of a nation's tribes turned against each other—it simply uses this loaded imagery because a superhero film must have a final, special effects-laden conflict. Again, however well-intentioned, the structure of the superhero narrative makes comparisons to reality inherently fraught, and the filmmakers stumble by including these images without truly contextualizing them.

Much of the discourse around the film focused on Jordan's portrayal of Killmonger and the call to Black liberation he represented. In a piece for *Shadow and Act*, Brooke Obie suggested that the character's pain and resentment over being abandoned reflect on the "rawest parts of being African American":

> If Wakanda is the Black Promised Land, then we are its forgotten children, sold away, left behind, rejected, condescended to. Swirling in constant reminders of worthlessness, of the specific anti-Black-American toxicity experienced by Black folk in the U.S.A., Killmonger is angry—not just at white supremacist oppressors or systemic racism, but also the Black Elite who left him behind. And he has every right to want vengeance.[63]

By comparison, Obie argues, T'Challa has the privilege and luxury of choosing to believe in justice and the law due to his regal station; Obie also expressed skepticism about T'Challa's outreach to the United Nations at the end of the film as a means of truly helping the oppressed.[64] This read of T'Challa as endorsing a status quo that does not actively challenge white power structures is one that has been present in much of the character's history, particularly in the Bronze Age *Avengers* stories, and the MCU depiction of the character opening up Wakanda to the world and its predominantly white heroes does not do much to challenge Obie's assertion.

Journalist Adam Serwer similarly lauded the film for its complex approach to the Killmonger character, suggesting that the film makes him sympathetic and ultimately the catalyst behind Wakandan efforts to benefit people of African descent around the world; all the while still criticizing his goal of hegemonic empire. As Serwer put it:

> It is remarkable that many viewers seem to have taken the "liberation" part at face value, and ignored the "empire" part, which Jordan delivers perfectly. [. . .] Killmonger's plan for "black liberation", arming insurgencies all over the world, is an American policy that has backfired and led to unforeseen disasters perhaps every single time it has been deployed; it is somewhat bizarre to see people endorse a comic-book version of George W. Bush's foreign policy [. . .] as long as the words "black liberation" are used in place of "democracy promotion."[65]

Serwer correctly notes that one of the first targets for Killmonger's effort is Hong Kong, hardly a traditional center of "white Western hegemony" and an unlikely target for a purely restorative attack.[66] Textually, at least, the film supports the idea that Killmonger's intent is noble even if his actions are contrary to that stated intent. This echoes the comics, where Killmonger is presented less as a revolutionary and more as a brutal and ruthless capitalist seeking power for his own right or out of personal vengeance against T'Challa, but it could be argued that this itself is a means by a predominantly white film studio to encourage the "right" kind of protest and liberation.

Journalist James Wilt took issue with what he felt was a confusing and contradictory depiction of Black nationalism and a lack of depth in the character of Killmonger, criticizing the film for using that character and the fictionalized history of Wakanda as a means of espousing neoliberal philosophy and politics for the comfort of a white audience. As Wilt puts it, the film "contains a fundamentally reactionary understanding of black liberation that blatantly advocates bourgeois respectability over revolution."[67] Critical race scholar and originator of the concept of intersectionality Kimberlé Crenshaw expressed frustration over the film's usage of a CIA agent shooting down "vessels carrying technology into the fight against an anti-black world order" as echoing the agency's real-world interference on the continent, as well as what she felt was a reinforcement of regressive views of Black power and liberation: "Black power has always been framed by its critics as dangerous, irrational, bloodthirsty revenge. Today's identity extremists were yesterday's Panthers and Pan Africanists. How did that libelous trope come to be the central tension in this celebration of Black superheroes?"[68]

These are legitimate criticisms of the film that suggest ultimately there are limits to how truly anti-colonialist and revolutionary a film released by one of the largest media conglomerates in the world that is expected to fit neatly into one of the most heavily regimented and carefully produced film franchises in history can be. Simply put, like most Marvel output, Black Panther is a product that carries significant economic burdens beyond simply being a unique celebration of Black identity and power. However, the film clearly tries to work within the limitations of these parameters to introduce complex questions about colonization and black identity in that blockbuster framework, an admirable effort even if it falls short in key areas. In one oft-cited scene set in South Korea as T'Challa, Okoye, and Nakia track down Ulysses Klaue, Coogler frames and dresses Nakia, T'Challa, and Okoye in red, green, and black clothing in one scene as an homage to the Pan-African flag and what it represents, and Ulysses Klaue in blue to represent the destructive force of colonization.[69] Coogler also clearly shows the ills of colonization as represented in actual force by Klaue and in effect by Killmonger; Shuri even uses the term "colonizer" to insult Ross when he startles her. While the metaphor is, as always, imperfect, it is hard to argue that the film does not genuinely believe in some form of meaningful Black liberation—and despite Killmonger's role as the film's antagonist, it is ultimately colonizing attitudes, trauma, and the drive for empire that are the true threat. Ultimately, the Black Panther film represented a pivotal moment in popular discourse about Africa and Black identity, where the vision of Wakanda was both celebrated and challenged. Historian N. D. B. Connolly championed the film's embrace of the historical dream of "free African nations" and anti-colonialism as well as its "literary and historical sinews tying us back to the black past, or better, to black past *dreams*."[70]

In short, the film is a powerful if fraught metaphor, building on the foundation established by Lee, Kirby, McGregor, Priest, and other writers. Unlike many other superhero films, it is aggressively trying to be about something and largely succeeds at introducing ideas and discourse rarely seen at the multiplex and exclusively unseen in major blockbusters. Personally, I have used it to introduce concepts like the African Diaspora and colonialism in college courses to students unlikely to have ever been exposed to these ideas. The film also has had a tremendous impact both on the prominence of Black voices and creatives in the superhero media space. After the film's success,

Ryan Coogler was not only brought on to write and direct the sequel but also landed a five-year exclusivity deal with Disney to produce programs for its various corporate divisions through his Proximity Media company, one of which will be a new dramatic series set in Wakanda for the Disney+ streaming service.[71] In this way, he and Boseman are set to become two of the most influential creators in the character's transmedia history.

A KING LONG REMEMBERED

The success of "Black Panther" was not overly surprising, yet the production timelines of the Marvel Cinematic Universe dictate that future films featuring the character were already in development concurrently with Coogler's flagship project—as such, a casual viewer may be confused why the hero of one of Marvel's biggest success stories to date only features briefly in *Avengers: Infinity War*, the penultimate film of the first ten years of the Avengers saga. Odds are you are familiar with the story, but to review—throughout the background of the previous Marvel Cinematic Universe films, the intergalactic tyrant Thanos has been collecting a set of cosmic MacGuffins known as the Infinity Stones, and as is revealed in this film his goal is to use them to erase half of life from existence to create balance and sustainability throughout the universe—an extremist utilitarian plan that is in practice effectively genocide. A full recitation of the film's events is not particularly helpful for our current discussion, but the plot comes to Wakanda because one of those stones is in the head of the android Avenger Vision. Faced with the prospect of forcing the Scarlet Witch to destroy the Stone and her lover in the process or finding a means to extract Vision's personality without destroying the stone, Captain America decides instead to travel to Wakanda in the hopes of seeking their aid. Despite the coordinated efforts of the Wakandans and the Avengers, Thanos claims the stone from Vision, completing his set, and with a snap of his fingers turns half of the population—including T'Challa—to dust.[72]

While the role of the Panther and Wakanda in "Infinity War" is slight, it provides a thematic aftermath to the consequences of the events in the Panther's solo film. Wakanda, now open to the world, has invited in the world's problems—echoing the traditionally isolationist words of Daniel Kaluuya's W'Kabi from the previous film in which he warned that inviting refugees into the country would bring the world's problems with them.[73] While that scene was clearly meant to demonstrate a regressive and ultimately counter-intuitive perspective, the events of "Infinity War" suggest that Wakanda does not necessarily benefit from this particular relationship with the outside world, though the threat is largely from the slavering alien hordes of an extraterrestrial tyrant as opposed to W'Kabi's more earthbound concerns. Again, the idea of Wakandan isolationism coming into conflict with global obligations and the unintended consequences of T'Challa's decisions become a major theme in the story.

As the heroes land in Wakanda, even the loyalist Okoye confides her skepticism to the king that she expected the opening of Wakanda to bring the Olympics and Starbucks rather than an alien invasion.[74] There is reason to be skeptical—Captain America's stated reason for seeking Wakandan help rather than simply having Scarlet Witch remove the stone is his resolve in not trading Vision's life for the lives of the world, yet the heroes seem to have no issue with surrounding the android with Wakandan soldiers and the Dora Milaje to slow down the attacking hordes of Thanos while Shuri attempts to remove the stone without killing him. Even with T'Challa's blessing and the consent of the Wakandan soldiers, it seems an oddly cruel calculus for Captain America, a hero David Roberts identified as particularly Kantian and who is canonically depicted as seeing value in all human beings onto themselves (especially after the Wakandans had already done so much to deprogram his best friend Bucky).[75] At worst, it serves as a mischaracterization that reinforces a subconscious belief about which lives matter more to the writers—are countless Wakandan lives truly worth one android?

The story has fun with the clash of cultures between Wakanda and the rest of the heroes—the lack of understanding of Wakandan culture to the outside world and white anxiety about it is represented by a quick humorous scene in which James "War Machine" Rhodes convinces Bruce "Hulk" Banner that T'Challa is a king and must be bowed to, only for T'Challa to tell Banner this is not a Wakandan custom and Rhodes to admonish the scientist.[76] This culture clash extended to the production itself, where after a lengthy shoot with a primarily Black cast and crew on "Black Panther" Boseman commented in a later interview how strange it was to see the main Avengers actors:

> Excuse me for how I say this, but it's just kind of what it is. We didn't have any white people in Wakanda. So all of a sudden, it was like this whole world has changed. It's like, what's going on? As characters, I had to be like "It's OK, it's fine. We opened our doors. They are visiting." [. . .] It was that weird juxtaposition. We are new on the (Avengers) set. But at the same time, this is our territory.[77]

That sense of ownership over a fictional terrain arguably informs Boseman's performance in the film—as does the necessity of creating Wakandan chants and rituals for the benefit of directors who had not yet seen the other film. It is also hard to ignore the unintentional symbolism of the Norse god Thor (a blonde, white man), arriving during the film's climactic battle to save the Wakandan forces. Yet at the same time, Wakanda's presence in the Marvel universe and its legitimacy goes unquestioned in the film, avoiding the narrative crutch so many writers have used of perpetuating paternalistic colonial viewpoints through white characters—Bucky stands in awe of Wakanda's defensive capabilities, Captain America shows T'Challa genuine gratitude, and T'Challa makes it clear that his homeland is not to be trifled with by telling one of Thanos' lieutenants "You are in Wakanda now. Thanos will have nothing but dust and blood."[78] In the span of a few months, the importance and legitimacy of the Black Panther and Wakanda's role in the new Marvel cinematic mythos was modernized and made immediately clear in a way that the comics had so often overlooked for so many years—making his apparent death at the end of the film as part of Thanos' plot even more shocking.

While Okoye, who had taken a significant role in many of the previous film's action beats, reappears as a representative of Wakanda staying in contact with the remaining Avengers in *Avengers: Endgame,* the sequel is largely the domain of the original Avengers team. However, at the pivotal moment where the heroes manage to reverse Thanos' erasure of life, T'Challa, Okoye, and Shuri are the first to appear through a portal on the battlefield to aid Captain America in his last stand against the villain, leading a contingent of Wakandan forces. The narrative choice of having the Wakandans appear before the rest of the reanimated heroes was largely a thematic connection to the Russos' earlier films—Sam "Falcon" Wilson was the first character the directors wanted to speak in that scene, likely due to their long history with the character and his relationship with Captain America, and as he was lost in Wakanda it made the most sense for the Wakandan portal to open first with the king leading the way.[79] A social media cottage industry of online reaction videos to the so called "Portals scene," dubbing a live opening night audience reaction over the film, tells the tale—T'Challa gets as big or a bigger reaction than even heroes like Spider-Man and Doctor Strange in most videos.[80] With a respectful nod and a renewed Wakandan war chant, T'Challa leads his forces alongside the rest of the universe's heroes in a CGI-laden final conflict that ends with Tony Stark sacrificing himself to use the Infinity Stones to erase Thanos and his armies from existence. Apart from an appearance at Stark's funeral, our last view of Wakanda and the Black Panther in the proper Marvel Cinematic Universe is a quiet moment in a montage of reunion and celebration around the globe as the king embracing his mother and sister as Wakanda celebrates the defeat of Thanos—a meaningful, poignant moment for the character and an implicit reminder of his new status as a pillar of the MCU and a celebration of Black power and excellence.

Sadly, it would also be the last time we saw Chadwick Boseman in a live-action MCU project. On August 28, 2020, Boseman passed away at the age of 43 following a secret, multi-year fight with colon cancer that had begun in 2016, shortly after his debut as the Black Panther.[81] The reaction was immediate, with fans, fellow actors, cast and crew all taking to social media to share their memories of the actor and his legacy. Fellow Howard University alum Ta-Nehisi Coates spoke of his commitment to "communicating Black humanity through Black heroism," while Oprah Winfrey celebrated his status as a role model, adding that Black children "see a reflection of themselves embodied in everything that he intended—they get to dream about and wish about and make wishes on the shooting star that was Chadwick Boseman."[82] Director Ryan Coogler spoke at length in his remembrance of Boseman about the actor's commitment to and involvement in the production, talking about filming T'Challa's scenes on the Ancestral Plane:

> We were in Atlanta, in an abandoned warehouse, with bluescreens, and massive movie lights, but Chad's performance made it feel real. I think it was because from the time that I met him, the ancestors spoke through him. [. . .] But it is with a heavy heart and a sense of deep gratitude to have ever been in his presence, that I have to reckon with the fact that Chad is an ancestor now. And I know that he will watch over us, until we meet again.[83]

That Boseman had shot nearly all of his roles as Black Panther—to say nothing of his vast body of other work in that time, culminating in his last live-action appearance on film in 2020's *Ma Rainey's Black Bottom*, for which he was posthumously recognized with numerous awards and an Oscar nomination—while battling the illness is nothing short of remarkable. It is perhaps a testament to the outsized role Boseman played in the formation of our public consciousness of Black Panther that the production of the inevitable sequel, *Black Panther: Wakanda Forever* was retooled following his death, with an official announcement in January of 2021 at the Disney Investor Day presentation that the role would not be recast or recreated with CGI. Instead, the focus of the rewrite will be placed on the larger world of Wakanda and its people, with no official word yet on who will ultimately step into the title role.[84]

At the time of this writing, it is unknown what this focus will look like, and the reader will probably have a better idea of what it is than I do now. In an interview with Yahoo! Entertainment, Lupita Nyong'o said Coogler's concept is "respectful of the loss" and feels "spiritually and emotionally correct," whatever it may be.[85] It seems inherently likely that an existing character will take on the role of the Black Panther—Shuri, Nakia, Okoye, and M'Baku being the most likely candidates—but not all agree with this move. Political scientist and MSNBC contributor Dr. Jason Johnson argued that T'Challa is too important a character to retire and that canonically the Panther mantle can and has been passed from one person to another, possibly providing a new young actor a huge opportunity.[86] More recently, a #RecastTChalla movement, centered on a petition started by fan Emmanuel Noisette, has made a similar argument, demanding Disney cast a new actor in the role, with Chadwick Boseman's brother Derrick offering his support and saying his brother would have also supported it.[87]

Such issues are ultimately a matter of opinion and the emotions and desire of Boseman's collaborators, but his impact continues to be felt in the Marvel Cinematic Universe material released since. Boseman's voice appeared one last time in late 2021 to reprise the role of T'Challa in the animated series *What If . . . ?*; while the character appears in several episodes, an alternate universe story where he becomes the intergalactic hero Star-Lord is the highlight, as is the fact that his innate nobility and decency reforms even the villainous Thanos and prevents his genocidal plot (the episode is also dedicated to Boseman's memory).[88] The Dora Milaje (led by Florence Kasumba's Ayo, a significant character in *Civil War* who took something of a backseat in the main *Panther* film) also appear in 2021's *The Falcon and the Winter Soldier* series, with Sam Wilson's new Captain America wings and costume coming as a gift from Wakanda—not hand-delivered and crafted by the Black Panther as they were in the comics, but spiritually playing the same role.[89]

The success of the Black Panther and the Marvel Cinematic Universe do not need to be relitigated—this very book begins with the raw numbers and details. That success means that the Marvel Cinematic Universe incarnation of the Black Panther is perhaps easily the most significant and visible incarnation of the character's transmedia identity. Along with the writers and artists working on the comics, the credit for this massively important incarnation of the Panther and what he represents must go to Boseman and Coogler—but also to the other actors, writers, directors, costume designers, and more that worked on these films in a collaborative effort. Entirely new audiences who would have never picked up a comic or even known where to start combing through Marvel's unnecessarily convoluted mythos were introduced to the character and the world of Wakanda through the films, an entrée point that suggests how important broadly accessible media is to the shape of transmedia characters—indeed, it is likely most of the people who saw the films have never opened a comic.

Boseman's Black Panther, simply put, is the prime Black Panther as put forth by Marvel and understood by the audience. All new comics, merchandise, video game appearances, and more bear the visual symbology of the cinematic version of the character's costuming in an example of transmedia synergy. Even this book started as a conference paper on the film, and you would not be holding it if the character had not been exposed to the wider audience through this work. The creative debt the collective cultural archetype of the Black Panther owes to these creators is incalculable, but it is also symbiotic, relying heavily on Lee, Kirby, McGregor, Priest, Hudlin, Coates, and countless others to provide the inspiration to make this populist media depiction.

Yet at the same time the MCU depiction of the Black Panther moves the character's perception forward by modernizing and streamlining it as so many of its interpretations of his fellow heroes have done, it also reiterates the same shortcomings of that perception. The Black Panther is everything said so far in this book—an inspiration to fans, a corrective slap to the face of long-standing tired racist stereotypes in the media, a means to comment with anger, resignation, and sly sarcasm on the zeitgeist as well as the long history of racism and oppression. It also remains fundamentally an asset to the parent company, and an extremely valuable one. The criticisms of the Panther film may be outweighed by its larger value in representation and encouragement in its audience, but they are nonetheless vestiges of a story of African identity and Blackness that does not come from an experience fully centered in these issues. This may not disqualify the story, but it complicates it—and as is so often the case with transmedia narratives, the story seen by the most people becomes the story.

NOTES

1. Mendelson, "Famous Flops."
2. Mendelson, "20 years later."
3. Gallagher, "How Happy Meals Killed Tim Burton's Batman."
4. Meslow, "Do Tim Burton's Batman Movies Hold Up?"; Weldon, *The Caped Crusade.*
5. Tucker, *Slugfest.*
6. Guerrasio, "Here's a look back"; Tucker, *Slugfest.*
7. Howe, "Avengers Assemble!"; Riesman, *True Believer.*
8. Ibid.
9. Sharf, "Scott Derrickson Fuels Rumor."
10. Parker & Couch, "Wesley Snipes Reveals."
11. Ibid.
12. Ibid.
13. Newby, "What Happened to 'Blade'?"
14. Hamman, "Marvel's Kevin Feige."
15. Howe, "Avengers."
16. Howe, "Avengers"; Robinson, "Secrets of the Marvel Universe."
17. Williams, "How Marvel Bounced Back."
18. Robinson, "Secrets."
19. Whitten, "Disney accounted for nearly 40%."
20. Heinz, "It's Time to Break Up Disney."

21. Lee, "What Exactly Does Disney's 'Reorganization' Mean for the Movie Industry?"

22. D'Alessandro, "Disney Closing Blue Sky Studios"; Donnelly & Lang, "Layoffs Hit Both Disney and Fox Film Groups."

23. Inoa, "Definitive Timeline."

24. Favreau, *Iron Man 2*; Johnston, *Captain America.*

25. Whedon, *Avengers: Age of Ultron.*

26. Labrecque, "Breaking Big."

27. Mohan, "Black Panther."

28. Chitwood, "How the MCU was made."

29. Russos, *Captain America: Civil War.*

30. Ibid.

31. Breznican, "Black Panther language."

32. Russo & Russo, *Captain America: Civil War.*

33. Chiorazzi, "The spirituality of Africa."

34. Russo & Russo, *Civil War.*

35. Ibid.

36. White, "Coogler."

37. Mu'min, "Ryan Coogler."

38. Boone, "Fruitvale Station."

39. Coogler, *Creed.*

40. Ibid.

41. Coogler, *Black Panther.*

42. Adebayo, "Nigerian army"; Coogler, *Black Panther*; Stephanie, "Black Panther makes a nod."

43. Coogler, *Black Panther*, 53:20.

44. Ibid, 32:44.

45. Ibid, 16:40.

46. Ibid, 1:11:29.

47. Ibid, 1:29:53.

48. Ibid, 1:18:15.

49. Ibid.

50. Ibid, 33:45.

51. Ibid.

52. Lewis, "Black Panther cast."

53. Coogler, *Black Panther*, 1:37:18.

54. Ibid, 1:50:30.

55. Priyadarshi, "Why Fruitvale Station."

56. Ibid.

57. Coogler, *Black Panther,* 1:56:19.

58. Ibid, 1:57:45.

59. Guglielmo, "Black Panther rules Marvel's world."

60. Fleming Jr., "'Black Panther' Director Ryan Coogler."

61. Coogler, *Black Panther*, 2:05:56.

62. De Waal, "Africa's 'Civil Wars.'"

63. Obie, "In Defense of Erik Killmonger."

64. Ibid.

65. Serwer, "The Tragedy of Erik Killmonger."

66. Ibid.

67. Wilt, "How Black Panther."

68. Crenshaw, personal Facebook page.

69. Janay, "Ryan Coogler."

70. Connolly, "How 'Black Panther' Taps Into 500 Years of History"; Emphasis original author's.

71. Fleming Jr., "Black Panther Helmer Ryan Coogler Stakes His Proximity Media Banner."

72. Russo & Russo, *Avengers: Infinity War.*

73. Coogler, *Black Panther.*

74. Russo & Russo, *Avengers: Infinity War.*

75. Roberts, "The irresolvable moral dilemma."

76. Russo & Russo, *Avengers: Infinity War*.

77. VanDenburgh, "Remembering Chadwick Boseman."

78. Russo & Russo, *Avengers: Infinity War*, 1:38:17.

79. Hickson, "Avengers: Endgame."

80. As a personal note, while there is much to be written and much of concern about the ouroboros of much of contemporary media being reactions to other contemporary media, these videos were still a strangely comforting reminder of seeing films in-person with others during the COVID-19 pandemic.

81. Ugwu & Levenson, "'Black Panther' Star Chadwick Boseman Dies of Cancer at 43."

82. FitzPatrick, "Robert Downey Jr. and more stars share memories of Chadwick Boseman."

83. Fleming Jr., "Coogler on Chadwick Boseman."

84. Jackson, "Black Panther 2 Script."

85. Polowy, "'Nyong'o."

86. Johnson, "How do we reconcile Black Panther."

87. Carras, "'Black Panther fans' implore Marvel."

88. Andrews, "What If . . . T'Challa Became a Star-Lord?"

89. Skogland, "Truth."

Chapter 10

What Makes a King?

The Transmedia Mythmaking
of Black Panther

In a 2018 interview with the website *SyFy Wire*, Christopher Priest reflected on his experiences with the Black Panther amid the excitement over the character's solo film debut, crediting his fellow writers and artists with the realization of what would eventually make its way to the big screen. Priest said that the work of Don McGregor laid much of the groundwork for what would become the film—he simply "painted the house" and updated it for a new audience, and then "a lot of people" contributed to it from there.[1] Priest's metaphor is apt—it is difficult to build a house on one's own and creating an enduring character that can stand the test of time is too. The long-standing creative nature of the Black Panther as a piece of corporate intellectual property is inherently collaborative, and the transmedia applications of that character are the sum of that creative work, from Lee and Kirby to McGregor and Cowan and Priest and Hudlin and Coates and beyond. But the Black Panther goes beyond a house—as a brand, he is an entire neighborhood subdivision of homes that follow a shared floorplan but make different aesthetic touches, all of which come together to create the notional concept of the neighborhood and what makes it different from adjacent metaphorical neighborhoods like Spider-Man or Captain Marvel. That this neighborhood exists within a massive (figurative and occasionally literal) city-state owned by the world's largest entertainment and media conglomerate also cannot be ignored.

In 2018, as part of that city-state's effort to promote its metaphorical neighborhood, Marvel published the Black Panther Annual, a self-contained anthology of stories, alongside the film that served to celebrate three of the most prolific Panther writers—Priest, McGregor, and Hudlin—and acted as a means through which each author could put their own spin on modern continuity or wrap up any loose threads from their own storylines. The

Annual makes it clear how much each writer contributed and how radically different their styles are. Priest's "Back in Black" storyline dips right back into the sardonic espionage realm in which his Panther was so comfortable, with Ross serving again as the chronologically-challenged narrator. Don McGregor's "Panther's Heart" acts as a post-script to his series, patching up many of the unresolved relationship questions from his run with the death of Monica Lynne, so long the linchpin of his stories and whose passing takes on poignancy because of the story's dedication to McGregor's late collaborators Rich Buckler and Billy Graham. Finally, Hudlin's "Black to the Future Part II" postulates a world in which his Black Power superhero has maneuvered Wakanda to the top of the geopolitical power structure, albeit at the cost of shaky alliances and the conquering of enemy nations and even allies—the story ends with a weary T'Challa lamenting the high cost of war in front of a destroyed Iron Man helmet.[2] Textually and meta-textually, the issue is a triumphant and yet also bittersweet reflection on the character's legacy and those that have built it—and a stark reminder of just how much every creative that has worked on the Black Panther has contributed to that metaphorical neighborhood in which so many fans wish to live.

In the first chapter, I argued for an alternative view of the Black Panther not as a transmedia narrative but a transmedia character. That alternative view suggests that it is not only serialized narratives that can be told across multiple forms of media, but rather that the larger concept of who a character is and what they represent is the sum of that character's transmedia interpretations—and that the manifestations of those representations exist at the intersection of narrative, economic, and social contexts. Such contexts cannot be ignored in the case of the Black Panther, a character defined from the beginning as a challenge to industry orthodoxy and its unease about Black heroes and stories and the ongoing profit made from regressive, often outright racist narratives about Black culture and Africa as a continent and diasporic people. In this chapter, I suggest that through analysis of what all these contributions have added to the Black Panther character, we can evaluate how the character acts as a successful counter-narrative to these ideas as well as where the character may directly or indirectly reify existing systems of power.

Here it is necessary to contextualize the remaining pages of this volume and address potential concerns the reader may have. It is undeniably true that the Black Panther is a fictional character, owned and published by one of the largest media companies in the world. There is good reason to be skeptical of his ability to truly speak to larger social issues, wary of the genre's tendency to trivialize those issues, and to ponder whether there is good faith behind the addressing of those issues if one wishes. It is foolish to suggest the character speaks the same for everyone or reflects a universal lived experience. But in a real sense, the character perhaps more than any other superhero serves as an important counter-narrative to a predominantly white social and political narrative in popular culture. As Mishelle Rodriguez argues in her analysis of the *Black Panther* film's possibility for encouraging healing and restoration, the film (and by extension the transmedia character) "encourages us to reconnect not only to our past but also to our limitless possibilities. To create new worlds and ways of being, we must first be able to imagine them."[3] The Black Panther allows for the imagination of these ways of being, and for that reason, it is worth recognizing his importance and how we can use the character to have these important and wide-ranging conversations.

IDENTIFYING THE TRANSMEDIA
CHARACTER OF BLACK PANTHER

In the first chapter, our working definition of transmedia characters posited that such characters consist of multiple dimensions that can be repeated over and over at the discretion of their creators and rights holders to be adapted to other forms of media to the point where they become less characters on a page or on a screen than living, breathing entities in the mind of the audience. The Black Panther is no exception. Again, applying Pearson's view of transmedia characters, we see the character exhibiting common recurring characteristics throughout his transmedia depictions—a noble, inquisitive, and occasionally arrogant man of regal bearing and dignity who grapples with his duty and familial legacy and the twin roles of superhero and king.[4] The multiplicity of those depictions—and which ones feel most accurate and true—can be a source of fan enjoyment and debate while simultaneously fueling the mass media engine of the intellectual property holders, as Jenkins suggests.[5] This book is certainly part of that conversation.

But as I have also argued in this book, the Black Panther is a counter-narrative to historically negative media depictions of Black culture and identity as well as Africa and the Diaspora more generally. Transmedia characters and stories offer unique opportunities to cultivate new perspectives on race and identity, as these elements can be repeated in different formats for different audiences to reinforce alternative and constructive viewpoints across viewer and reader lifespans. The Black Panther is no different. The works analyzed and presented in this book are a thorough but incomplete sample of the broader transmedia corpus of the Black Panther. However, through generative analysis of the present texts, it is possible to identify specific consistent elements that make up the character and can often act as a response to Eurocentric and colonialist narratives. I turn again here to Bertetti to analyze what he calls the fictional and existential elements of the character, and to expand on his model. Bertetti suggests that the *existential* identity consists of the character's proper identity—their "figurative attributes" that separate them from other characters as well as the role they play in the text, as well as their relational identity, or relationships between the *fictional* world and characters around them. At the same time, he speaks of the character's *fictional* identity, consisting of the character's roles and expression in different forms.[6] In these terms, the Panther has a proper identity—he is T'Challa, the king of Wakanda, a superhero wearing a black cat suit who fights to protect his homeland, its resources, and its people, and these elements separate him from Iron Man or Captain America, and he has specific relationships with his family as well as the world around him as the ruler of an isolated nation. Throughout this book, we have also explored the fictional identity of the character, and how that fictional identity has evolved over time and in different media from centrist side character to warrior poet to revolutionary to reluctant leader of a democracy. These existential and fictional elements come together to create the Black Panther as a transmedia character and repeated across multiple media forms they serve to reinforce the values and ideas the character represents. I have identified significant areas of commonality and consistency throughout that development.

The first is *exceptionalism.* The Black Panther, in all depictions and regardless of the face under the cowl, is represented as an exemplar of the superhero genre through his intellect, athleticism, and competency. This is a marked change from the Black characters that existed at the time of his creation in the mid-1960s. From the outset, T'Challa is presented as a noble and self-sufficient leader, even as the white heroes around him make ethnocentric comments about Africa and African people and was never portrayed as speaking in the exaggerated slang or behaved in the stereotyped fashion of many of his contemporaries. As journalist Jesse J. Holland puts it in his introduction to the *Tales of Wakanda* collection of short stories:

> There, on the pages of a comic book, was an unapologetic, proud, intelligent paragon of Blackness, our own personal King Arthur. [. . .] With the Panther's Ascension, many of us found the courage to define for ourselves who our heroes would be, what they would look like, and what they represented, not only to us but to the world.[7]

However, because of the lack of internal champions at Marvel for much of the character's first few decades of life, that exceptionalism gave way to simply having the character appear in the background while white heroes got the focus—Don McGregor's run being a notable exception. As the character's publishing history wore on, the relevance and significance of that exceptionalism—and the character manifesting it—became more obvious as Black writers took over. Consider, for instance, Christopher Priest's efforts to present the Black Panther as a hyper-competent and capable superspy who is always twelve steps ahead of his foes, Dwayne McDuffie and later Reginald Hudlin's simultaneous embrace of African-American culture and their explorations of how T'Challa's metatextual role as the world's first major Black superhero would make him act as a role model and aspirational figure for Marvel's other Black heroes, and Ta-Nehisi Coates' exploration of the character's philosophical and intellectual side. Moreover, Wakanda itself is uniformly presented as a remarkable marvel in its own right, exceeding much of the white Marvel universe's considerable fictional technology and power. Far from the colonized worldview—most often represented in the form of the Panther's villains, particularly Klaw—of Africa as a backward continent or a savage land, Wakanda represents a progressive technological and social haven much closer to the actual reality of many African tribes and nations throughout history. Because Wakanda and the Black Panther are so closely intertwined, so does the character. The rejection of Africa as a "lesser" and celebration of what it represents in the context of the Black Panther mythos is one way in which these stories challenge prevailing cultural narratives.

Second is a focus on *identity tension.* Here the idea of "double consciousness" is useful as a starting point, though one again must be careful to clarify that T'Challa is not an example of "double consciousness" as Du Bois defines it in *Souls of Black Folk*.[8] T'Challa is often within his own homeland and wields a significant amount of power and influence as a diplomat and politician, luxuries not afforded in the original understanding of the concept. Yet the tension between who T'Challa is and who he is trying to be is inherent throughout these narratives. The entire narrative grist for Don McGregor's *Jungle Action* series consists of T'Challa dealing with the fact that his own Western education and romance with Monica Lynne serve to make him an outsider in his own home; the later arc pitting him against Klansmen illustrates his status as a clear and defined Other on American soil, bearing the insults and symbolic attacks that those of a similar skin color and heritage have experienced for centuries on these shores. Removed from his Wakandan context, T'Challa becomes acutely aware of his identity in a way he arguably had not before, echoing if not exactly mirroring Du Bois' discussion of the inherent tension of finding a sense of place where one is not welcomed. Christopher Priest illustrates this pointedly in the scene in his run where the Panther is identified by a gathered Black crowd as their hero, a fact which puzzles him as he sees himself as a global hero; however, he and the audience are consistently reminded of how the responsibilities to his nation and culture cause tensions in his role as a superhero. Moreover, Priest's work specifically touches on black stereotyping and tokenism, particularly in how it offers a critique of the Thomas-era *Avengers* version of the character as a background character—the character must both be African and a superhero, and in Thomas' view that tension is at surface level. For Priest and later writers, however, it is crucial to how the character should be read, and that T'Challa rejects this binary to create his own outcome by spying on the Avengers from within and working outside the parameters of that relationship could serve as a means of rejecting that inherent tension. The duality of the superhero has always played a role in the conflict and struggle these characters face—from Spider-Man trying to make rent while fighting Electro to Iron Man trying to be the face of a company while leading the Avengers.

In the case of the Black Panther, that duality comes with additional resonance due to the character's status as the first Black superhero and still one of the most prominent in the genre, as unlike most white heroes he does not have the luxury of ever having a truly "secret" identity due both to his race and his existential and fictional roles. Superman, an extraterrestrial from another world, somehow appears as a white Midwesterner and as such is less alien to his contemporaries and readers—his personal and racial identity does not carry with it the same weight. The Black Panther represents a nation and a people in a way most heroes do not. From a critical race theory perspective, race is built into all aspects of the Black Panther—it cannot and arguably should not ever be fully removed from his stories, and the existence of those stories are a counter-storytelling proposition.

The third major trend is a clear history of *anti-colonialism* as well as open recognition of foreign interference in Africa. This is perhaps one of the most overt elements of the Black Panther's transmedia character, dating back to his 1966 debut as what Adilifu Nama called an "unprecedented and upbeat" depiction of Africa and its people at a time when Black pride and political consciousness were on the rise and depictions of Africa as a "backward" continent were commonplace in the media.[9] The history of global foreign policy toward Africa is one primarily of advancing the economic and political goals of primarily European and Western interests, from the slave trade to proxy wars and CIA interference in the country, and so too the motivations of many a Black Panther antagonist align with the goal of exploitation and conquest of Wakanda's African utopia. It is telling that the villain who reoccurs more than any other in Black Panther storylines is Klaw/Klaue, who is often explicitly coded as a colonizer that sees the technology and resources of Wakanda as a sort of divine birthright to be seized from the "savage" natives. Both Coates and Hudlin imagine concerted efforts by racist supervillains from around the globe—whether as part of a warped moral crusade in the form of Hudlin's Black Knight or pure capitalist greed as in Coates' Zeke Stane—seeking to overthrow the sovereign government and take the country's natural resources for itself. As a metaphor, it is hard to miss.

Yet, as history suggests, the exploitation of African land, people, and resources comes not at the hand of cartoonish supervillains but government officials and massive corporations. It is no accident that as Black writers and creators began taking over, this became an explicit element of the Panther stories. Hudlin's run, published at the height of the Bush administration's "war on terror," opens with a top-secret meeting of US government officials and generals salivating over the opportunity to invade Wakanda and take its vibranium and oil, and in Priest's run the government routinely interferes on Wakandan soil at the same time villain Killmonger is reimagined as a ruthless capitalist seeking not only to defeat his adversary but make Wakanda a more business-friendly nation. Even the kid-friendly Panther cartoons do not shy away from this—consider *Iron Man: Armored Adventures'* "blood vibranium" subplot, which posits a shadow government of corporate interests making backdoor deals to ensure access to vital resources via regime destabilization only to be punished with mere fines when caught. The connection to real historical systems of exploitation and subjugation is obvious. Coogler's film is perhaps the most overt on this issue, challenging the audience by making its villain an open anti-colonialist revolutionary who also uses the same tactics of destabilization and upheaval to destroy Wakanda; it complicates this further by the villain playing a role in changing Wakandan policy while also recognizing how the very colonialism he rails against shaped his twisted worldview. However, Coates brilliantly flips the idea on its head by showing the blurry line between self-defense and empire-building in his "Intergalactic Empire of Wakanda" storyline, where T'Challa's desperate search for the origins of vibranium inadvertently creates a fascist empire colonizing and conquering worlds in the name of a Wakandan utopia, illustrating the damage fanatical adherence to a manifest destiny can cause (and, implicitly, challenging the doctrine of "self-defense" and nation-building that has led to so much American military adventurism). If fascism is Captain America's cause to rally against and crime is Batman's, it is quite clear that colonization and foreign interference are the Panther's *raison d'etre*.

I return once again to Evan Narcisse's assertion that the Black Panther shapes history as he moves through it. To that end, it is impossible to ignore that the Black Panther *reflects white attitudes and perspectives toward Blackness* throughout his publishing history. I speak here not just of the micro-aggressive barbs and quips thrown about by the Panther's ostensible allies, standing in disbelief of Wakandan technological superiority because of ingrained prejudice, but also how the character has evolved in his existential identity over time. The Black Panther, while certainly created by sympathetic outsiders under the liberal auspices of the Marvel offices, was still written and conceptualized from a predominantly white and male perspective until the 1990s and reflects in many ways the ways in which such perspectives view Blackness and the African Diaspora. You can tell a great deal about those mindsets not only through the stories, but also through the character's

appearance. In his 2015 chapter on the evolution of costumes and appearances for Black superheroes in *The Blacker the Ink*, Blair Davis remarks that
the costumes for such characters often tell us little about who they actually
are and the designs and attitudes toward the characters change as cultural
beliefs do—such outfits can be hokey or even "bizarre fetish objects of white
mainstream representations of black identities" that fans come to ridicule
over time (consider Luke Cage's 1970s ensemble of an open bright yellow
shirt, silver tiara, and chain around his waist to his more modern plainclothes
vigilante look in comics and the Netflix series).[10] The Black Panther is no
exception here—while his uniform has not changed radically over the years
it must be understood that it is the product of an era where the character's
skin had to be hidden to appear on newspaper stands. It is arguably not an
accident that the outfit gets ripped and torn as much to reveal Black skin as it
does in McGregor's run with a Black artist like Billy Graham at the helm, as
a means of pushing back. Nor is it an accident that as the character becomes
more self-sustained and regal, so too does his appearance, from Mark Texeira
re-adding the cloak and cowl from Kirby's original design and including gold
accoutrements to the more modern look from artists like Brian Stelfreeze
that add more tribal accoutrements and feline attributes to the black bodysuit
design and inspire the high-tech outfit of the films. The modern Panther habit
more closely reflects the character's identity as a scientist and leader in no
small part because more writers and artists of color are working on the character and view him as important.

Moreover, the character reflects the paternalism and racism, both soft and
overt, of the white majority toward Black identity and excellence. Consider
the Thomas *Avengers* series, in which the character is used as a mouthpiece
for white centrist views on race relations, or how quickly Marvel changed his
name to avoid association with the Black Panther Party. While the Panther
often does battle with overtly racist villains like Klaw, the Ku Klux Klan,
Nazis, and the white supremacist Strucker Twins he is also the target of soft
racism and lowered expectations from his own allies, dating all the way back
to the quips from Lee and Kirby's Fantastic Four referencing Tarzan films.
While generally used to demonstrate the wrong-headedness of such perspectives (as the Panther and Wakanda continually exceed these stereotypes),
the fact that they are still in the mouths of characters to this day illustrates a
strawman and writers' crutch that too many writers still rely on, particularly
on the television side. While these perspectives can be played for laughs, as
Priest did with the express intent of addressing a perceived hesitance on the
part of the white audience to enjoy the adventures of a Black hero and using
Everett Ross as the "ugly American" foil, they can occasionally reach to the
level of polemic. Consider Hudlin's run, which cast Doctor Doom as an open
eugenics enthusiast speculating that Wakandans are superior to other Africans

due to differences in their DNA, white soldiers claiming Captain America as "their" hero, and Confederate vampires scheming to use the disarray and destruction of Hurricane Katrina to reclaim New Orleans. These stories reflect genuine historical white antagonism toward Black advancement and achievement and Nama suggests they represent a heightened racial consciousness for the character than seen in previous iterations—but Nama also critiques many of those storylines as "clumsy" and invoking the polemical stereotyping of blaxploitation films that cast "white villains as racist simpletons."[11] By exaggerating racist attitudes, white audiences can be inadvertently let off the hook in a way that Coates' more nuanced critiques of gentrification in *Black Panther & The Crew* do not allow for—note the "real estate agent" in issue who tries to ingratiate himself to T'Challa and Storm by referencing his Black Studies major and the music of Frank Ocean while representing a company trying to destroy a historic Black neighborhood, appreciating the surface level of Black culture while devastating its roots for financial gain.[12] At the same time, the publication history of the character and the lack of appearances in other media for decades—his villains and allies appeared in arcade games well before he did and it took the efforts of Larry Houston to get him on television—suggest an ongoing lack of interest in the character on the part of the predominantly white studios and license holders until fairly recently, when the film and recent comic series proved his marketability. In many ways, the Black Panther, textually and meta-textually, represents the larger challenge of representing Black characters in media when the inertia of structural forces makes change slow.

This is, of course, the sort of structural problem the Black Panther exists to fix, even if only in a film or the pages of a comic. I suggest the fifth major transmedia dimension of the character is that of *correction and recuperation.* The Panther, from the beginning, exists to do battle against the forces that would subjugate his people and take their resources. As such, it is hard not to see the character as enforcing primarily a corrective or recuperative narrative. Corrective and alternative-history narratives are not uncommon in popular culture—Quentin Tarantino as of late has made a cottage industry of them, killing Adolf Hitler in *Inglorious Basterds* and more recently using his characters to foil the Manson murders in *Once Upon a Time in Hollywood*—but the Black Panther has centuries of systematic injustice to rail against, and we know from historical evidence he was created to challenge these perspectives. From the first Lee and Kirby comic onward, T'Challa is meant to represent something of an apology on the part of a predominantly white set of creators for long-standing racist media depictions and tropes of Africa that serve to justify its subjugation. As the character goes on, that subtext becomes explicit—McGregor uses the hero specifically to imagine what would have happened had someone with power stood up to the cruelty of lynching and racial hatred in the early twentieth century, Priest uses the character to send up stereotypes and bigotry, Hudlin sends him to help the Black victims of Hurricane Katrina, and Coogler opens his film with the hero doing battle with a clear analogue for Boko Haram. The Black Panther therefore takes on responsibility many other heroes do not—he must not only do battle with the villains, but also generations of prejudice and pain. There is value in this—as media scholar Frances Gateward suggests, the success of the Black Panther and Black-owned comics companies offers heroism and hope "by showing Black communities surviving and thriving."[13]

However, the powers of a superhero are limited to enact genuine social change. In many ways, the characters act as wish fulfillment or propaganda—Superman did not win World War II any more than Black Panther stopped apartheid. Instead, it may be most valuable to consider these restorative narratives as part of creating a space where such crimes are not forgotten or marginalized (indeed, they are immortalized in infamy) but are also not the sum of a lived experience. The Black Panther is particularly important here, as the metaphor of Wakanda has acted in this way. John Jennings, a media scholar, member of the Black Kirby art collaborative, and co-founder of Harlem's Black Comic Book Festival, spoke about the importance of the franchise's Afrofuturist tendencies and their connection to social justice by creating a sovereign, unconquered space:

> The future for black people in America was supposed to be connected to only three spaces: one, the hold of a slave ship; two, the plantation; and three, the grave. The construction of a space of agency, joy, and true freedom has always been the central focus of black speculative culture. [. . .] The notion of a black future in our country is still a radical political idea.[14]

If nothing else, the idea of the Black Panther allows a vision of a world in which those wrongs were righted, and a new way of thinking took its place, and as creators from these experiential backgrounds write his adventures, so too does that recuperative narrative evolve. Consider, for instance, Nnedi Okorafor's deeply personal and politically engaged use of her Ngozi character as a participant in the ENDSARS movement in Nigeria, a protest against government corruption and police brutality on the part of the country's "Special Anti-Robbery Squad." Okorafor's story, published in the 2021 special *Marvel's Voices: Legacy* #1, casts Ngozi—her universe's Black Panther and host to the Venom symbiote—as a defender of the protestors when police open fire on them.[15] Like McGregor using the Panther as an imaginary corrective to the wrongs of the Ku Klux Klan or Hudlin imagining a world where the Panther's resources help the people of New Orleans, Okorafor's story references a real-world tragedy in which the Nigerian army and local police opened fire on protestors at the Lekki toll gate—it remains unclear how many actually died but Amnesty International suggests as many as 12 were killed.[16] In this way, she too uses a Black Panther-related character as a corrective against real-world injustice.

Such things are, of course, a heavy responsibility, and the Panther bears that burden consistently. The sixth major transmedia dimension of the character, then, is *a heavy crown*. The difficulties of leadership and the rightness of command are seen throughout the Black Panther stories. Admittedly, this is not unique to the character—reluctant leaders and kings are prominent throughout popular narratives, mythology, and the like—but it is nonetheless worth mentioning because the inherent challenge and tension of T'Challa's rule and his constant battle not only with external foes, but internal strife and distrust of his policies are a means through which many of these other elements are explored. The character regularly questions his own willingness to lead—he is as much joyful and inquisitive scientist, explorer, and adventurer as he is head of state, and the two drives are in constant conflict. McGregor and Coates both get a significant amount of dramatic mileage out of the question of whether he would rather be a king or a superhero, and Coates makes his position on that tension explicit by outright stating he is better suited to the latter. This level of complexity and where it come from makes the character uniquely suited to a variety of transmedia adaptations, where he can fulfill multiple roles in different stories.

The character is also used to interrogate the difficult decisions that must be made when a leader balances the needs of a people and his nation against other responsibilities and desires, often to a degree that challenges his humility and morality, starting with McGregor's Panther balancing Wakandan tradition and his own progressivism. Priest's Panther, at least the one we see for most of his run, is a singular island onto himself, combining competence and occasional arrogance as he jeopardizes the economic health of Wakanda and the entire world just to stop Killmonger; similarly, Hickman's approach to the character has him uncertain about turning power over to his sister at the same time he grapples with the rightness of consigning entire dimensions to destruction to protect his own. Coates sees the Panther stuck at a crossroads between monarchy and democracy, with his nation turned against him and coming face-to-face with that nation's history. The cinematic Panther allows Wakandan tradition and his own anger to get the better of him, only succeeding in being the hero and king Wakanda needs by rejecting its dogma and embracing the world. That ongoing tension between nationalistic duty and progress for the greater good speaks to inherent tensions in the broader sociopolitical reality and can make the character both an effective protagonist and an effective ideological foil across multiple media forms, as well as one uniquely equipped to comment on political issues.

In a 2021 essay criticizing sports pundit Stephen A. Smith for apologizing for comments Smith made about Japanese baseball player Shohei Otani, fellow pundit Jason Whitlock suggested Smith was called out because he was paid more than his female fellow talent at ESPN, calling the network "Wakanda" and saying that the point of the *Black Panther* film was that "T'Challa [. . .] was nothing more than a puppet for the black women of Wakanda" and that he sought their "advice, counsel, and support" at every turn.[17] The tortured and confused metaphor aside, Whitlock's comments betray an breathtaking ignorance of the source material in making an unrelated talking point. Yet, despite his fumbling attempt at using the idea of a world in which the perspective of Black women is valued as a pejorative, he is correct in that Black and African women are crucial to the Black Panther mythology. Indeed, I argue that *feminism* is a significant element of the Panther's transmedia character and a necessary one to address just this sort of worldview.

From the beginning, the Black Panther has been defined by the influence of the women in his life, from his romantic interests like Monica Lynne, the film version of Nakia, and most significantly Ororo "Storm" Munroe to his fellow heroes like Misty Knight to the members of his family, like his sister Shuri and mother/stepmother Ramonda. This is consistent across all versions of the character. McGregor goes to great lengths to show the love, faith, and trust T'Challa has in Monica Lynne and his attempts to bring her into the Wakandan fold. Priest specifically introduces the Dora Milaje as warriors and bodyguards for the king that are the rival of any male warrior. Hudlin spends a great deal developing the relationship of Storm and T'Challa as loving equals who value each other romantically, intellectually, and professionally, treating their union like a major event and even eventually giving the Black Panther mantle to Shuri, who had worked so hard to get it. The work of Coates and Roxane Gay centers the Midnight Angels in the narrative as not only queer Black women—a rarity in superhero media—but equally significantly as political agents onto themselves who instigate a rebellion that evokes meaningful democratic and social change. Nnedi Okorafor brought a politically active Africanfuturist and African feminist approach to her work on the *Shuri* series and the character of Ngozi. Coogler builds his film around a deep and strong female supporting cast, giving each of the main female characters a full arc and using the treatment of women as a key point of differentiation between Killmonger and T'Challa. Even the animated *Avengers Assemble* series centers an entire episode around Yemandi, one of the female Black Panthers from Wakanda's history, and positions Shuri as crucial to saving Wakanda and an equal partner to her brother.

This conscious effort to center women in the Black Panther narrative is important, as it is unique among many of the character's contemporaries and respectful of the many women who played crucial roles in Black history.

In an essay on the film, Marjorie Morgan stated the women in the movie are "central to the story" and the "scaffolding, spine, and substance of the action" and their "actions and individual choices are essential to the shape of the narrative."[18] Claudia Bucciferro championed *Black Panther*'s female cast as "break[ing] common stereotypes of Black women in film," stating their complexity and power offered the opportunity to promote positive social learning in children as well as "[reposition] narratives involving empowered Black women and men in the popular imagination."[19] At the same time, as scholar Michaela Meyer notes, the Marvel Cinematic Universe has erased Ayo's queer identity, a common problem in the Marvel Cinematic Universe more broadly but more significant here because of her status as a rare queer Black woman in the comics (Aneka is nowhere to be found in the films or the *Falcon and the Winter Soldier* TV series in which Ayo appears).[20] This criticism is warranted and the inevitable consequence of a film brand designed to be consumed in a variety of different, less LGBTQ-friendly countries. One could also point at Priest's depiction of Nakia/Malice as a crazed and obsessive jilted woman as one of the low points in the franchise's depiction of women, despite his stories' inclusion of other more complex and empowered female characters.

It is crucial to get this right, of course, as these representations matter. A 2018 study found a possible connection between the underrepresentation of female superheroes in media and significant gaps in confidence, STEM interest, and leadership opportunities between young girls and young boys, a gaps pronounced even more for young women of color.[21] In the character of Shuri alone, viewers can see a capable, confident and brilliant young scientist every part the equal of anyone in Wakanda, and actress Letitia Wright signified her hope in a 2018 *Huffington Post* interview that the character would inspire young Black girls in particular to pursue careers in science.[22] Even if occasionally fraught, the celebration of African and African American womanhood, and the centrality of these characters in Black Panther's stories, serves to challenge the sexism and bigotry that has historically been levied against African and black women in general as well as chart a path forward.

Finally, more than any other superhero—and indeed, perhaps unlike any other superhero—the Black Panther franchise at its best is a *recognition and celebration of the African Diaspora and its people.* The African Diaspora is a central concept in the stories and motivation of the Black Panther, as well as a key point in the complexity of the intellectual exercise of Wakanda as a concept. Wakanda, depicted as a nation that has closed itself off from the rest of the world to avoid the same fate that colonialism had wrought upon its neighboring countries, is crucial to this narrative. However, each of these stories brings that same isolationist attitude into direct conflict with reality and challenge the responsibilities of such a place in the sociohistorical context of reality.

The very origin story of the Black Panther illustrates both why Wakandan isolationism was seen as necessary, but also untenable. Priest illustrates the perception many black members of the Marvel universe (and in a metatextual way, black fans) have of the Panther as "their hero," even if the Panther often does not see himself in that way—he acts as a unifying focal point both in a fictional sense and a real one for people of African descent around the world. Hudlin embraces this idea fully, turning his Black Panther into a celebration of contemporary Black culture where Priest by his own admission was more cautious about the idea.[23] Coates writes at length about Wakanda as an ideal but also a myth, challenging the idea of an all-knowing king and celebrating the democratization of the utopia at the same time Okorafor introduces the idea of the Pan-African Egungun council in the *Shuri* series to create a more cohesive vision of a fictional Africa and the real continent's influence on Wakanda. Kendrick Lamar's *Black Panther* album featured African artists and musicians performing in their native language and African American rappers relating their lived experiences to the films' characters. In Coogler's film, the real pain and struggle of a people spread to the winds by centuries of colonialism, slavery, and exploitation comes to Wakanda's doorstep and acts as the pivotal philosophical conflict between the hero and antagonist while at the same time the costume design of the film and the cultural practices of Wakanda draw from the various nations and tribes across the African continent. Yet at the same time the film also offers a view of Black liberation that can be seen as retrograde or even harmful and positions a CIA agent as a hero—both loaded ideas in real-world context. As illustrated throughout this book, when considering the transmedia depiction of this character as a restorative counter-narrative, that counter-narrative cannot be separated from the cultural contexts in which it operates. Wakanda matters because, for so many, the home and culture of their ancestors can feel as distant as those fictional shores, and its contemporary place in popular fiction speaks to the efforts of place-making and celebration of that culture.

So why do these elements matter? They matter because these are the elements that have caused the Black Panther to become, as Marrone put it, a character who "exceeds the narrative proper" and becomes an object of discourse.[24] Fans tune into *Black Panther* series, dress up in costume to go to conventions and premieres, play video games with his likeness, and read his comics not just because the character is available and interesting but also because he and what he represents strike a fundamentally human chord. Through the broader definition of the Black Panther as a transmedia character, we can interrogate the complex history of colonialism and Diaspora, the realities of Black identity and place, the legacies of slavery, and more while also enjoying the adventures both grounded and fantastical of a man who may be a superpowered king, but whose struggles are recognizable. The character allows for the discussion of these complex issues in an accessible and entertaining way. The Black Panther matters also as a transmedia character because those elements identified above—as well as others the reader may have identified over the course of this volume—lend themselves to a multiplicity of platforms and interpretations from children's television to video games to comics and short stories, all of which can find different audiences but speak to them about the subject matter in differing ways. He matters also because no other character speaks to these issues in this way, and he matters because the existence of the character has also given countless writers, artists, actors, directors, programmers, creatives, and fans license to express themselves and speak to issues that matter to them through the creation and consumption of transmedia materials—particularly the Black writers and artists who have created definitive and lasting takes on the character.

He matters also because on a critical level the Marvel culture has become the monoculture. There are few media enterprises that speak to audiences at the same mass level as the Marvel brand, particularly the Marvel Cinematic Universe. In a fragmented media landscape where we are all watching, doing, and believing different things the MCU franchise has become a rare unifying touchstone, and the Black Panther becoming a pivotal part of that is significant because that is the gateway for broader audiences to be introduced to these characters and the ideological payloads they carry. Such an arrangement consolidates power even further in the hands of Marvel's parent company Disney, already a clearinghouse for perhaps the largest and most lucrative collection of intellectual property in human history, a fact which gives the company almost unprecedented control and sway over exhibition and creator relationships. Moreover, the same malleability and multiplicity of the character in these different formats and tones also means that the character can be marketed to different audiences and ages and in different contexts, creating a product ecosystem that enriches its parent company in perpetuity.

I would be remiss if I did not mention that despite the billions of dollars in box office and home video sales, merchandise, and theme park revenue that Black Panther and his Marvel ilk have raised for the company, the actual people who created these wonderful characters remain woefully undercompensated. The Marvel Comics publishing arm is far from the most significant part of the Disney pantheon despite its significance in generating ideas and characters for the company's other branches. And thanks to the comics industry's practice of "work for hire" contracts in which creators are compensated only for the work they do on the page, all revenue from films, merchandise and intellectual property rights to the characters and stories stay with Marvel. That means the creators of some of the most lucrative characters in existence see little to no money—one of the most generous Marvel compensations could amount to just $5,000 to a creator whose character generates billions of dollars in revenue on screen and in merchandise—and the expectation is that the creator "shuts up" about their compensation and contribution as a result.[25] Moreover, the ready-made conceit of the multiverse—in which infinite versions of a character can exist—means that actors or creators associated with a particular character or version of that character could be cut out entirely simply by focusing on another one for a new audience. It is cynical but not inaccurate to think of the Marvel pantheon as a rotating set of products for Disney, with each character acting as a brand tailored to target demographics and psychographics. Even as we celebrate what the Black Panther means for representation and inclusivity, it is impossible to ignore the role the character—and Marvel as an intellectual property mill—play in consolidating media power in the hands of a few elite corporate entities, and all the conversations must play out against that backdrop.

SEARCHING FOR WAKANDA

On May 25, 2020, Black birdwatcher Christian Cooper was threatened by a white woman for asking her to put her dog on a leash while watching birds in New York's Central Park. The woman, in an incident caught on camera, called the police on Cooper, who went out of his way to remain calm and non-threatening during the encounter. Ultimately, both parties left the scene before the police arrived, but the video went viral and sparked a national conversation about race, white privilege, and police brutality in no small part because it happened the same day that George Floyd was murdered by police in Minnesota, sparking nationwide protests.[26] Cooper, as it happens, was also a long-time Marvel writer. There, he worked on X-Men titles like *Excalibur* and the Marvel swimsuit specials of the 1990s and was part of several other firsts: creating the first gay character in *Star Trek* history (Yoshi Mishima from the *Star Trek: Starfleet Academy* series), Marvel's first openly lesbian character Victoria Montesi, and as editor of the *Alpha Flight* series oversaw the coming out of its hero Northstar.[27] In short, Cooper is an unsung comics legend, particularly among the comparatively small number of LGBTQIA+ creators working for the big superhero companies. Yet, in that moment, none of that was known (nor would it have likely mattered) to the woman on the phone, whose first instinct was to call the police on a Black man. Cooper would later write a comic about the situation for DC Comics' *Represent* digital series, but the incident threw many things into sharp relief about the subject matter of this book—what good is the fantasy of a superhero in addressing racism and inequality when even the men and women who create them are not immune to these issues?[28]

This book was written primarily between the early spring of 2020 and the summer of 2021, an era of time marked by the global COVID-19 pandemic as well as a national reckoning with America's history of racism. Instrumental civil rights leaders like minister C.T. Vivian and Representative John Lewis passed away in the summer of 2020, causing the public to revisit and discuss the sacrifices and challenges they faced. That same summer, decades of the death and maiming of Black bodies as the result of police brutality were punctuated by the protests over the death of George Floyd (his killer, now-former Minneapolis police officer Derek Chauvin, was convicted in 2021), the tragic and unpunished murder of Breonna Taylor, and countless other Black men and women who were the victims of an unjust system. At an unprecedented level, popular culture became part of the discussion—cable networks went off the air, and kids tuning into Nickelodeon to see reruns of *SpongeBob SquarePants* instead saw messages aimed at informing their audiences of the need for equity and anti-racist action—Viacom's other networks also aired a black screen reading "I can't breathe" for just under nine minutes (the amount of time Chauvin knelt on Floyd's neck).[29] A year before they would win the NBA championship, the Milwaukee Bucks refused to play a 2020 NBA Playoff game to protest a police shooting that left Kenosha, WI resident Jacob Blake paralyzed from the waist down—their opponents, the Orlando Magic, followed suit, leading to a league-wide postponement of games that echoed throughout the rest of the sports world.[30] In protests that followed in Kenosha, 17-year-old Kyle Rittenhouse opened fire, killing two protestors—the police simply walked past him as he attempted to surrender, and he was ultimately acquitted in 2021.[31] The duality of the American justice system came into sharp relief—Rittenhouse was eventually taken into custody, intact and unharmed, and given bail, becoming a conservative folk hero framed in those circles as a kid as simply trying to defend his neighborhood—that he, being from Illinois, was not actually part of that neighborhood scarcely seemed to matter.[32] The unrest and the protests became a flashpoint for the 2020 election, with Republican candidates across the spectrum but most notably former President Donald Trump beating their metaphorical chests about the crime and unrest and promising a strong, authoritarian solution while trying to paint the unrest as the inevitable result of electing his rival Joe Biden despite it happening on Trump's watch—voters disagreed and elected Biden president with a massive popular vote lead and a narrow Electoral College victory.

Amid all of this, Chadwick Boseman—the physical embodiment of the Black Panther in the eyes of many and a symbol in his own right—passed away in August 2020 following a secret battle with colon cancer (as discussed in chapter 9). His death at a young age led to national conversations about public health and differing outcomes based on race, along with reverential and occasionally heated discussions about his contributions to the world of Marvel and if anyone could possibly replace him.[33] The tributes to Boseman and his body of work, often with rhetoric declaring him a "king," signified the importance of the Black Panther as a symbol in this time of tumult and restarted conversations about the character's resonance outside of the page or screen. I do not seek to say the Black Panther is a perfect restorative symbol or that he is inherently revolutionary in a real sense—as the intellectual property of the world's largest entertainment company, shepherded through much of his existence by white creators and executives until recently, such claims may be a stretch. But I think back to Evan Narcisse's words about the character taking significant evolutionary leaps under Black creators who found such meaning in him, and while the old saying "you cannot dismantle the master's house with the master's tools" is still apt, perhaps they can instead continue to build and widen the door in Priest's metaphorical "house" to continue exploring these larger existential issues of race, colonization, politics, and identity.

After all, in the relative context of superhero comics, the Black Panther was a revolutionary act—a significant if imperfect rejection of the notional idea of African and Black inferiority and the implicit white orthodoxy of the media. From Black Panther came Luke Cage, the Falcon, Storm, and countless other Black heroes to uplift generations—many of whom would get into the industry themselves and make their own contributions or go on to create other works in various fields inspired by these characters. We cannot ignore the treatment of the character as an afterthought or lesser figure for most of his existence, but we cannot ignore the contributions and opportunities the existence of the character has given to so many. The Black Panther cannot solve the impact of centuries of slavery or the effect decades of statutory and implicit apartheid, segregation, police brutality, redlining, or the myriad of other ills inflicted on African Americans and other members of the African Diaspora. But the idea, fictional or otherwise, that there can be a world where such things are not forgotten but not defining of the Black identity and experience can be powerful, and the symbol matters.

More than just about any other superhero, the Black Panther represents an idea and a consciousness that has been largely reappropriated and given new life by those he purports to represent, speaking to an identity that simply is not addressed by Batman, Superman, Spider-Man, or any other contemporary. The Panther is important because what he addresses is important, and how the franchise has arrived at where it is today is important, and because where and why the character succeeds and fails both in-text and outside of it is important. In Ta-Nehisi Coates' final issue of *Black Panther*, the hero assures an ally worried about the heroes' collective fate and hoping for a miracle that "The miracle is Wakanda."[34] By giving writers, artists, filmmakers, actors, actresses, programmers, designers, critics, scholars, and fans a means for creative expression, interrogation of complex ideas, and a space in which to introduce and have challenging discussions about the weight of history and how the burden of that weight differs, the transmedia character of the Black Panther moves beyond simple entertainment and toward that same miracle.

NOTES

1. SyFy Wire, "Building Black Panther," 11:17–12:10.
2. Priest et al., "Back in Black"; McGregor et al., "Panther's Heart," Hudlin et al., "Black to the Future Part 2," 31.
3. Rodriguez, "Vibranium Healing," 167.
4. Pearson, "World Building Logics and Copyright."
5. Jenkins, "Revenge of the Origami Unicorn."
6. Bertetti, "Toward a Typology of Transmedia Characters," 2348–9.
7. Holland, "An Unexpected Gift," 11–12.
8. Du Bois, *The Souls of Black Folk.*
9. Nama, *Super Black*, 42.
10. Davis, "Bare Chests," 211.
11. Nama, *Super Black,* 51–53.
12. Coates et al., "We Are the Streets Part 3 – Black Against the Empire."
13. Pineda, "Yes, lots of comics were racist."
14. Reese, "How the Afrofuturism."
15. Okorafor, "A Luta Continua."
16. BBC News, "Nigeria's Lekki shooting."
17. Whitlock, "Fearless."
18. Morgan, "The Women of Wakanda."
19. Buccifero, "The Symbolic, the Real, and the Ladies of Wakanda," 19 & 29–30.
20. Meyer, "*Black Panther*, erasure, and intersectional representation in popular culture."
21. Women's Media Center & BBC America, *Superpowering Girls.*
22. Finley, "'Black Panther' Actress."
23. Nama, *Super Black.*
24. Marrone, "Montalbano," 2–3.
25. Couch, "Marvel and DC's 'Shut-Up Money'"; Thielman, "Marvel and DC face backlash over pay."
26. Betancourt, "Christian Cooper hopes American can change."
27. Ibid.
28. Betancourt, "Christian Cooper has written a comic book."
29. Wynne, "Nickelodeon Went Off the Air."
30. Goldman, "'Tired of the Killings.'
31. Sullivan, "Kyle Rittenhouse"; Williams, "Kyle Rittenhouse: American Vigilante."

32. Williams, "American Vigilante."
33. Flier et al., "Did disparities kill the king of Wakanda?"
34. Coates et al., "Wakanda Unbound Issue #24," 4.

Bibliography

"72 Best Superhero Movies of All Time." *Rotten Tomatoes.* Accessed May 6, 2020. https://editorial.rottentomatoes.com/guide/best-superhero-movies-of-all-time.

"Mtcheew." *Naija Lingo,* n.d, http://naijalingo.com/words/mtcheew.

Aaron, Jason, Kubert, Adam, Dell, John, Martin, Laura, & Molinar, Larry. "Avengers vs. X-Men (Part Nine)." New York: Marvel Comics (2012). Marvel Unlimited.

Aaron, Jason, Raney, Tom, & Charalampidis, Jim. "Black Panther vs. Storm." *AvX: Vs.* 1, no. 5. New York: Marvel Comics (2012). Marvel Unlimited.

Adebayo, Bukola. "Nigerian army hands over nearly 200 Boko Haram child 'foot soldiers' to UN." *CNN,* July 10, 2018. https://www.cnn.com/2018/07/10/africa/nigerian-army-child-soldiers-released/index.html.

Adekoya, Remi. "Why Africans worry about how Africa is portrayed in western media," *The Guardian,* November 28, 2013. https://www.theguardian.com/commentisfree/2013/nov/28/africans-worry-how-africa-portrayed-western-media.

African Union Commission. "The Diaspora Division." *African Union Commission,* n.d. https://au.int/en/Diaspora-division.

Alemán, Sonya M., & Alemán, Jr., Enrique. "Critical Race Media Projects: Counterstories and Praxis (Re)claim Chicana/o Experiences," *Urban Education* 51, no. 3 (2016): 287–314.

Allen, Douglas, Lawhon, Mary, & Pierce, Joseph. "Placing race: On the resonance of place with black geographies," *Progress in Human Geography* 43, no. 6 (2019): 1001–19.

American Society of News Editors. "2019 Diversity Survey," *News Leaders Association.* September 10, 2019, https://www.newsleaders.org/2019-diversity-survey-results.

Amorosi, A. D. "Little Steven on the Apartheid-Smashing 'Sun City' – and Trading Fiery Polemics for Fun." *Variety,* March 13, 2020. https://variety.com/2020/music/news/little-steven-interview-sun-city-apartheid-political-1203528043/.

Anderson, Joshua. "A Tension in the Political Thought of Huey P. Newton," *Journal of African American Studies* 16, no. 2 (2011): 249–67.

Andrews, Penelope. "ICE Raids Bear a Disturbing Resemblance to the 'Pass Raids' of Apartheid." *Slate,* July 25, 2019. https://slate.com/news-and-politics/2019/07/ice-raids-south-africa-pass-laws.html.

Anna, Cara. "Post-apartheid South Africa is world's most unequal country." *Associated Press*, May 7, 2019. https://apnews.com/a1cd5ebc5ed24a7088d970d3 0bb04ba1.

Avengers Assemble. "Atlantis Attacks." Directed by Tim Eldred. Written by Trevor Devall. Disney XD, February 24, 2019.

———. "Bashenga." Directed by Tim Eldred. Written by Geoffrey Thorne. Disney XD, January 27, 2019.

———. "Civil War, Part 2: The Mighty Avengers." Directed by Tim Eldred. Written by Elliott Casey. Disney XD, January 28. 2017.

———. "Descent of the Shadow." Directed by Tim Eldred. Written by Margaret Dunlap. Disney XD, December 2, 2018.

———. "Into the Deep." Directed by Micah Gunnell. Written by Eugene Son. Disney XD, September 30, 2018.

———. "King Breaker, Part 2." Directed by Tim Eldred. Written by Brandon Easton. Disney XD, February 10, 2019.

———. "Panther's Rage." Directed by Micah Gunnell. Written by Eugene Son. Disney XD, September 25, 2016.

———. "T'Chanda," Directed by Tim Eldred. Written by Eugene Son. Disney XD, January 13, 2019.

———. "T'Challa Royale." Directed by Micah Gunnell. Written by Mark Henry. Disney XD, October 28, 2018.

———. "The Last Avenger." Directed by Kalvin Lee. Written by Zach Craley. Disney XD, December 2, 2018.

———. "The Panther and the Wolf." Directed by Tim Eldred. Written by Eugene Son. Disney XD, October 7, 2018.

———. "The Zemo Sanction." Directed by Micah Gunnell. Written by Akela Cooper. Disney XD, October 14, 2018.

———. "Widowmaker." Directed by Kalvin Lee. Written by Akela Cooper. Disney XD, February 17, 2019.

———."Yemandi." Directed by Kalvin Lee. Written by Denise Downer. Disney XD, January 20, 2019.

Bailey, Jason. "'Gone With the Wind' and Controversy: What You Need to Know." *The New York Times,* June 10, 2020. https://www.nytimes.com/2020/06/10/movies/ gone-with-the-wind-controversy.html.

Barker, Karlyn. "Stevie Wonder Arrested in Apartheid Protest." *Washington Post,* February 15, 1985. https://www.washingtonpost.com/archive/politics/1985/02/15/ stevie-wonder-arrested-in-apartheid-protest/84a1c736-2847-469a-b5d9-aaf305843f17/.

Bassett, Mary T. "Beyond Berets: The Black Panthers as Health Activists," *American Journal of Public Health* 106, no. 10 (2016): 1741–43.

BBC News. "Nigeria's Lekki shooting: What has happened so far at Lagos judicial panel." *BBC News,* November 27, 2020. https://www.bbc.com/news/ world-africa-55099016.

Bendis, Brian Michael, Guice, Jackson, & Ponsor, Justin. "Ultimate Origins (Part V)." *Ultimate Origins* 1, no. 5. New York: Marvel Comics (2008). Marvel Unlimited.

Beresford, David. "Row over 'mother of the nation' Winnie Mandela." *The Guardian,* January 27, 1989. https://www.theguardian.com/century/1980-1989/Story/0,110268,00.html.

Bergerson, Amy Aldous. "Critical race theory and white racism: Is there room for white scholars in fighting racism in education?" *International Journal of Qualitative Studies in Education* 16, no. 1 (2003): 51–63.

Berman, Nicolas, Couttenier, Mathieu, Rohner, Dominic, and Thoenig, Mathias. "How minerals fuel conflicts in Africa." *Africa Times,* March 17, 2017. https://africatimes.com/2017/03/17/how-minerals-fuel-conflicts-in-africa/.

———. "This Mine is Mine! How Minerals Fuel Conflicts in Africa," *American Economic Review* 107 no. 6 (2017): 1564–610.

Berr, Jonathan. "'Black Panther" merchandise is also striking gold." *CBS News,* March 8, 2018. https://www.cbsnews.com/news/black-panther-merchandise-is-also-striking-gold/.

Bertetti, Paolo. "Toward a Typology of Transmedia Characters," *International Journal of Communication* 8 (2014), 2344–361.

Betancourt, David. "Christian Cooper has written a comic book partly inspired by his viral Central Park moment." *The Washington Post,* September 9, 2020. https://www.washingtonpost.com/arts-entertainment/2020/09/09/christian-cooper-comic-central-park-birding/.

———. "Christian Cooper hopes American can change. Because he's not going to." *The Washington Post,* June 23, 2020. https://www.washingtonpost.com/arts-entertainment/2020/06/23/christian-cooper-central-park-birder-comics/.

———. "Miles Morales is a Spider-Man who's biracial like me. So why wasn't I more excited for his movie?" *The Washington Post,* December 13, 2018.

Biesecker, Barbara A. "Rethinking the Rhetorical Situation from within the Thematic of 'Différance,'" *Philosophy and Rhetoric,* 22 no. 2 (1989): 110–30.

Bloem, Jeffrey R. "The Unintended Consequences of Regulating 'Conflict Minerals' in Africa's Great Lakes Region." *World Bank Blogs,* November 25, 2019. https://blogs.worldbank.org/impactevaluations/unintended-consequences-regulating-conflict-minerals-africas-great-lakes-region.

Bloom, Joshua, & Martin Jr., Waldo E. *Black Against Empire: The History and Politics of the Black Panther Party.* Oakland, CA: University of California Press, 2016.

Boone, Steven. "Fruitvale Station." *RogerEbert.com,* July 15, 2013. https://www.rogerebert.com/reviews/fruitvale-station-2013.

Borrelli, "How Nnedi Okorafor is building the future of sci-fi from Flossmoor. (Being George R. R. Martin's protégé doesn't hurt.)" *Chicago Tribune,* May 23, 2019. https://www.chicagotribune.com/entertainment/ct-ae-nnedi-okorafor-sci-fi-0526-story.html.

Bowcott, Owen. "Thatcher dismissive of Mandela after first phone chat, files reveal." *The Guardian,* December 27, 2018. https://www.theguardian.com/uk-news/2018/dec/28/thatcher-dismissive-of-mandela-after-first-phone-chat-files-reveal.

Bradley, Bill. "How Chadwick Boseman Helped Create The 'Wakanda Forever' Salute." *Huffington Post,* September 2, 2020. https://www.huffpost.com/entry/chadwick-boseman-wakanda-forever-salute_n_5f4f8fd7c5b6250f655d7395.

Bramlett-Solomon, Sharon, & Carstarphen, Meta G. "American Press and Multiculturalism: Legacy and Changes." In *Race, Gender, Class and Media: Studying Mass Communication and Multiculturalism,* edited by Sharon Bramlett-Solomon and Meta G. Carstarphen, 57–68. Dubuque, IA: Kendall Hunt Publishing, 2017.

Brandon, George. "Orisha." *Britannica.com,* n.d. https://www.britannica.com/topic/orisha.

Braxton, Greg. "Black Panther battles ethics." *The Los Angeles Times,* July 26, 2008. https://www.latimes.com/archives/la-xpm-2008-jul-26-et-comic26-story.html.

Breznican, Anthony. "Black Panther language: Where Captain America: Civil War found the words of Wakanda." *Entertainment Weekly,* May 5, 2016. https://ew.com/article/2016/05/05/black-panther-language-wakanda-xhosa/.

British Broadcasting Corporation. "Four More Ways the CIA Has Meddled in Africa." *BBC.com,* May 17, 2016. https://www.bbc.com/news/world-africa-36303327.

Brod, Harry. *Superman is Jewish? How Comic Book Superheroes Came to Serve Truth, Justice, and the Jewish-American Way.* New York: Free Press, 2012.

Bryant, Howard. *Full Dissidence: Notes from an Uneven Playing Field.* Boston, MA: Beacon Press, 2020.

Buccifero, Claudia. "The Symbolic, the Real, and the Ladies of Wakanda." In *Why Wakanda Matters: What Black Panther Reveals About Psychology, Identity, and Communication,* edited by Sheena C. Howard. Dallas, TX: Smart Pop (2021): 17–33.

Bullington, Jonathan. "White supremacy in America: Can parents stop online radicalization?" *USA Today,* August 23, 2019. https://www.usatoday.com/story/news/nation/2019/08/23/white-supremacy-america-can-parents-stop-online-radicalization/2092314001/.

Bump, Philip. "15 years after the Iraq War began, the death toll is still murky." *Washington Post,* March 20, 2018. https://www.washingtonpost.com/news/politics/wp/2018/03/20/15-years-after-it-began-the-death-toll-from-the-iraq-war-is-still-murky/.

———. "FBI Director Wray reconfirms the threat posed by racist extremists." *Washington Post,* March 2, 2021. https://www.washingtonpost.com/politics/2021/03/02/fbi-director-wray-reconfirms-threat-posed-by-racist-extremists/.

Bunce, Mel, Franks, Suzanne and Paterson, Chris. "Introduction: A new Africa's media image?" In *Africa's Media Image in the 21st Century: From the "Heart of Darkness" to "Africa Rising,"* edited by Mel Bunce, Suzanne Franks, and Chris Paterson, 1–13. New York: Routledge, 2017.

Burroughs, Todd Steven. "Black Panther, Black Writers, White Audience: Christopher Priest and/vs. Reginald Hudlin." *Fire!!!* 4 no. 2, "Paneling Blackness" (Fall 2018), 55–93.

———. *Marvel's Black Panther: A Comic Book Biography, From Stan Lee to Ta-Nehisi Coates.* New York: Diasporic Africa Press, 2018. [Kindle Edition].

Butler, Bethonie. "Everyone was talking about 'Roots' in 1977 – including Ronald Reagan." *Washington Post,* May 30, 2016. https://www. washingtonpost.com/news/arts-and-entertainment/wp/2016/05/30/ everyone-was-talking-about-roots-in-1977-including-ronald-reagan/.

Capcom. *Marvel vs. Capcom: Infinite.* Capcom. PC. 2017.

Carlson-Ghost, Mark. "Before Black Panther, there was Lothar!" *MarkCarlson-Ghost.com,* n.d. https://www.markcarlson-ghost.com/index.php/2018/02/10/ before-the-black-panther-lothar.

Carmichael, Rodney, & Madden, Sidney. "'Black Panther: The Album' Is Kendrick Lamar's Parallel, Pan-African Universe." *All Songs Considered.* https://www.npr.org/sections/allsongs/2018/02/21/587334273/ black-panther-the-album-is-kendrick-lamar-s-parallel-pan-african-universe.

Carr, Bryan J. "Playing Like a Girl: The Ludic Representation of Gender in Video Games," in *What is a Game? Essays on the Nature of Videogames,* ed. Gaines S. Hubbell (Jefferson, NC: McFarland & Company, 2020), 189–209.

Carras, Christi. "'Black Panther' fans implore Marvel to #RecastTChalla after Chadwick Boseman's death." *Los Angeles Times,* December 28, 2021. https://www.latimes.com/entertainment-arts/movies/story/2021-12-28/ chadwick-boseman-black-panther-recast-tchalla-marvel.

CBR Staff. "Hudlin & Dickey Talk Black Panther / Storm Wedding." *CBR.com,* January 26, 2006. https://www.cbr.com/hudlin-dickey-talk-black-pantherstorm-wedding/.

Center for Media Literacy, "MediaLit Kit: Five Key Questions of Media Literacy/ Five Core Concepts of Media Literacy." *MediaLit.org,* 2005. http://www.medialit. org/sites/default/files/14B_CCKQPoster+5essays.pdf.

Chambers, Veronica. "When Blackness is a Superpower." *New York Times,* April 23, 2021. https://www.nytimes.com/2021/04/23/arts/black-superheroes.html.

Chiorazzi, Anthony. "The spirituality of Africa." *The Harvard Gazette,* October 6, 2015. https://news.harvard.edu/gazette/story/2015/10/the-spirituality-of-africa/.

Chitwood, Adam. "How the MCU was made: 'Black Panther' and the creation of Marvel's first Oscar contender." *Collider,* August 28, 2019. https://collider.com/ how-black-panther-became-marvels-first-oscar-winner/.

Claremont, Chris, Byrne, John, & McLeod, Bob. "Cry . . . Vengeance!" In *Marvel Team-Up* 1, no. 100, ed. Jim Shooter (New York: Marvel Comics, 1980), 32–41. Marvel Unlimited.

Clark, Alexis. "How the History of Blackface is Rooted in Racism." *History.com,* April 20, 2021. https://www.history.com/news/blackface-history-racism-origins.

———. "Returning From War, Returning to Racism." *The New York Times,* July 30, 2020. https://www.nytimes.com/2020/07/30/magazine/black-soldiers-wwii-racism.html.

Clayton, Aubrey. "The statistical paradox of police killings." *Boston Globe,* June 11, 2020. https://www.bostonglobe.com/2020/06/11/opinion/ statistical-paradox-police-killings/.

Coates, Ta-Nehisi. *Between the World and Me.* New York: Spiegel & Grau, 2015.

———. *We Were Eight Years in Power: An American Tragedy.* New York: One World, 2017.

Coates, Ta-Nehisi, & Acuña, Daniel. "Book I: Many Thousands Gone, Issue #1." *Black Panther* 7, no. 1. New York: Marvel Comics (2018). Marvel Unlimited.

———. "Book I: Many Thousands Gone, Issue #3." *Black Panther* 7, no. 3. New York: Marvel Comics (2018). Marvel Unlimited.

———. "Book 1: Many Thousands Gone, Issue #4." *Black Panther* 7, no. 4. New York: Marvel Comics (2018). Marvel Unlimited.

———. "Book 3: Two Thousand Seasons, Issue #14." *Black Panther* 7, no. 14. New York: Marvel Comics (2019). Marvel Unlimited.

———. "Book 3: Two Thousand Seasons, Issue #15." *Black Panther* 7, no. 15. New York: Marvel Comics (2019). Marvel Unlimited.

———."Book 3: Two Thousand Seasons, Issue #16." *Black Panther* 7, no. 16. New York: Marvel Comics (2019). Marvel Unlimited.

———. "Book 3: Two Thousand Seasons, Issue #17." *Black Panther* 7, no. 17. New York: Marvel Comics (2019). Marvel Unlimited.

———. "Book 4: Wakanda Unbound, Issue #24." *Black Panther* 7, no. 24. New York: Marvel Comics (2021). Marvel Unlimited.

Coates, Ta-Nehisi, Acuña, Daniel, Bodenheim, Ryan, & O'Halloran, Chris. "Book 4: Wakanda Unbound, Issue #23." *Black Panther* 7, no. 23. New York: Marvel Comics (2021). Marvel Unlimited.

Coates, Ta-Nehisi, Acuña, Daniel, Stelfreeze, Brian, & Martin, Laura. "Book 4: Wakanda Unbound, Issue #25." *Black Panther* 7, no. 25. New York: Marvel Comics (2021).

Coates, Ta-Nehisi, Bartel, Jen, Anka, Kris, & Farrell, Triona Tree. "Book 2: The Gathering of My Name, Issue #12." *Black Panther* 7, no. 12. New York: Marvel Comics (2019). Marvel Unlimited.

Coates, Ta-Nehisi, Bartel, Jen, Reinwand, Paul, & Farrell, Triona Tree. "Book I: Many Thousands Gone, Issue #6." *Black Panther* 7, no. 6. New York: Marvel Comics (2019). Marvel Unlimited.

Coates, Ta-Nehisi, Guice, Butch, Hanna, Scott, & Brown, Dan. "We Are the Streets—Part 1: Double Consciousness." *Black Panther & The Crew* 1, no. 1. New York: Marvel Comics (2017).

Coates, Ta-Nehisi, Guice, Butch, Chater, Mack, Hanna, Scott, & Brown, Dan. "We Are the Streets—Part 3: Black Against the Empire." *Black Panther & The Crew* 1, no. 3. New York: Marvel Comics (2017).

Coates, Ta-Nehisi, Harvey, Yona, Guice, Butch, Hanna, Scott, & Brown, Dan. "We Are the Streets Part 4 – Nothing but A Man." *Black Panther & The Crew* 1, no. 4. New York: Marvel Comics (2017).

Coates, Ta-Nehisi, Kirk, Leonard, & Martin, Laura. "Avengers of the New World: Part 11." *Black Panther* 6, no. 170. New York: Marvel Comics (2018). Marvel Unlimited.

Coates, Ta-Nehisi, Kirk, Leonard, Deering, Marc, & Martin, Laura. "Avengers of the New World: Part 7." *Black Panther* 6, no. 166. New York: Marvel Comics (2017). Marvel Unlimited.

Coates, Ta-Nehisi, Kirk, Leonard, Deering, Marc, Martin, Laura, & Milla, Matt. "Avengers of the New World Part 8." *Black Panther* 6, no. 167. New York: Marvel Comics (2018). Marvel Unlimited.

Coates, Ta-Nehisi, Kirk, Leonard, Deering, Marc, Wong, Walden, Martin, Laura, & Milla, Matt. "Avengers of the New World: Part 13." *Black Panther* 6, no. 172. New York: Marvel Comics (2018). Marvel Unlimited.

Coates, Ta-Nehisi, Sprouse, Chris, Story, Karl, & Martin, Laura. "A Nation Under Our Feet: Part 5." *Black Panther* 6, no. 5. New York: Marvel Comics (2016). Marvel Unlimited.

———. "A Nation Under Our Feet: Part 6." *Black Panther* 6, no. 6. New York: Marvel Comics (2016). Marvel Unlimited.

———. "A Nation Under Our Feet: Part 7." *Black Panther* 6, no. 7. New York: Marvel Comics (2016). Marvel Unlimited.

———. "A Nation Under Our Feet: Part 10." *Black Panther* 6, no. 10. New York: Marvel Comics (2017). Marvel Unlimited.

Coates, Ta-Nehisi, Sprouse, Chris, Story, Karl, & Menyz, Marcio. "Book 3: Two Thousand Seasons, Issue #18." *Black Panther* 7, no. 18. New York: Marvel Comics (2020). Marvel Unlimited.

Coates, Ta-Nehisi, Sprouse, Chris, Story, Karl, Vines, Dexter, Martin, Laura, & Crossley, Andrew. "Avengers of the New World: Part 5." *Black Panther* 6, no. 17. New York: Marvel Comics (2017). Marvel Unlimited.

Coates, Ta-Nehisi, Sprouse, Chris, Story, Karl, Wong, Walden, & Martin, Laura. "A Nation Under Our Feet: Part 8." *Black Panther* 6, no. 8. New York: Marvel Comics (2017). Marvel Unlimited.

Coates, Ta-Nehisi, Sprouse, Chris, Torres, Wilfredo, Story, Karl, & Martin, Laura. "Avengers of the New World: Part 6." *Black Panther* 6, no. 18. New York: Marvel Comics (2017). Marvel Unlimited.

Coates, Ta-Nehisi, Sprouse, Chris, Story, Karl, Wong, Walden, Vines, Dexter, Martin, Laura, & Crossley, Andrew. "Avengers of the New World: Part 4." *Black Panther* 6, no. 16. New York: Marvel Comics (2017). Marvel Unlimited.

Coates, Ta-Nehisi, Sprouse, Chris, Sudzuka, Goran, Wong, Walden, Story, Karl, Poggi, Martin, Laura, Milla, Matt, Molinar, Larry, Rosenberg, Rachelle, & Mounts, Paul. "A Nation Under Our Feet: Part 11." *Black Panther* 6, no. 11. New York: Marvel Comics (2017). Marvel Unlimited.

Coates, Ta-Nehisi, Stelfreeze, Brian, & Martin, Laura. "A Nation Under Our Feet: Part 1." *Black Panther* 6, no. 1. New York: Marvel Comics (2016). Marvel Unlimited.

———. "A Nation Under Our Feet: Part 2." *Black Panther* 6, no. 2. New York: Marvel Comics (2016). Marvel Unlimited.

———. "A Nation Under Our Feet: Part 3." *Black Panther* 6, no. 3. New York: Marvel Comics (2016). Marvel Unlimited.

———. "A Nation Under Our Feet: Part 9." *Black Panther* 6, no. 9. New York: Marvel Comics (2017). Marvel Unlimited.

Coates, Ta-Nehisi, Stelfreeze, Brian, Martin, Laura, & Milla, Matt. "A Nation Under Our Feet: Part 4." *Black Panther* 6, no. 4. New York: Marvel Comics (2016). Marvel Unlimited.

Coates, Ta-Nehisi, Stelfreeze, Brian, Sprouse, Chris, Story, Karl, Hanna, Scott, Martin, Laura, & Milla, Matt. "A Nation Under Our Feet: Part 12." *Black Panther* 6, no. 12. New York: Marvel Comics (2017). Marvel Unlimited.

Coates, Ta-Nehisi, Torres, Wilfredo, Burrows, Jacen, Pallot, Terry, & Martin, Laura. "Avengers of the New World: Part 2." *Black Panther* 6, no. 14. New York: Marvel Comics (2017). Marvel Unlimited.

Coates, Ta-Nehisi, Torres, Wilfredo, Martin, Laura, & Crossley, Andrew. "Avengers of the New World: Part 1." *Black Panther* 6, no. 13. New York: Marvel Comics (2017). Marvel Unlimited.

Coates, Ta-Nehisi, Walker, Kevin, & Paitreau, Stephane. "Book 2: The Gathering of My Name, Issue #7." *Black Panther* 7, no. 7. New York: Marvel Comics (2019). Marvel Unlimited.

Coates, Ta-Nehisi, Walker, Kevin, Tartaglia, Java, & Paitreau, Stephane. "Book 2: The Gathering of My Name, Issue #10." *Black Panther* 7, no. 10. New York: Marvel Comics (2019). Marvel Unlimited.

Cobb, Jelani. "'Black Panther' and the invention of 'Africa.'" *The New Yorker,* February 18, 2018. https://www.newyorker.com/news/daily-comment/black-panther-and-the-invention-of-africa.

Cole, Peter. "Remember the Massacre at Wounded Knee." *Jacobin Magazine,* December 29, 2016. https://www.jacobinmag.com/2016/12/wounded-knee-massacre-lakota-us-army.

Color of Change. "Not to be Trusted: Dangerous Levels of Inaccuracy in TV Crime Reporting in NYC." *ColorofChange.org,* March 2015. https://s3.amazonaws.com/s3.colorofchange.org/images/ColorOfChangeNewsAccuracyReportCardNYC.pdf.

Connolly, N. D. B. "How 'Black Panther' taps into 500 years of history." *The Hollywood Reporter,* February 16, 2018. https://www.hollywoodreporter.com/heat-vision/black-panther-taps-500-years-history-1085334.

Coogan, Peter. "The Hero Defines the Genre, the Genre Defines the Hero," in *What is a Superhero?,* edited by Robin S. Rosenberg and Peter Coogan. New York: Oxford University Press (2013): 3–10.

Coogler, Ryan, dir. *Black Panther.* 2018, Burbank CA: Marvel Studios.

Coogler, Ryan, dir. *Creed.* 2015, Burbank CA: Warner Bros. Pictures.

Coogler, Ryan, dir. *Fruitvale Station.* 2013, New York NY: The Weinstein Company.

Corley, Shaun. "Who is DC's Version of Black Panther, the Red Lion?" *ScreenRant,* October 4, 2020. https://screenrant.com/who-is-dcs-version-of-black-panther-the-red-lion/.

Couch, Aaron. "Marvel and DC's 'Shut-Up Money': Comic Creators Go Public Over Pay." *The Hollywood Reporter,* July 16, 2021. https://www.hollywoodreporter.com/movies/movie-news/marvel-and-dcs-shut-up-money-comic-creators-go-public-over-pay-1234983043/.

———. "Why Didn't 'Black Panther' Get A TV Show 20 Years Ago?" *The Hollywood Reporter,* February 28, 2018. https://www.hollywoodreporter.com/movies/movie-news/black-panther-animated-series-almost-happened-1088069/.

Crenshaw, Kimberlé Williams. *Facebook* [Personal Page]. Retrieved from https://www.facebook.com/kimberle.crenshaw/posts/10156138000853851.

———. "Twenty years of critical race theory: Looking back to move forward." *Conn. L. Rev.* 43 (2010): 1253.

Cronin, Brian. "Comic Book Legends Revealed #263." *CBR.com,* June 3, 2010. https://www.cbr.com/comic-book-legends-revealed-263/.

———. "Comic Legends: Was Kirby Behind Black Panther's First Series Ending?" *CBR.com,* February 19, 2018. https://www.cbr.com/black-panther-jack -kirby-canceled/.

———. "The Abandoned An' Forsaked—Whitewashing Whitewash Jones." *CBR.com,* March 30, 2013. https://www.cbr.com/ the-abandoned-an-forsaked-whitewashing-whitewash-jones/.

Croteau, David, & Hoynes, William. *Media/Society: Technology, Industries, Content, and Users.* 6th ed. Thousand Oaks, CA: Sage Publications (2019).

Crystal Dynamics. *Marvel's Avengers.* Square Enix. PlayStation 5. 2020.

Culver, Dennis. *Black Panther: The Illustrated History of a King.* San Rafael, CA: Insight Comics, 2018.

Culverson, Donald R. "The Politics of the Anti-Apartheid Movement in the United States, 1969–1986." *Political Science Quarterly* 111, no. 1 (1996): 127–49.

D'Alessandro, Anthony. "Disney Closing Blue Sky Studios, Fox's Once-Dominant Animation House Behind 'Ice Age' Franchise." *Deadline,* February 9, 2021. https://deadline.com/2021/02/ blue-sky-studios-closing-disney-ice-age-franchise-animation-1234690310/.

Dar, Taimur. "Comics Writer Don McGregor Talks 'Black Panther.'" *School Library Journal,* January 31, 2018. https://www.slj. com/?detailStory=comics-writer-don-mcgregor-talks-black-panther.

Dash, Mike. "Dahomey's Women Warriors." *Smithsonian Magazine,* September 23, 2011. https://www.smithsonianmag.com/history/dahomeys-women-warriors -88286072/.

Dates, Jannette L. and Pease, Edward C. "Warping the World—Media's Mangled Images of Race," in *The Media in Black and White,* edited by Everette E. Dennis and Edward C. Pease. New Brunswick, NJ: Transaction Publishers (2000): 77–82.

David, Saul. "Slavery and the 'Scramble for Africa.'" *BBC,* February 17, 2011. http:// www.bbc.co.uk/history/british/abolition/scramble_for_africa_article_01.shtml.

Davis, Blair. "Bare Chests, Silver Tiaras, and Removable Afros: The Visual Design of Black Comic Book Superheroes," in *The Blacker the Ink: Constructions of Black Identity in Comics & Sequential Art,* edited by Frances Gateward & John Jennings. New Brunswick, NJ: Rutgers University Press (2015): 193–212.

———. "Why the first black superhero was not the one you think." *Washington Post,* January 27, 2020, NA. Gale Academic OneFile (accessed June 26, 2020). https:// link-gale-com.ezproxy.uwgb.edu/apps/doc/A612372971/AONE?u=greenbay&sid =AONE&xid=12336a7.

Delgado, Richard. "Storytelling for Oppositionists and Others," *Michigan Law Review* 87, no. 8 (1989): 2411–41.

Demiurge Studios. *Marvel Puzzle Quest.* D3. Mobile. 2013.

De Waal, Alex. "Africa's 'Civil Wars' Are Regional Nightmares." *Foreign Policy,* October 22, 2019. https://foreignpolicy.com/2019/10/22/africas-civil-wars-are-regional-nightmares/.

Dickerson, Caitlin, "Overlooked: Ida B. Wells." *New York Times,* March 9, 2018. https://www.nytimes.com/interactive/2018/obituaries/overlooked-ida-b-wells.html.

Dixon, Marcus James. "Black Oscar winners: Every actress, actor who won Academy Awards." *GoldDerby,* June 10, 2020. https://www.goldderby.com/feature/black-oscar-winners-halle-berry-denzel-washington-1203522323/.

Donnelly, Matt and Lang, Brent. "Layoffs Hit Both Disney and Fox Film Groups." *Variety,* May 15, 2019. https://variety.com/2019/film/news/disney-fox-layoffs-1203216165/.

Du Bois, W. E. B. *The Souls of Black Folk.* Project Gutenberg [Digital Version], 1903. Retrieved from https://www.gutenberg.org/files/408/408-h/408-h.htm.

Dunn, Kevin. "Lights . . . Camera . . . Africa: Images of Africa and Africans in Western Popular Films of the 1930s." *African Studies Review,* 39 no. 1 (1996): 149–75.

Dyson, Michael Eric. "Ta-Nehisi Coates on education, religion, and Obama." *The Washington Post,* October 13, 2017. https://www.washingtonpost.com/outlook/ta-nehisi-coates-on-education-religion-and-obama/2017/10/13/adc054c6-ae84-11e7-be94-fabb0f1e9ffb_story.html.

Elbein, Asher. "The Secret Identity of Marvel Comics' Editor." *The Atlantic,* December 17, 2017. https://www.theatlantic.com/entertainment/archive/2017/12/the-secret-identity-of-marvel-comics-editor/547829/.

Elderkin, Beth. "Nnedi Okorafor Remarks on the Past, Present, and Future of Afrofuturism in New TED Talk." *Gizmodo,* November 2, 2017. https://io9.gizmodo.com/nnedi-okorafor-remarks-on-the-past-present-and-future-1820077413.

Elliott, Justin. "Reagan's embrace of apartheid South Africa." *Salon,* February 5, 2011. https://www.salon.com/2011/02/05/ronald_reagan_apartheid_south_africa/.

Ellison, Harlan, Thomas, Roy, & Buscema, Sal. "The Summons of Psyklop." *Avengers* 1, no. 88. New York: Marvel Comics (1971). Marvel Unlimited.

Englehart, Steve, & Colletta, Vinnie. "J'Accuse!" *Captain America* 1, no. 170. New York: Marvel Comics (1974). Marvel Unlimited.

English, Daylanne K., & Kim, Alvin. "Now We Want Our Funk Cut: Janelle Monáe's Neo-Afrofuturism." *American Studies* 52 no. 4 (2013): 217–30.

Epic Games. *Fortnite.* Epic Games. PlayStation 5. 2017.

Ertan, Arhan, Fiszbein, Martin, & Putterman, Louis. "Who was colonized and when? A cross-country analysis of determinants." *European Economic Review,* 83 (2016): 165–84.

Evanier, Mark. *Kirby: King of Comics.* New York: Abrams ComicArts, 2008. Kindle.

Evans Jr., George J. "Lion Man." In *All-Negro Comics* 1, edited by Orrin C. Evans. Philadelphia, PA: All-Negro Comics, Inc (June, 1947): 28–37.

Evans, Orrin C. "All-Negro Comics: Presenting Another First in Negro History." In *All-Negro Comics* 1, edited by Orrin C. Evans. Philadelphia, PA: All-Negro Comics, Inc (June, 1947): 1.

Fantastic Four: The Animated Series. "Prey of the Black Panther." Directed by Thomas McLaughlin Jr. Written by Glenn Leopold. Syndicated, November 11, 1995.

Favreau, Jon, dir. *Iron Man 2.* 2010, Burbank CA: Marvel Studios.

Feeny, Michael J. "Harlem's Hue-Man bookstore to close doors on July 31." *New York Daily News,* July 2, 2012. https://www.nydailynews.com/new-york/manhattan/harlem-hue-man-bookstore-close-doors-july-31-article-1.1106665.

Fihlani, Pumza. "Is necklacing returning to South Africa?" *BBC News,* October 12, 2011. https://www.bbc.com/news/world-africa-14914526.

Finley, Taryn. "'Black Panther' Actress Letitia Wright Hopes Shuri Inspires More Girls to Pursue STEM." *Huffington Post,* February 20, 2018. https://www.huffpost.com/entry/black-panther-actress-letitia-wright-hopes-shuri-inspires-more-girls-in-stem_n_5a8ba183e4b09fc01e02b764.

Fitzpatrick, Alex. "It's Not Just Black Panther. Afrofuturism is Having a Moment." *Time,* April 20, 2018. https://time.com/5246675/black-panther-afrofuturism/.

FitzPatrick, Hayley. "Robert Downey Jr. and more stars share memories of Chadwick Boseman." *ABC News,* August 31, 2020. https://abcnews.go.com/GMA/Culture/robert-downey-jr-stars-share-memories-chadwick-boseman/story?id=72719085.

Flanagan, Andrew. "Kendrick Lamar's 'DAMN.' Wins Historic Pulitzer Prize in Music." *NPR.org,* April 16, 2018. https://www.npr.org/sections/therecord/2018/04/16/602948758/kendrick-lamars-damn-wins-historic-pulitzer-prize-in-music.

Fleming Jr., Mike. "'Black Panther' Director Ryan Coogler on Chadwick Boseman: 'Because He Was a Caretaker, A Leader, And A Man of Faith, Dignity and Pride, He Shielded His Collaborators from His Suffering.'" *Deadline,* August 30, 2020. https://deadline.com/2020/08/black-panther-director-ryan-coogler-on-chadwick-boseman-black-panther-caretaker-a-leader-and-a-man-of-faith-dignity-and-pride-he-shielded-his-collaborators-from-his-suffering-1203027062/.

———. "'Black Panther' Helmer Ryan Coogler Stakes His Proximity Media Banner To 5-Year Exclusive Disney Television Deal; Wakanda Series in Works for Disney+." *Deadline,* February 1, 2021. https://deadline.com/2021/02/black-panther-ryan-coogler-wakanda-series-disney-plus-exclusive-disney-television-deal-proximity-media-1234684707/.

Flier, Lydia A., Rico, Gabriela, & Connor, Yamicia D. "Did disparities kill the king of Wakanda? Chadwick Boseman and changing landscape of colon cancer demographics." *Stat,* August 31, 2020. https://www.statnews.com/2020/08/31/disparities-kill-king-of-wakanda-chadwick-boseman-changing-landscape-colon-cancer-demographics/.

Ford, Angela, McFall, Kevin, & Dabney, Bob. "African American Media Today: Building the Future from the Past." *Democracy Fund,* February 2019. https://www.democracyfund.org/media/uploaded/2019_DF_AfricanAmericanMediaToday.pdf.

Ford, Matt. "Racism and the Execution Chamber." *The Atlantic.* June 23, 2014, https://www.theatlantic.com/politics/archive/2014/06/race-and-the-death-penalty/373081/.

Fortnite. "Marvel's Greatest Warriors and Royalty Come to Fortnite." YouTube video. 0:38. December 21, 2020. https://www.youtube.com/watch?v=yHDXUT6EU8A.

Foss, Sonja K. "Generative Criticism." In *Rhetorical Criticism: Exploration and Practice* (5th Ed.), 367–440. Long Grove, IL: Waveland Press, 2009.

———. "Metaphor Criticism." In *Rhetorical Criticism: Exploration and Practice* (5th Ed.), 267–306. Long Grove, IL: Waveland Press, 2009.

Foster, Elizabeth A. "How Africa is transforming the Catholic Church." *The Washington Post,* September 9, 2019. https://www.washingtonpost.com/outlook/2019/09/09/how-africa-is-transforming-catholic-church/.

Foucault, Michel. "The Archaeology of Knowledge," *Social Science Information* 9 no. 1 (1970): 175–85.

Fowler, Hayley. "Nazis, Klansmen killed 5 people in NC 40 years ago during the Greensboro Massacre." *The Charlotte Observer,* November 4, 2019. https://www.charlotteobserver.com/news/state/north-carolina/article237007024.html.

Frissell, Peregrine, Ibrahim, Ala'a, Raghavendran, Sheila, & Yang, Avery. "Missed deadline: The delayed promise of newsroom diversity." *Asian-American Journalists Association Voices.* July 27, 2017, https://voices.aaja.org/index/2017/7/25/missed-deadlines.

Gallagher, Simon. "How Happy Meals Killed Tim Burton's Batman." *WhatCulture,* June 27, 2019, https://whatculture.com/film/how-happy-meals-killed-tim-burtons-batman-2.

Gamer's Little Playground, "Marvel Ultimate Alliance 3 Movie (Cutscenes Only) 1080p HD." YouTube video, 1:34:14, July 19, 2019, https://www.youtube.com/watch?v=wYOpWdnu2jo&ab_channel=Gamer%27sLittlePlayground.

Gavaler, Chris. "The Ku Klux Klan and the birth of the superhero." *Journal of Graphic Novels & Comics* 4, no. 2 (2013): 191–208.

Gay, Roxane, Coates, Ta-Nehisi, Martinez, Alitha, Poggi, Roberto, & Rosenberg, Rachelle. "Dawn of the Midnight Angels: Part 2." *Black Panther: World of Wakanda* 1, no. 2. New York: Marvel Comics (2016).

———. "Dawn of the Midnight Angels: Part 5." *Black Panther: World of Wakanda* 1, no. 5. New York: Marvel Comics (2016).

Gay, Roxane, Martinez, Alitha, Rosenberg, & Rosenberg, Rachelle. "Dawn of the Midnight Angels: Part 1." *Black Panther: World of Wakanda* 1, no. 1. New York: Marvel Comics (2016).

Generic Gaming. "Marvel vs. Capcom: Infinite—Black Panther Scenes." YouTube video, 6:56, September 19, 2017. https://www.youtube.com/watch?v=Hi9IwBnx_VA&ab_channel=GenericGaming.

George, Alice. "The 1968 Kerner Commission Got It Right, But Nobody Listened." *Smithsonian Magazine.* March 1, 2018, https://www.smithsonianmag.com/smithsonian-institution/1968-kerner-commission-got-it-right-nobody-listened-180968318/.

Glass, Andrew. "House overrides Reagan apartheid veto, Sept 29, 1986." *Politico,* September 29, 2017. https://www.politico.com/story/2017/09/29/house-overrides-reagan-apartheid-veto-sept-29-1986-243169.

Godsil, Rachel D., & Johnson, Alexis McGill. "Transforming Perception: Black Men and Boys." *Perception Institute.* March 2013, https://perception.org/publications/transforming-perception/.

Goessling, Kristen. "Increasing the Depth of Field: Critical Race Theory and Photovoice as Counter Storytelling Praxis," *The Urban Review* 50, no. 4. (2018): 648–74.

Goff, Phillip Atiba, Eberhardt, Jennifer L., Williams, Melissa J., & Jackson, Matthew Christian. "Not Yet Human: Implicit Knowledge, Historical Dehumanization, and Contemporary Consequences." *Journal of Personality and Social Psychology* 94, no. 2 (2008): 292–306.

Goldberg, Susan. "To Rise Above the Racism of the Past, We Must Acknowledge It." *National Geographic,* April 2018: 4–6.

Goldman, Tom. "'Tired of the Killings': Pro Athletes Refuse to Play to Protest Racial Injustice." *National Public Radio,* August 26, 2020. https://www.npr.org/sections/live-updates-protests-for-racial-justice/2020/08/26/906496470/a-dramatic-day-in-pro-sports-where-the-action-was-no-action.

Gomez, Michael A. "Africans, Religion, and African Religion through the Nineteenth Century." *Journal of Africana Religions* 1, no. 1. (2013): 78–90.

Good, Owen S. "The Rise of Skywalker's opening crawl references an event you could only hear in Fortnite." *Polygon,* December 20, 2019. https://www.polygon.com/fortnite/2019/12/20/21031513/star-wars-the-rise-of-skywalker-fortnite-opening-crawl-palpatines-message.

Gough, Bob. "Interview with Don McGregor." *Mile High Comics* [Internet Archive], n.d. https://web.archive.org/web/20110716194521/http://www.milehighcomics.com/interviews/donmcgregor.html.

Graham, David A. "The New Black Panther Party is the New ACORN." *Newsweek,* July 14, 2010. https://www.newsweek.com/new-black-panther-party-new-acorn-74927.

Groth, Gary. "TCJ Archive: Jack Kirby Interview." *The Comics Journal.* May 23, 2011 (originally published February 1990), http://www.tcj.com/jack-kirby-interview/.

Guariglia, Matthew. "Senators Demand Answers on the Dangers of Predictive Policing." *Electronic Frontier Foundation,* April 19, 2021. https://www.eff.org/deeplinks/2021/04/senators-demand-answers-dangers-predictive-policing.

Guerrasio, Jason. "Here's a look back at the unreleased 1994 'Fantastic Four' movie that has since become a cult classic." *Business Insider,* August 10, 2015. https://www.businessinsider.com/how-1994-fantastic-four-became-a-cult-classic-2015-8.

Guglielmo, Connie. "Black Panther rules Marvel's world. Literally." *CNet,* August 29, 2020. https://www.cnet.com/features/black-panther-chadwick-boseman-marvel-king-of-wakanda/.

Gustines, George Gene. "Marvel Announces a New Black Panther Series." *The New York Times,* May 18, 2021. https://www.nytimes.com/2021/05/18/arts/marvel-black-panther-john-ridley.html.

———. "Marvel's World of Wakanda Will Spotlight Women, on the Page and Behind It." *New York Times,* July 22, 2016. https://www.nytimes.com/2016/07/23/books/black-panther-marvel-comics-roxane-gay-ta-nehisi-coates-wakanda.html?_r=0.

———. "Ta-Nehisi Coates to Write Black Panther Comic for Marvel." *New York Times,* September 22, 2015. https://www.nytimes.com/2015/09/23/books/ta-nehisi-coates-to-write-black-panther-comic-for-marvel.html.

Hall, Peter A. "Of Neon, Road Signs, and Head Shapes: A Case for Generative Criticism," in *The Routledge Companion to Criticality in Art, Architecture, and Design,* edited by Chris Brisbin and Myra Thiessen, 315–29. New York: Routledge, 2018.

Hallwalls Contemporary Art Center. "John Jennings & Stacey Robinson *Black Kirby.*" *Hallwalls.com,* n.d. https://www.hallwalls.org/visual/5278.html.

Hamman, Cody. "Exclusive: Marvel's Kevin Feige Says Blade Will Return Someday." *Jo Blo,* June 26, 2017. https://www.joblo.com/horror-movies/news/exclusive-marvel-s-kevin-feige-says-blade-will-return-someday-323.

Hannigan, Ed and Bingham, Jerry. "Journey Through the Past!" *Marvel Premiere,* no. 52. New York: Marvel Comics (1980).

———. "The Beasts in the Jungle!" *Black Panther* 1, no. 14. New York: Marvel Comics (1979).

———. "The Ending, in Anger!" *Marvel Premiere* 1, no. 53. New York: Marvel Comics (1980).

———. "The Killing of Windeagle!" *Marvel Premiere* 1, no. 51. New York: Marvel Comics (1979).

Hansler, Jennifer. "What Martin Luther King Jr.'s death did to civil rights leaders." *CNN,* April 4, 2018. https://www.cnn.com/2018/04/04/politics/civil-rights-activists-martin-luther-king-jr-legacy/index.html.

Hardt, Hanno. *Critical Communication Studies: Communication, History, & Theory in America.* New York: Routledge, 1992.

Harris, Beth. "Daniel Kaluuya wins supporting actor, his 1st Oscar." *Associated Press,* April 26, 2021. https://apnews.com/article/oscars-2021-best-supporting-actor-daniel-kaluuya-e1c4b816637e4cf1030ee4223eed8c0.

Harris, Joseph E. "Introduction." In *Global Dimensions of the African Diaspora*, edited by Joseph E. Harris, 3–8. 2nd ed. Washington, D. C.: Howard University Press, 1993.

Harris-Perry, Melissa. *Sister Citizen: Shame, Stereotypes, and Black Women in America.* New Haven, CT: Yale University Press, 2011.

Harvey, Jim. "The World's Finest Presents Static Shock: Backstage—Interviews—Dwayne McDuffie." *The World's Finest,* (n.d.). https://dcanimated.com//WF/staticshock/backstage/interviews/mcduffiewf.php

Heinz, Brett. "It's Time to Break Up Disney." *The American Prospect,* October 1, 2019. https://prospect.org/power/time-to-break-up-disney-monopoly/.

Hickman, Jonathan, Camuncoli, Giuseppe, Kesel, Karl, & Mounts, Paul. "City of the Dead." *Fantastic Four* 1, no. 608. New York: Marvel Comics (2012). Marvel Unlimited.

———. "Inert." *Fantastic Four* 1, no. 607. New York: Marvel Comics (2012). Marvel Unlimited.

Hickman, Jonathan, Deodato, Mike, & Martin Jr., Frank. "Builders." *New Avengers* 3, no. 11. New York: Marvel Comics (2013). Marvel Unlimited.

———. "What Maximus Made." *New Avengers* 3, no. 8. New York: Marvel Comics (2013). Marvel Unlimited.

Hickman, Jonathan, Epting, Steve, Magyar, Rick, & D'Armata. "Memento Mori." *New Avengers* 3, no. 1. New York: Marvel Comics (2013). Marvel Unlimited.

Hickman, Jonathan, Ribić, Esad, & Svorcina, Ive. "Beyond." *Secret Wars* 1, no. 9. New York: Marvel Comics (2016). Marvel Unlimited.

———. "King of the Dead." *Secret Wars* 1, no. 7. New York: Marvel Comics (2016). Marvel Unlimited.

———. "The End Times." *Secret Wars* 1, no. 1. New York: Marvel Comics (2015). Marvel Unlimited.

Hickman, Jonathan, Schiti, Valerio, & Martin Jr., Frank. "Into the Breach." *New Avengers 3,* no. 18. New York: Marvel Comics (2014). Marvel Unlimited.

———. "We Are All Monsters Now." *New Avengers* 3, no. 19. New York: Marvel Comics (2014). Marvel Unlimited.

Hickman, Jonathan, Schiti, Valerio, Martin Jr., Frank, & Mounts, Paul. "Blu'Dakorr." *New Avengers* 3, no. 20. New York: Marvel Comics (2014). Marvel Unlimited.

Hickman, Jonathan, Schiti, Valerio, Larroca, Salvador, Martin Jr., Frank, & Mounts, Paul. "The Bomb." *New Avengers* 3, no. 21. New York: Marvel Comics (2014). Marvel Unlimited.

Hickman, Jonathan, Walker, Kev, & Martin Jr., Frank. "All the Angels Have Fallen." *New Avengers* 3, no. 23. New York: Marvel Comics (2014). Marvel Unlimited.

———. "We Are Not Brothers." *New Avengers* 3, no. 22. New York: Marvel Comics (2014). Marvel Unlimited.

Hickson, Colin. "Avengers: Endgame Had Black Panther Return First—Here's Why." *Comic Book Resources,* August 10, 2019. https://www.cbr.com/avengers-endgame-black-panther-return-first-why/.

Hirsch, Afua. "Racist African stereotypes are as prevalent as ever on TV." *The Guardian,* August 28, 2019. https://www.theguardian.com/commentisfree/2019/aug/28/racist-africans-stereotypes-tv-colonial.

Holland, Jesse J. "An Unexpected Gift," in *Black Panther: Tales of Wakanda,* edited by Jesse J. Holland. London: Titan Books (2021): 10–15.

Holligan, Anna. "I'll be at front of queue to change my slave name." *BBC News,* September 10, 2021. https://www.bbc.com/news/world-europe-58492848.

Hoskin, Michael. "Exploring White Privilege in Christopher Priest's Black Panther: Part 2, Hunter, the White Wolf." August 3, 2020. http://sequart.org/magazine/70527/exploring-white-privilege-in-christopher-priest-black-panther-part-2-hunter-white-wolf/.

———. "Panther's Range: The History of the Black Panther Prior to Christopher Priest." *Sequart Organization,* September 7, 2020. http://sequart.org/magazine/70539/panthers-range-history-black-panther-prior-to-christopher-priest/.

Howard, Sheena C. *Encyclopedia of Black Comics.* Golden, CO: Fulcrum Publishing, 2017.

Howe, Sean. "Avengers Assemble!: How Marvel went from Hollywood also-ran to mastermind of a $1 billion franchise." *Slate,* September 28, 2012. https://slate.com/business/2012/09/marvel-comics-and-the-movies-the-business-story-behind-the-avengers.html.

———. *Marvel Comics: The Untold Story.* New York: Harper Perennial, 2012.

Hudlin, Reginald. "Looking Back at Black Panther with Reginald Hudlin." Disc 1. *Marvel Knights: Black Panther*, DVD. Directed by Mark Brooks and Jon Schnepp. Los Angeles, CA: Shout! Factory, LLC, 2010.

Hudlin, Reginald. "The Black Panther: A Historical Overview and a Look to the Future." In *Black Panther: Who Is the Black Panther?* [Barnes & Noble Edition]. Written by Reginald Hudlin, Art by John Romita Jr., Klaus Janson, and Dean White. New York: Marvel Worldwide, 2018.

Hudlin, Reginald, CAFU, Bit, & Staples, Val. "Endgame—Conclusion." *Black Panther* 4, no. 34. New York: Marvel Comics (2008). Marvel Unlimited.

Hudlin, Reginald, Cowan, Denys, Janson, Klaus, & Pantazis, Pete. "Part I." *Captain America/Black Panther: Flags of our Fathers* 1, no. 1. New York: Marvel Comics (2010). Marvel Unlimited.

———. "Part II." *Captain America/Black Panther: Flags of our Fathers* 1, no. 2. New York: Marvel Comics (2010). Marvel Unlimited.

Hudlin, Reginald, Cowan, Denys, Palmer, Tom, & Pantazis, Pete. "Part 4." *Captain America/Black Panther: Flags of our Fathers* 1, no. 4. New York: Marvel Comics (2010). Marvel Unlimited.

Hudlin, Reginald, Cowan, Denys, Palmer, Tom, Florea, Sandu, & Pantazis, Pete. "Part III." *Captain America/Black Panther: Flags of our Fathers* 1, no. 3. New York: Marvel Comics (2010). Marvel Unlimited.

Hudlin, Reginald, Di Vito, Andrea, & Staples, Val. "Ready to Die (Part 3)." *Black Panther* 4, no. 33. New York: Marvel Comics (2008). Marvel Unlimited.

Hudlin, Reginald, Eaton, Scot, Janson, Klaus, & White, Dean. "Black Steel in the Hour of Chaos." *Black Panther* 4, no. 12. New York: Marvel Comics (2006). Marvel Unlimited.

———. "Bride of the Panther, Part One." *Black Panther* 4, no. 14. New York: Marvel Comics (2006). Marvel Unlimited.

———. "Bride of the Panther Part Two." *Black Panther* 4, no. 15. New York: Marvel Comics (2006). Marvel Unlimited.

———. "Two the Hard Way Part One." *Black Panther* 4, no. 10. New York: Marvel Comics (2006). Marvel Unlimited.

———. "White Light, Black Heat." *Black Panther* 4, no. 13. New York: Marvel Comics (2006). Marvel Unlimited.

Hudlin, Reginald, Eaton, Scot, Andrews, Kaare, Janson, Klaus, & White, Dean. "Here Come a Storm." *Black Panther* 4, no. 18. New York: Marvel Comics (2006). Marvel Unlimited.

Hudlin, Reginald, Eaton, Scot, Hennessy, Andrew, & White, Dean. "World Tour, Part 1: Holiday in Latveria." *Black Panther* 4, no. 19. New York: Marvel Comics (2006). Marvel Unlimited.

Hudlin, Reginald, Eaton, Scot, Janson, Klaus, Bradstreet, Tim, & White, Dean. "Bride of the Panther Part Three." *Black Panther* 4, no. 16. New York: Marvel Comics (2006). Marvel Unlimited.

Hudlin, Reginald, Garcia, Manuel, Leisten, Jay, & Milla, Matt. "Aqua-Boogie." *Black Panther* 4, no. 21. New York: Marvel Comics (2006). Marvel Unlimited.

Hudlin, Reginald, Garcia, Manuel, Leisten, Jay, Parsons, Sean, & Milla, Matt. "Inside Man." *Black Panther* 4, no. 22. New York: Marvel Comics (2007). Marvel Unlimited.

Hudlin, Reginald, Garcia, Manuel, Morales, Mark, Florea, Sandu, & Milla, Matt. "World Tour Part Two: Fly Me to the Moon." *Black Panther* 4, no. 20. New York: Marvel Comics (2006). Marvel Unlimited.

Hudlin, Reginald, Lashley, Ken, & Milla, Matt. "Black to the Future Part II." *Black Panther Annual* 2, no. 1. New York: Marvel Comics (2018). Marvel Unlimited.

Hudlin, Reginald, Lashley, Ken, Mounts, Paul. "The Deadliest of the Species, Part 5." *Black Panther* 5, no. 5. New York: Marvel Comics (2009).

Hudlin, Reginald, Lashley, Ken, Neary, Paul, & Mounts, Paul. "The Deadliest of the Species, Part 1." *Black Panther* 5, no. 1. New York: Marvel Comics (2009).

———. "The Deadliest of the Species, Part 2." *Black Panther* 5, no. 2. New York: Marvel Comics (2009).

———. "The Deadliest of the Species, Part 3." *Black Panther* 5, no. 3. New York: Marvel Comics (2009).

———. "The Deadliest of the Species, Part 4." *Black Panther* 5, no. 4. New York: Marvel Comics (2009).

———."The Deadliest of the Species, Part 6." *Black Panther* 5, no. 6. New York: Marvel Comics (2009).

Hudlin, Reginald, Romita Jr., John, Janson, Klaus, & White, Dean. "Who is the Black Panther?" *Black Panther* 4, no. 1. New York: Marvel Comics (2005). Marvel Unlimited.

———. "Who is the Black Panther? Part Two." *Black Panther* 4, no. 2. New York: Marvel Comics (2005). Marvel Unlimited.

———. "Who is the Black Panther? Part Three." *Black Panther* 4, no. 3. New York: Marvel Comics (2005). Marvel Unlimited.

———. "Who is the Black Panther? Part Four." *Black Panther* 4, no. 4. New York: Marvel Comics (2005). Marvel Unlimited.

———. "Who is the Black Panther? Part Five." *Black Panther* 4, no. 5. New York: Marvel Comics (2005). Marvel Unlimited.

———. "Who is the Black Panther? Part Six." *Black Panther* 4, no. 6. New York: Marvel Comics (2005). Marvel Unlimited.

Hudlin, Reginald, Turnbull, Koi, Ho, Don, Regla, Sal, de los Santos, Jeff, & Smith, J.D. "War Crimes Part 1." *Black Panther 4,* no. 23. New York: Marvel Comics (2007). Marvel Unlimited.

Hudlin, Reginald, Yardin, David, Leisten, Jay, & White, Dean. "Wild Kingdom (Part 2): House of Paine." *Black Panther* 4, no. 8. New York: Marvel Comics (2005). Marvel Unlimited.

Hunt, Darnell, & Ramón, Ana-Christina. "Hollywood Diversity Report 2020: A Tale of Two Hollywoods." *UCLA Social Sciences,* 2020. https://socialsciences. ucla.edu/wp-content/uploads/2020/02/UCLA-Hollywood-Diversity-Report-2020-Film-2-6-2020.pdf.

Hurley, Leon. "Here's how many people play Fortnite." *Games Radar,* November 3, 2021. https://www.gamesradar.com/how-many-people-play-fortnite/.

Inoa, Christopher. "A Definitive Timeline of Wesley Snipes' Attempts to Make Black Panther." *SyFy Wire,* February 9, 2018. https://www.syfy.com/ syfywire/a-definitive-timeline-of-wesley-snipes-attempts-to-make-black-panther.

Internet Movie Database. "Reginald Hudlin." *IMDB.com,* n.d., https://www.imdb. com/name/nm0399737/.

Iron Man: Armored Adventures. "Line of Fire." Directed by Stéphane Juffé & Philippe Guyenne. Written by Mark Henry & Clelia Constantine. Nicktoons, August 17, 2011.

———. "Panther's Prey." Directed by Stéphane Juffé. Written by Andrew R. Robinson & Craig Kyle. Nicktoons, August 28, 2009.

———. "The Makluan Invasion Part 1: Annihilate!" Directed by Philippe Guyenne. Written by Mark Henry & Thomas Barichella. Nicktoons. July 18, 2012.

———. "The Makluan Invasion Part 2: Unite!" Directed by Stéphane Juffé & Philippe Guyenne. Written by Brandon Auman. Nicktoons. July 25, 2012.

Jackson, Matthew. "Black Panther 2 Script in the Works With 'Respect and Love,' Says Kevin Feige of Wakanda-Focused Sequel." *SyFy Wire,* January 11, 2021. https://www.syfy.com/syfywire/kevin-feige-black-panther-2-will-not-cg-chadwick-boseman.

James, C. L. R. *The Black Jacobins: Touissant L'Ouverture and the San Domingo Revolution.* 2nd ed. New York: Vintage Books, 1963.

Janay, Malinda. "Ryan Coogler Included a Subtle but Powerful Message on Pan-Africanism in 'Black Panther.'" *Blavity,* February 21, 2018. https:// blavity.com/ryan-coogler-included-a-subtle-but-powerful-message-on-pan-africanism-in-black-panther?category1=culture&category2=r ace-identity.

Janik, Rachel. "'Writing History with Lightning': The Birth of a Nation at 100." *Time,* February 8, 2015. https://time.com/3699084/100-years-birth-of-a-nation/.

Jefferson, J'na. "Wakanda Forever: The 'Black Panther' Soundtrack Goes Platinum." *Vibe,* May 25, 2018. https://www.vibe.com/music/music-news/ black-panther-soundtrack-platinum-587836/.

Jenkins, Henry. *Convergence Culture: Where old and new media collide.* New York: New York University Press, 2006.

———. "The Revenge of the Origami Unicorn: Seven Principles of Transmedia Storytelling (Well, Two Actually. Five More on Friday)." *Henryjenkins.org,* December 12, 2009.

———. "Transmedia 202: Further Reflections." *Henryjenkins.org,* July 31, 2011. http://henryjenkins.org/2011/08/defining_transmedia_further_re.html.

Johnson, Jason. "How do we reconcile Black Panther without our King Chadwick Boseman?" *The New Tri-State Defender,* September 3, 2020. https://

tri-statedefender.com/how-do-we-reconcile-black-panther-without-our-king-chadwick-boseman/09/03/.

Johnson, Victoria. "Black Panther Writer Reginald Hudlin on T'Challa and the Future of Black Superheroes." *Vulture,* February 13, 2018. https://www.vulture.com/2018/02/black-panther-reginald-hudlin-interview.html.

Johnston, Joe, dir. *Captain America: The First Avenger.* 2011, Burbank CA: Marvel Studios.

Johnston, Rich. "Chris Claremont on Why X-Men Writers Aren't Allowed to Create New Characters Now." *Bleeding Cool,* October 7, 2014. https://bleedingcool.com/comics/chris-claremont-on-why-x-men-writers-arent-allowed-to-create-new-characters-now/.

Joyner, Jazmine. "Who Are the Dora Milaje? What You Need to Know About the Badass Women of 'Black Panther.'" *Slashfilm,* February 15, 2018. https://www.slashfilm.com/who-are-the-dora-milaje/.

Juddery, Mark. "How Superman Defeated the Ku Klux Klan." *Mental Floss,* October 31, 2009. https://www.mentalfloss.com/article/23157/how-superman-defeated-ku-klux-klan.

Kai, Maiysha. "Digging the Dora Milaje? Then Love the Dahomey Women Warriors." *The Root,* February 18, 2018. https://theglowup.theroot.com/digging-the-dora-milaje-then-love-the-dahomey-women-wa-1823114028.

Kanjunju, Amini. "Africa's secret weapon: The Diaspora." *CNN,* November 1, 2013. https://www.cnn.com/2013/11/01/opinion/africas-secret-weapon-Diaspora/index.html.

Kasinof, Laura. "An ugly truth behind 'ethical consumerism.'"

Keech, Marc, & Houlihan, Barrie. "Sport and the End of Apartheid." *The Round Table* 88, no. 349 (1999): 109–21.

Kempley, Rita. "Bebe's Kids." *Washington Post,* August 1, 1992. https://www.washingtonpost.com/wp-srv/style/longterm/movies/videos/bebeskidspg13kempley_a0a2ce.htm.

Kendall, G. "Don't Look for These Spider-Man Shows on Disney+." *CBR.com,* January 26, 2020. https://www.cbr.com/spider-man-tv-shows-not-on-disney-plus/.

Kent, Clarkisha. "On Black Panther, Black Leopard, and the Politics of Being a Black Superhero." *The Root,* January 30, 2018. https://www.theroot.com/on-black-panther-black-leopard-and-the-politics-of-bei-1822489281.

Khan, Imran. "Marvel Ultimate Alliance Games Delisted Without Notice." *Game Informer,* July 26, 2018. https://www.gameinformer.com/2018/07/26/marvel-ultimate-alliance-games-delisted-without-notice.

Kinder, Marsha. *Playing with Power in Movies, Television, and Video Games: From Muppet Babies to Teenage Mutant Ninja Turtles.* Los Angeles, CA: University of California Press, 1991.

King, LaGarrett. "The media and black masculinity: Looking at the media through race [d] lenses." *Critical Education* 8, no. 2 (2017).

Kinos-Goodin, Jesse. "9 Key Moments in the Black Panther's 50-year Evolution." *CBC.ca,* February 14, 2018. https://www.cbc.ca/radio/q/blog/9-key-moments-in-the-black-panther-s-50-year-evolution-1.4529109.

Kirby, Jack. "Black Musketeers." *Black Panther* 1, no. 9. New York: Marvel Comics (1978). Marvel Unlimited.

———. "Kiber the Cruel." *Black Panther* 1, no. 11. New York: Marvel Comics (1978). Marvel Unlimited.

Kleiner, Sam. "Apartheid Amnesia." *Foreign Policy,* July 19, 2013, https://foreignpolicy.com/2013/07/19/apartheid-amnesia/.

Klose, Kevin. "Soviets, in Shift, Criticize Amin's Rule in Uganda." *The Washington Post,* April 30, 1979. https://www.washingtonpost.com/archive/politics/1979/04/30/soviets-in-shift-criticize-amins-rule-in-uganda/8da7e457-5b22-48c9-9fb6-9f44290ea890/.

Kraft, David, Wilson, Ron, & Marcos, Pablo. "Voodoo and Valor!" *Marvel Two-in-One* 1, no. 41. New York: Marvel Comics (1978). Marvel Unlimited.

Kreitner, Richard. "October 15, 1966: The Black Panther Party Is Founded." *The Nation,* October 15, 2015. https://www.thenation.com/article/archive/october-15-1966-the-black-panther-party-is-founded/.

Labrecque, Jeff. "Breaking Big: Welcome to The Show, Chadwick Boseman." *Entertainment Weekly,* November 20, 2014. https://ew.com/article/2014/11/20/chadwick-boseman-black-panther/.

Lamar, Kendrick. *Black Panther: The Album.* Top Dawg/Aftermath/Interscope. Recorded 2017. Released February 9, 2018. Digital.

Lamar, Kendrick & XXL Staff. "Position of Power: Kendrick Lamar's XXL Cover Story in His Own Words." *XXL,* December 22, 2015. https://www.xxlmag.com/kendrick-lamar-xxl-magazine-winter-2015-cover-story/.

Lamerichs, Nicolle. "An Introduction to Character Studies." *NicolleLamerichs.com,* November 10, 2019. https://nicollelamerichs.com/2019/11/10/character-studies/.

Lawson, Aurich. "Marvel vs. Capcom: Infinite isn't the same without arcade-era pixel art." *Ars Technica,* September 18, 2017. https://arstechnica.com/gaming/2017/09/marvel-vs-capcom-infinite-isnt-the-same-without-arcade-era-pixel-art/.

Lee, Chris. "What Exactly Does Disney's 'Reorganization' Mean for the Movie Industry?" *Vulture,* October 14, 2020. https://www.vulture.com/2020/10/what-exactly-does-disneys-reorganization-mean-for-movies.html.

Lee, Stan, & Kirby, Jack. "Doomsday." *Fantastic Four* 1, no. 59 (1967). New York: Marvel Comics. Marvel Unlimited.

———. "The Black Panther!" *Fantastic Four* 1, no. 52 (1966). New York: Marvel Comics. Marvel Unlimited.

———. "The Way It Began . . . !" *Fantastic Four* 1, no. 53 (1966). New York: Marvel Comics. Marvel Unlimited.

———. "When Strikes the Silver Surfer!" *Fantastic Four* 1, no. 55 (1966). New York: Marvel Comics. Marvel Unlimited.

Lego Marvel Super Heroes: Black Panther—Trouble in Wakanda. Directed by Michael D. Black. Written by Mark Hoffmeier. Disney XD, May 11, 2018.

Lehr, Dick. *The Birth of a Movement: How Birth of a Nation Ignited the Battle for Civil Rights.* New York: PublicAffairs, 2014.

Lenker, Maureen Lee. "*Black Panther* cast and crew respond to Trump's Africa comments." *Entertainment Weekly,* January 30, 2018. https://ew.com/movies/2018/01/30/black-panther-team-responds-trumps-africa-comments/.

Leone, Matt. "X-Men: Children of the Atom: An oral history." *Polygon,* April 14, 2021. https://www.polygon.com/2021/4/14/22336505/x-men-children-of-the-atom-an-oral-history.

Lewis, Rebecca. "Black Panther cast had no idea they were auditioning for a Marvel movie." *Metro,* March 15, 2019. https://metro.co.uk/2019/03/15/black-panther-cast-no-idea-auditioning-marvel-movie-8908849/.

Liss, David, & Francavilla, Francesco. "Fear and Loathing in Hell's Kitchen Part 1." *Black Panther: The Man Without Fear* 1, no. 521. New York: Marvel Comics (2011). Marvel Unlimited.

———. "Urban Jungle." *Black Panther: The Man Without Fear* 1, no. 513. New York: Marvel Comics (2010). Marvel Unlimited.

Liss, David, Martinbrough, Shawn, Palo, Jeffe, Serrano, Felix, Aburto, Jesus, & Beaulieu, Jean-Francois. "The Kingpin of Wakanda: Conclusion." *Black Panther: The Most Dangerous Man Alive!* 1, no. 529. New York: Marvel Comics (2012). Marvel Unlimited.

Liss, David, Martinbrough, Shawn, & Serrano, Felix. "Kingpin of Wakanda (Part 1)." *Black Panther: The Most Dangerous Man Alive!* 1, no. 525. New York: Marvel Comics (2012). Marvel Unlimited.

———. "The Kingpin of Wakanda, Part 2." *Black Panther: The Most Dangerous Man Alive!* 1, no. 526. New York: Marvel Comics (2012). Marvel Unlimited.

Liss, David, Palo, Jeffe, & Beaulieu, Jean-Francois. "Storm Hunter, Part 2." *Black Panther: The Man Without Fear* 1, no. 520. New York: Marvel Comics (2011). Marvel Unlimited.

———. "True Sons." *Black Panther: The Most Dangerous Man Alive!* 1, no. 523.1. New York: Marvel Comics (2011). Marvel Unlimited.

Little, Becky. "How a Movement to Send Freed Slaves to Africa Created Liberia." *History.com,* April 5, 2019. https://www.history.com/news/slavery-american-colonization-society-liberia.

———. "Why Nelson Mandela Was Viewed as a 'Terrorist' by the U.S. Until 2008." *Biography.com,* May 19, 2020. https://www.biography.com/news/nelson-mandela-terrorist-reagan-thatcher.

Locke, John. *Second Treatise of Government.* Online: Project Gutenberg (1690/2010). https://english.hku.hk/staff/kjohnson/PDF/LockeJohnSECONDTREATISE1690.pdf.

Loeb, Jeph, & Djurdjevic, Marko. "Favorite Son." *Ultimate Captain America Annual* 1, no. 1. New York: Marvel Comics (2008). Marvel Unlimited.

Loeb, Jeph, Madureira, Joe, & Lichtner, Christian. "Robots in Disguise." *The Ultimates* 3, no. 5. New York: Marvel Comics (2008). Marvel Unlimited.

Loeb, Jeph, Sandoval, Rafa, Bonet, Roger, & Gracia, Marte. "Training Day." *Ultimate Captain America Annual* 1, no. 1. New York: Marvel Comics (2008). Marvel Unlimited.

Lopez, German. "Hurricane Katrina, in 7 essential facts." *Vox,* August 28, 2015. https://www.vox.com/2015/8/23/9191907/hurricane-katrina.

Lund, Martin. "'Introducing the Sensational Black Panther!': Fantastic Four #52-#53, the Cold War, and Marvel's imagined Africa," *Comics Grid* 6 no. 1 (2016): 1–21.

Maberry, Jonathan, Eaton, Scot, Campanella, Robert, Mendoza, Jaime, Melkis, Dave, & Beaulieu, Jean-Francois. "Doomwar (Part 6)." *Doomwar* 1, no. 6. New York: Marvel Comics (2010).

Maberry, Jonathan, Eaton, Scot, Lanning, Andy, & Beaulieu, Jean-Francois. "Doomwar (Part 1)." *Doomwar* 1, no. 1. New York: Marvel Comics (2010).

Maberry, Jonathan, Eaton, Scot, Lanning, Andy, Campanella, Robert, & Beaulieu, Jean-Francois. "Doomwar (Part 2)." *Doomwar* 1, no. 2. New York: Marvel Comics (2010).

Madrigal, Alexis. "When the Revolution was Televised," *The Atlantic,* April 1, 2018. https://www.theatlantic.com/technology/archive/2018/04/televisions-civil-rights-revolution/554639/.

Mahmoud, Yahia. "Modernism in Africa." *Routledge Encyclopedia of Modernism,* September 5, 2016. https://www.rem.routledge.com/articles/overview/modernization-development-studies-and-modernity-in-current-african-debates.

Maloney, Nora. "Backstage at the Black Panther New York Fashion Week presentation." *Vanity Fair,* February 13, 2018. https://www.vanityfair.com/style/2018/02/backstage-at-the-black-panther-new-york-fashion-week-presentation.

Manovich, Lev. "Database as a Symbolic Form." *Convergence: The International Journal of Research into New Media Technologies,* vol. 5, 1999, 80–97.

———. *The Language of New Media.* Boston, MA: MIT Press, 2001.

Margolin, Emma. "David Duke, Former KKK Leader, Announces Senate Run." *NBC News,* July 22, 2016. https://www.nbcnews.com/politics/politics-news/david-duke-former-kkk-leader-announces-senate-run-n615006.

Marrone, Gianfranco. "Montalbano: Affirmations and transformations of a media hero: Introduction." *Montalbano: Affirmations and Transformations of a Media Hero.* Turin, Italy: RAI Libri (2004). Translated via Google Translate from https://digilander.libero.it/marrone/pdf_testi/montalbano_introduzione.pdf.

Marvel Future Avengers. "Black Panther." Directed by Yūzō Satō. Written by Ryū King. Dlife/Disney+, September 23, 2017 (Japan) / February 28, 2020 (U.S.).

———. "The Final Fateful Battle." Directed by Yūzō Satō. Written by Ryū King. Dlife/Disney+, January 13, 2018 (Japan) / February 28, 2020 (U.S.).

Marvel Super Hero Adventures. "Family Friendly." Directed by Svend Gregori. Disney Channel, February 2, 2018.

Massie, Victoria M. "The most radical thing the Black Panthers did was give kids free breakfast." *Vox,* October 15, 2016. https://www.vox.com/2016/2/14/10981986/black-panthers-breakfast-beyonce.

McDuffie, Dwayne. "To Be Continued #3." *To Be Continued.* 1999. https://web.archive.org/web/20020317100339/http://homepage.mac.com/dmcduffie/site/TBC3.html.

McDuffie, Dwayne, & McDaniel, Walter. "And We Are Not Saved!" *Deathlok* 1, no. 23. New York: Marvel Comics (1993).

McDuffie, Dwayne, & Miehm, Grant. "Vices Pass for Virtues." *Deathlok* 1, no. 24. New York: Marvel Comics (1993).

McDuffie, Dwayne, & Wozniak, Chris. "Protect and Defend." *Deathlok* 1, no. 25. New York: Marvel Comics (1993).

McGee, Michael Calvin. "Text, Context, and the Fragmentation of Contemporary Culture." *Western Journal of Speech Communication,* 54 no. 3 (1990): 274–89.

McGregor, Don. "Living Inside the Head of the King of Wakandans." In *Black Panther Psychology: Hidden Kingdoms*, edited by Travis Langley and Alex Simmons, xvi–xxv. New York: Sterling, 2019.

———. "Panther's Spoor." In *Black Panther: Panther's Prey Book 4*, Don McGregor (writing) and Dwayne Turner (art). New York: Marvel Comics (1991).

McGregor, Don, & Acuña, Daniel. "Panther's Heart." *Black Panther Annual* 2, no 1. New York: Marvel Comics (2018).

McGregor, Don, & Buckler, Rich. "Panther's Rage." *Jungle Action featuring the Black Panther* 2, no. 6. New York: Marvel Comics (1973). Marvel Unlimited.

McGregor, Don, & Colan, Gene. *Black Panther: Panther's Quest.* New York: Marvel Comics (1988; 2017).

McGregor, Don, & Graham, Billy. "A Cross Burning Darkly Blackening the Night!" *Jungle Action featuring the Black Panther* 2, no. 21. New York: Marvel Comics (1976).

———. "Blood and Sacrifices!" *Jungle Action featuring the Black Panther* 2, no. 19. New York: Marvel Comics (1976). Marvel Unlimited.

———. "Of Shadows and Rages." *Jungle Action featuring the Black Panther* 2, no. 17. New York: Marvel Comics (1975). Marvel Unlimited.

———. "Once You Slay the Dragon!" *Jungle Action featuring the Black Panther* 2, no. 11. New York: Marvel Comics (1974). Marvel Unlimited.

———. "They Told Me a Myth I Wanted to Believe." *Jungle Action featuring the Black Panther* 2, no. 20. New York: Marvel Comics (1976). Marvel Unlimited.

McGregor, Don, Graham, Billy, & Janson, Klaus. "King Cadaver is Dead and Living in Wakanda!" *Jungle Action Featuring the Black Panther* 2, no. 10. New York: Marvel Comics (1974).

McGregor, Don, Graham, Billy, & Buckler, Rich. "Death Riders on the Horizon." *Jungle Action featuring the Black Panther* 2, no. 22. New York: Marvel Comics (1976). Marvel Unlimited.

McGregor, Don, Kane, Gil, & Janson, Klaus. "But Now the Spears are Broken." *Jungle Action featuring the Black Panther* 2, no. 9. New York: Marvel Comics (1974). Marvel Unlimited.

McGregor, Don, & Turner, Dwayne. *Black Panther: Panther's Prey Pt. Four of Four.* New York: Marvel Entertainment Group, 1991.

McLellan, Dennis. "Dwayne McDuffie dies at 49; comic book and animation writer." *Los Angeles Times,* February 24, 2011. https://www.latimes.com/local/obituaries/la-me-dwayne-mcduffie-20110224-story.html.

McMillan, Graeme. "'Black Panther' Creators Shed Light on Industry Prejudice at New York Comic Con." *The Hollywood Reporter,* October 7, 2016. https://www.hollywoodreporter.com/heat-vision/new-york-comic-con-explores-936112.

———. "Ta-Nehisi Coates Leaving Marvel's 'Black Panther.'"

Mendelson, Scott. "20 years later, how Batman changed the movie business . . . " *Open Salon,* June 24, 2009 [Internet Archive]. https://web.archive.org/web/20090627032037/http://open.salon.com/blog/scott_mendelson/2009/06/24/20_years_later_how_batman_changed_the_movie_business.

———. "Box Office: 'Black Panther' tops 'Last Jedi' and 'Avengers.'" *Forbes,* March 25, 2018. https://www.forbes.com/sites/scottmendelson/2018/03/25/box-office-black-panther-tops-last-jedi-and-avengers/#16d1d1a31c50.

———. "Famous Flops: 'Supergirl' Doomed Girl-Powered Comic Book Movies." *Forbes,* May 8, 2015. https://www.forbes.com/sites/scottmendelson/2015/05/08/famous-flops-supergirl-doomed-girl-powered-comic-book-movies/?sh=5ac0f3136d4d.

Mercurio, Eugenio, & Filak, Vincent F. "Roughing the Passer: The Framing of Black and White Quarterbacks Prior to the NFL Draft." *The Howard Journal of Communications* 21 (2010): 56–71.

Meslow, Scott. "Do Tim Burton's Batman Movies Hold Up?" *GQ,* February 7, 2018. https://www.gq.com/story/do-tim-burtons-batman-movies-hold-up.

Metz, Cade. "Who Is Making Sure the A.I. Machines Aren't Racist?" *The New York Times,* March 15, 2021. https://www.nytimes.com/2021/03/15/technology/artificial-intelligence-google-bias.html.

Meuginot, Will, & Sebast, Richard, dirs. *Ultimate Avengers 2: Rise of the Panther.* 2006, Santa Monica, CA: Lionsgate Films [DVD].

Meyer, Michaela D. E. "*Black Panther*, queer erasure, and intersectional representation in popular culture." *Review of Communication* 20 no. 3 (2020): 236–43.

Miller, Matt. "Stan Lee's Powerful 1968 Essay About the Evils of Racism is Still Necessary Today." *Esquire,* November 12, 2018. https://www.esquire.com/entertainment/movies/a25022397/stan-lee-marvel-racism-1968-essay/.

Mohan, Megha. "Black Panther: The 'weird signs' that led Chadwick Boseman to Wakanda." *BBC News,* September 5, 2020. https://www.bbc.com/news/stories-54014997.

Molly, David, & Kelion, Leo. "Fortnite Movie Nite: Christopher Nolan's hit films screen in-game." *BBC News,* June 26, 2020. https://www.bbc.com/news/technology-53176946.

Morgan, Marjorie H. "The Women of Wakanda." *Cinema Femme,* January 22, 2019. https://cinemafemme.com/2019/01/22/the-women-of-wakanda/.

Morrison, Grant. *Supergods.* New York: Spiegel & Grau, 2011.

Mu'min, Huda. "Ryan Coogler on 'Fruitvale Station.'"

Myre, Greg. "The Day Nelson Mandela Walked Out of Prison." *NPR Parallels,* June 27, 2013. https://www.npr.org/sections/parallels/2013/06/11/190671704/the-day-nelson-mandela-walked-out-of-prison.

Nama, Adilifu. *Super Black: American Pop Culture and Black Superheroes.* Austin, TX: University of Texas Press, 2011.

Narcisse, Evan. "'The miracle is Wakanda': Ta-Nehisi Coates says goodbye to Black Panther." *Polygon,* May 26, 2021. https://www.polygon.com/interviews/22454722/black-panther-comics-ending-ta-nehisi-coates-interview.

———. "Ta-Nehisi Coates is Trying to Do Right by Marvel Comics' First Black Superhero." *Kotaku,* April 9, 2016. https://kotaku.com/ta-nehisi-coates-is-trying-to-do-right-by-marvel-comics-1769418783.

———. "The Natural: The Trouble Portraying Blackness in Video Games." *Kotaku,* February 13, 2017. https://kotaku.com/the-natural-the-trouble-portraying-blackness-in-video-1736504384.

———. "Wakanda was the way Stan lee spoke to me." *Polygon*, November 16, 2018. https://www.polygon.com/comics/2018/11/16/18098440/stan-lee-black-panther-wakanda.

———. in Zoom discussion with the author, June 15, 2021.

Narcisse, Evan, Coates, Ta-Nehisi, Pina, Javier, & Hollowell, Morry. "Underground Spiritual Game." *Rise of the Black Panther* 1, no. 6. New York: Marvel Comics (2018). Marvel Unlimited.

Narcisse, Evan, Coates, Ta-Nehisi, Pina, Javier, & Paitreau, Stéphane. "Coffin for Head of State." *Rise of the Black Panther* 1, no. 2. New York: Marvel Comics (2018). Marvel Unlimited.

National Advisory Commission on Civil Disorders. *Report of the National Advisory Commission on Civil Disorders.* New York: Bantam Books, 1968.

Naughtie, Andrew. "Former KKK Leader endorses Trump for president again—and Tucker Carlson for VP." *The Independent,* July 9, 2020. https://www.independent.co.uk/news/world/americas/kkk-trump-david-duke-tucker-carlson-election-2020-a9609491.html.

Netmarble Monster. *Marvel: Future Fight.* Netmarble Games. Mobile. 2015.

Newby, Richard. "'Falcon and the Winter Soldier' Uncovers Marvel's Original Sin." *The Hollywood Reporter,* March 26, 2021. https://www.hollywoodreporter.com/movies/movie-news/falcon-and-the-winter-soldier-uncovers-marvels-original-sin-4156851/.

———. "What Happened to 'Blade'?" *The Hollywood Reporter,* August 18, 2018. https://www.hollywoodreporter.com/heat-vision/blade-started-a-revolution-was-abandoned-by-marvel-1135703.

Newkirk, Pamela. "The Minority Press: Pleading Our Own Cause." In *The Press: Institutions of American Democracy,* edited by Geneva Overholser and Kathleen Hall Jamieson, 81–91. New York: Oxford University Press, 2005.

Norwood, Rico. "Coding Blackness: A History of Black Video Game Characters." *Wired,* February 26, 2021. https://www.wired.com/story/black-character-history-video-games/.

NPR Staff. "Ta-Nehisi Coates Hopes 'Black Panther' Will Be Some Kid's 'Spider-Man.'" *NPR Code Switch,* April 6, 2016. https://www.npr.org/sections/codeswitch/2016/04/06/473224606/a-reluctant-king-ta-nehisi-coates-takes-on-marvels-black-panther.

Nurnberger, Ralph D. "The United States and Idi Amin: Congress to the Rescue." *African Studies Review* 25, no. 1 (1982): 49–65.

Nyberg, Amy Kiste. "Comics Code History: The Seal of Approval." *CBLDF.org.* Retrieved July 27, 2020. http://cbldf.org/comics-code-history-the-seal-of-approval/.

Obie, Brooke. "In Defense of Erik Killmonger and the Forgotten Children of Wakanda." *Shadow and Act,* February 17, 2018. https://shadowandact.com/erik-killmonger-forgotten-wakanda.

Okorafor, Nnedi, Araújo, André Lima, & O'Halloran, Chris. "Obinna's Folly." *Black Panther: Long Live the King* 1, no. 5. New York: Marvel Comics (2018). Marvel Unlimited.

Okorafor, Nnedi, Cross, Chris, & Rosenberg, Rachelle. "A Luta Continua." *Marvel's Voices: Legacy* 1, no. 1. New York: Marvel Comics (2021). Marvel Unlimited.

Okorafor, Nnedi, Ford, Tana, Hanna, Scott, & Kniivila, Irma. "Under the Bridge." *Black Panther: Long Live the King* 1, no. 6. New York: Marvel Comics (2018). Marvel Unlimited.

Okorafor, Nnedi, Romero, Leonardo, & Bellaire, Jordie. "Timbuktu." *Shuri* 1, no. 4. New York: Marvel Comics (2019). Marvel Unlimited.

Okorafor, Nnedi, Stott, Rachael, & Lopez, Carlos. "Godhead." *Shuri* 1, no. 10. New York: Marvel Comics (2019). Marvel Unlimited.

Olsson, Ola. "On the democratic legacy of colonialism." *Journal of Comparative Economics,* 37 no. 4 (2009): 534–51.

Opam, Kwame. "Wakanda Reborn: Tour Black Panther's reimagined homeland with Ta-Nehisi Coates." *The Verge,* May 15, 2017. https://www.theverge.com/a/marvel-black-panther.

Oreskes, Michael. "Civil Rights Act Leaves Deep Mark on the American Political Landscape." *New York Times,* July 2, 1989. https://www.nytimes.com/1989/07/02/us/civil-rights-act-leaves-deep-mark-on-the-american-political-landscape.html.

Palmer, Colin. "Defining and Studying the Modern African Diaspora." *Perspectives on History,* September 1, 1998. https://www.historians.org/publications-and-directories/perspectives-on-history/september-1998/defining-and-studying-the-modern-african-Diaspora.

Panels to Pixels, "History of Black Panther in Video Games." YouTube video, 4:01, February 12, 2018. https://www.youtube.com/watch?v=_Rv_nT5QuWo&ab_channel=PanelstoPixels.

Parker, Ryan, & Couch, Aaron. "Wesley Snipes Reveals Untold Story Behind His 'Black Panther' Film." *The Hollywood Reporter,* January 30, 2018. https://www.hollywoodreporter.com/heat-vision/black-panther-wesley-snipes-reveals-untold-story-behind-90s-film-1078868.

Pearson, Roberta. "World-Building Logics and Copyright: The Dark Knight and the Great Detective." In *World Building Transmedia, Fans, Industries,* edited by Marta Boni, 109–28. Amsterdam, Netherlands: Amsterdam University Press, 2017.

Peters, Mark. "8 Ways Comic Book Legend Jack Kirby Fought Fascism." *Paste,* February 16, 2017. https://www.pastemagazine.com/comics/jack-kirby/8-ways-comic-book-legend-jack-kirby-fought-fascism/.

Phillips, Tom. "Fortnite storyline has plans for 'many years of Marvel integration.'" *Eurogamer,* October 20, 2020. https://www.eurogamer.net/articles/2020-10-26-fortnite-storyline-has-plans-for-many-years-of-marvel-integration.

Pineda, Dorany. "Yes, lots of comics were racist. A new generation of Black artists is reinventing them." *Los Angeles Times,* April 29, 2021. https://www.latimes.com/entertainment-arts/books/story/2021-04-29/yes-lots-of-comics-were-racist-a-new-generation-of-black-artists-is-reinventing-them.

Polo, Susana. "Allow us to Explain: Why the Movie Green Lantern Is White." *The Mary Sue,* November 22, 2010. https://www.themarysue.com/why-movie-green-lantern-white/.

Polowy, Kevin. "'Super Sema' star Lupita Nyong'o: 'Black Panther 2' without Chadwick Boseman 'feels spiritually and emotionally correct." *Yahoo! Entertainment,* April 28, 2021. https://www.yahoo.com/entertainment/lupita-nyongo-super-sema-youtube-black-panther-2-chadwick-boseman-150021866.html.

Priest, Christopher, & Bennett, Joe. "Snapped." *Captain America and the Falcon* 1, no. 6. New York: Marvel Comics, 2004. Marvel Unlimited.

Priest, Christopher, & Breyfogle, Norm. "The Story Thus Far." *Black Panther* 3, no. 30. Marvel Comics, 2001. Marvel Unlimited.

Priest, Christopher, Bright, Mark, & DeCastro, Nelson. "Enemy of the State: Book Four—The Taking of Wakanda 1–2–3." *Black Panther* 3, no. 12. New York: Marvel Comics, 1999. Marvel Unlimited.

Priest, Christopher, Bright, Mark, & Wong, Walden. "Beloved." *Black Panther* 3, no. 24. New York: Marvel Comics, 2000. Marvel Unlimited.

———. "Enemy of the State: Book Three." *Black Panther* 3, no. 11. New York: Marvel Comics, 1999. Marvel Unlimited.

Priest, Christopher, Calafiore, Jim, & Livesay, John. "Gorilla Warfare Book One: Hell(O), I Must Be Going." *Black Panther* 3, no. 34. New York: Marvel Comics, 2001. Marvel Unlimited.

———. "Gorilla Warfare Book Two: Masks." *Black Panther* 3, no. 35. New York: Marvel Comics, 2001. Marvel Unlimited.

Priest, Christopher, Calafiore, Jim, & McKenna, Mark. "Ascension: Part 4 of 4." *Black Panther* 3, no. 62. Marvel Comics, 2003. Marvel Unlimited.

———. "Black and White: Conclusion: Ol' Boy Enters the Life." *Black Panther* 3, no. 56. Marvel Comics, 2003. Marvel Unlimited.

Priest, Christopher & Evans, Vince. "Lord of the Damned." *Black Panther* 3, no. 5. New York: Marvel Comics, 1999.

Priest, Christopher & Hotz, Kyle. "Legacy." *Black Panther* 3, no. 18. New York: Marvel Comics, 2000.

Priest, Christopher & Jusko, Joe. "Caged." *Black Panther* 3, no. 7. New York: Marvel Comics, 1999. Marvel Unlimited.

———. "Hunted." *Black Panther* 3, no. 6. New York: Marvel Comics, 1999. Marvel Unlimited.

———. "That Business with the Avengers!" *Black Panther* 3, no. 8. Marvel Comics, 1999. Marvel Unlimited.

Priest, Christopher & Lucas, Jorge. "Black and White: Chapter 1: The Last Temptation of Joe Pushead." *Black Panther* 3, no. 51. Marvel Comics, 2003. Marvel Unlimited.

———. "Black and White: Chapter 4: Kasper Cole Buys a Clue." *Black Panther* 3, no. 54. Marvel Comics, 2003. Marvel Unlimited.

———. "Saddles Ablaze." *Black Panther* 3, no. 46. New York: Marvel Comics, 2002. Marvel Unlimited.

Priest, Christopher, & Manley, Mike. "Enemy of the State." Black Panther 3, no. 9. New York: Marvel Comics, 1999. Marvel Unlimited.

———. "Enemy of the State: Book Two." Black Panther 3, no. 10. New York: Marvel Comics, 1999. Marvel Unlimited.

Priest, Christopher, Perkins, Mike, & Troy, Andy. "Back in Black." Black Panther Annual 2, no. 1. New York: Marvel Comics (2018). Marvel Unlimited.

Priest, Christopher, & Texeira, Mark. "Original Sin." Black Panther 3, no. 3. New York: Marvel Comics, 1999. Marvel Unlimited.

———. "The Client." Black Panther 3, no. 1. New York: Marvel Comics (1998). Marvel Unlimited.

———. "The Price." Black Panther 3, no. 5. New York: Marvel Comics (1999). Marvel Unlimited.

Priest, Christopher, Velluto, Sal, & Almond, Bob. "Enemy of the State II—Book One: Mirror." Black Panther 3, no. 41. Marvel Comics, 2002. Marvel Unlimited.

———. "Enemy of the State II—Book Two: Alliance." Black Panther 3, no. 42. Marvel Comics, 2002. Marvel Unlimited.

———. "Enemy of the State II—Book Three: The Kiber Chronicles." Black Panther 3, no. 43. Marvel Comics, 2002. Marvel Unlimited.

———. "Enemy of the State II—Book Four: 60 Minutes." Black Panther 3, no. 44. Marvel Comics, 2002. Marvel Unlimited.

———. "Enemy of the State II—Conclusion: All the President's Men." Black Panther 3, no. 45. Marvel Comics, 2002. Marvel Unlimited.

———. "Freefall." Black Panther 3, no. 19. New York: Marvel Comics, 2000. Marvel Unlimited.

———. "Local Hero." Black Panther 3, no. 16. New York: Marvel Comics, 2000. Marvel Unlimited.

———. "More of that Business with the Avengers!" Black Panther 3, no. 23. New York: Marvel Comics, 2000. Marvel Unlimited.

———. "Nightmare." Black Panther 3, no. 21. New York: Marvel Comics, 2000. Marvel Unlimited.

———. "Passage." Black Panther 3, no. 25. New York: Marvel Comics, 2000. Marvel Unlimited.

———. "Retribution." Black Panther 3, no. 20. New York: Marvel Comics, 2000. Marvel Unlimited.

———. "Seduction of the Innocent, Book 2: Innocent Blood." Black Panther 3, no. 32. Marvel Comics, 2001. Marvel Unlimited.

———. "Seduction of the Innocent, Conclusion: War and Love." Black Panther 3, no. 33. Marvel Comics, 2001. Marvel Unlimited.

———. "Stürm und Drang: A Story of Love & War, Book 1: Echoes." Black Panther 3, no. 26. Marvel Comics, 2001. Marvel Unlimited.

———. "Stürm und Drang: A Story of Love & War, Book 2: An Epidemic Insanity." Black Panther 3, no. 27. Marvel Comics, 2001. Marvel Unlimited.

———. "Stürm und Drang: A Story of Love & War, Book 3: The Trade of Kings." Black Panther 3, no. 28. Marvel Comics, 2001. Marvel Unlimited.

———."The Death of the Black Panther Book 2 of 2: The King is Dead." Black Panther 3, no. 49. Marvel Comics, 2002. Marvel Unlimited.

———. "The End." Black Panther 3, no. 13. New York: Marvel Comics, 1999. Marvel Unlimited.

———. "Turbulence." Black Panther 3, no. 14. New York: Marvel Comics, 2000. Marvel Unlimited.

———. "Smash." Black Panther 3, no. 15. New York: Marvel Comics, 2000. Marvel Unlimited.

———. "Uptown." Black Panther 3, no. 17. New York: Marvel Comics, 2000. Marvel Unlimited.

Priest, Christopher, Zircher, Patrick, & Rapmund, Norm. "Ascension: Part 1 of 4." *Black Panther* 3, no. 59. Marvel Comics, 2003. Marvel Unlimited.

Priest, Christopher J. "black panther faq." *DigitalPriest.com,* 2011. https://digitalpriest. com/legacy/comics/panther/faq.html.

———. "black panther series commentary." *DigitalPriest.com,* June 2001. https:// digitalpriest.com/legacy/comics/panther/start.html.

———. "black panther series commentary: year one." *DigitalPriest.com,* November 2002. https://digitalpriest.com/legacy/comics/panther/panther1.html.

———. "black panther series commentary: year two" *DigitalPriest.com,* November 2002. https://digitalpriest.com/legacy/comics/panther/panther2.html.

———. "black panther series commentary: year three." *DigitalPriest.com,* November 2002. https://digitalpriest.com/legacy/comics/panther/panther3.html.

———."black panther series commentary: year four." *DigitalPriest.com,* November 2002. https://digitalpriest.com/legacy/comics/panther/panther4.html.

———. "black & white: a crime novel." *DigitalPriest.com,* April 2003. https:// digitalpriest.com/legacy/comics/panther/bw/index.htm.

———. "the death of the black panther." *DigitalPriest.com,* 2008. https://digitalpriest. com/legacy/comics/panther/panther_death.html.

———. "the last time priest discussed the viability of black characters." *DigitalPriest.com,* May 2002/April 2003. https://digitalpriest.com/legacy/comics/ chips3.html.

———. "What I Forgot to Mention." *DigitalPriest.com,* September 2011. https:// digitalpriest.com/comics/panther/.

Priyadarshi, Mohit. "Why Fruitvale Station—and not Black Panther—remains Ryan Coogler's most important film?" *Medium,* February 27, 2018. https://medium. com/@priyadarshi.mohit/why-fruitvale-station-still-remains-my-favorite-ryan-coogler-movie-35d406ae4995.

Public Broadcasting System. "Biographies: Ida B. Wells." *PBS.org.* https://www.pbs. org/blackpress/news_bios/wells.html.

Pulliam-Moore, Charles. "Chris Claremont Thinks Black Panther's Marriage to Storm Was a Bad Idea, and He's Right." *Gizmodo/io9.com,* January 31,

2018. https://gizmodo.com/chris-claremont-thinks-black-panthers-marriage-to-storm-1822598048.

———. "The New Black Panther in Marvel's *Venomverse: War Stories* Needs Her Own Comic Book." *Gizmodo/io9,* September 8, 2017. https://gizmodo.com/the-new-black-panther-in-marvels-venomverse-war-storie-1802758682.

RandomBlackGamer, "Marvel Ultimate Alliance 2 – All Cutscenes/Full Movie (Full 1080p)." YouTube video, 2:13:23, October 28, 2015, https://www.youtube.com/watch?v=gG73KVxx_y4&ab_channel=RandomBlackGamer.

Rasool, Amira. "Why I'm dressing up to see Black Panther." *Teen Vogue,* February 14, 2018. https://www.teenvogue.com/story/black-panther-dress-up-african-fashion.

Raven Software. *Marvel: Ultimate Alliance.* Activision. Xbox 360. 2006.

Reese, Hope. "How the Afrofuturism behind Black Panther and Get Out combines social justice and sci-fi." *Vox,* February 27, 2018. https://www.vox.com/conversations/2018/2/26/17040674/black-panther-afrofuturism-get-out.

Reign, April. "#OscarsSoWhite Creator: With a Mostly White Academy, What Could We Expect?" *Variety,* January 15, 2020. https://variety.com/2020/film/news/oscarssowhite-nominations-diversity-april-reign-1203467389/.

Rico, Don, & Pike, Jay Scott. "Fanged Fury!" In *Jungle Tales* 4, edited by Stan Lee. New York: Atlas Comics (1955): 1–6.

———. "Rampage!" In *Jungle Tales* 1, edited by Stan Lee. New York: Atlas Comics (1954): 1–6.

———. "The Screaming Terror!" In *Jungle Tales* 3, edited by Stan Lee. New York: Atlas Comics (1955): 1–6.

Rico, Don, & Maneely, Joe. "The Trail of Sudden Death!" In *Jungle Action* 1, edited by Stan Lee. New York: Atlas Comics (1954):

Ridley, John. "Hey, HBO, 'Gone With the Wind' romanticizes the horrors of slavery. Take it off your platform for now." *Los Angeles Times,* June 8, 2020. https://www.latimes.com/opinion/story/2020-06-08/hbo-max-racism-gone-with-the-wind-movie.

Riesman, Abraham. "How an Untested Young Comics Writer Revolutionized Black Panther." *Vulture*, February 16, 2018. https://www.vulture.com/2018/02/don-mcgregor-panthers-rage-black-panther.html.

———. "The Man Who Made Black Panther Cool." *Vulture,* January 22, 2018. https://www.vulture.com/2018/01/christopher-priest-made-black-panther-cool-then-disappeared.html.

———. *True Believer: The Rise and Fall of Stan Lee.* New York: Penguin Random House, 2021.

Roberts, David. "The irresolvable moral dilemma at the heart of Avengers: Infinity War." *Vox,* May 17, 2018. https://www.vox.com/summer-movies/2018/5/17/17343442/avengers-infinity-war-captain-america-thanos-sequel-moral-dilemma.

Robinson, Joanna. "Secrets of the Marvel Universe." *Vanity Fair,* November 27, 2017. https://www.vanityfair.com/hollywood/2017/11/marvel-cover-story.

Robinson, Randall. *An Unbroken Agony: Haiti, from Revolution to the Kidnapping of a President.* New York: Basic Books, 2007.

Robinson, Raz. "Toy companies have not kept up with demand for 'Black Panther' merch." *Fatherly,* April 9, 2018. https://www.fatherly.com/news/black-panther-toy-shortage/.

Rodriguez, Mishelle. "Vibranium Healing." In *Why Wakanda Matters: What Black Panther Reveals About Psychology, Identity, and Communication,* edited by Sheena C. Howard. Dallas, TX: Smart Pop (2021): 149–70.

Romano, Aja. "Art Spiegelman, creator of Maus, calls out Marvel Comics for its 'apolitical' politics." *Vox,* August 20, 2019. https://www.vox.com/culture/2019/8/20/20812333/art-spiegelman-marvel-comics-backlash-essay-trump.

Romano, Nick. "Selma star says Oscar voters blacklisted film over casts' 'I Can't Breathe' T-shirts." *Entertainment Weekly,* June 5, 2020. https://ew.com/movies/selma-oscar-voters-blacklisted-i-cant-breathe-t-shirts/.

Rothenberg, Paula S. and Mayhew, Kelly S. "Maintaining Race, Class, and Gender Hierarchies: Reproducing 'Reality.'" In *Race, Class, and Gender in the United States,* 9th ed., edited by Paula S. Rothenberg and Kelly S. Mayhew. New York: Worth Publishers (2014): 575–78.

Rothmyer, Karen. "Hiding the Real Africa," *Columbia Journalism Review,* March/April, 2011. https://archives.cjr.org/reports/hiding_the_real_africa.php.

Ruiz, Steven. "It's already too late for the NFL to make up for blackballing Colin Kaepernick." *USA Today,* June 11, 2020, https://ftw.usatoday.com/2020/06/colin-kaepernick-nfl-blackballed-qb-development.

Russo, Anthony, & Russo, Joe, dirs. *Avengers: Endgame.* 2019, Burbank CA: Marvel Studios.

———. *Avengers: Infinity War.* 2018, Burbank CA: Marvel Studios.

———. *Captain America: Civil War.* 2016, Burbank CA: Marvel Studios.

Russonello, Giovanni. "Fascination and Fear: Covering the Black Panthers." *The New York Times,* October 15, 2016. https://www.nytimes.com/2016/10/16/us/black-panthers-50-years.html.

Saunders, Robert A. "(Profitable) imaginaries of black power: The popular and political geographies of *Black Panther,*" *Political Geography* 69 (2019): 139–49.

Sayej, Nadja. "Beyond Black Panther: afrofuturism takes flight at Chicago museum." *The Guardian,* April 10, 2018. https://www.theguardian.com/artanddesign/2018/apr/10/afrofuturism-exhibition-in-their-own-form-museum-contemporary-photography-chicago.

Schwartz, Daniel. "1960: The Year of Africa." *CBC.ca,* June 8, 2010. https://www.cbc.ca/news/world/1960-the-year-of-africa-1.909381.

Scopely/FoxNext. *Marvel Strike Force.* Scopely/FoxNext. Mobile. 2018.

Seay, Laura and Dionne, Kim Yi. "The long and ugly tradition of treating Africa as a dirty, diseased place." *The Washington Post,* August 25, 2014. https://www.washingtonpost.com/news/monkey-cage/wp/2014/08/25/othering-ebola-and-the-history-and-politics-of-pointing-at-immigrants-as-potential-disease-vectors/.

Serwer, Adam. "The Tragedy of Erik Killmonger." *The Atlantic,* February 21, 2018. https://www.theatlantic.com/entertainment/archive/2018/02/black-panther-erik-killmonger/553805/.

Sharf, Zack. "Scott Derrickson Fuels Rumor Over Namor Joining MCU in 'Doctor Strange 2.'" *Indiewire,* March 13, 2019. https://www.indiewire.com/2019/03/doctor-strange-scott-derrickson-namor-mcu-sequel-1202050965/.

Shen, Kona. "French Rule and Tensions in the Colony 1750–1784." *History of Haiti 1492–1805*, October 27, 2015. https://library.brown.edu/haitihistory/2frt.html/.

Silfer, Roger, DeFalco, Tom, Wilson, Ron, & Marcos, Pablo. "Conjure Night!" *Marvel Two-In-One* 1, no. 40. New York: Marvel Comics (1978). Marvel Unlimited.

Simmons, Alex, & Langley, Travis. "The First Panther: Interview with actor Keith David." In *Black Panther Psychology: Hidden Kingdoms,* edited by Travis Langley and Alex Simmons. New York: Sterling (2019), 11–20.

Smedley, Audrey, & Smedley, Brian D. *Race in North America: Origin and Evolution of a Worldview.* 4th ed. Boulder, CO: Westview Press, 2012.

Smiley, CalvinJohn, & Fakunle, David. "From 'brute' to 'thug': the demonization and criminalization of unarmed Black male victims in America." *Journal of Behavior & Social Environment* 26 no. 3–4 (2016): 350–66.

Smith, Zack. "PRIEST on BLACK PANTHER, Pt. 1: Everyone Kind of Forgot Who PANTHER Was" [Archived]. *Newsarama,* August 10, 2015. https://web.archive.org/web/20200519045723/https://www.newsarama.com/25496-priest-looks-back-at-black-panther.html.

———. "PRIEST on BLACK PANTHER, Pt. 2: 'It's Not Arrogance, it's Competence.'" [Archived]. *Newsarama,* August 11, 2015. https://web.archive.org/web/20150817005304/https://www.newsarama.com/25506-priest-on-black-panther-pt-2.html.

———. "PRIEST on BLACK PANTHER, Pt. 3: 'Hubris & Arrogance' Would Kill BLACK PANTHER Movie." [Archived]. *Newsarama,* August 12, 2015. https://web.archive.org/web/20150815024135/http://www.newsarama.com/25518-priest-on-black-panther-pt-3-enemy-of-the-state-and-the-panther-film.html.

SOB x RBE & Contributors. "Paramedic!" *Genius.* https://genius.com/13838503

Solórzano, Daniel G. "Images and words that wound: Critical race theory, racial stereotyping, and teacher education." *Teacher Education Quarterly* 24, no. 3 (1997): 5–19.

Solórzano, Daniel G., & Yosso, Tara J. "Critical race methodology: Counter-storytelling as an analytical framework for education research," *Qualitative Inquiry* 8, no. 23 (2002): 23–44.

Southern Poverty Law Center. *Ku Klux Klan: A History of Racism and Violence.* Montgomery, AL: The Southern Poverty Law Center. https://www.splcenter.org/sites/default/files/Ku-Klux-Klan-A-History-of-Racism.pdf.

Spangler, Todd. "'Gone With the Wind' Hits No. 1 on Amazon Best-Sellers Chart After HBO Max Drops Movie." *Variety,* June 10, 2020. https://variety.com/2020/digital/uncategorized/gone-with-the-wind-amazon-best-seller-hbo-max-1234630577/.

Spears, Arthur K. "Race and Ideology: An Introduction." In *Race and Ideology: Language, Symbolism, and Popular Culture,* edited by Arthur K. Spears. Detroit, MI: Wayne State University Press (1999): 11–60.

Stallworth, Ron. *Black Klansman.* New York: Flatiron Books, 2014.

Staples, Brent. "The Racist Trope That Won't Die." *New York Times,* June 17, 2018. https://www.nytimes.com/2018/06/17/opinion/roseanne-racism-blacks-apes.html.

Stephanie, Shanice. "Black Panther makes a nod to the Boko Haram kidnapping in Nigeria." *The Source,* February 20, 2018. https://thesource.com/2018/02/20/black-panther-film-makes-nod-boko-haram-kidnapping-nigeria/.

Stevens, J. Richard. *Captain America, Masculinity, and Violence: The Evolution of a National Icon.* Syracuse, NY: Syracuse University Press, 2015.

Stilwell, Blake. "Marvel legend Stan Lee was a World War II vet who got his start fixing telephone poles." *Business Insider.* November 13, 2018, https://www.businessinsider.com/marvel-comics-legend-stan-lee-was-world-war-ii-veteran-2018-11.

Stone, Sam. "Green Lantern: Geoff Johns Looks Back at His DC Legacy, Teases Reis Reunion." *CBR.com.* May 22, 2020, https://www.cbr.com/geoff-johns-green-lantern-anniversary/.

Sullivan, Becky. "Kyle Rittenhouse is acquitted of all charges in the trial over killing 2 in Kenosha." *NPR,* November 19, 2021. https://www.npr.org/2021/11/19/1057288807/kyle-rittenhouse-acquitted-all-charges-verdict.

Sung, Lydia. "Marvel Ultimate Alliance 2 DLC gets Black Panther and release date." *Neoseeker,* October 30, 2009. https://www.neoseeker.com/news/12180-marvel-ultimate-alliance-2-dlc-gets-black-panther-and-release-date/.

Suttner, Raymond. "The African National Congress centenary: A long and difficult journey." *International Affairs* 88, no. 4 (2012): 719–38.

SyFy. "Building Black Panther: The Work of Christopher Priest (Behind the Panel) | SYFY WIRE." YouTube Video, 16:03. June 18, 2018. https://www.youtube.com/watch?v=5A-U2NFWcVc.

Syvertsen, Jennifer L., Ohaga, Spala, Agot, Kawango, Dimova, Margarita, Guise, Andy, Rhodes, Tim, & Wagner, Karla D. "An ethnographic exploration of drug markets in Kisumu, Kenya." *International Journal of Drug Policy* 30 (2016): 82–90.

Team Ninja. *Marvel Ultimate Alliance 3: The Black Order.* Nintendo. Nintendo Switch. 2019.

Tejada, Andrew. "Representation Without Transformation: Can Hollywood Stop Changing Cartoon Characters of Color?" *Tor.com,* July 14, 2020. https://www.tor.com/2020/07/14/representation-without-transformation-can-hollywood-stop-changing-cartoon-characters-of-color/.

Tenreyro, Tatiana. "Jessie Washington Was a Real Person & 'BlacKkKlansman' Brings His Horrific Story to Light." *Bustle,* August 9, 2018. https://www.bustle.com/p/jesse-washington-was-a-real-person-blackkklansman-brings-his-horrific-story-to-light-10041824.

The Avengers: Earth's Mightiest Heroes. "Behold . . . The Vision!" Directed by Roy Burdine. Written by Michael Ryan. Disney XD, July 29, 2012.

———. "Live Kree or Die." Directed by Steve Gordon. Written by Christopher Yost. Disney XD, November 4More, 2012.

———. "Living Legend." Directed by Vinton Heuck. Written by Kevin Burke & Chris Wyatt. Disney XD, November 3, 2010.

———. "Operation: Galactic Storm." Directed by Boyd Kirkland. Written by Christopher Yost. Disney XD, October 21, 2012.

———. "Panther's Quest." Directed by Sebastian Montes. Written by Paul Giacoppo. Disney XD, November 17, 2010.

———. "The Man in the Ant Hill." Directed by Vinton Heuck. Written by Christopher Yost. Disney XD, October 24, 2010.

———. "Who Do You Trust?" Directed by Gary Hartle. Written by Brian Reed. Disney XD, May 13, 2012.

The Ezra Klein Show. "What's Really Behind the 1619 Backlash? An Interview with Nikole-Hannah Jones and Ta-Nehisi Coates" [Transcript]. *New York Times,* July 30, 2021, https://www.nytimes.com/2021/07/30/opinion/ezra-klein-podcast-ta-nehisi-coates-nikole-hannah-jones.html?searchResultPosition=5.

The Falcon & The Winter Soldier. "Truth." Directed by Kari Skogland. Written by Dalan Musson. Disney+, April 16, 2021.

The Fortnite Team. "Black Panther, Captain Marvel, and Taskmaster Join Fortnite in the Marvel Royalty and Warriors Pack." *EpicGames.com,* December 21, 2020. https://www.epicgames.com/fortnite/en-US/news/black-panther-captain-marvel-and-taskmaster-join-fortnite-in-the-marvel-royalty-and-warriors-pack.

The Super Hero Squad Show. "Tremble at the Might of . . . M.O.D.O.K.!" Directed by Patty Shinagawa. Written by Mark Hoffmeier. Cartoon Network, November 14, 2009.

Thielman, Sam. "Marvel and DC face backlash over pay: 'They sent a thank you note and $5,000 – the movie made $1bn.'" *The Guardian,* August 9, 2021. https://www.theguardian.com/books/2021/aug/09/marvel-and-dc-face-backlash-over-pay-they-sent-a-thank-you-note-and-5000-the-movie-made-1bn.

Thomas, Roy, & Buscema, John. ". . . And We Battle for the Earth!" *Avengers* 1, no. 68. New York: Marvel Comics (1969). Marvel Unlimited.

———. "Death Be Not Proud!" *Avengers* 1, no. 56. New York: Marvel Comics (1968). Marvel Unlimited.

———. "Death Calls for the Arch-Heroes!" *Avengers* 1, no. 52. New York: Marvel Comics (1968). Marvel Unlimited.

———. "In Battle Joined!" *Avengers* 1, no. 53. New York: Marvel Comics (1968). Marvel Unlimited.

———. "Pursue the Panther!" *Avengers* 1, no. 74. New York: Marvel Comics (1970). Marvel Unlimited.

———. "Some Say the World Will End in Fire . . . Some Say in Ice!" *Avengers* 1, no. 61. New York: Marvel Comics (1969). Marvel Unlimited.

———. "The Monarch and the Man-Ape!" *Avengers* 1, no. 62. New York: Marvel Comics (1969). Marvel Unlimited.

———. "The Name Is . . . Yellowjacket!" *Avengers* 1, no. 59. New York: Marvel Comics (1968). Marvel Unlimited.

———. "Three Stood Together!" *Fantastic Four* 1, no. 119. New York: Marvel Comics (1972). Marvel Unlimited.

———. "When Strikes the Squadron Sinister!" *Avengers* 1, no. 70. New York: Marvel Comics (1969). Marvel Unlimited.

Thomas, Roy, & Colan, Gene. "A Life on the Line." *Daredevil* 1, no. 69. New York: Marvel Comics (1970). Marvel Unlimited.

Thomas, Roy, & Giacoia, Frank. "The Sting of the Serpent!" *Avengers* 1, no. 73. New York: Marvel Comics (1970). Marvel Unlimited.

Thomas, Roy, Giacoia, Frank, & Buscema, Sal. "Look Homeward, Avenger!" *Avengers* 1, no. 87.

Traveller's Tales. *Lego Marvel Super Heroes.* Warner Bros. Interactive. Xbox 360. 2013.

———. *Lego Marvel's Avengers.* Warner Bros. Interactive. Multiplatform. 2016.

———. *Lego Marvel Super Heroes 2.* Warner Bros. Interactive. PC. 2017.

Tucker, Reed. *Slugfest: Inside the Epic 50-Year Battle Between Marvel and DC* (New York: Hachette, 2017).

Tunç, Hakan. "Preemption in the Bush Doctrine: A Reappraisal." *Foreign Policy Analysis* 5 (2009), 1–16.

Tyler-Ameen, Daoud, & Madden, Sidney. "Here's How 'Black Panther: The Album' Came Together." *NPR.org,* February 6, 2018. https://www.npr.org/sections/therecord/2018/02/06/582841574/heres-how-black-panther-the-album-came-together.

Ugwu, Reggie, & Levenson, Michael. "'Black Panther' Star Chadwick Boseman Dies of Cancer at 43." *New York Times,* August 28, 2020. https://www.nytimes.com/2020/08/28/movies/chadwick-boseman-dead.html.

VanDenburgh, Barbara. "Remembering Chadwick Boseman: His best quotes on 'Black Panther,' James Brown and Angela Bassett." *USA Today,* August 29, 2020. https://www.usatoday.com/story/entertainment/celebrities/2020/08/28/chadwick-boseman-best-quotes-black-panther-james-brown/5664070002/.

Vest, Jason P. *Spike Lee: Finding the Story and Forcing the Issue.* Santa Barbara, CA: Praeger, 2014.

Vicarious Visions. *Marvel: Ultimate Alliance 2.* Activision. Xbox 360. 2009.

Vitali, Ali, Hunt, Kasie, & Thorp V, Frank. "Trump referred to Haiti and African nations as 'shithole' countries." *NBC News,* January 12, 2018, https://www.nbcnews.com/politics/white-house/trump-referred-haiti-african-countries-shithole-nations-n836946.

Walsh, Kenneth T. "50 Years After Race Riots, Issues Remain the Same." *U.S. News & World Report.* July 12, 2017, https://www.usnews.com/news/national-news/articles/2017-07-12/50-years-later-causes-of-1967-summer-riots-remain-largely-the-same.

Watercutter, Angela. "Black Panther's Oscar wins made history." *Wired,* February 25, 2019. https://www.wired.com/story/black-panthers-oscar-wins-made-history/.

Webster, Andrew. "Fortnite's Galactus event was a giant arcade shooter—and now the game is down." *The Verge,* December 1, 2020. https://www.theverge.com/2020/12/1/21747893/fortnite-galactus-event-chapter-2-season-5-release-date#:~:text=The%20Marvel%2Dthemed%20season%20of,with%20a%20Galactus%2Dsized%20bang.&text=It%20was%20a%20strange%20event,explosives%20to%20feed%20the%20supervillain.

Weeks, Jerome. "Tarzan and the race card; The ape-man's creator might have believed in white superiority, but the new Disney film goes out of its way to avoid the black and white issues." *The Baltimore Sun,* June 27, 1999. https://www.baltimoresun.com/news/bs-xpm-1999-06-27-9906280262-story.html.

Welch, Kelly. "Black Criminal Stereotypes and Racial Profiling." *Journal of Contemporary Criminal Justice* 23, no. 3 (2007): 276–88.

Weldon, Glen. *The Caped Crusade: Batman and the Rise of Nerd Culture* (New York: Simon & Schuster, 2016).

Wells, Veronica. "Roxane Gay and Yona Harvey to Write Companion Series to Black Panther Focused on Black Women." *Madame Noire,* July 26, 2016, https://madamenoire.com/708318/roxane-gay-and-yona-harvey-to-write-companion-series-to-black-panther-focused-on-black-women/.

Welsh-Huggins, Andrew, & Associated Press. "David Duke Agrees to Pay $5K to Man Hurt at Charlottesville Rally." *NBC Washington,* January 23, 2020. https://www.nbcwashington.com/news/david-duke-agrees-to-pay-5k-to-man-hurt-at-charlottesville-rally/2203246/.

What If . . . ? "What If . . . T'Challa Became a Star-Lord?" Directed by Bryan Andrews. Written by Matthew Chauncey. Disney+, August 18, 2021.

Whedon, Joss, dir. *Marvel's Avengers: Age of Ultron.* 2015, Burbank CA: Marvel Studios.

Wheeler, Andrew. "Trace the Lineage of Marvel's Black Super Heroes." *Marvel.com,* February 28, 2014. https://www.marvel.com/articles/comics/trace-the-lineage-of-marvel-s-black-super-heroes.

Whitbrook, James. "Batman's in *Fortnite* Now, and He's Just as Lost as You Are." *Io9/Gizmodo,* April 20, 2021. https://io9.gizmodo.com/batmans-in-fortnite-now-and-hes-just-as-lost-as-you-ar-1846726290.

———. "Marvel Made *Fortnite* Canon and I Have Lost My Entire Mind." *Io9/Gizmodo,* August 29, 2020. https://io9.gizmodo.com/marvel-made-fortnite-canon-and-i-have-lost-my-entire-mi-1844881735.

White, Abbey. "'Black Panther' wins two Grammys." *The Hollywood Reporter,* February 10, 2019. https://www.hollywoodreporter.com/news/black-panther-album-soundtrack-win-at-2019-grammys-awards-1185173.

White, Brett. "Coogler Calls 'Black Panther' a 'Personal' Project." *Comic Book Resources,* January 13, 2016. https://www.cbr.com/coogler-calls-black-panther-a-personal-project/.

Whitlock, Jason. "Fearless: Stephen A. Smith's Shohei apology really bows to globalists, 'Black Twitter,' and the black matriarchy." *The Blaze,* July 13, 2021. https://www.theblaze.com/op-ed/fearless-stephen-a-smiths-shohei-apology-really-bows-to-globalists-black-twitter-and-the-black-matriarchy.

Whitney, Ogden. "Fire Spirit!" In *Jungle Tales* 1, edited by Stan Lee. New York: Atlas Comics (1954): 8–14.

Whitten, Sarah. "Disney accounted for nearly 40% of the 2019 US box office." *CNBC,* December 29, 2019. https://www.cnbc.com/2019/12/29/disney-accounted-for-nearly-40percent-of-the-2019-us-box-office-data-shows.html.

Whitty, Stephen. "Looking back at 'blaxploitation' films." *NJ.com,* July 5, 2009. https://www.nj.com/entertainment/tv/2009/07/looking_back_at_blaxploitation. html.

Wiacek, Stephen. *Black Panther: The Ultimate Guide.* New York: DK Publishing, 2018.

Williams, Dmitri, Martins, Nicole, Consalvo, Mia, & Ivory, James D. "The virtual census: representations of gender, race, and age in video games." *New Media & Society* 11, no. 5 (2009), 815–34.

Williams, Paige. "Kyle Rittenhouse, American Vigilante." *The New Yorker,* June 28, 2021. https://www.newyorker.com/magazine/2021/07/05/ kyle-rittenhouse-american-vigilante.

Williams, Trey. "How Marvel Bounced Back from Bankruptcy to Become Hollywood's Biggest Brand." https://www.thewrap.com/ how-marvel-went-from-bankruptcy-to-hollywoods-most-successful-franchise/.

Wilson, Carl. "Kendrick Lamar's *Black Panther* Album Is Rich with Meaning You Can Only Appreciate After the Movie." *Slate,* February 16, 2018. https://slate.com/ culture/2018/02/kendrick-lamars-black-panther-soundtrack-album-reviewed.html.

Wilt, James. "How Black Panther Liberalizes Black Resistance for White Comfort," *Canadian Dimension*, February 21, 2018. https://canadiandimension.com/articles/ view/how-black-panther-liberalizes-black-resistance-for-white-comfort.

Womack, Ytasha. *Afrofuturism: The World of Black Sci-fi and Fantasy Culture.* Chicago: Lawrence Hill Books, 2013.

Women's Media Center & BBC America. *Superpowering Girls: Female Representation in the Sci-Fi/Superhero Genre.* October 2018. https://www.womensmediacenter. com/assets/site/reports/bbca-wmc-superpowering-girls/Superpowering_Girls_ BBCA_Womens_Media_Center.pdf.

Worger, William. "Afri-Comics, South Africa, 1970s." *UCLA Library International Digital Ephemera Project,* May 1, 2018. https://idep.library.ucla.edu/afri-comics.

World Bank. "African Diaspora." April, 2012. http://siteresources.worldbank.org/ INTDIASPORA/Resources/AFR_Diaspora_FAQ.pdf.

Wright, Bradford W. *Comic Book Nation: The Transformation of Youth Culture in America.* 2nd ed. Baltimore, MD: Johns Hopkins University Press (2003).

Wright, Joshua K. "Black Outlaws and the Struggle for Empowerment in Blaxploitation Cinema." *Spectrum: A Journal on Black Men* 2, no. 2 (Spring 2014), 63–86.

Wynne, Kelly. "Nickelodeon Went Off the Air for Almost 9 Minutes to Support Equality and Share a 'Declaration of Kids' Rights.'"

Yarm, Mark. "Ta-Nehisi Coates Fights the Power—Literally—With Black Panther." *Wired,* April 6, 2016. https://www.wired.com/2016/04/ ta-nehisi-coates-black-panther-comics/.

Yates, Brian. "Twenty-First-Century Race Man: Reginald Hudlin's Black Panther." *Fire!!* 4 no. 2, "21st Century Black Studies: Digital Publications (Part Two)" (Fall 2017), 85–133.

Yosso, Tara J. "Critical Race Media Literacy: Challenging Deficit Discourse about Chicanas/os," *Journal of Popular Film & Television* 30, no. 1 (2002), 52–62.

Zoller Seitz, Matt. "Why *Roots* Is the Single Most Important Piece of Scripted Television in Broadcast History." *Vulture,* May 27, 2016. https://www.vulture.com/2016/05/why-roots-was-so-important.html.

Index

About the Author

Bryan J. Carr is associate professor in the Communication and Information Science departments at the University of Wisconsin–Green Bay, where he specializes in mass media and critical studies of popular culture. Dr. Carr's research focuses primarily on critical questions of identity and its intersection with social and economic forces, primarily in superhero media and video games. He is co-editor of the upcoming *Gendered Defenders: Marvel Superheroines in Transmedia Spaces*, and his work has appeared in edited volumes such as *Parasocial Politics, What is a Game?* and *From Jack Johnson to LeBron James: Sports, Media, and the Color Line*, as well as in journals like the *Journal of Entertainment and Media Studies* and *Public Relations Review*. He also hosts and produces the podcast *Serious Fun* on the Phoenix Studios podcast network. He lives in northeast Wisconsin with his wife and two cats.